THE RATIONAL BIBLE: EXODUS

THE RATIONAL BIBLE

EXODUS

God, Slavery, and Freedom

DENNIS PRAGER

EDITED BY JOSEPH TELUSHKIN

THE ALPERSON EDITION

REGNERY
FAITH

Regnery Faith™ is a trademark of Salem Communications Holding Corporation
Regnery® is a registered trademark of Salem Communications Howlding Corporation

All Scripture taken from New JPS Translation, Jewish Publication Society. Philadelphia, PA 1985. Used by permission.

Cataloging-in-Publication data on file with the Library of Congress

ISBN 978-1-62157-772-0

Published in the United States by
Regnery Faith
An imprint of Regnery Publishing
A Division of Salem Media Group
300 New Jersey Ave NW
Washington, DC 20001
www.RegneryFaith.com

Manufactured in the United States of America

10 9 8 7 6 5 4 3 2 1

Books are available in quantity for promotional or premium use.
For information on discounts and terms, please visit our website: www.Regnery.com.

CONTENTS

To Sue
"It is not good for man to be alone.
I will make him a helper who is his equal."
—Genesis 2:18 (literal translation)

INTRODUCTION

To the reader: Reading this Introduction will greatly enhance your understanding and enjoyment of this commentary.

MOST PEOPLE—ESPECIALLY IN THEIR YOUNGER YEARS—PASS THROUGH A DIFFICULT time with one or both of their parents. In my teen years and twenties, I was one of them. But no matter how I felt, there was never a time I did not honor my parents. For example, from the age of twenty-one, when I left my parents' home, I called my parents every week of their lives.

I treated my parents with such respect because I always believed God had commanded me to do so: "Honor your father and mother" (Commandment Five of the Ten Commandments). The Torah —as the first five books of the Bible have always been known in Hebrew—commands us to love our neighbor, to love God, and to love the stranger; but we are never commanded to love our parents. We are commanded to honor them (and we are not commanded to honor anyone else).

Why do I begin this introduction to a Bible commentary with this personal story?

Because it encapsulates why I have devoted so much of my life to explaining the Torah: because its central message—that God is good and demands we be good—is the only belief that will enable us to make a good world.

WHY THIS COMMENTARY?

I have been teaching the Torah for much of my adult life and have devoted decades to writing this explanation of, and commentary on, the Torah.

I have done so because I believe if people properly understand the Torah and attempt to live by its values and precepts, the world will be an infinitely kinder and more just place.

All my life I have been preoccupied—almost obsessed—with the problem of evil: people deliberately hurting other people. At the age of sixteen, I wrote in my diary that I wanted to devote my life "to influencing people to the good." That mission has animated my life. In a nutshell, I love goodness and hate evil. My favorite verse in the Bible is "Those of you who love God—hate evil" (Psalms 97:10).

Because of my (and the Torah's) preoccupation with evil, in this commentary I frequently cite the two most recent examples of mass evil—Nazism and communism. I assume all readers of this commentary have some acquaintance with Nazi evil. Tragically, however, relatively few people have much knowledge of communist evil. So, I should note here that communist regimes murdered about 100 million people and enslaved and destroyed the lives of more than a billion. If you hate evil, you must confront what Nazis and communists wrought in the twentieth century (and what others wrought before them and are doing at this time).

I have had one other mission: to understand human beings. The two missions—promoting goodness and attaining wisdom—are linked, because it is almost impossible to do good without wisdom. All the good intentions in the world are likely to be worthless without wisdom. Many of the horrors of the twentieth century were supported by people with good intentions who lacked wisdom.

Here, too, because it has so much wisdom, the Torah is indispensable.

However, we live in an age that not only has little wisdom, it doesn't even have many people who value it. People greatly value knowledge and intelligence, but not wisdom. And the lack of wisdom —certainly in America and the rest of the West—is directly related to the decline in biblical literacy. In the American past, virtually every home, no matter how poor, owned a Bible. It was the primary vehicle by which parents passed wisdom on to their children.

In the modern period, however, people have increasingly replaced Bible-based homes and Bible-based schools with godless homes and with schools in which the Bible is never referred to. As a result, we are less wise and more morally confused. As I show in my discussion of secular education as a potential "false god," the best educated in the West have often both lacked wisdom and been among the greatest supporters of evil ideologies and regimes.

Given the supreme importance of goodness and the indispensability of wisdom to goodness, the Torah, the greatest repository of goodness and wisdom in human history, is the most important book ever written. It gave birth to the rest of the Bible, to Christianity, and to Western civilization. It gave us "Love your neighbor as yourself," the Ten Commandments, a just and loving God, and every other bedrock of humane civilization.

Who Is This Torah Commentary For?

I have written this book for people of every faith, and for people of no faith. Throughout my years teaching the Torah, I would tell my students, "The Torah either has something to say to everyone or it has nothing to say to Jews." The idea that the Torah is only for Jews is as absurd as the idea that Shakespeare is only for the English or Beethoven is only for Germans.

That is why, over time, half the people taking my Torah classes—at a Jewish university no less—were not Jews.

Nevertheless, I would like to address some groups specifically.

To Jewish Readers:
Because the Torah has formed the basis of Jewish life for 3,000 years, there are very many Jewish commentaries, a good number of which have passed the hardest test: the test of time. However, the modern world poses intellectual and moral challenges that did not exist when the classic Jewish commentaries—most

dating to the Middle Ages—were written. Therefore, most modern Jews read neither those commentaries nor the Torah. I hope this commentary will address nearly all the intellectual and moral objections of these Jews.

In general, it has not gone well for Jews (or the world) when Jews ceased believing in the Torah. Belief in the Torah as a divine document has probably been the single most important reason Jews have stayed alive for 3,000 years and it has formed the core of Jews' moral values. When Jews abandoned belief in the Torah, they or their offspring almost always ceased being Jews; and, too often, they created or joined social movements with non-Torah, or even anti-Torah, values.

To Jews who already believe in the Torah as a divine document: I hope this commentary gives you *chizuk* (strengthened faith). And I hope it encourages you to go into the world to teach Torah-based values. To all other Jews, I hope this commentary leads you to an intellectual appreciation of the Torah's unique greatness and consequently causes you to at least entertain the possibility that God is its ultimate author.

TO CHRISTIAN READERS:

One cannot be a serious Christian without being familiar with the Hebrew Bible (or Old Testament, as the Christian world named it). Nor can one understand Jesus, a Jew who was not only observant of Torah law, but asserted he came not to change "a jot or a tittle" of it.

For the many Christians who already believe the Torah embodies the word of God, I hope this commentary strengthens your faith in the Torah. As Maimonides, the greatest Jewish philosopher, wrote 900 years ago, his differences with Christian theology notwithstanding, it is Christians who have been primarily responsible for disseminating knowledge of the Torah to so much of the world.

I should also add I have greatly benefited from reading Christian Bible scholars.

At the same time, the Bible scholar who most influenced my understanding of Genesis and Exodus was a Jew, the late Professor Nahum Sarna, chair of the department of Near Eastern and Judaic Studies at Brandeis University. His Jewish Publication Society commentaries on Genesis and Exodus are masterful. And my understanding of Leviticus and Numbers was deeply influenced by the late great Jewish Bible scholar Jacob Milgrom, who was also a dear friend.

To Non-Religious Readers:
I have had you most in mind when writing this commentary. With every passing generation in the West, fewer and fewer people believe in God, let alone in the Bible. This is a catastrophe for the West, and it is a tragedy for you. Having God, religion, a religious community, and a sacred text in one's life enables one to have a far deeper and richer—not to mention wiser—life. If you keep an open mind when reading this commentary, that life will, hopefully, become appealing to you.

To readers outside of the West, the Torah has as much to say to you as to anyone in the West. I look forward to your reactions. They will surely influence my writing of the subsequent volumes.

In writing this commentary, I have no hidden agenda. My agenda is completely open: I want as many people as possible to take the Torah seriously, to entertain the possibility it is God-given, or, at the very least, to understand why so many rational people do.

Nor do I have a parochial agenda. I am a believing Jew, but neither God, nor the Torah, nor later Judaism ever obligated Jews to make non-Jews Jewish. Jews have always welcomed—and until prohibited from doing so, even sought—converts; but what God and the Torah obligate Jews to do is to bring humanity to the God of the Torah, to His basic moral rules, and to the Torah's values and insights. People can and have lived according to the Torah's moral values as Christians, members of other faiths, or simply as non-denominational believers in God (such as the American founder Benjamin Franklin).

THE TORAH IS NOT MAN-MADE

For reasons I develop throughout the commentary, I am convinced the Torah is divine, meaning God, not man, is its ultimate source. The Torah is so utterly different—morally, theologically, and in terms of wisdom—from anything else preceding it and, for that matter, from anything written since, that a reasonable person would have to conclude either moral supermen or God was responsible for it.

To cite just a few examples of what the Torah introduced to the world:

- A universal God (the God of all people): This began the long road to human beings believing that with one "Father in Heaven," all human beings are brothers and sisters.

- An invisible, incorporeal God: Therefore, the physical is not the only reality. Life is infinitely more than the material world in which we live during our brief lifetime on earth.

- A moral God: All gods prior to the Torah's God were capricious, not moral. A just and moral God meant, among other things, ultimately justice will prevail (if not in this life, in the next). It also meant human beings, imbued with a sense of justice, can argue with, and question, this just God (the name "Israel" means "wrestle with God").

- A God beyond nature: God made nature, and is therefore not natural. This led to the end of the universal human belief in nature gods (such as rain gods). And sure enough, as belief in the Torah's God declines, nature worship seems to be returning.

- A God Who loves and Who wants to be loved: This was another world-changing concept introduced by the Torah to the world.

- Universal human worth: Every human being is "created in God's image." Nothing like this had ever been posited prior to the Torah.
- Universal human rights: Another world-altering consequence of universal human worth.

Another major reason I am convinced the Torah is not man-made is it so often depicts the people of the Book, the Jews, in a negative light. Had Jews made up what is, after all, their book and their story, they would never have portrayed themselves as critically and even negatively as the Torah (and the rest of the Hebrew Bible) often does. There is no parallel to this in any ancient national, or any religious, literature in the world.

A contemporary Jewish thinker, Rabbi Saul Berman, stated his position on the divinity of the Torah in words as close to my own as I could imagine:

> The more I study the Torah, the more I am convinced that it is the revealed word of God. The more I study ancient cultures, the more I see the absolutely radical disparity between the values of pagan civilizations and the values which Torah brought into the world. Torah was God's weapon in the war against idolatrous culture; and war it was.

I would only add that the Torah's battle, and sometimes war, with many of the dominant ideas of our time is as great as it was with the cultures of three millennia ago, when the Torah came into the world.

MAN-MADE OR GOD-MADE: WHY IT MATTERS

What difference does it make if the Torah is man-made or God-made?

The first difference has already been noted: There is no comparison between "God commanded" and "Moses (or anyone else) commanded." If I believed the Ten Commandments were written by men, I would not have honored my parents as much as I did during periods of emotional ambivalence. Those who believe God is the source of the Torah's commandments are far more likely to obey them than those who believe they are all man-made.

A second difference is that only because I believe the Torah is God-made have I worked to understand and explain difficult passages of the Torah. If you believe the Torah is man-made, when you encounter a morally or intellectually problematic verse or passage, you have an easy explanation: Men wrote it (Ancient men, at that). And you are then free to dismiss it. But those of us who believe God is the source of the Torah don't have that option. We need to try to understand the verse or passage morally and intellectually.

Let me offer one of many examples. There is a Torah law that says if you have a particularly bad—a "wayward" —son, you may take him to the elders (the court) of your city; and if they find him guilty, they are to stone him to death. When modern men and women read that, they dismiss it as morally primitive: "What do you expect from something people wrote 3,000 years ago?"

But since I don't believe it's "something people wrote," I don't have that option. Consequently, I have had to look for rational explanations for seemingly irrational laws and passages and for moral explanations for seemingly immoral laws and passages.

And I have almost always found them. In this case, for example, I came to understand this law was one of the great moral leaps forward in the history of mankind. In this law, the Torah brilliantly preserved parental authority while permanently depriving parents of the right to kill their children, a commonplace occurrence in the ancient world and even today (for example, "honor killings" in the Muslim world). The law permits only a duly established court ("the elders")—not parents—to take the life of their child. And we have no record of any court in Jewish history ever executing a "wayward" son.

My belief in the divinity of the Torah led me to seek a moral explanation of what appears to us to be an immoral law, and it was solely because of that belief I found one. This has happened repeatedly regarding seemingly immoral or irrational laws, verses, and passages.

A third difference is that only those who believe in the text as God-given will continue to live by it, carefully study it, and try to impart its wisdom generation after generation. There will always be a few individuals who believe the Torah is man-made who will nevertheless diligently study it. But it is doubtful their grandchildren will. If Jews long ago believed the Torah was man-made, there would be no Jews today.

I would go further: If you believe in God, but you don't believe in any divinely revealed text, how do you know what your God wants of you? How do you know what God wants of humanity? Of course, you or your society can make up laws and values, including some good ones the Torah would approve of. But if God told us nothing, we would bcome our own gods when it comes to determining moral values.

HOW WAS THE TORAH TRANSMITTED?

I take no position on how God revealed the Torah. What concerns me most is not how God transmitted the Torah. *Who* wrote the Torah is infinitely more important than *how* it was written.

REASON, TORAH, AND GOD

The title of this commentary is, "The Rational Bible." There are two reasons for this.

First, my approach to understanding and explaining the Torah is reason-based. I never ask the reader to accept anything I write on faith alone. If something I write does not make rational sense, I have not done my job. On those few—thankfully, very few—occasions I do not have a rational explanation for a Torah verse, I say so.

Second, reason has always been my primary vehicle to God and to religion. My beliefs—in God, the revelation at Sinai, the Torah, etc.—are not rooted in faith alone. *We Have Reason to Believe*, the title of a book written in 1958 by the British Jewish theologian Louis Jacobs, had a deep impact on me.

The title has an important double meaning. The obvious one is that reason can lead one to religious faith. The less obvious meaning of the title is the one I cherish: we human beings have the faculty of reason—and are to use it *in order* to believe.

Of course, there is a faith component to my religious life. The primary example is the foundation of this commentary—my belief in the Torah as a divine document. It is reason that has led to this belief, but I acknowledge there are a few verses or passages that challenge this belief. Whenever I encounter such passages, however, I am not prepared to say, "'Love the stranger' is divine, but this difficult part is man-made."

Once one says that, the Torah not only ceases to be divine, it ceases to be authoritative. As I put it in a number of public dialogues with a secular Jewish scholar, Professor Alan Dershowitz of Harvard Law School: "I think I can sum up our basic difference this way: When Professor Dershowitz differs with the Torah, he thinks the Torah is wrong and he is right. When I differ with the Torah, I think the Torah is right and I am wrong." Professor Dershowitz agreed with that summation.

My approach is to abandon neither faith nor reason. I neither abandon the claim of reason because of the dictates of faith, nor abandon the faith claim because of reason. In the Torah, faith and reason nearly always live together in harmony. And when they do not, I do not deny either.

Moreover, there is a faith component to everyone's life, including atheists' lives. Any atheist who believes good and evil really exist, or life has a purpose beyond one he or she has made up, or that free will exists, or, for that matter, that science alone will explain how the universe came about, or how life arose from non-life, or how intelligence arose from non-intelligence, has suspended reason in favor of faith.

WHY READ THIS COMMENTARY?

Why should people devote time to reading my explanation of the Torah?

Here is my answer: I have devoted more than fifty years to studying and teaching the Torah. That includes a life-long immersion in Torah Hebrew—both its grammar and its vocabulary. I could not have written this commentary without this extensive knowledge of Hebrew. But most importantly, I have sought to make the Torah completely relevant to my life and to the lives of others. And by "others," I mean—literally—millions of others. Every good teacher learns from his or her students, and I am no exception—the thinking and experiences of myriad people inform this commentary. But I have been blessed to have something very rare among teachers or scholars: millions of students—and of almost every nationality, ethnicity, religion, and philosophy.

For over three decades, I have been a radio talk show host, broadcasting for more than half of that time on radio stations throughout America and on the Internet internationally. This has enabled me to discuss virtually every subject imaginable with a large number of people—live on the radio and through many thousands of emails. It also has enabled me to dialogue about religious matters with many of the leading theologians and scholars of our time and to debate many contemporary leading atheists. I have been able to bounce ideas off, and learn from, lay people and scholars of every background.

Given this uncommon, if not unique, background, after much soul-searching, I decided to write this commentary from the first-person perspective where appropriate. I became convinced that showing how the Torah's ideas and values have played themselves out in one individual's life makes the commentary more interesting, more real, and more relevant.

Shortly before finishing this first volume—on Exodus—I had the great honor of being invited to speak about my Torah commentary to the Bible faculty and students of Israel's religious university, Bar-Ilan University. They did not invite me because they thought I know more than, or even as much as, any one of them about the Torah. They invited me because they believe I bring a fresh understanding of the Torah. That is why I wrote this commentary.

DID THE EXODUS HAPPEN?

Many scholars believe the Israelites were enslaved in Egypt. Many do not.

There are strong logical and historical arguments for the Jews having been enslaved in Egypt. One I find particularly compelling was offered by the distinguished scholar Professor Richard Elliott Friedman in his commentary on the Exodus. He notes the Torah repeats one law more than any other: to love the stranger and not to oppress him. And in every case the Torah adds the words, "because you were strangers in the land of Egypt." Why, Friedman asks, would the Torah make repeated reference to the Israelites having been strangers in Egypt if they were never there? Why would one of the greatest of the Torah's moral innovations—a law to love the foreigner—be based on a premise no Israelite could relate to?

Similarly, why would any people make up origins so lowly as being slaves? No other nation did. And why would the Israelites in the wilderness complain that they ate better in Egypt if they were never there? Of course, one could argue that was also made up out of whole cloth. But if it never happened, why bother making it up?

A FEW DETAILS

Why Exodus Is Volume 1

The primary reason I began my commentary with the second book of the Torah, Exodus, and not the first, Genesis, is that Exodus contains the Ten Commandments, the most important moral code in world history, and the central moral code of the Torah. If people lived by those ten laws alone, the world would be almost devoid of all man-made suffering.

In addition, Genesis is almost all narrative, while Exodus is, in equal parts, narrative, laws, and theology.

BC or BCE?

Some readers will wonder why I use the letters "BCE" rather than the more familiar "BC" in dates. I struggled with this issue because I have no problem with "BC." But virtually all academic works and many general works now use "BCE." BCE stands for "Before the Common Era," but any reader who prefers to read the letters as "Before the Christian Era," is certainly welcome to—that is, after all, what "Common Era" denotes.

God as "He"

I refer to God as "He" because that is how the Torah refers to God. As the Torah was the first religious work in the world to completely desexualize God and religion, the Torah needs no defense in this matter.

Using "He or She" would not only be dishonest to the text, it would also incline people to think of God in gender terms. "She" always refers to a female, but "he" or "man" frequently refers to both sexes. "The rights of man" means "human rights"; the word "mankind" includes women; and so on. And using "It" would render the God of the Torah something else entirely, akin to Aristotle's Unmoved Mover. One does not pray to, love, or otherwise relate to an "It."

Moreover, as I will explain at length in another volume of this commentary, rendering God a "He" taught generations of males that to be compassionate and loving is part of being masculine.

On How to Read This Commentary

The reader can benefit from reading this commentary in any way he or she desires. It can, of course, be read straight through, or be used as a reference work for one's own study of the Torah. But those are not the only ways to read it. Readers can equally benefit from choosing to read any subject heading that strikes them as interesting. And that is made easier by simply perusing the table of contents to see the subjects covered here.

The Use of Post-Biblical Jewish Sources

I frequently cite post-biblical Jewish sources—most especially, the Talmud —because they aid greatly in understanding various laws and texts. The Jews, after all, had the Torah for more than a thousand years prior to the rise of Christianity. The Talmud is the encyclopedia-sized compendium of Jewish law and philosophy that reflects those thousand-plus years of Jews' studying and living the Torah.

ACKNOWLEDGMENTS

This is the most difficult part of this introduction because so many people have influenced me with their insights into life and the Bible that I am certain to unwittingly omit names that should be included.

I attended yeshivas (all-day religious Jewish schools) from first grade until twelfth; and I continued formal study thereafter as well. That formal education made my Torah teaching possible. Two teachers at the Yeshiva of Flatbush High School in Brooklyn, New York who particularly influenced me were the principal, Rabbi David Eliach, and my Torah teacher Rabbi Amnon Haramati.

In my late twenties and early thirties (1976–83), as the director of the Brandeis-Bardin Institute, a Jewish educational center in California, I had the unique opportunity to meet and have extended dialogues with most of the influential Jewish thinkers of the time—Orthodox, Conservative, Reform, and secular, from North and South America, Europe, and Israel. They included (in alphabetical order) Yehuda Bauer, Eliezer Berkovits, Saul Berman, Eugene Borowitz, Emil Fackenheim, Norman Frimer, Martin Gilbert, Arthur Hertzberg, Louis Jacobs, Norman Lamm, Julius Lester, Hyam Maccoby, Jacob Milgrom, Pinchas Peli, Jakob Petuchowski, Gunther Plaut, Emanuel Rackman, Richard L. Rubenstein, Uriel Simon, David W. Weiss (the Israeli immunologist), and Elie Wiesel.

From 1982 until 1992, I was given another unique opportunity—a true gift—to discuss religion for two hours every Sunday night with clergy and spokesmen of virtually every religion in the world. I was the moderator of a radio show, "Religion on the Line," broadcast on the ABC radio station in Los Angeles. This constituted a decade-long immersion in religious conversation with people who devoted their lives to their respective religions—Reform,

Conservative, Orthodox, and Reconstructionist rabbis; mainstream and evangelical Protestant ministers; Roman Catholic priests; Eastern Orthodox priests; Mormon bishops; Muslim imams; Seventh Day Adventist ministers; Buddhist priests, and others. It was a life-shaping and life-changing experience. I ended up speaking in at least a hundred synagogues, in scores of churches, and at the largest mosque in the Western United States.

I not only learned from all these people: I was also able to test my religious beliefs with lucid minds of all faiths. And of no faith; I regularly invited atheist and humanist spokesmen on the show as well.

After 1992, I continued to routinely raise religious issues on my daily radio shows and to discuss religious matters regularly with highly knowledgeable Jewish friends such as Izzy and Rita Eichenstein, Allen and Susan Estrin, Rabbi Leonid Feldman, Rabbi Mordecai Finely, Rabbi Michael and Jill Gotlieb, Dr. Stephen and Dr. Ruth Marmer, Rabbi Eyal and Tzippy Ravnoy, Rabbi David Wolpe, and Rabbi David and Beverly Woznica. I would be particularly remiss if I did not mention the role Chabad rabbis the world over have played in my religious life. I would like to mention all of them, but I must at least mention my family's four Chabad rabbis and their wives at whose homes my sons and/or I have spent many Shabbat evenings talking about God, the Torah, and just about everything else—Rabbi Simcha and Shterny Backman of Glendale, California, Rabbi Moshe and Matty Bryski of Agoura Hills, California, Rabbi Berl and Chani Goldman of Gainesville, Florida, and Rabbi Yosef and Chana Lipsker of Reading, Pennsylvania.

Special mention must be made of a man who combines uncompromising intellectual honesty, Jewish religious faith and practice, and extraordinary biblical scholarship. Professor Leeor Gottlieb of the Department of Bible at Bar-Ilan University. His contribution has been indispensable.

Likewise, knowledgeable and wise Christian friends such as Father Gregory Coiro, Joshua Charles, Gregory Koukl, Dr. Wayne Grudem, Pastor John Hagee, Eric Metaxas, Msgr. Jorge Mejia, Michael Nocita, and Dr. Hugh Ross have helped me form my thoughts on the Bible and religion generally.

Two Christians, Joshua Charles and Holly Hickman, were among the few individuals who read large parts of this commentary. They provided important insights for which I am deeply grateful.

Ilana Kurshan, a prominent writer and serious thinker, edited the hundreds of hours of tapes of my eighteen-year teaching of the Torah verse-by-verse. She was instrumental in making this commentary a reality. I cannot thank her enough. She was indeed an editor of this commentary.

Then there is Joel Alperson. Aside from being a close friend since 1982, when we met at a speech I gave in Kansas City, Kansas, I want to first acknowledge that without Joel there would be no commentary. It was Joel who found the company to transcribe my Torah tapes, resulting in the creation of 5,000 pages of text. Debbie Weinberger was one of the transcriptionists who did a magnificent job and this work is written in her memory. Joel then searched for an editor and ultimately found Ilana Kurshan, whose work he carefully reviewed.

Joel was determined that my Torah commentary be put into print. But I knew, as it stood, even after Ilana's superb editing of my lectures, I had much more to say. So, one day, Joel, not one to ever give up, put the question to me directly: "What would it take for you to complete and publish the commentary?"

I told him I would do so under one condition—that Joseph Telushkin serve as editor. He is a fount of biblical, rabbinic/Talmudic, and historical knowledge; no one knows my thinking on the Torah as well as Joseph and we had already written two books together. If Joseph worked with me, I would put all other writing aside for years to write this commentary.

I did not think that would happen, but Joel makes things happen. He brought Joseph on board to work full time for three years on this commentary. And even after this, Joel managed all of the business affairs and carefully read through every draft of this volume. Thank you, Joel. And thank you as well for your intellectual input and your constant insistence that I always live up to the name of the commentary—the name you came up with—The Rational Bible.

Joseph Telushkin and I met in our second year of high school at the Yeshiva of Flatbush. We met one day after school at a nearby bookstore. We both loved books because we loved ideas—we wanted to understand life. That was an immediate bond. And there was one other: Neither of us did almost any schoolwork. Instead, we read books and magazines (and, in my case, attended classical music concerts and studied scores).

At the age of twenty-six, we wrote and published our first book, *Eight Questions People Ask about Judaism*, which was soon thereafter expanded and published as *The Nine Questions People Ask about Judaism*. The book became one the most widely read introductions to Judaism and remains in print nearly forty-five years later. Working with him on this commentary was a reminder of the joy we experienced when we wrote our first two books together at the outset of our careers. Joseph constantly contributed information that influenced and deepened my arguments—even on those occasions when we disagreed.

From the earliest days of our friendship, people would often say about Joseph and me: "They're as close as brothers." And we have always responded: "Would that all brothers be that close."

Finally, a word about the person to whom I have dedicated this book—my wife, Susan. She was the final editor of every word of this book, not just for grammar and syntax, but primarily for her specialty: logic. She is trained as a lawyer, but her ability to think rigorously is an innate gift—as rare a gift as perfect pitch is to the few musicians who have that innate ability. The number of less than clear assertions she uncovered is so great I am almost embarrassed to think this book might have been published without her input. And that is only one of the many reasons everyone who knows Sue knows how blessed I am to have her in my life.

I will end with a thank you to the people I mentioned at the beginning of the introduction. My parents, Max and Hilda Prager, raised my brother, Kenneth, and me to take the Torah and God seriously. My love of the Torah is in no small part due to them. And, the aforementioned difficulties notwithstanding, I loved them. I wish I could hand deliver this commentary to them.

Dennis Prager
January 2018

PREFACE

Joel Alperson

I'VE ALWAYS TRIED TO FIND THE ANSWERS TO THE BIG QUESTIONS OF LIFE.

When I was all of nine years old, after a close friend showed me some magic tricks, I found the magic book he had read so I could perform the same magic he showed me.

Later, as a college freshman, I discovered Plato, who addressed many of the "big questions" I deeply cared about, with arguments that were linear and well thought through. Later, as a college senior, I studied one-on-one with a professor who told me of a legend which held that Plato had written a book on "the good." I was so excited. I thought if I could only read this book, I could learn "the secret" of leading a good life. Unfortunately, the legend also held that this volume had been lost in a great fire. So, my search for "the good" began and ended in the span of that one-hour study session.

Who would have guessed that decades later I would not only find myself reading a brilliant explanation of what I have come to regard as the greatest book ever written, but that I would also have helped to make this work possible? My Sunday school and Hebrew school teachers certainly would not have guessed. Given my awful grades and even worse behavior, they'd be shocked. My grandfather, an Orthodox rabbi, would also be shocked. He had given me a five-volume set of the Torah when I was a teen, but whenever he would open one of those volumes, he would hear the binding crack. He knew I hadn't even touched the books.

My story is hardly unique. The majority of those living in the West have dismissed the Torah and the rest of the Bible as little more than ancient religious fairy tales. And why not? Ten plagues? The creation of the world by a super-natural God? A giant flood wiping out virtually all of mankind? Ten Commandments from 3,000 years ago? Why would people choose to study, let alone think their lives could be transformed by, such stories?

I certainly didn't.

Then, one weekend in 1982, I heard Dennis Prager speak at a retreat outside of Kansas City. I remember arguing with him all weekend. But he had answers. And they stayed with me. So began my long journey of realizing that the Torah had more meaning than I ever imagined.

Eventually, Dennis taught the Torah to a class in Los Angeles, line-by-line, over the course of eighteen years, and I started listening to recordings of those classes in my car as I drove around my hometown of Omaha, Nebraska. Realizing that I couldn't focus on the material and driving at the same time, I asked him if I could transcribe some of those recordings. That was in 2002. Little did I know at the time his agreement would start the process of creating this remarkable work. I was able to enlist the help of Ilana Kurshan, a very talented student of the Torah. For one year she took approximately 5,000 pages of Dennis's Torah class transcripts and converted them into a first draft of this commentary. Her work was excellent and enormously helpful.

It was also our very good fortune that Rabbi Joseph Telushkin was available to help with this project. For all the reasons Dennis listed in his introduction, no one else could have added to this great work as Rabbi Telushkin has. The finished product, as Dennis is the first to acknowledge, was made possible because of Rabbi Telushkin's passionate involvement.

Helping Dennis Prager author this work has been an honor for me. I helped the wisest man I know comment on the wisest book ever written. Having carefully and repeatedly listened to Dennis's Torah lectures, I expected this book to be an edited version of all the wonderful ideas he offered over the years. But I was surprised by the many new and important insights he added to this project. I think even he was surprised. This work captured him. It was obvious from his tremendous investment of time, thought, and research that this was not another book. This is arguably his greatest work, and his legacy. You have only to read a few essays or a single chapter to see the profundity of his writing.

Dennis has repeatedly said how grateful he is to me for helping to make his, as he likes to put it, "magnum opus" possible. He says it is one of the greatest gifts he's ever received. Ironically, after working so closely with him over so many years, I believe the greatest gift I've given was to myself.

I've come to realize the book on "the good" was not lost in a fire.

It's here for you to read.

Acknowledgments: This remarkable project could never have been completed without the help of so many wonderful and devoted individuals. In addition to Dennis's acknowledgments, I would like to thank some of those individuals with whom I worked. I can't possibly give them all the credit they're due, but these individuals' efforts were indispensable in creating this book:

Talia Gordis, Emily Sirotkin, Helen Lin, and Katrina Chen devoted many hours to reviewing lecture transcripts to identify and organize the essay topics which were used throughout this commentary.

Thanks to Scott Dugan for carefully and accurately accounting for the expenses related to this commentary.

Thanks to Pete Sirotkin whose great work at our office in Omaha allowed me the freedom to work on this book. He is an exemplary human being and exemplary Christian—and he believes this is the greatest Bible commentary he's ever read.

While many people were involved in transcribing hundreds of Dennis's Torah lecture recordings, one transcriptionist stands out. Debbie Weinberger lived in Israel and transcribed much of Dennis's work. Very sadly, this young woman died of cancer in 2007. Her feelings about being remembered in this work were expressed in the following email:

"When he said it was Dennis Prager on the line, I think my heart stopped for a nanosecond! We had a lovely conversation and we agreed that our biggest prayer is that I get to see or receive a copy of Leviticus personally—in other words, that I stick around.... So very touched deep in my soul that Dennis wants to add a note about me and my working on the project/book."

When I was struggling to decide whether to devote the necessary time and expense to this commentary, my dear friend Ron Carson asked how I would feel on my deathbed if this book were never published. Thank you, Ron, for helping me to make the right decision.

To my dear friend Dr. Howard Gendelman (Howie), who constantly amazes me with his tremendous courage, passion, and persistence. His life has been a *Kiddush Hashem* (a sanctification of God's name).

To my dear friend Dennis Prager: There is no one else on the planet for whom I would have involved myself so deeply in such a project. It is your life-changing ideas and the promise they hold of making so many people better human beings that continue to inspire and excite me. What greater goal could one have and how many others could make such a goal attainable? Thank you for allowing me to share in your remarkable dream.

And finally to Conny—my beautiful wife and the mother of our children. Thank you so much for your encouragement, for listening to me endlessly discuss the details of this work and for celebrating its many successes with me. As I've told you so often, no one's support and enthusiasm means as much to me. How can I possibly thank you for your endless love, kindness, and devotion? May we spend many happy hours teaching our children the lessons contained within this great work. And may our children teach them to their children.

Joel Alperson
January 2018

THE STORY THUS FAR

THE FIRST FIVE BOOKS OF THE BIBLE HAVE ALWAYS BEEN KNOWN AS THE TORAH, which is Hebrew for "Teaching" or "Law." Exodus is the second book. The first book, Genesis, begins with a description of the creation of the world. Every nation and religion in the world had a creation story, but the creation story in Genesis was unique in important ways. Only one God created the world; there was no sex and no violence involved in creation, and God was not part of nature—God created nature. As you will see, each of those unique things will play a huge role in the Torah's transformation of the world.

One other unique element in the Genesis creation story is that although the Torah is, among other things, the story of the Jewish people, it is probably the only national history ever written that begins with the creation of the world. One reason is the subject of the Torah is all mankind, not just the Jews. That, too, is a major feature of the Torah and this commentary.

After the Creation, Genesis describes how the human race immediately descended into evil (good and evil are another preoccupation of the Torah). God is so angered by humans hurting one another He destroys the world, saving but one man, Noah, and his family. Noah is saved solely because he is a good man (in other flood stories, the hero is usually saved because he is good looking, and the gods like him).

Eventually God reveals Himself to the father of the Jewish people, Abraham. God says that through Abraham and his offspring, all the families and nations of the earth will be blessed. Abraham is the father of Isaac, and Isaac is the father of Jacob. The latter is renamed "Israel," which, the Torah explains, means "struggle with God." Very early on, the Torah makes it clear people are allowed, indeed expected, to argue with God—another major theme of the Torah.

Even an atheist who doesn't believe that either the Exodus or the giving of the Ten Command- ments at Sinai actually occurred would have to acknowledge that the Western world has been largely shaped by the belief that these events did occur.

One of Israel's (Jacob's) twelve sons was Joseph, whose story is the second longest biographical story in the Torah (the first is Moses). Joseph's brothers, intensely jealous of their father Jacob's love for him, abandoned their brother to die in a pit. But Joseph was saved by a passing caravan, then sold as a slave, and eventually wound up in Egypt. There he deciphered the Pharaoh's dreams, saved Egypt from a seven-year fam- ine, and arose from slave to viceroy of Egypt, second in power only to the Pharaoh himself. Joseph's broth- ers, who went to Egypt from famine-stricken Canaan looking for food, met with their brother Joseph. That meeting may be the most dramatic scene in Western literature.

And that brings us to the first verse in Exodus.

1.1 These are the names of the sons of Israel who came to Egypt with Jacob, each coming with his household:

1.2 Reuben, Simeon, Levi, and Judah;

1.3 Issachar, Zebulun, and Benjamin;

1.4 Dan and Naphtali, Gad and Asher.

1.5 The total number of persons that were of Jacob's issue came to seventy, Joseph being already in Egypt.

1.6 Joseph died, and all his brothers, and all that generation.

The "sons of Israel" (*b'nei yisrael*) is how the Israelites are referred to in the Torah. *Israel* was the name given to the Jewish patriarch Jacob after he wrestled with an angel (Genesis 32:29). As noted above, "Israel" means "wrestle (or struggle) with God."

Why should non-Jews care about the story of one of the smallest nations on earth? Because the Israelites' move to Egypt set the stage for two of the most important events in world history: the Israelites' Exodus from Egyptian slavery and the revelation of the Ten Commandments at Mount Sinai.

Even an atheist who believes neither event occurred would have to acknowledge that the Western world—and those parts of the non-Western world influenced by the West—has been largely shaped by belief that these events did occur. For example, Thomas Jefferson and Benjamin Franklin, two of the founders of America, neither of whom believed in a literal reading of the Bible, commissioned a design for the Great Seal of the United States of America which depicted the Israelites leaving Egypt. (Franklin proposed the scene be surrounded by the words, "Resistance to tyrants is obedience to God.") Not only did these men deem the Exodus to be civilization-defining, they also believed America was founded in a second Exodus—of people leaving Europe and establishing the United States.

> *Nations, like people, are their memories. A nation that doesn't remember its past, like the man who fell on his head, ceases to be the nation it was.*

That these two events—the Exodus and the giving of the Ten Commandments—are the two seminal events (other than Creation itself) of the Torah means liberty and morality are the twin pillars of the Torah. They became the twin pillars of America as well, which is not surprising, given that America was, outside of Israel, the most Bible-based (particularly the Hebrew Bible) country ever founded.

ESSAY: THE JEWS: A SECOND CREATION

1.7 But the Israelites were fertile and prolific; they multiplied and increased very greatly,

Professor Nahum Sarna, the author of important commentaries on Exodus and Genesis, points out the language used in this verse— "multiplied and increased" —echoes the opening chapter of Genesis, in which God instructs all living creatures to "multiply and increase" over all the earth (Genesis 1:28). Just as the world was created by God in the beginning of Genesis, a new creation is now taking place with the formation of the Jewish people as a nation.

THE JEWS: GOD'S THIRD ATTEMPT TO CREATE A MORAL WORLD

The Exodus followed by the revelation of the Ten Commandments at Sinai and the subsequent writing of this Torah may be considered God's third attempt to create a moral world.

God's first attempt to make a good world was creating human beings with a conscience. That didn't work: Cain, the firstborn child of the first couple, Adam and Eve, killed his brother, Abel. After this, a general moral deterioration of humanity followed, and God came to regret creating human beings (Genesis 6:5-6).

Consequently, God sent the flood, destroying all mankind except for one particularly good man—Noah—and his family. Since the human conscience was insufficient to make a good world, God then *revealed* some basic moral laws and principles such as not to murder, to take the life of those who deliberately murder, to have children, not to consume the blood of any creature, and every human being is created in the image of God (Genesis 9:1-7).

Once again, people murdered and plundered and engaged in other evils. God, therefore, initiated a third effort to morally improve mankind by revealing Himself to one specific group who would be charged with spreading ethical monotheism to the world. This group was first known as Hebrews, then as Israelites, then as Jews. They descended from a man named Abraham to whom God revealed Himself and His desire that the entire world be blessed through Abraham and his descendants.

Abraham's descendants were enslaved in Egypt for hundreds of years. The process by which they became enslaved begins in this chapter, and is followed midway in the book by the Exodus from Egypt and the revelation of the Ten Commandments at Mount Sinai.

WHY DIDN'T GOD GIVE THE TEN COMMANDMENTS TO THE FIRST HUMAN BEINGS?

Of course, one might ask, why would God have to keep trying? Doesn't God know what works and what doesn't? Why didn't He just begin the world with the Ten Commandments or with a Chosen People as conduits of His moral will?

I would offer three responses:

First, in creating a being (the human) with free will, it is arguable that God could not predict what this creature would always do. Genesis 6:6 says that, after seeing how much evil men do, "God regretted that He had created man on earth." That verse implies God did know how man would turn out.

Second, God made these multiple attempts at having people act decently to show why revelation was necessary, and why specifically the revelation at Sinai and the Torah were necessary. Precisely because prior attempts—the making of the human conscience and basic moral "Noahide" principles—did not work, God gave the Ten Commandments and the Torah.

Third, this third attempt at making a good world establishes the raison d'être of the Jewish people—"to be a nation of priests and a holy nation" (Exodus 19:6) and to bring the world to the Ten Commandments and ethical monotheism.

WHY DO PEOPLE THINK THERE ARE SO MANY JEWS IN THE WORLD?

1.7 (cont.) so that the land was filled with them.

The words, "the land was filled with them" imply that although the Israelites were granted permission to live in an area of Egypt known as Goshen (Genesis 45:10), the Egyptians perceived them as everywhere. Throughout history, Jew-haters—and even many non-Jews sympathetic to Jews—have often wildly overstated the number of Jews in their country. I remember once, in my early years of lecturing, sitting next to a non-Jewish woman on an airplane on the way to Louisville, Kentucky. She asked me why I was visiting her city. I told her I was going to speak to the Jewish community there. As the conversation continued—on the subject of Jews—it became apparent to me this woman thought there were far more Jews in Kentucky than there actually were.

I told her (at that time) there were 280 million Americans, and then asked her, "How many of them do you think are Jews?"

She thought for a moment, and responded, "About fifty million."

When I told her there were about six million Jews in America, she was clearly startled. She pondered this, and then said, "I guess they must all live in Kentucky."

As of this writing, there are about fourteen million Jews in a world population of about seven and a half billion. That means that about .0018 percent, or fewer than two out of every thousand people in the world, are Jews. But few people would guess this—because the influence of the Jews has always been so great. *And the reason for that influence is this Torah, its God, its Ten Commandments, and its Exodus story.* In short, the stories and values of this Book of Exodus have transformed the world.

THE INDISPENSABLE IMPORTANCE OF REMEMBERING

1.8 A new king arose over Egypt who did not know Joseph.

Joseph, about whom more is written than any other figure in the Torah except for Moses, was the Israelite who rose from slavery, followed by imprisonment, to become the second most powerful man in Egypt. He is credited with saving Egypt (from famine). Given that Joseph's role in Egyptian history was so profound, the words "who did not know Joseph" are extraordinary.

One of humanity's most common character traits is ingratitude—people either not acknowledging the good another does for them or quickly forgetting that good. The latter is what this verse describes.

Human beings tend to much more quickly forget the good others have done *for* them than the bad others have done *to* them. That's human nature. It is, therefore, one of the very many reasons that to become a good person involves fighting one's nature—a theme developed often in the Torah, in the rest of the Bible, and in this commentary.

The American writer Bruce Feiler has an additional insight into this verse—the recurring emphasis on remembering in the Torah and specifically the Book of Exodus:

"The story begins with forgetting. The pharaoh does not remember how a son of Israel saved Egypt from famine. The rest of the Five Books of Moses becomes an antidote to this state of forgetfulness. God hears the groaning of Israel and '*remembers* His covenant' (Exodus 2.24). Moses leads the Israelites from Egypt and urges them to '*remember* this day' (Exodus 13.3). The Israelites are ordered to '*remember* the Sabbath day' (Exodus 20.8), and to observe Passover as a 'day of *remembrance*' (Exodus 12.14). Moses's goal is to build a counter-Egypt...to construct a society that offers an alternative to ignorance and unknowingness. He must devise a community that *remembers*"[1] (emphases added).

Remembering—the good others have done, the evil others have done, and one's moral obligations—is an indispensable aspect of a good and meaningful life.

Who are we, if not our memories? I once interviewed a man who, as the result of a fall on his head, had lost virtually all long-term memory. He did not even remember who his wife and children were. In the interview he acknowledged that, for all intents and purposes, because of his loss of memory, the man he had been had died.

The same holds true for nations. Nations, too, are their memories. A nation that doesn't remember its past, like the man who fell on his head, ceases to be the nation it was. This may be happening now in a number of Western European nations that teach their young people to consider themselves "world citizens" or Europeans rather than members of a specific nation. It is also happening in the United States, where the level of ignorance of the American past among young Americans is unprecedented.[2]

What can be stated for certain is a major reason for the survival of the Jewish people has been memory. The Jewish religion is replete with prayers and rituals that reinforce that memory, the most obvious being the Passover Seder, the retelling of the Exodus in Jewish homes for over 3,000 years.

THE INDIVIDUAL AND MASSIVE EVIL

1.9 And he [Pharaoh] said to his people,

Samson Raphael Hirsch, a nineteenth-century German Jewish thinker, pointed out it was the Egyptian leader, not the Egyptian people, who initiated the campaign against the Israelites that ultimately came to include attempted genocide.

This is a profound insight.

The terrible truth is individuals are capable of inflicting massive evils—because individuals are far more capable of doing great evil than great good.

Were it not for Lenin, it is unlikely communism would have taken over Russia and ultimately the Soviet Union, where it enslaved over 150 million people and murdered tens of millions. The same holds true for Mao Zedong in China. This one man was responsible for the deaths of over sixty million Chinese men, women, and children. The same can be said of Kim Il-Sung, who created the most totalitarian state in human history, North Korea. And were it not for Adolf Hitler, the Holocaust would almost certainly not have taken place.

Understandably, people are very uncomfortable with acknowledging how much evil one individual can perpetrate. That is one reason people concoct and believe conspiracy theories. The assassination of the American President John F. Kennedy in 1963 is one example. The overwhelming evidence is that one man, Lee Harvey Oswald, an American Communist, murdered Kennedy. But the assassination had so many destructive consequences and was so emotionally difficult for Americans to accept that many came to believe there was a conspiracy to assassinate President Kennedy. They simply could not believe so much damage could be done by just one person—a pathetic misfit, no less. Oswald proves the unhappy truth that you don't even have to be particularly talented to do great evil.

1.9 (cont.) "Look, the Israelite people are much too numerous for us.

Pharaoh refers to the Israelites using the rare phrase *am b'nei Yisrael*, which literally means "the nation of the children of Israel." There are two words for "nation" in biblical Hebrew—*am* and *goy*. *Am* refers to a nation defined by blood ties, a common ancestry, history, and language (see, for example, the book of Esther 8:9) as opposed to *goy*, which refers to a nation defined as a political unit (see Isaiah 2:4). In using "am," Pharaoh is saying, in effect, the purity of the Egyptian people is being threatened by an alien presence, the children of Israel, who are of a different bloodline.

Throughout history, blood beliefs have been a great source of cruelty: Those who are not part of the right group are deemed worthy of persecution. The Torah, in contrast, did not place much value on blood ties. As Joseph Telushkin points out, Jacob is regarded as the third patriarch of the Jewish people, but his twin brother, Esau, who did not share Jacob's religious beliefs, is not even regarded as a Jew. In Exodus (19:6), God tells the Jews to be a holy *goy* (national unit), not a holy *am* (blood-group or ethnicity).

Human beings tend to much more quickly forget the good others have done for them than the bad others have done to them.

The Hebrew Bible holds, and later Judaism held, that anyone of any blood can become a Jew—just like the first Jew, Abraham, who was not born a Jew but became one late in life. Likewise, centuries later, Ruth, a Moabite woman, becomes a Jew, and subsequently becomes the ancestor of Israel's great king, David (Ruth 4:13-22), the man from whom, according to Jewish (and Christian) tradition, the Messiah will descend.

1.10 Let us deal shrewdly with them, so that they may not increase; otherwise in the event of war they may join our enemies in fighting against us and rise from the ground."

THE GUILT OF THE EGYPTIAN PEOPLE

1.11 So they set taskmasters over them to oppress them with forced labor;

The Torah indicts the Egyptians four times in the next four verses:

The Egyptians set taskmasters over the Israelites (verse 11).

They ruthlessly impose hardships on them (verse 13).

They make them perform harsh labors (verse 14).

They make life bitter for them (verse 14).

The Torah is emphasizing the collective guilt of the Egyptians. Even though it is Pharaoh who initiates the slavery and annihilation campaign, the Egyptian people are the ones who execute it. Individuals initiate mass evil, but they need the collaboration of many people to carry it out. This explains the collective national punishments the Egyptian people will experience.

1.11 (cont.) and they built garrison cities for Pharaoh: Pithom and Raamses.

1.12 But the more they were oppressed, the more they increased and spread out, so that the [Egyptians] came to dread the Israelites.

1.13 The Egyptians ruthlessly imposed upon the Israelites

Most Egyptians were not as evil as Pharaoh, just as most Germans in the 1930s and 1940s were not as evil as Hitler. There are relatively few truly evil people in the world. However, you don't need a great number of truly evil people to carry out massive evil. You only need:

1) ordinary people who have allowed themselves to be indoctrinated by the truly evil;
2) people who benefit from the evil (to cite one obvious example, during World War II, not only were six million Jews murdered, but their assets were stolen as well; and these assets enriched large numbers of Europeans;
3) a paucity of courageous good people.

I am convinced courage is the rarest of all good traits. There are far more kind and honest people than there are courageous people. Unfortunately, however, in the battle against evil, all the good traits in the world amount to little when not accompanied by courage.

Two verses later, the Torah depicts precisely this trait—courage.

1.14 the various labors that they made them perform. Ruthlessly they made life bitter for them with harsh labor at mortar and bricks and with all sorts of tasks in the field.

WERE THE MIDWIVES WHO DISOBEYED PHARAOH EGYPTIANS OR HEBREWS? I

1.15 The king of Egypt spoke to the Hebrew midwives,

The Torah emphasizes Pharaoh's direct order to the midwives to highlight their courage in defying his edict. The meaning of the Hebrew phrase *m'yaldot ha'ivriyot* is ambiguous: it may be translated either as "the Hebrew midwives" (meaning the midwives were Hebrews), or as "midwives of the Hebrews" (meaning the midwives could have been of any nationality). But there are several clues in the text (which shall be noted) that clearly suggest that the women were not Hebrews. The most obvious clue, however, is not rooted in the text but in common sense: Given that Pharaoh intended to murder every male Hebrew baby, it is unreasonable to expect he would rely on Hebrew women to murder their own.

THE TORAH GIVES THE MIDWIVES' NAMES, BUT NOT THE PHARAOH'S

1.15 (cont.) one of whom was named Shiphrah and the other Puah,

In listing the names of the heroic midwives, the Torah is making a powerful moral point. We tend to remember the names of villains, but not of the truly good. The Torah wants to correct that and to ensure the names of moral heroes are also remembered. Thus, Shifrah (the modern spelling) and Puah are mentioned by name, yet the Torah never mentions the name of the evil Pharaoh. To this day the names of two lowly midwives are better known than the name of the demigod Pharaoh. Moreover, Shifrah remains a common name for Jewish girls (Puah, less euphonious, is rarely used).

1.16 saying, "When you deliver the Hebrew women, look at the birthstool: if it is a boy, kill him; if it is a girl, let her live."

ESSAY: THE MORAL SIGNIFICANCE OF FEARING GOD

1.17 The midwives, fearing God, did not do as the king of Egypt had told them; they let the boys live.

The Torah does not say the midwives saved the babies because they could not bear to harm them, nor does it say the midwives saved the Hebrew babies because they loved God. They saved the babies because "they feared God."

Fear of God—when that God is the moral God of the Torah, the God of the Ten Commandments, the God Who commanded, "Love your neighbor as yourself" —is necessary to make a society of moral individuals. Of course, there are moral atheists, just as there were moral pagans, and moral individuals in even the worst cultures. But you cannot build a good world with a handful of individuals who happen to be good people. You need a universal moral code from a universal God Who is the source of that moral code, and this God must judge all people accordingly. Consequently, "fear of God" is as inevitable as it is necessary. If God judges how moral we are, of course there will be fear of Him—just as there is of a human judge. Conversely, if God does not judge people, there is no reason to fear Him.

There is another important moral aspect to fear of God. People fear those who are more powerful than they are. Therefore, the only way not to fear powerful people is to fear God. Thus, in the instance recorded here, those who feared God saved Hebrew babies, while those who feared Pharaoh helped drown Hebrew babies.

Remember, it was not love of God that prompted the midwives' moral heroism. In our time, many people invoke the commandment to love God but ignore or even disparage the commandment to fear God. While many God-believers will engage in heroic self-sacrifice out of love of God, most God-believers are moral on a day-to-day basis because they believe they will be judged by God. That's why, for example, in traditional Western societies, the finest people were routinely described as "God-fearing," not "God-loving."

It was the midwives' fear of God that liberated them from fear of the Egyptian tyrant. This point is often overlooked: Fear of God is a *liberating* emotion, freeing one from a disabling fear of evil, powerful people. This needs to be emphasized because many people see fear of God as onerous rather than liberating.

This fear is what gave the midwives the strength to carry out what is, as far as we know, the first recorded act of civil disobedience in history. Indeed, fear (and sometimes love) of God explains why a disproportionately high number of dissidents in totalitarian societies have been believers in God. When I visited the Soviet Union in 1969, I smuggled out a Soviet Jewish dissident song whose lyrics included the words: "I fear no one except God, the only one" ("*Nye byusa nikovo krome boga odnavo*").

Those words were all the more remarkable in that the vast majority of Soviet Jewish dissidents were not religious. But they understood the simple moral and logical fact that if one "fears no one except God," one can muster the courage not to fear a totalitarian state. And these simple words also explain why totalitarian states like the Soviet Union so feared and fought against belief in God. Because belief in God posits there is something higher than the Party, it constitutes a fatal threat to secular totalitarian societies (that's why North Koreans have been horribly punished for owning a Bible).

Those who feared God saved Hebrew babies. Those who feared Pharaoh helped drown Hebrew babies.

In the Torah, the term "fear of God" is generally used when describing non-Jews. For example, when Abraham worries Sarah will be mistreated in Gerar, he explains: "there is no fear of God in this place" (Genesis 20:11). Thus, the use of this phrase to account for the midwives' behavior provides yet another indication that the midwives were likely not Hebrews.

Finally, it is important to point out that the Torah's account of the moral heroism of the midwives is part of a pattern present throughout the opening chapters of Exodus—the depiction of both non-Jews and women as moral heroes (see commentary on Exodus 2:1). This is another of the many examples of the Torah's uniqueness. Other holy works have rarely portrayed either people of other nations, other religions, or women—let alone women of other nations and religions—as the moral heroes of their epic stories. This unique aspect of the Torah—one of so many examples of such—is among the many reasons why I do not regard the Torah as man-made.

WERE THE MIDWIVES WHO DISOBEYED THE PHARAOH EGYPTIANS OR HEBREWS? II

1.18 So the king of Egypt summoned the midwives and said to them, "Why have you done this thing, letting the boys live?"

The fact that Pharaoh seems puzzled by their behavior is yet another indication the women were not Hebrews: His question, "Why have you done this thing...?" suggests that he is truly mystified by their behavior. It is unlikely he would have been so perplexed had the women been Hebrews. Even a Pharaoh would understand why women might not want to kill the babies of their own people.

Surprisingly, Pharaoh does not kill the midwives for disobeying him; he simply pleads with them like a plaintive husband whose wife has not done what he has asked of her. There is a parallel to the Holocaust here. Just as the midwives were not killed or even punished for refusing to participate in the murder of all Jewish boys, the few German soldiers who refused to participate in the Holocaust were also neither killed nor persecuted by the Nazi regime; they were either assigned other tasks or sent to the front (admittedly a very perilous option). Often standing up to great evil leads to death—as, for example, Poles who were caught hiding Jews during World War II—but it also often does not.

This does not, it should be emphasized, in any way reduce the moral greatness of those who did resist Hitler or other tyrants, many of whom suffered terribly, or—like Pastor Dietrich Bonhoeffer—were executed for their moral courage. It is only to note that there are also times when standing up for the good does not lead to terrible persecution.

WHEN LYING IS MORAL

1.19 The midwives said to Pharaoh, "Because the Hebrew women are not like the Egyptian women: they are vigorous. Before the midwife can come to them, they have given birth."

The midwives lie to Pharaoh, offering as an excuse the supposedly rapid nature of Hebrew women's manner of giving birth. This passage offers guidance to all people confronting criminals or evil political regimes. The midwives want to save the infants, but they don't want to die; so they don't tell Pharaoh what they are really thinking: *We fear God more than you and therefore have disobeyed you and your evil decree.*

We can infer from this episode that one is not obligated to speak truthfully to murderers and die—or have other innocents die—as a result. Rather, we are not only permitted, but morally obligated, to lie to the evil in order to save ourselves or other innocents. The notion that it is always immoral to lie is itself immoral.

To explain why this is so—why lying is sometimes moral and telling the truth is sometimes immoral—it is necessary to explain the concept of moral absolutes.

ESSAY: MORAL ABSOLUTES, MORAL RELATIVISM, AND SITUATIONAL ETHICS

Many religious people think that if you believe in moral absolutes, you cannot believe in situational ethics; they think situational ethics and moral relativism are synonymous.

This is a serious mistake. Moral relativism and situational ethics are not at all the same. In fact, if you believe in moral absolutes, you must also believe in situational ethics.

The doctrine of moral absolutes—or "objective morality" or "moral truth"—means there is an objective moral standard that transcends personal or societal opinion. To cite three examples, murder, the sexual abuse of a child, and lying are morally wrong not because many people or even an entire society believe they are wrong but because they *are* wrong—in the same way two plus two equals four, not because many (or even all) people think they equal four, but because they do equal four. There are moral truths just as there are mathematical, scientific, and historical truths. (However, there is one big difference: unlike scientific and historical truths, moral truths require God—because while scientific and historical truths can be proven, moral truths cannot be proven. You can argue murder is wrong, but you cannot prove it is wrong the way you can prove, for example, the earth is round. Moral truths depend entirely upon the existence of a Moral Source higher than mankind. Murder is wrong because God says so. If there is no God, all notions of right and wrong are subjective opinion.)

> *Courage is the rarest of all the good traits. There are far more kind and honest people than there are courageous people.*

One more way to describe the existence of moral absolutes is "universal morality." This means that just as two-plus-two-equals-four is universally true, so, too, moral truths are universal. If it is a truth that murder is wrong, it is wrong for all people. Moral relativism holds the opposite. It holds that morality is not universal but determined by each individual or each society: "what you think is wrong is wrong—for *you*; and what I think is wrong is wrong—for *me*."

> *There are moral truths just as there are mathematical, scientific, and historical truths.*

"Situational ethics" is not at all the same as moral relativism. Situational ethics does not mean every individual determines what is moral; it means *only by knowing the situation can we know whether an act is moral or immoral.* This should be clear to anyone who gives it a moment's thought. Take, for example, killing a person. Is that morally wrong? It depends entirely on the situation. If it is done in self-defense or to defend other innocents, or in a moral war, it is a moral act. Otherwise it is not "killing," but "murder." And murder, by definition, is immoral killing.

Or, take sexual intercourse. That act can be the most beautiful form of physical human bonding, but the same exact act can be the evil act known as rape. What determines whether sexual intercourse is beautiful and even holy or evil? The answer is—the situation.

The situation is what makes it possible for us to determine what the moral absolute is. Very few acts are in and of themselves morally wrong. It is the situation that enables us to determine what is right and wrong.

Lying is another example. The situation enables us to determine whether lying is wrong. If a murderer asks you where his intended victim is hiding, and you know the answer, it is not only alright to lie to the murderer, it is morally imperative to do so—because saving an innocent person's life is a greater moral good than refraining from lying.

That is why the midwives' lie was moral. And the biblical proof that this is what God wanted is two verses later when God rewards their behavior. God approved of both their conduct and their lie.

MORE ON THE MIDWIVES: EGYPTIAN OR HEBREW? III

Ilana Pardes, professor of Comparative Literature at the Hebrew University, noted the words translated here as "they are vigorous" (*ki chayyot hei-nah*) also mean "they are animals." In this instance, the latter translation makes more sense. The midwives understand Pharaoh, like most slave-owners, had a racist view of the enslaved people, and was therefore willing to believe the Hebrews were like animals. So he was readily convinced that, unlike the refined women of Egypt, the Hebrew women—like animals—could give birth without requiring assistance.

Ironically, it was Pharaoh's racism that enabled him to accept as true the lie the midwives told him.

This verse is another indication the midwives were not Hebrews. They speak of Hebrew women in the third person—"they."

1.20 And God dealt well with the midwives; and the people multiplied and increased greatly.

1.21 And because the midwives feared God, He established households for them.

God rarely rewards people so immediately and directly—or even rewards many people at all in this life. The preeminent Jewish philosopher Moses Maimonides (1135–1204), in a discussion of divine intervention in individuals' lives (known in Hebrew as *hashgacha pratit,* literally "divine supervision"), posits that God generally intercedes only in the lives of those who involve themselves with Him, and/or those whose lives are involved in something much greater than themselves. The midwives met both of these criteria, which may account for their divine reward. Or, perhaps their rewards are cited to show how unequivocally God approved of their behavior.

1.22 Then Pharaoh charged all his people, saying, "Every boy that is born you shall throw into the Nile,

> The whole Egyptian people are now implicated in the cruel treatment of the Israelites. Cruel as Pharaoh is, he could not have carried out murder on this scale alone; and the Torah once again reminds us it is only through the cooperation of the masses that massive evil is committed.

1.22 (cont.) but let every girl live."

> We do not know for certain why the Pharaoh ordered newborn boys killed, but not newborn girls. But we can speculate.
>
> One likely explanation is offered by a Midrash (a rabbinic story that illuminates a biblical story), which relates that Pharaoh was warned by his sorcerers and astrologers that a male savior of the Israelites was about to be born. This would also explain why Pharaoh only sought to kill the newborn male infants, and why Moses's older brother, Aaron, though only three years old at the time, was not considered a risk. As we shall see in the next chapter, it is only Moses whom their mother feels the need to hide.
>
> It is also possible Pharaoh spared the girls because in a patriarchal society they would not be able to cause as much trouble as boys. Pharaoh likely presumed if the Hebrew males were eliminated, despite any racial misgivings he had, the girls would eventually marry Egyptian or other non-Hebrew men and assimilate, and the Hebrew people would disappear.

CHAPTER 2

2.1 A certain man of the house of Levi went and married a Levite woman.

The "house of Levi" refers to one of the twelve tribes of Israel, the Levites.

The Torah does not mention here the names of this husband and wife—which is remarkable given the monumental role they played as the parents of Moses, the most important figure in the Hebrew Bible and one of the most important figures in world history. They are named later in Exodus 6:20. One possible reason is the Torah's desire to emphasize that Moses was born to ordinary people, not to illustrious, famous, rich, or even particularly holy parents. The most likely reason is to focus attention exclusively on the child, not the parents.

The Torah also wishes to emphasize that Moses's birth was in no way miraculous. God chose Moses to lead the Jews out of Egypt because of his exceptional moral and leadership traits (see, for example, comments on verses 13 and 17). He was not preordained to lead and he was a normal mortal.

THE PREEMINENT ROLE OF WOMEN IN MOSES'S LIFE— AND IN THE TORAH

It is Moses's mother who played the critical role in saving him. Indeed, women played central and heroic roles in the early chapters of Exodus:

The midwives, who defied Pharaoh's edict to drown the Hebrews' male babies; Pharaoh's daughter, who, we will see, saved Moses;

19

The preeminent role of women in Moses's life, like the prominent role of women in Genesis, is striking, particularly in light of the common dismissal of the Torah as a sexist document.

Miriam, Moses's sister, who intervened with the Egyptian princess to have Moses's mother, Yocheved, appointed to nurse and care for Moses until he was weaned;

Zipporah, Moses's Midianite wife, who saved either Moses or their son (the text is not clear) from God's deadly wrath by circumcising their baby (Exodus 4:24-26).

The preeminent role of women in Moses's life, like the prominent—and occasionally preeminent—role of women in the founding of the Jewish people in Genesis, is striking, particularly in light of the common dismissal of the Torah as a sexist document. Some laws in the Torah inevitably reflected the patriarchal culture of its time, but the Torah often portrays women as playing a more important role than men. It is adamant about the equal value of women and men—as reflected in its stories, in the woman as the final act of creation (all creation is in ascending order of sophistication and complexity), in the equal role of mothers and fathers, and elsewhere.

THERE IS NO MIRACLE IN MOSES'S BIRTH

2.2 The woman conceived and bore a son; and when she saw how beautiful he was, she hid him for three months.

The Torah continues its mundane description of Moses's birth. This is in keeping with the Torah's profound desire to prevent Moses from being regarded as divine and therefore worshipped by the Jewish people after his death (or even while alive). This is also the probable reason—as we shall see much later—why Moses is not allowed into the Promised Land, and why his burial place will forever remain unknown.

WHY MOSES WAS SAVED IN THE SAME TYPE OF VESSEL NOAH WAS SAVED IN

2.3 When she could hide him no longer, she got a wicker basket [*tevah*] for him and caulked it with bitumen and pitch.

In order to show a relationship between the stories of Noah and Moses, the Torah uses the same Hebrew word, *tevah*, to refer both to Moses's basket and to Noah's ark (despite the vast discrepancy in size between them).

This is another example of the Torah communicating that the Exodus (which includes the revelation of the Ten Commandments at Sinai) begins a new creation. Just as God saved Noah in a *tevah* set in the water, He will save Moses in a *tevah* set in water. Just as in Genesis, God started a new world with Noah, He is, in effect, starting a new world with Moses and the Jews. And just as God attempted to morally improve the world by revealing moral laws to Noah (i.e., all humanity) after the flood, He will attempt to do the same by revealing specific laws to humanity through Moses and a particular people.

2.3 (cont.) She put the child into it

In the face of this early attempt at genocide, Moses's mother gave up her child to save his life.

2.3 (cont.) and placed it among the reeds by the bank of the Nile.

2.4 And his sister stationed herself at a distance, to learn what would befall him.

The Daughter of the Israelites' Killer Saves the Man Who Will Save the Israelites

2.5 The daughter of Pharaoh came down to bathe in the Nile, while her maidens walked along the Nile. She spied the basket among the reeds and sent her slave girl to fetch it.

2.6 When she opened it, she saw that it was a child, a boy crying. She took pity on it and said, "This must be a Hebrew child."

The Torah specifies that Pharaoh's daughter is aware the baby is a Hebrew to emphasize her moral greatness—she takes pity on the baby knowing he is a Hebrew boy, the group her own father has targeted for annihilation.

If one believes the Torah narrative, how remarkable it is the daughter of the man who set out to annihilate the Hebrews is the one who saves them—and how remarkable of the Torah to relate that fact. If one does not believe the Torah narrative, the Torah, in making up such a story, is even more impressive in its lack of racism, ethno-centrism, and hatred of Egyptians.

In any case, the message is clear: though Pharaoh had a genocidal hatred for the Israelites, his daughter was a great humanitarian, the very person who thwarted her father's evil campaign. Biology is not destiny; you can be the child of an evil person and be a good person.

2.7 Then his sister said to Pharaoh's daughter, "Shall I go and get you a Hebrew nurse

Moses's sister, Miriam, demonstrates considerable courage and boldness: She is not afraid to come forward and make a suggestion to the daughter of the king, even though she is a lowly slave girl.

2.7 (cont.) to suckle the child for you?"

It is only natural to suggest finding a Hebrew wet-nurse for a Hebrew child. Among other reasons, presumably an Egyptian woman would not (any more than a white woman in the nineteenth-century American South would) have breastfed an infant black slave child. Moreover, because of the killing of the Hebrew infants, there were many Hebrew women who still had milk in their breasts. Miriam was, of course, eager to restore the baby to his mother, though she could not share this with Pharaoh's daughter.

2.8 And Pharaoh's daughter answered, "Yes." So the girl went and called the child's mother.

2.9 And Pharaoh's daughter said to her, "Take this child and nurse it for me, and I will pay your wages." So the woman took the child and nursed it.

In another extraordinary display of decency, Pharaoh's daughter offers to pay wages to a slave.

2.10 When the child grew up, she brought him to Pharaoh's daughter, who made him her son. She named him Moses, explaining, "I drew him out of the water."

The name Moses comes from the root of the Hebrew word *m'shi-tihu*, "I drew him out." Moses is also an Egyptian name, and presumably Pharaoh's daughter chooses the name for an Egyptian reason rather than a Hebrew one. The Torah is providing a Hebrew explanation for a name most likely chosen for its Egyptian significance (which we do not know).

2.11 Some time after that, when Moses had grown up,

We do not learn anything about Moses's upbringing or his relationship with either his adopted or birth mother. The Torah was not written in the age of psychology; it is less concerned with the inner lives of its characters than with imparting moral teaching and wisdom to its readers.

2.11 (cont.) he went out to his kinsfolk and witnessed their labors. He saw an Egyptian beating a Hebrew, one of his kinsmen.

Despite being raised an Egyptian, Moses apparently recognized he was (also) a Hebrew. Children in the ancient world were often nursed until three years of age, and Moses's mother would have likely wanted to maximize her time with him. It is quite possible she taught him he was a Hebrew. Perhaps he also had some continuing contact with his sister, since the Torah makes it clear he knew his brother Aaron (Exodus 4:14).

> *Biology is not destiny; you can be the child of an evil person and be a good person.*

Perhaps resentful Egyptians in Pharaoh's court regularly reminded Moses of his lowly (Hebrew) background.

And perhaps the daughter of Pharaoh, the mother who raised him, told him.

It is also possible, though less likely, Moses did not know he was a Hebrew, and the Torah's words "one of his brothers" (translated here as "kinsmen") is the Torah speaking, not Moses's mind.

OUR MOTHER IS THE WOMAN, AND OUR FATHER IS THE MAN, WHO RAISES US

Regarding the role of Pharaoh's daughter in Moses's life, the Talmud—the holiest Jewish body of literature after the Bible, edited between the years 200 and 500, and comprising sixty-three volumes of philosophy, theology, ritual and ethical law, and stories—states: "Yocheved gave birth to Moses, Batya [the Hebrew name given to Pharaoh's daughter, meaning 'daughter of God'] raised him; therefore he is identified as her child."[1]

In other words, even though Yocheved gave birth to Moses and even nursed him, the Jewish tradition regards Pharaoh's daughter as Moses's mother. As important as birth parents almost always are (and Yocheved was), in most cases blood is less important than actually raising a child when it comes to assigning the title "mother" or "father."

WHY MOSES WILL BE CHOSEN TO LEAD IS ALREADY APPARENT

Verse 11 alone suggests at least three reasons why Moses was the exceptional man who would be chosen to deliver the Israelites from bondage:

1. Moses fights evil. He is instinctively intolerant of suffering and injustice. As soon as he sees a slave being beaten by an overseer, he doesn't move on, as most people in his situation (a prince) would. He does whatever he can to stop the evil. Most people, when confronted with evil directed against others, look away. They are too afraid to confront it. Moral courage, as noted, is the rarest of all good traits (see commentary to Exodus 1:13).

2. Moses will later command the respect of the Israelites in part because he was not raised among them. That made him far more worldly than people who were raised as slaves. Also, the Israelites must have admired this man who *chose* to be one of them, when he could have led an utterly charmed life as an Egyptian prince.

3. Moses does not have a slave mentality. Unlike his fellow Hebrews, who were so demoralized that they could only cry out (see 2:23, 3:7, 9), Moses does not share their demoralization and does not merely cry out; he takes action.

2.12 He turned this way and that and, seeing no one about,

Moses looks around to make sure there is no one to witness the illegal act he is about to commit. To protect a slave, let alone to kill an Egyptian, was a major transgression of Egyptian law. If he were caught, he would be executed (see verse 15).

Another possible reading is that he checked to see whether there was "a man"—someone who might intercede on behalf of the slave. Only when Moses saw there was "no man" who would, did he intervene. The Hebrew word *ish* ("man") is sometimes used in Hebrew—as in English ("Be a man!") and other languages—to refer to a morally upstanding individual. As the Talmud states: "In a place where there is no man, be a man [*ish*]."[2]

GOD APPARENTLY STRONGLY APPROVED OF MOSES'S ACT OF HOMICIDE

2.12 (cont.) he struck down the Egyptian and hid him in the sand.

Moses killed the Egyptian and buried him. Many people have criticized Moses for this homicide. But what else should Moses have done? Should he have walked away? He would have been turning his back on a terrible injustice.

Should he have tried to persuade the Egyptian overseer to stop? The idea borders on the absurd. Should he have attacked the Egyptian without killing him? The Egyptian would either have fought back and quite possibly killed Moses or informed on Moses, which would have resulted in his being accused of subversion for trying to stop an overseer from punishing a slave (see commentary to verse 15).

Clearly, God approved of what Moses did. This is the first of three stories told about Moses to convey what sort of man Moses was and, implicitly, why God chose him to lead the Israelites out of Egypt.

To more fully appreciate what Moses did, one should see the film that won the 2013 Academy Award for Best Picture, *Twelve Years a Slave*, especially the scene in which a master whips a slave woman to the brink of death. Watching this scene, one can only wish there was a Moses-like character to do what he did here.

2.13 When he went out the next day, he found two Hebrews fighting; so he said to the offender,

The word translated here as "offender" literally means "the evil one." The Torah does not hesitate to describe a Jew as evil. Much of the Torah's—and the entire Hebrew Bible's—greatness and credibility lies in its willingness to critique the Jewish people. At the same time, it is to the Jews' credit that they canonized books so critical of them.

MOSES'S THREE RESPONSES TO INJUSTICE

2.13 (cont.) "Why do you strike your fellow?"

This is the second of three stories told about Moses before God appears to him.

In the first story, Moses witnessed injustice and responded by killing. In this second story, when he witnessed injustice, he spoke. The next time, he will simply stand.

These are the three possible responses to evil: fighting back (and killing if necessary), speaking out, and standing.

Moses is chosen by God not just because he fights against evil, but because he knows which response is most appropriate in any given situation.

2.14 He retorted, "Who made you chief and ruler over us? Do you mean to kill me as you killed the Egyptian?" Moses was frightened, and thought: Then the matter is known!

When Moses asked the Hebrew offender why he hit his fellow, the man did not respond to the question; instead he verbally attacked Moses. This is a classic response of guilty people when challenged about what they have done—to attack their accuser.

2.15 When Pharaoh learned of the matter, he sought to kill Moses; but Moses fled from Pharaoh. He arrived in the land of Midian, and sat down beside a well.

Given that Moses was raised at the royal court, we might have thought he would be spared punishment for killing a mere overseer. But killing an Egyptian overseer and identifying with the Hebrews would have branded him a traitor and warranted the death penalty.

2.16 Now the priest of Midian had seven daughters. They came to draw water, and filled the troughs to water their father's flock;

2.17 but shepherds came and drove them off. Moses rose to their defense, and he watered their flock.

For the third time, Moses refuses to tolerate the evil he sees around him. This time he does not kill or speak out; he simply stands—in defense of Midianite women. This third event demonstrates Moses is not simply a Hebrew nationalist, concerned with fighting evil only when a Hebrew is the victim. And he is as offended by injustice toward women as men.

In the first instance, he intervenes when a non-Hebrew oppresses a Hebrew; in the second instance he intervenes when one Hebrew wrongs another Hebrew; and now he intervenes when non-Hebrew men oppress non-Hebrew women. All injustice infuriates him and prompts him to act.

2.18 When they returned to their father Reuel,

Elsewhere in the Torah, this man is called Jethro (see, for example, Exodus 3:1 and 18:1), on one occasion Jether (Exodus 4:18), and on another Hobab (Numbers 10:29). He was known by each of these names.

2.18 (cont.) he said, "How is it that you have come back so soon today?"

Apparently, the women were often detained by bullying shepherds at the well, so their father grew accustomed to their late return. Jethro and his daughters have learned to accept the shepherds' harassment as a matter of course. Moses has not.

2.19 They answered, "An Egyptian rescued us from the shepherds; he even drew water for us and watered the flock."

The Midianites understandably identify Moses as an Egyptian, which suggests he resembled an Egyptian in speech, dress, and mannerism.

2.20 He said to his daughters, "Where is he then? Why did you leave the man? Ask him in to break bread."

Like any father who has daughters to marry off, Reuel is eager to welcome an eligible bachelor into his home, particularly one who has demonstrated such noble characteristics.

2.21 Moses consented to stay with the man,

After a long flight through the desert from a place where he was wanted for murder, one can assume Moses was overjoyed to be invited home by seven single women.

2.21 (cont.) and he gave Moses his daughter Zipporah as wife.

The Torah never states Moses loved Zipporah (or the reverse) or that he found her beautiful. We are simply told he was given her hand in marriage (in Hebrew the "Zi" in her name is pronounced "Tzee").

2.22 She bore a son whom he named Gershom, for he said, "I have been a stranger in a foreign land."

2.23 A long time after that, the king of Egypt died, and the Israelites were groaning under the bondage and cried out; and their cry for help from the bondage rose up to God.

IF GOD INTERVENED DURING THE EXODUS, WHY DIDN'T HE INTERVENE AT OTHER TIMES?

2.24 God heard their moaning, and God remembered His covenant with Abraham and Isaac and Jacob.

God works according to His own inscrutable timetable. But from our perspective God never seems to step in early enough. When the Torah describes God as "remembering," it does not mean the same as humans remembering, that He'd forgotten. God did not forget and then remember. God's "remembering" means God has decided to act.

However, even accepting that meaning, the obvious question remains: why didn't God decide to act earlier—whether in ancient Egypt or elsewhere since then? Indeed, it would appear that when it comes to rescuing the just from the unjust, much of the time God doesn't act at all.

To such questions, we have no answer. Ever since the biblical Book of Job, people have asked why the God of the Bible allows the just to suffer. One can only say, as the medieval Hebrew saying goes, "If I knew God, I'd be God" (*lu yidativ, hayitiv*).

The Exodus raises an additional question however—especially, for obvious reasons, among Jews: If God intervened to stop the suffering of the Jews in Egypt, why didn't He intervene to stop the suffering of the Jews in Europe during the Holocaust? One can, of course, ask the identical question regarding other nations' mass murders: the sixty million-plus Chinese at the hand of their own communist regime; the twenty to thirty million murdered by Stalin's communist regime; the six million Ukrainians also killed by Stalin's regime; the one out of every four Cambodians killed by Pol Pot and his communist regime; the mass killings of Armenians by the Ottoman Turks; the slaughter of Tutsis by Hutus in Rwanda, and so many others.

But when Jews ask this question, it is often in light of a divine intervention many Jews do believe occurred—the Exodus. One possible answer to bear in mind is God allowed centuries to elapse before intervening to stop the enslavement and mass murder of the Israelite children in Egypt. On that basis, one could argue God also intervened in Europe—though only after allowing six million Jews to be murdered. That, of course, is in no way an emotionally satisfying answer. But it does illustrate why citing God's intervention in ancient Egypt may not be a valid basis on which to challenge God about the Holocaust. A Hebrew in ancient Egypt whose son had been drowned in the Nile could just as validly have asked, "Why didn't God intervene sooner?"

> *The Torah does not hesitate to describe a Jew as evil. Much of the Torah's—and the entire Hebrew Bible's—greatness and credibility lie in its willingness to critique the Jewish people.*

In the final analysis, regarding God's not intervening to stop unjust human suffering, I have three responses:

First, if God always intervened to stop evil, human beings would not have free will; we would be robots.

> *We all want to know why God allows the just to suffer. One can only say, as the medieval Hebrew saying goes, "If I knew God, I'd be God."*

Second, the only possible answer to the problem of unjust suffering is ultimate justice in an afterlife. As I will demonstrate later, if God is good, it is axiomatic there is an afterlife. Moreover, as we will see on a number of occasions, the Torah does affirm an afterlife, despite its relative silence on the issue—because of its desire to keep us human beings preoccupied with this life.

Third, I have always been moved by an argument put forward by the late American Rabbi Milton Steinberg: The believer has to account for the existence of one thing—unjust suffering; the atheist has to account for the existence of everything else.

2.25 God looked upon the Israelites, and God took notice of them.

CHAPTER
3

3.1 Now Moses, tending the flock of his father-in-law Jethro, the priest of Midian, drove the flock into the wilderness,

> The most likely explanation for this is Moses drove his flock to ungrazed land where plant life was plentiful. Presumably the area where the Midianites were concentrated was over-grazed by the flocks of others.
>
> Perhaps there is another reason altogether. Winston Churchill had this to say about prophets and wilderness: "Every prophet has to come from civilization, but every prophet has to go into the wilderness. He must have a strong impression of a complex society and all that it has to give, and then he must serve periods of isolation and meditation. This is the process by which psychic dynamite is made."[1]

3.1 (cont.) and came to Horeb, the mountain of God.

> Although the Torah does not specify Moses's exact location, Horeb refers to the region of Mount Sinai where God later reveals the Ten Commandments (see also I Kings 19:8 which describes the prophet Elijah journeying to the "mountain of God at Horeb").

3.2 An angel of the Lord appeared to him in a blazing fire out of a bush. He gazed,

> Nahum Sarna notes that in ensuing dialogues between God and Moses, it is God, not an angel, who speaks. But the angel is necessary at this point because God could not appear in the bush; this would be too jolting for Moses (or any other mortal).

The Midrash—rabbinic commentaries on the Bible dating from the first millennium— notes that God makes His first appearance to Moses not from an awesome mountaintop or a giant tree, but from a humble little bush, to teach that "no place is devoid of God's presence, not even a thorn bush."[2]

3.2 (cont.) and there was a bush all aflame, yet the bush was not consumed.

This image became the most famous metaphor for the Jewish people: like the bush that burns but is not consumed, the Jewish people, too, have been burned (literally and metaphorically) but never destroyed. A divine fire sustains the Jews.

ESSAY: BELIEF IN GOD IS A CHOICE—AND WHY TO MAKE IT

3.3 Moses said, "I must turn aside to look at this marvelous sight; why doesn't the bush burn up?"

One can assume just about anyone who keeps looking at a burning bush will eventually wonder why the fire isn't burning the bush and what is sustaining the fire. But it is also true most people would not keep looking. After a first glance, and the realization the fire seemed contained, there would be nothing to prompt most people to continue to look. But Moses did continue looking and he noticed something unique, even miraculous, was taking place.

If you wait for God to contact you before you lead a God-centered life, you will almost surely never lead a life with God in it.

In a sense, Moses's behavior exemplifies a choice we all have when looking at life—am I seeing a miracle? Is the birth of a baby a miracle? Is thought, consciousness, great art—and, for that matter, all existence—a miracle? That is our choice to make.

The Victorian-era British poet, Elizabeth Barrett Browning, commented on this verse:

> Earth's crammed with heaven,
> And every common bush afire with God
> But only he who sees takes off his shoes.... [3]

"Only he who sees…"

That's the great question: Who sees the miracles of daily life?

And the answer is: Whoever chooses to see.

One of the most important lessons of life—one I believe most people never learn—is that almost everything important is a choice. We choose whether to be happy (or, at the very least whether to act happy), whether to be a hard worker, whether to be honest, whether to be kind, whether to see miracles, and, yes, whether to believe in God (or, at the very least, live as if there is a God).

At an early age, I decided to believe in God and lead a God-centered and religious life. I was well aware of all the arguments against belief in God. And God never directly appeared to me.

I made this decision because:

1. I came to realize the terrible consequences of a world without God.

- If there is no God, life is ultimately pointless—the product of mere random chance. We humans therefore have no more ultimate meaning than rocks. Just as rocks came about by chance, will eventually cease to exist, and leave behind no record of their existence, if there is no God, the same holds true for every one of us—we, too, came about by chance, will cease to exist (much sooner than rocks), and leave behind no lasting record of our existence. (How many of our ancestors can we name, let alone know anything about? Start with any of your sixteen great-great-grandparents.)

  A secular scholar of Greek philosophy writing in the *New York Times* perfectly captured this view:

  "Eventually everything ends in heat death. The universe certainly started with a bang, but it likely ends with a fizzle.

What's the purpose in that, though?

There isn't one. The universe as we understand it tells us nothing about the goal or meaning of existence, let alone our own. In the grand scheme of things, you and I are enormously insignificant.

I will never see my Papa again. One day I will die. So will you. [We] will decay along with everything in the universe as the fundamental particles we're made of return to the inert state in which everything began."[4]

Since I do not believe existence in general and human life in particular are nothing more than a purposeless coalescing of stellar dust, I have to conclude there is a God.

- If there is no God, good and evil do not objectively exist because if there is no God, there is no non-material reality. Only the physical exists, and good and evil are not physical properties; they are moral properties. Therefore, if there is no God, the terms "good" and "evil" are subjective opinions, not objective realities. People and societies call "good" what they approve of, and call "evil" what they disapprove of. To be sure, this does not mean an atheist cannot be a good person or a God-believer cannot be a bad person. It only means the existence of a moral God is necessary for morality to objectively exist. People will counter, "To which God are you referring?" since not all conceptions of God agree on what is good or evil. The answer is the God introduced to the world by this Torah: the God of Creation and of the Ten Commandments. Many people and religions use the word

"God," but the "God" about whom they are speaking is not necessarily the original one—the one introduced by this Torah.

Honest people can debate God's existence. But what is not debatable is the absence of an objective good and evil if there is no God. Atheist philosophers acknowledge this. When I debated the subject, "Can We Be Good without God?" at Oxford University with the eminent British moral philosopher Professor Jonathan Glover, an atheist, one of the first things he said was "…if there isn't a God, there is only subjective morality. That's absolutely true."

The eminent Princeton philosopher Richard Rorty acknowledged that for secular liberals such as himself, "there is no answer to the question, 'Why not be cruel?'"[5]

Therefore, believing good and evil really do exist, I have no logical choice but to believe in a moral God.

- If there is no God, the only reality is material (physical). Only if there is a God (Who is not material) does anything non-material actually exist—including everything we most cherish, such as love and the mind. If there is no God, love is nothing more than the interaction of neurons in the brain or the effects of hormones on the brain. And if there is no God, the "mind" is just the material brain deceiving itself into believing it exists. If only matter is real, the mind is merely another physical part of the brain. Therefore, as I do not believe love is only the interplay of neurons

or the effect of hormones, I believe in God. And as I
believe there is a mind, not only a physical brain, I
believe there is a God.

2. I chose to believe in God because I wanted to lead the
deepest, richest, and most hope-filled life possible.

All that is provided only by a God-centered and religion-centered life. Virtually every poll measuring the happiness of people living in the West finds religious individuals are more at peace, happier, live longer, and enjoy a more communal life.[6]

In the words of a study conducted by the Austin Institute for the Study of Family and Culture, "Research has suggested that religious faith may be adept in its ability to offer significance and meaning to life, that religious coping mechanisms can improve physical and emotional health, that faith can be a powerful motivating force, and that congregants may receive emotional support from others in their congregations."[7]

You can be an agnostic intellectually. But you cannot live as an agnostic. You live as either a believer or as an atheist.

In light of this, the most important question to ask an atheist is this: "Do you hope you are right or wrong?"

Virtually every atheist I have debated (and I have debated many) has said that while they cannot, for intellectual (and emotional) reasons, believe in God, they certainly would wish God did exist. How could they not? Who wouldn't want to believe life has ultimate meaning, good and evil really exist, the good are rewarded and the evil punished, death doesn't end everything, and we will be reunited with those we love?

It is a deeper life to begin each meal with a blessing.

It is a deeper life to have a community to which you are attached and which cares about you. In theory, such secular communities can exist, but they rarely do.

It is a deeper life to gather with people and study holy texts such as the Torah. Of course, secular people can gather and regularly study, let us say,

Shakespeare. But for every Shakespeare study group, there are probably a thousand Bible study groups.

It is a deeper life to have a weekly Sabbath, during which normal work ceases and one spends hours with loved ones and/or members of one's religious community.

Therefore, deeply wanting to live such a richer life, I chose to believe in God.

3. I want to live with hope.

This world is saturated with injustice. Enormous numbers of good people suffer horribly, and a great number of unjust people are never brought to justice. Only if the just God of the Torah exists can there be ultimate justice. Only if this God exists, do the good receive their just rewards and the evil receive their just punishments. That, of course, can only happen if there is an afterlife (the existence of which is discussed on a number of occasions in this commentary). And only if there is a God is there an afterlife—the only hope that death doesn't end our existence, and that of everyone we love.

Therefore, as I want to live with hope, I have chosen to believe in God.

Of course, there are those who dismiss such a choice as mere wishful thinking.

I readily admit I wish there is a good God, ultimate justice, an afterlife, and meaning to my life. Every normal person wishes the same. But that does not make belief in God solely a product of wishful thinking. I believe in God for a host of rational reasons, one of which is the unique greatness of the Torah and the Bible. Moreover, all those atheists who believe there is (or, more precisely, who manufacture) some ultimate purpose to their lives should recognize their entire philosophy of a meaningful life really is based on wishful thinking—precisely what they accuse believers of.

Moreover, while I readily admit that for all these reasons I made the choice to believe in God, these are not the only reasons. The arguments for God's existence are far more rationally powerful than the atheist argument that everything—life, intelligence, consciousness, the entire universe—came about by itself.

Science would seem to confirm the miracle of life. The more science reveals about the brain, the further it is from understanding how it operates; the inability of science to explain the development of life from non-life (the organic from the inorganic); the immeasurable odds against intelligent life existing; or the latest insoluble puzzle, as revealed by CERN, the European Organization for Nuclear Research:

> All of our observations find a complete symmetry between matter and antimatter, which is why *the universe should not actually exist.*[8]

So, again, I acknowledge that belief in God—or in atheism—is indeed a choice. But as noted at the beginning of this essay, virtually everything worthwhile is a choice. Love is a choice, leading a good life is a choice, marriage is a choice, (for most people) having children is a choice, working hard is a choice, taking care of others is a choice, learning a musical instrument or a foreign language instead of playing video games is a choice.

"All of our observations find a complete symmetry between matter and antimatter, which is why the universe should not actually exist."

—CERN, the European Organization for Nuclear Research

I see no good reason not to make this choice—and myriad reasons to do so.

Yet, while an ever-increasing number of people consider themselves agnostic, the great majority of these people *live* as if they are atheists, bereft of all the magnificent life-enhancing benefits a God-centered life provides. These individuals are agnostics intellectually, but atheists behaviorally.

Such people need to make a choice: Will I live as if there is a God or as if there is no God? You can be an agnostic intellectually, but you cannot *live* as an agnostic; you live as either a believer or as an atheist. You live either as if life is random chance or as if it is infused with ultimate meaning.

Moses *chose* to look carefully and see a miracle in that burning bush. If we look carefully, we, too, will see a miracle—in everything.

3.4 When the Lord saw that he had turned aside to look,

> God waits to call out to Moses until Moses first notices God. For nearly every human being (Abraham was a rare exception), that is how the divine-human encounter takes place: God communicates with us after, or if, we make the effort to notice His presence. Again, this is our choice to make. If you wait for God to contact you before you lead a God-centered life, you will almost surely never lead a life with God in it.

> Here's an almost precise analogy: Shakespeare will speak to you only after you make the effort to read and understand him. And the more effort you make to understand him, the more meaningful he will be in your life.

> That is the case regarding God: Bringing God into your life takes effort. What worthwhile thing in life doesn't require effort? Why should God be different?

3.4 (cont.) God called to him out of the bush: "Moses! Moses!" He answered, "Here I am."

> God's call to Moses is an echo of God's call to Abraham just before He commands the binding of Isaac, and Moses answers with the same word as Abraham: *Hineni* ("Here I am," Genesis 22:1).

3.5 And He said, "Do not come closer. Remove your sandals from your feet, for the place on which you stand is holy ground.

> Of course, this random spot in some wilderness is not inherently holy. It is holy because God appears there. Any place or situation into which we bring God or where we encounter God (as Moses does here) becomes holy. Almost nothing is intrinsically holy. This, too, is a matter of choice (see the essay on holiness in Leviticus 19:2).

3.6 I am," He said, "the God of your father, the God of Abraham, the God of Isaac, and the God of Jacob."

> God is, of course, the God of all people, not just the God of Moses's ancestors. But God does not introduce Himself as the universal Creator of Heaven and

Earth and of all humankind, because this designation is not relevant or meaningful to the task at hand. God is revealing Himself to Moses to have him take the Israelites out of Egypt, a task rooted in the promises God made to Abraham, Isaac, and Jacob.

Furthermore, the primitive Israelites to whom Moses will convey God's words will be much more comfortable with the familiar notion of an ancestral God than with the revolutionary and highly sophisticated notion of a single Author of all of creation.

3.6 (cont.) And Moses hid his face, for he was afraid to look at God.

Moses did not really have to fear seeing God, because God is invisible. However, it is unlikely Moses knew that. And Moses might have simply been overwhelmed by the awe-inspiring moment and instinctively covered his face.

3.7 And the Lord continued, "I have marked well the plight of My people in Egypt

God repeatedly refers to the Israelites as "My people."

3.7 (cont.) and have heeded their outcry because of their taskmasters; yes, I am mindful of their suffering.

3.8 I have come down to rescue them from the Egyptians and to bring them out of that land to a good and spacious land, a land flowing with milk and honey,

Sarna explains these terms are used somewhat differently in the Torah than in modern parlance. Milk here refers to goat's milk: "a land flowing with milk therefore suggests ample pasturage and the prospect of much meat, hide, and wool. And honey here refers to the thick, sweet syrup produced from dates, not to the honey produced from bees. Milk and honey were considered among the chief necessities of human life in the ancient Near East, and their combination was thought to constitute a highly nutritious diet—milk being rich in protein and the dried date rich in carbohydrates." Indeed, "some Arab tribes are known to subsist for months at a time solely on milk and honey."

THE ONLY SOVEREIGN STATES THAT HAVE EVER EXISTED IN CANAAN WERE JEWISH STATES

3.8 (cont.) the region of the Canaanites, the Hittites, the Amorites, the Perizzites, the Hivites, and the Jebusites.

Note that Canaan was not the land or country of the Canaanites. It was a land with seven nations (see Deuteronomy 7:1), meaning the land of Canaan was never historically identified with one people until the Israelites/Jews made it their state. The Israelites were the first to claim Canaan as a national homeland; and for more than three thousand years since, the only sovereign states in Canaan have been Jewish states.

The first one lasted from the time of King David (around 1000 BCE) until 586 BCE, when the Babylonians destroyed the First Temple.

The second Jewish state lasted from about two generations after 586 BCE until its destruction by the Romans in about the year 70.

And the third Jewish state was established in 1948 as the modern state of Israel.

3.9 Now the cry of the Israelites has reached Me; moreover, I have seen how the Egyptians oppress them.

This verse is essentially a repetition of verse 7. Perhaps God refers again to the suffering of Israelites in order to impress upon Moses the need for him to step up and lead the people.

3.10 Come, therefore, I will send you to Pharaoh, and you shall free My people, the Israelites, from Egypt."

3.11 But Moses said to God, "Who am I that I should go to Pharaoh and free the Israelites from Egypt?"

One can only imagine Moses's shock. He is leading a completely normal shepherd's life when, out of nowhere, God Himself appears to him, and asks him to lead the Israelites out of Egypt.

Moses responds with a statement of total humility. It is often said that in order to successfully run for president of the United States, a person has to have the requisite "fire in the belly." Moses was the antithesis of this model. During the American Revolution, a relatively common phrase was the "meekness of Moses," which described the humility many were looking for in their prospective leaders. In a 1776 letter to a fellow revolutionary, John Adams, later to be the second president of the United States, wrote: "The management of so complicated and mighty a machine, as the United Colonies, requires the Meekness of Moses, the Patience of Job and the Wisdom of Solomon, added to the Valor of Daniel."[9]

In that sentence, the reader will also note (once again) the central role the Hebrew Bible played for the founders of the United States.

3.12 And He said, "I will be with you;

In addition, Moses knows he is wanted for murder in Egypt (Exodus 2:15). He is presumably terrified of appearing before a king who wants to kill him. Nevertheless, he does not object to God's assignment on the grounds it would endanger his life. But God knows fear plays a role in Moses's thinking and reassures him, "I will be with you."

In the next chapter, God is more explicit in addressing this fear: "All the men who sought to kill you are dead" (Exodus 4:16).

These words, "I will be with you," seem to be a non-sequitur. Moses just asked God who is he to be chosen for such an awesome task, yet instead of listing Moses's qualifications, God says, "I will be with you." Perhaps God is telling Moses that who he is and what his qualifications are do not matter; he was chosen for his qualifications, but he will succeed because God will be with him.

3.12 (cont.) that shall be your sign that it was I who sent you. And when you have freed the people from Egypt, you shall worship God at this mountain."

The "sign that it was I who sent you" is the people will be freed from Egypt and worship God at this mountain.

That is how things usually work: God's "signs"—His interventions in individuals' or nations' lives—are seen most clearly only in retrospect. In the case of the Jews, for example, when one reflects on over 3,600 years of Jewish survival and influence on the world, it is difficult not to see the hand of God. However, given the terrible suffering Jews have endured at the hands of Jew-haters for millennia, for a Jew at any particular moment, it has not been easy to see God's hand. Perhaps this is one meaning of the biblical verse that we can only see God from the back (Exodus 33:23)—only after an event happens can we see God's hand in it.

> *The Torah has the almost impossible task of being relevant to primitive slaves living in the Bronze Age and to highly educated people living thousands of years later.*

The Israelites have to be released from serving Pharaoh in order to serve God. This is consistent with Moses's later demand to Pharaoh—made in God's name—"Let My people go that they may worship [serve] Me" (Exodus 9:1).

3.13 Moses said to God, "When I come to the Israelites and say to them, 'The God of your fathers has sent me to you,' and they ask me, 'What is His name?' what shall I say to them?"

Moses's first objection to God's command was "Who am *I*?" In this verse, he raises his second objection: "Who are *You*?"

Moses's question signifies the Israelites have strayed so far from their faith they probably no longer even know God's name (or much else about God); they know only that they have an ancestral God. The medieval commentator Rashbam assumed Moses did not know God's name at this point. After all, why would he? *How* would he? Having grown up in the Egyptian royal household presumably the gods he knew of were the Egyptian gods—and, now, the Midianite gods.

Therefore, Moses might have put the question in the mouths of the Israelites to cover his own ignorance. On the other hand, Moses might have simply been expressing an honest desire to more fully understand God—a quest we should all undertake.

Rabbi Harold Kushner comments: "It may be hard for the modern reader to understand the point of this question. Moses is not changing the subject and saying to God: 'Excuse me, what is Your name? I didn't get it the first time.' In ancient times, a name was more than an identifying label. Your name was your essence, what you were all about, your identity rather than just your identification. To ask, 'What is God's name?' is to ask, 'What is God all about? What does He stand for?'"

GOD'S NAME IS A VERB—"TO BE"

3.14 And God said to Moses, "Ehyeh-Asher-Ehyeh." He continued, "Thus shall you say to the Israelites, 'Ehyeh sent me to you.'"

This is one of the great moments of the Torah. Just like Moses, we are all expectantly awaiting God's answer.

At this sublime moment of divine revelation, God identifies Himself with a name having four possible meanings, each one perfectly accurate.

"I am what I am";

"I am who I am";

"I will be what I will be";

"I will be who I will be."

The reason all four translations are accurate is Hebrew does not have a word for the present tense of the verb "to be." In other words, there is no Hebrew word for "am" or "is" or "are." Therefore, in order to say, "I am Joseph," for example, one would say, "Ani Joseph" ("I Joseph"). The absence of the present tense of "to be" is not unique to Hebrew; it is also true of Arabic and Russian, among other languages. So, here, when God uses the future tense of the verb "to be," it literally means, "I will be." But it is often translated as "I am" because there is no present tense of the verb "to be" in Hebrew.

Importantly, this name, "I am who I am," or "I will be who I will be," is never again mentioned in the Torah. This suggests God was giving Moses an answer for Moses, not for the Israelites. Such an abstract name would have made no sense to the theologically primitive Israelites. Even though God tells Moses to tell the Israelites "Ehyeh" ("Am" or "Will Be") sent him, that name is really for Moses. Moses is not going to get the Israelites to follow him by telling them, "'I am' sent me to lead you" —as is made clear in the next verse, when God gives Moses a far more relatable name to use.

God's response is not only for Moses. It is also for us who are reading this thousands of years later. It is important to remember the Torah has the almost impossible task of being relevant to slaves living in the Bronze Age, to people in our time, and to our descendants. That it has succeeded in doing so is another reason I regard the Torah as not man-made.

While the term "I am what I am" or "I will be who I will be" is not used again, the most commonly used name for God in the Torah and the rest of the Hebrew Bible is essentially the verb "to be." It is composed of the Hebrew letters, YHVH (from where we get the word "Jehovah"), and it is always translated "Lord" because it is pronounced *Adonai*, meaning "Lord" even though YHVH actually means "Being," or "Will Be," or even just "Is."

Given that in the Torah names indicate essence, "YHVH" tells us the essence of God is being. God simply cannot be explained any further; anything else anthropomorphizes God. God simply "Is."

3.15 And God said further to Moses, "Thus shall you speak to the Israelites: The Lord [YHVH], the God of your fathers, the God of Abraham, the God of Isaac, and the God of Jacob, has sent me to you:

This shall be My name forever,

This My appellation for all eternity.

God recognizes that a tribal, ancestral identity is absolutely necessary for the Israelite slaves to be able to relate to Him, and to know Who He is. Therefore, God tells Moses to identify Him in these terms—and not, for example, as "Creator of the universe," let alone as "I am who I am"—when speaking to the people.

3.16 "Go and assemble the elders of Israel and say to them:

Moses has three groups of people to convince of God's message: Pharaoh, the Israelite slaves, and the elders of Israel, a category whose identity is not clear. Were they also slaves? Presumably yes, but we don't know.

In any case, the term "elders" suggests they were credited with wisdom and therefore regarded with respect, which is how older people have been regarded in almost every society. In recent years, many societies have lost reverence for the old. The reason is wisdom, certainly in comparison with knowledge, is often undervalued or not valued at all. And one reason for that is knowledge is far more valued due to extraordinary advances in technology, medicine, and science. Likewise, intelligence is far more valued than wisdom—think of how many parents want their children to be "brilliant" versus how many parents want their children to be wise (in truth, few parents even think in terms of wise, a term that cannot be measured on tests).

In our time, intelligence is far more valued than wisdom. Think of how many parents want their children to be "brilliant" versus how many parents want their children to be wise.

The loss to society has been immeasurable. Societies need wisdom far more than knowledge; indeed, knowledge without wisdom is likely to lead to catastrophe. Think of how societies like Nazi Germany, the USSR, North Korea, and the Iranian mullahs misused both their intelligence and their knowledge.

3.16 (cont.) The Lord [YHVH], the God [Elohei] of your fathers, the God of Abraham, Isaac, and Jacob, has appeared to me and said

God is telling Moses to use both the personal name YHVH ("Jehovah") and the universal name Elohim in introducing God to the elders.

3.16 (cont.) 'I have taken note of you and of what is being done to you in Egypt,

At the end of Genesis, Joseph uses these same words in his deathbed prophecy to his brothers: He promises them that God will take note of them and deliver them from Egypt to the Promised Land (see Genesis 50:24.) Given that traditions about Joseph probably still circulated in the Israelite community, these words would have been very comforting, and would have given Moses credibility when he introduced himself to the Israelites.

3.17 and I have declared: I will take you out of the misery of Egypt to the land of the Canaanites, the Hittites, the Amorites, the Perizzites, the Hivites, and the Jebusites, to a land flowing with milk and honey.'

3.18 They will listen to you; then you shall go with the elders of Israel to the king of Egypt and you shall say to him, 'The Lord, the God of the Hebrews, manifested Himself to us.

God tells Moses to refer to Him as "the God of the Hebrews" because this was a term Pharaoh would understand. In the ancient world, gods were only gods of clans and peoples. There was no concept of a single God of all mankind; this was among the revolutionary ideas the Torah introduced to humanity.

3.18 (cont.) Now therefore, let us go a distance of three days into the wilderness

God does not want Moses to ask for the complete freeing of the Israelites from slavery; Pharaoh would never accede to such a radical request. Instead, Moses is told to ask Pharaoh to permit the Israelites at least a weeklong sabbatical (three days out, time for sacrifices, and three days back). The Hebrew word, *nah*, which appears in the Hebrew text, and which means "please," is not translated here. God is actually instructing Moses to be polite in his request of Pharaoh: "Now therefore, please, let us go.... "

3.18 (cont.) to sacrifice to the Lord our God.'

Moses's request will be anathema to Pharaoh for several reasons. One is it is an affront to Egyptian religion, in which many animals were worshipped as gods. Essentially Moses would be asking Pharaoh for permission to slaughter Egyptian gods as an offering to the Israelite God.

The Torah views animal sacrifice as an appropriate way of serving God. As previously noted, the Torah's view is animals were created for human beings to *use* for morally legitimate purposes, and not to *abuse*. (It is also worth noting, according to Torah law, nearly all sacrificed animals were to be eaten, meaning sacrifices were also a form of public slaughter.) My understanding of the rationale for animal sacrifice is explained in the commentary on the Book of Leviticus, large sections of which deal with sacrifice.

3.19 Yet I know that the king of Egypt will let you go only because of a greater might

God tells Moses Pharaoh will only free the Israelites after Pharaoh is confronted by a formidable show of force. In predicting Pharaoh's behavior, God may seem to be curtailing Pharaoh's freedom of choice. However, the Jewish notion of free will allows for divine foreknowledge. As one of the greatest teachers in Jewish history, Rabbi Akiva, explains in the Talmud, "All is foreseen, yet free will is granted" (*ha-kol tzafui v'ha reshut nituna*).[10] To put it in contemporary terms, God stands outside of time.

3.20 So I will stretch out My hand and smite Egypt with various wonders which I will work upon them; after that he shall let you go.

In the final analysis, all of the negotiating is ultimately a charade; Pharaoh will free the Israelites only because of the plagues God will inflict on Egypt. However, God and Moses must first offer Pharaoh the option of freeing the slaves without having to suffer those plagues. God must act justly and therefore cannot inflict the plagues until Pharaoh has made them morally justified.

3.21 And I will dispose the Egyptians favorably toward this people, so that when you go, you will not go away empty-handed.

3.22 Each woman shall borrow from her neighbor and the lodger in her house objects of silver and gold, and clothing, and you shall put these on your sons and daughters, thus stripping the Egyptians."

The word translated here as "shall borrow" literally means "ask," and can also be translated as "request." God does not say the women should make demands of their neighbors, even though they are surely entitled to these valuables after hundreds of years of slavery. The women must behave with decency even toward their oppressors. *Even victims must act ethically.* And that surely is one of the great Torah lessons relevant to the time in which we live.

Ironically, it was almost certainly that jewelry the Israelites later used in building the Golden Calf (Exodus 32:2-3).

CHAPTER

4

4.1 But Moses spoke up and said, "What if they do not believe me and do not listen to me, but say: The Lord did not appear to you?"

Moses raises a third objection.

He first objected that he did not consider himself—a shepherd in Midian—the appropriate person to go before Pharaoh (see Exodus 3:11).

He then objected that he did not even know God's right name, or how to refer to the deity who was sending him (see Exodus 3:13).

Moses's third objection presents a more serious challenge. God will now give Moses a demonstration of how He will prove to doubters in Egypt both His presence and power.

4.2 The Lord said to him, "What is that in your hand?" And he replied, "A rod."

Before converting Moses's rod into a snake, God has Moses confirm it is an ordinary rod.

4.3 He said, "Cast it on the ground." He cast it on the ground and it became a snake; and Moses recoiled from it.

4.4 Then the Lord said to Moses, "Put out your hand and grasp it by the tail" —he put out his hand and seized it, and it became a rod in his hand—

In asking Moses to grasp the snake by its tail, God is testing Moses's faith. As a shepherd, Moses knows a snake should be held by the neck to prevent it from striking. He is therefore taking a risk in obeying God's command.

4.5 "that they may believe that the Lord, the God of their fathers, the God of Abraham, the God of Isaac, and the God of Jacob, did appear to you."

4.6 The Lord said to him further, "Put your hand into your bosom." He put his hand into his bosom; and when he took it out, his hand was encrusted with snowy scales!

Throughout history, this skin disease of "snowy scales" has often been translated as leprosy, though we now know that, while it is an affliction of the skin, it is not leprosy. The comparison to snow is not about its whiteness but its flakiness.

Sarna notes: "Apart from the startling phenomenon of the sudden appearance and [in the next verse] disappearance of the encrustation, this particular sign had an ominous aspect to it. It is seen in the Bible as a divine punishment for human behavior."

God's "hardening" of Pharaoh's heart is precisely what allowed Pharaoh to exercise his free will.

(Numbers 12:10-16 describes Moses's sister, Miriam, being afflicted with this punishment; and II Chronicles 26:16-21 depicts the Judean king, Uzziah [8th century BCE] as being similarly punished: "*tzara'at* [this skin disease] broke out on his forehead…for the Lord had struck him with a plague.")

It is likely God performs this miracle to warn Moses that He is starting to tire of all his objections, and to subtly remind him He has the power to punish those who do not obey Him.

4.7 And He said, "Put your hand back into your bosom." —He put his hand back into his bosom; and when he took it out of his bosom, there it was again like the rest of his body. —

4.8 "And if they do not believe you or pay heed to the first sign, they will believe the second.

4.9 And if they are not convinced by both these signs and still do not heed you, take some water from the Nile and pour it on the dry ground, and it—the water that you take from the Nile—will turn to blood on the dry ground."

Unlike the first two signs, this one cannot be performed before Moses's eyes because he is standing in the desert rather than beside the Nile. Moses takes the promise of this sign on faith.

4.10 But Moses said to the Lord, "Please, O Lord, I have never been a man of words, either in times past or now that You have spoken to Your servant; I am slow of speech and slow of tongue."

In the three stories related about Moses in Chapter 2, he intervened successfully by smiting the Egyptian overseer who was beating the Hebrew slave and he intervened successfully when he stood up on behalf of the bullied shepherdesses of Midian. The one time he was unsuccessful was when he tried to use words to stop the two quarreling Israelites (Exodus 2.13-14).

4.11 And the Lord said to him, "Who gives man speech? Who makes him dumb or deaf, seeing or blind? Is it not I, the Lord?

When Moses pleads that he is inarticulate, God is not impressed.

4.12 Now go,

The Hebrew is very direct, even abrupt. God essentially says to Moses, "Get going!"

ONE OF THE MOST INFLUENTIAL LEADERS IN HISTORY DIDN'T SPEAK WELL...

4.12 (cont.) and I will be with you as you speak and will instruct you what to say."

Moses is chosen for his moral greatness rather than for his charisma or eloquence. He is chosen not because he sounds good, but because he *is* good. It does not matter to God that Moses does not speak well, because he is, in any event, going to be a vehicle for God's words. Indeed, perhaps God deliberately chooses a leader who does not speak well to show that the message is so much more important than the medium. In our day, the opposite is often the case: "The medium," in Marshall McLuhan's famous words, "is the message."

In any event, it is only fair to note it is God's plagues, more than Moses's (and Aaron's) words that convince Pharaoh to allow the Jews to leave Egypt.

...AND DIDN'T WANT TO BE A LEADER

4.13 But he said, "Please, O Lord, make someone else Your agent."

After four carefully reasoned objections, Moses finally admits the truth: He just doesn't want this dangerous, arduous, all-consuming mission that will completely change his life. He is like the child who gives a dozen reasons to explain why he cannot do his homework, and then finally gets to the truth, "I just don't want to do it!" This fifth objection is a final desperate plea.

In this sense, Moses is an ideal leader—because he doesn't really want the job. Throughout history, most national leaders ached to be powerful, influential, famous, rich. Moses either preferred to lead a simple life with his family, or feared returning to Egypt, or both.

4.14 The Lord became angry with Moses, and He said, "There is your brother Aaron the Levite. He, I know, speaks readily. Even now he is setting out to meet you,

Finally, God loses patience with Moses's objections, though He does offer him a significant consolation. Moses will not have to undertake the mission alone; and his partner, his brother Aaron, does speak well.

4.14 (cont.) and he will be happy to see you.

4.15 You shall speak to him and put the words in his mouth—I will be with you and with him as you speak, and tell both of you what to do—

4.16 and he shall speak for you to the people. Thus he shall serve as your spokesman, with you playing the role of God to him,

4.17 and take with you this rod, with which you shall perform the signs."

That rod will accompany Moses for the rest of his life, serving both as a link to his first encounter with God at the burning bush, and as a reminder of his humble origins as a shepherd. Moses will remain a shepherd, though his new flock will be the Hebrew nation.

That Moses wages the battle with the Egyptians using a simple shepherd's rod rather than sophisticated weaponry is reminiscent of the sling and the five smooth stones with which the young shepherd David confronted and prevailed over the Philistine giant Goliath (I Samuel 17:40-51). With God on their side, Moses and David overcame foes far mightier than the Israelites on whose behalf they fought.

4.18 Moses went back to his father-in-law Jether and said to him, "Let me go back to my kinsmen in Egypt and see how they are faring."

There are two possible explanations as to why Moses solicits his father-in-law's permission.

One is he may have needed his father-in-law's official permission to take Zipporah from her father's house. The other more likely explanation is Moses was exhibiting good manners in formally making this request. Moses was, as we shall see later (Exodus 18), extremely close to Jethro.

WHY DOESN'T MOSES TELL HIS FATHER-IN-LAW ABOUT HIS ENCOUNTER WITH GOD?

Moses deliberately neglects to mention he has just had a divine encounter in which God told him to confront Pharaoh and deliver the Israelites from Egyptian bondage. Moses probably feared such a declaration would not have been well received by his father-in-law. Jethro might well have regarded him as emotionally unbalanced, or, if he did believe Moses, might object to Moses taking on such a dangerous mission, and bringing Jethro's daughter and two grandchildren with him. It is hard to imagine another reason Moses would not have told his father-in-law about his encounter with God.

4.18 (cont.) And Jethro said to Moses, "Go in peace."

Jethro could understand and relate to the importance of brotherly and tribal bonds, so he permits Moses to return to his kin without hesitation. We cannot know how much Jethro knew regarding the persecution of the Israelites or the possible danger to his son-in-law once he returned to Egypt.

4.19 The Lord said to Moses in Midian, "Go back to Egypt, for all the men who sought to kill you are dead."

God, who knows people's thoughts, understood Moses was likely afraid of being executed if he returned to Egypt. Therefore, God reassures him he no longer has reason to fear for his life.

4.20 So Moses took his wife and sons, mounted them on an ass, and went back to the land of Egypt; and Moses took the rod of God with him.

The Torah has until now only mentioned the birth of a single son. Apparently, Moses has at least one other (see Exodus 18:4).

DID GOD DEPRIVE PHARAOH OF FREE WILL?

4.21 And the Lord said to Moses, "When you return to Egypt, see that you perform before Pharaoh all the marvels that I have put within your power. I, however, will stiffen his heart so that he will not let the people go.

The Torah refers twenty times to the stiffening or hardening of Pharaoh's heart; half of them are attributed to Pharaoh's decisions to harden his heart and half of them attributed to God hardening Pharaoh's heart. The latter instances have troubled readers throughout the ages: Is it fair to punish someone—in this case, Pharaoh—who is not acting freely because God has strengthened his heart?

There are at least two ways of dealing with this problem.

1. God believed Pharaoh deserved to be punished.

Had Pharaoh released the Israelites after a single plague, God would not have been able to adequately punish him and the Egyptian nation for enslaving the Israelites for hundreds of years and for the mass murder of the infant boys—all of which, it should be noted, they did out of free will, well before God hardened Pharaoh's heart.

2. Strengthening Pharaoh's heart is precisely what gave Pharaoh free will.

Had God not strengthened Pharaoh's heart, Pharaoh would have released the Israelites after one or, at most, two or three plagues. But such a release would have no more been an act of free will than it is free will when a man gives a confession while being tortured, or signs a contract with a gun pointed at his head (as in the famous words from Mario Puzo's novel, *The Godfather*, "I'll make him an offer he can't refuse"). God's strengthening allowed Pharaoh to do what, in his heart, he really wanted to do: refuse to give up his slaves.

> *Moses is chosen not because he sounds good, but because he is good.*

See the commentary to Exodus 10.7 for proof that God's hardening of Pharaoh's heart did not deprive the king of his free will.

4.22 Then you shall say to Pharaoh, 'Thus says the Lord: Israel is My first-born son.

All the nations of the world are God's children. Israel is the firstborn because the Israelites were the people to whom God first introduced Himself.

4.23 I have said to you, "Let My son go, that he may worship Me," yet you refuse to let him go.

ESSAY: THE DIFFERENCE BETWEEN BELIEF IN GOD AND FAITH IN GOD

4.23 (cont.) Now I will slay your first-born son."'

Few readers, even veteran students of the Bible, recall the killing of Pharaoh's firstborn son, which transpired during the tenth plague, was mentioned by God to Moses even before the plagues began. But Moses does not repeat those words to Pharaoh at this point. Perhaps he feared it would provoke Pharaoh to kill him.

If that is indeed the reason Moses does not fulfill this explicit order from God, it would reveal that, at that point, he lacked complete faith God would protect him. He would come to faith later; but at this point, both God and His promises were quite new to Moses. In a sense, then, one could say even God has to establish credibility to be fully trusted.

Which raises the issue of trust, or faith, in God.

There are two distinct meanings to the statement, "I believe in God."

The first meaning is, "I believe God exists."

The second meaning is, "I trust in God."

The first is the most common meaning, but it is not nearly as important as the second. To believe God exists but not have trust, or faith, in Him is the same as believing another person exists but not having trust in that person.

The importance of trust in God has been so fundamental to American history, for example, that one of the two mottos of the United States since the nineteenth century has been, "In God We Trust" (the other is *e pluribus unum*—Latin for "from many, one"). The motto's words were carefully chosen; they were not "We Believe in God."

So, then, what does trust, or faith, in God mean?

Does it mean, as many people assume, trusting God will help us whenever we are in trouble? Clearly, that cannot be the case. An innumerable number of people who have trusted in God have not been helped—certainly not in any direct way—by God when they were in trouble. If God always intervened as we wished, there would be no unjust suffering in this world—no disease, no evil, and no death (and, one should add, no free will). But, of course, there is an immeasurable amount of unjust suffering: If pain were water, the world would drown.

Therefore, trust in God must mean, first and foremost, that we believe God cares about each one of us and in some way He will ultimately do right by us. And that in turn means—in the final analysis—since injustice often prevails in this world, there must be an afterlife, a life in which a just God makes sure justice prevails.

But trust in God also means more than belief in an afterlife. Believers also trust that God will, at times of His choosing, intervene in this world, though not necessarily in the lifetime of any specific individual who might beseech God's intervention. For example, Jews have trusted for thousands of years that God would ensure the Jews would one day return to their homeland—and they did. And, of course, such trust does not only apply to Jews. Many people, myself included, believe God intervened in some way to inspire the founding of the United States of America, a country founded by Christians rooted in the Hebrew Bible. It is not surprising, therefore, that the only verse inscribed on the most iconic symbol of the American Revolution, the Liberty Bell, is from the Torah: "You shall proclaim liberty throughout the land for all its inhabitants" (Leviticus 25:10). America became the one truly Judeo-Christian country.

> *To believe God exists but not have trust, or faith, in Him is the same as believing another person exists but not having trust in that person.*

4.24 At a night encampment on the way, the Lord encountered him and sought to kill him.

In an age when the rite of circumcision is under attack in some non-traditional circles, this episode reminds us how seriously God takes the one specific commandment He enjoined on Abraham (Genesis 17:9-12).

Nahum Sarna maintains that the obscure incident documented in this verse and the two following it are probably a truncated version of a larger, popular story circulated orally in Israel. The story is missing several important details: Most notably, we cannot be certain whom God sought to kill or why.

Umberto Cassuto, an Italian Jewish Bible scholar who was a professor of Bible at the Hebrew University, argued it was Moses, not the son, God sought to kill, perhaps as a punishment for failing to circumcise his son. In either case, Zipporah understood that circumcising their son was necessary, and Moses's life—or, according to some, his son's life—is once again saved by a woman.

4.25 So Zipporah took a flint and cut off her son's foreskin, and touched his legs with it, saying, "You are truly a bridegroom of blood to me!"

The story underscores the centrality of circumcision to Jewish identity. Thousands of years after this event, the philosopher Benedict Spinoza—a Jew who was so alienated from the Jewish community and so hostile to Judaism, he was among the few Jews ever to be excommunicated from, and never readmitted to, the Jewish community—maintained that as long as the Jews practice circumcision they will survive as a distinct people.

The only verse inscribed on the most iconic symbol of the American Revolution, the Liberty Bell, is from the Torah.

Although circumcision was widely practiced among the ancient Semites and in Egypt, the Torah elevated the act by infusing it with new meaning. (For the religious meaning of circumcision, see the essay, "In Defense of Circumcision," at the end of the commentary to Genesis 17).

The fact circumcision was practiced in other cultures demonstrates the vitally important point that it is the significance of a ritual, not the ritual itself, that matters.

Anti-religious writers often cite religious rituals and holy days that were also practiced by pagans in order to denigrate those rituals and holy days and, by extension, religion. But what higher religion does is use familiar rituals, practices, and themes and infuses them with moral and elevated spiritual meaning.

4.26 And when He let him alone, she added, "A bridegroom of blood because of the circumcision."

It is unclear what this phrase "a bridegroom of blood" really means or even whom Zipporah is addressing, especially since *chatan* (bridegroom) also means "to protect" in Arabic. Sarna contends Zipporah is in effect telling their son, "You are now circumcised and so protected for me by means of the blood—the blood of circumcision." Others hold she is addressing Moses (who is, after all, her bridegroom).

4.27 The Lord said to Aaron, "Go to meet Moses in the wilderness." He went and met him at the mountain of God, and he kissed him.

> The repetition of the words "mountain of God" suggest Aaron met Moses at the same mountain where God appeared to Moses in the burning bush (Exodus 3:1).

4.28 Moses told Aaron about all the things that the Lord had committed to him and all the signs about which He had instructed him.

> There are three signs: the transformation of the rod into a snake; the transformation of a healthy hand into a diseased hand; and the transformation of water into blood (Exodus 4:1-9).

4.29 Then Moses and Aaron went and assembled all the elders of the Israelites.

4.30 Aaron repeated all the words that the Lord had spoken to Moses, and he performed the signs in the sight of the people,

4.31 and the people were convinced. When they heard that the Lord had taken note of the Israelites and that He had seen their plight, they bowed low in homage.

> The people believed Moses and Aaron after they witnessed the signs.
>
> Today, such signs would likely be dismissed by most people—myself among them—as magic tricks. This is not to say God no longer directly communicates with human beings; only that in an age of science and skepticism, people are less likely to be persuaded by miracles and revelations than in the past.

WHERE DID ALL THE ELDERS GO?

5.1 Afterward Moses and Aaron went and said to Pharaoh,

God had told Moses to go to Pharaoh with the elders (Exodus 3:18), but the elders are not mentioned in this verse. According to Rashi, the leading medieval Jewish Bible commentator (France, 1040–1105), the elders started out with Moses and Aaron, but they dropped out "one by one, two by two" as they grew increasingly fearful of appearing before the god-king who was not likely to take kindly to Moses's demands. By the time Moses and Aaron reached Pharaoh, none of the elders remained to accompany them (Exodus 5:4).[1]

Whether or not this is precisely what happened, their fear of confronting the king of Egypt is the best explanation I can think of to account for the elders' absence.

Why, then, did they drop out?

One possible reason is people tend to grow more fearful with age. As we get older, the reality of death becomes ever clearer, and with it a greater appreciation for the value of life. Older people are therefore less likely than young people to undertake a life-endangering mission. If you want caution, wisdom, and strategic thinking, you are more likely to get it from older people. If you want physical courage and risk-taking, you are more likely to get it from younger people. And there are times, such as is the case here, when physical courage is the more valuable attribute.

Another possible reason for the elders not accompanying Moses has not so much to do with courage as it does with faith. Moses was assured by God that He would take care of him ("I will be with you," Exodus 3:12), and even enabled him to perform miracles. The elders had no such direct assurance from God.

MOSES DOESN'T TALK TO PHARAOH AS HE WAS TOLD TO

51. (cont.) "Thus says the Lord, the God of Israel:

Moses does not use the name God instructed him to use: "The Lord, God of the Hebrews" (Exodus 3:18). As becomes apparent in the next comment, this is one of several ways in which Moses initially fails to heed the exact instructions given by God at the burning bush.

The universal practice of slavery, and the accompanying horrible treatment of slaves, is one of the many reasons it is absurd to believe people are basically good.

5.1 (cont.) Let My people go that they may celebrate a festival for Me in the wilderness."

God had told Moses to politely ask Pharaoh for permission to leave Egypt for a brief period. Moses was even supposed to use the word "please" (*nah* in Hebrew—see Exodus 3:18). Instead, Moses and Aaron simply demand that Pharaoh release the Israelites. They also neglect to specify they are asking permission for only a limited period (about a week—see commentary on Exodus 3:18). This is not to suggest that had Moses spoken precisely as God instructed, he would have elicited a different response from Pharaoh. But given the demanding tone, and the unspecified amount of time, it is no wonder Pharaoh immediately responds so dismissively.

5.2 But Pharaoh said, "Who is the Lord that I should heed Him and let Israel go? I do not know the Lord, nor will I let Israel go."

Sarna points out an interesting juxtaposition: When God appeared before Moses at the burning bush, Moses's first response was a rather humble, "Who am I?" Pharaoh, in contrast, responds to the idea of God with "Who is the

Lord?" These opposing responses of Moses and Pharaoh highlight their fundamentally different orientations. Moses sees himself as a simple human being, "the most humble of men" as the Torah later tells us (Numbers 12:3). In contrast, Pharaoh sees himself, as do the Egyptians, as a divine being. His arrogance, as reflected in his contemptuous statement, "Who is the Lord?" is what God recognizes needs to be crushed.

MOSES THEN SAYS WHAT HE WAS TOLD TO SAY

5.3 They answered, "The God of the Hebrews has manifested Himself to us. Let us go, we pray, a distance of three days into the wilderness to sacrifice to the Lord our God, lest He strike us with pestilence or sword."

Apparently, Moses realizes he has not followed God's exact instructions, tries again, and gets it right. First, he uses the name God instructed him to use when speaking to Pharaoh. It makes more sense for Moses to refer to God as "God of the Hebrews" rather than as "God of Israel," because Pharaoh uses the term "Hebrews" to refer to his slaves. Second, Moses speaks politely as God originally directed—"Let us go, we pray .... " Third, he now says, as instructed, "lest He [God] strike us with pestilence or sword." This is obviously a threat to the Israelites: If Pharaoh doesn't acquiesce, the Hebrews will suffer at the hands of God (for neglecting their obligations to Him). But it also threatens Pharaoh with a work-stoppage if the slaves are struck with pestilence or sword.

5.4 But the king of Egypt said to them, "Moses and Aaron, why do you distract the people from their tasks? Get to your labors!"

Pharaoh blames Moses and Aaron for the punishment he is about to inflict on the Israelites. So will the Israelites.

5.5 And Pharaoh continued, "The people of the land are already so numerous, and you would have them cease from their labors!"

A form of the Hebrew word *hishbatem* (translated here as "cease from their labors") is still used to refer to a workers' strike (*shvita*)—the root of both is *shavat* (the Hebrew consonants for Sabbath). Pharaoh is essentially accusing Moses and Aaron of trying to rally the Hebrew slaves to go on strike—which is an overstatement on Pharaoh's part, since Moses and Aaron were asking for only a few days off from work.

5.6 That same day Pharaoh charged the taskmasters and foremen of the people, saying,

Pharaoh issues his decree on the very same day Moses and Aaron come before him, to make it clear they are to blame for the increased workload. He is trying to turn the Hebrews against Moses and Aaron.

5.7 "You shall no longer provide the people with straw for making bricks as heretofore; let them go and gather straw for themselves.

5.8 But impose upon them the same quota of bricks as they have been making heretofore; do not reduce it, for they are shirkers; that is why they cry, 'Let us go and sacrifice to our God!'

5.9 Let heavier work be laid upon the men; let them keep at it and not pay attention to deceitful promises."

5.10 So the taskmasters and foremen of the people went out and said to the people,

The Hebrew slaves had two levels of overseers who supervised them: the Hebrew foremen and, above them, the Egyptian taskmasters. Thousands of years later, the Nazis adopted a similar governing structure in their concentration camps. They appointed *kapos*, prisoners who were themselves often Jews, over the Jewish prisoners, and appointed Nazi soldiers over the *kapos*.

5.10 (cont.) "Thus says Pharaoh: I will not give you any straw.

"Thus says" is often used in the Bible in referring to a royal pronouncement. Moses uses the term when referring to God to communicate that God is King—indeed, the King of Kings.

5.11 You must go and get the straw yourselves wherever you can find it; but there shall be no decrease whatever in your work."

5.12 Then the people scattered throughout the land of Egypt to gather stubble for straw.

5.13 And the taskmasters pressed them, saying, "You must complete the same work assignment each day as when you had straw."

5.14 And the foremen of the Israelites, whom Pharaoh's taskmasters had set over them, were beaten. "Why," they were asked, "did you not complete the prescribed amount of bricks, either yesterday or today, as you did before?"

According to Rashi, the Israelite foremen were beaten because they could not bear to force their fellow Hebrews to fulfill the impossible quotas the Egyptians demanded. The foremen therefore had to face the beatings of the Egyptian taskmasters. As noted, Pharaoh and his taskmasters sought to induce hatred of Moses among the Hebrew foremen—and presumably among the slaves as well—and, as verse 21 makes clear, they understandably succeeded. When the Hebrew foremen came upon Moses and Aaron they said to them, "May the Lord look upon you and punish you for making us loathsome to Pharaoh...."

5.15 Then the foremen of the Israelites came to Pharaoh and cried: "Why do you deal thus with your servants?

The word "servants" (or "slaves"—the Hebrew uses the same word for both, and it is not possible to always know when the Torah is referring to servants or slaves)—appears three times in the next two verses, highlighting the submissive stance of the Hebrew foremen relative to the Egyptian taskmasters.

A sociological note: That the Hebrew word for "servants" is the same as the word for "slaves" may help explain why Jews have historically been reluctant to take on positions of servitude or positions that even imply servitude. Thus, while most people, when speaking of their employment, say, "I work *for* so-and-so," Jews are more apt to say, "I work *with* so-and-so."

5.16 No straw is issued to your servants, yet they demand of us: Make bricks! Thus your servants are being beaten, when the fault is with your own people."

5.17 He replied, "You are shirkers, shirkers! That is why you say, 'Let us go and sacrifice to the Lord.'

5.18 Be off now to your work! No straw shall be issued to you, but you must produce your quota of bricks!"

Throughout history, slaves were almost always regarded as less than human. Therefore, they could be subjected to great cruelty, sometimes emanating from sheer sadism. (The universal practice of slavery, and the accompanying horrible treatment of slaves, is one of the many reasons it is absurd to believe people are basically good—see the commentary on Genesis 8:21).

5.19 Now the foremen of the Israelites found themselves in trouble because of the order, "You must not reduce your daily quantity of bricks."

The foremen are the ones who must now relay Pharaoh's cruel and impossible orders to their fellow Hebrews.

5.20 As they left Pharaoh's presence, they came upon Moses and Aaron standing in their path,

5.21 and they said to them, "May the Lord look upon you and punish you for making us loathsome to Pharaoh and his courtiers—putting a sword in their hands to slay us."

The foremen's anger is completely understandable: They would have much preferred that Moses and Aaron never went before Pharaoh; all it seems to have done is make matters worse.

IT CAN BE DIFFICULT TO LOVE BOTH HUMANS AND GOD AT THE SAME TIME

5.22 Then Moses returned to the Lord and said, "O Lord, why did You bring harm upon this people?

Moses witnesses the suffering of the slaves, and because of his hatred of evil, he cries out against God. Moses's cry to God exemplifies the reality that it can be difficult to simultaneously love both humans and God. If we truly love human beings, we can become so upset by the pain they endure we have trouble loving the God who allows such suffering.

> *It can be difficult to love both humans and God at the same time.*

On the other hand, there are people who are so preoccupied with God they don't permit themselves to fully feel the pain of human beings. One example is those—in any religion—who leave the world to immerse themselves in a religious life and ignore human suffering.

The Torah's goal is that we love both man and God.

This is Moses's predicament. But it is Pharaoh, not God, who is the one responsible for the Hebrews' suffering. All anger should be directed at him.

It Is OK to Get Angry with God

5.22 (cont.) Why did You send me?

Moses criticizes God both for making his mission unsuccessful and for sending him to Egypt in the first place. On some level, however, God has already responded to this charge. At the burning bush, God told Moses Pharaoh would refuse to let the Israelites leave.

God does not become angry with Moses for his outburst. He understands that, in the face of great evil, it can be very difficult to trust Him or to understand His seeming passivity. God's non-reaction to Moses's outburst means all of us, not just Moses, are allowed to cry out against God when we are confronted with great evil, whether done to us or others. It is important to recall the name of the Jewish people, "Israel," means "struggle [or wrestle] with God" (Genesis 32:29).

Of course, Moses's anger with God does not lead him to doubt God's existence; he had, after all, spoken with God (at the burning bush). But Moses does doubt God will deliver on His promise to save the Israelites. His reaction illustrates the two types of faith: faith in God's existence and faith in God's trustworthiness.

Like Moses, we, too, can become angry with God and even doubt His trustworthiness; these are perfectly understandable responses to the reality of evil in the world. However, evil should not lead us to doubt God's existence. We need to be intellectually consistent. If the existence of evil argues for no God, then the existence of goodness must argue for God.

> *If the existence of evil argues for no God, then the existence of goodness must argue for God.*

5.23 Ever since I came to Pharaoh to speak in Your name, he has dealt worse with this people; and still You have not delivered Your people."

When we want something good to happen we can become very impatient. The words, "ever since I came to Pharaoh" suggests Moses's effort had been going on for a long time. But, of course, this was only his first meeting with Pharaoh. We all want good to prevail over evil immediately. And it would be nice if it did. But more often—this case being one of them—it doesn't. Hence the need for perseverance, faith, and hope.

6.1 Then the Lord said to Moses, "You shall soon see what I will do to Pharaoh: he shall let them go because of a greater might; indeed, because of a greater might he shall drive them from his land."

God does not respond to Moses's accusations at the end of the previous chapter—that the mission has not only not succeeded, it has increased the suffering of the enslaved Israelites. There is an important Talmudic principle that states silence in the face of an accusation is, in effect, acknowledgment that the accusation is true.[1] By saying nothing, God may be acknowledging it is understandable. Moses harbors doubts that God will carry out what He promised to do, and at least thus far, following God's instructions has actually made things worse for the Israelites.

Now God does respond, not to the accusations, but, more likely, to build up Moses's trust and hope. God even more emphatically promises to deliver on His word, and tells Moses He will do so *now*.

6.2 God spoke to Moses and said to him, "I am the Lord.

6.3 I appeared to Abraham, Isaac, and Jacob as El Shaddai, but I did not make Myself known to them by My name [YHVH].

As related in Exodus 3:15, God reveals the name YHVH to Moses.

6.4 I also established My covenant with them, to give them the land of Canaan, the land in which they lived as sojourners.

The Israeli Bible scholar Nehama Leibowitz (1905–1997) notes that God describes the Promised Land in different terms when speaking to the patriarchs

The number seven is the most important and most recurring number in the Torah because God created the world in seven days. And everything else rests on that.

than to the Israelites. When Abraham was promised the land of Canaan, he was not told anything about its beauty and riches because he did not need evidence of the greatness of God's promise (Genesis 12:1). However, the Israelites, who were more skeptical, not to mention more theologically primitive, were promised a land "flowing with milk and honey." Given the depth of Moses's faith, the patriarchal description of Canaan now offered—the one without any mention of the land's beauty or riches—is sufficient for Moses.

6.5 I have now heard the moaning of the Israelites because the Egyptians are holding them in bondage, and I have remembered My covenant.

God tells Moses He can be fully trusted to deliver the Israelites from slavery because He "remembers" the promise He made to the patriarchs. When God "remembers" it is the Torah's way of saying God has decided to act at that moment.

6.6 Say, therefore to the Israelite people: I am the Lord. I will free you from the labors of the Egyptians and deliver you from their bondage. I will redeem you with an outstretched arm and through extraordinary chastisements.

This verse is the traditional reason why Jews drink four cups of wine at the Passover Seder. Each cup represents the three divine promises in this verse and the divine promise in the following verse:

"I will free you...."

"I will deliver you...."

"I will redeem you..."

"I will take you to be My people..."

There are actually three more promises in the following two verses (then again, four cups of wine is quite sufficient):

"I will be your God..."

"I will bring you into the land..."

"I will give it to you for a possession..."

WHY SEVEN IS THE MOST IMPORTANT NUMBER IN THE TORAH

God thus makes a total of seven promises. Once again, the number seven appears in the Torah. It is the most significant and recurring number in the Torah.

To cite only some examples:

- The world is created in seven days.
- The Sabbath is on the seventh day.
- Every seventh year is a Sabbatical year for the land (Leviticus 25:3-6) and every Jubilee Year (Leviticus 25:8-12) begins after every forty-ninth year (seven times seven).
- The festivals of Pesach (Passover) and Succot (Tabernacles) are each seven days long.

The reason, of course, is the number seven signifies God is the Creator. This greater significance of seven—representing God's creation of the world in seven days—argues for my belief, that the first verse of the Torah ("In the beginning God created the heavens and the earth") is the most important verse in the Bible. (Even that verse, in the Hebrew, contains seven words!)

In brief, the reason that verse, and the recurring number seven, is so important is that everything in the Torah and the Bible rests on the belief God is the Creator. If one does not accept that, the God of the Bible is a fairy tale, and all life is just a natural coincidence devoid of ultimate meaning.

6.7 And I will take you to be My people, and I will be your God.

The language of this verse ("And I will take you to be My people") is reminiscent of the language of the ancient Jewish marriage contract (*ketubah*) in which a man takes a woman for his wife and the woman accepts his proposal. This husband/wife metaphor is commonly used throughout the literature of the prophets to describe the relationship between God and Israel. Most famously, the prophet Hosea speaks of God saying to the Jewish people: "I will betroth you unto Me forever; I will betroth you unto Me with righteousness and justice; and with goodness and mercy. And I will betroth you unto Me with faithfulness and you shall know God" (Hosea 2:21). Again, the number seven is alluded to by the seven statements of betrothal in Hosea's verse. (To this day, in the Jewish wedding ceremony, seven blessings are recited under the wedding canopy, and those seven blessings are repeated daily on the seven days following the wedding.)

Sometimes a father casts so large a shadow he makes it hard for his children to find the sunshine they need to grow and flourish.

In this verse, God is also telling the Jewish people they are a nation only insofar as God is their God. Many secular Jews have made significant contributions to modern Jewish history—it was largely secular Jews, for example, who founded the modern State of Israel. But secular Jews who wish to perpetuate a secular Jewish identity have rarely been successful; their descendants either come to embrace some form of God-centered Judaism, or ultimately cease identifying as Jews.

6.7 (cont.) And you shall know that I, the Lord, am your God who freed you from the labors of the Egyptians.

6.8 I will bring you into the land which I swore to give to Abraham, Isaac, and Jacob, and I will give it to you for a possession, I the Lord."

6.9 But when Moses told this to the Israelites, they would not listen to Moses, their spirits crushed by cruel bondage.

6.10 The Lord spoke to Moses, saying,

6.11 "Go and tell Pharaoh king of Egypt to let the Israelites depart from his land."

God no longer tells Moses to speak to Pharaoh politely, or to request permission for the Israelites to sacrifice to God for about a week.

6.12 But Moses appealed to the Lord, saying, "The Israelites would not listen to me; how then should Pharaoh heed me, a man of impeded speech!"

> Moses raises three objections: the Israelites will not listen to him; Pharaoh will not listen to him; and he does not speak well.

6.13 So the Lord spoke to both Moses and Aaron in regard to the Israelites and Pharaoh king of Egypt, instructing them to deliver the Israelites from the land of Egypt.

> This time God speaks to Aaron as well.

6.14 The following are the heads of their respective clans. The sons of Reuben, Israel's first-born: Enoch and Pallu, Hezron and Carmi; those are the families of Reuben.

6.15 The sons of Simeon: Jemuel, Jamin, Ohad, Jachin, Zohar, and Saul the son of a Canaanite woman; those are the families of Simeon.

6.16 These are the names of Levi's sons by their lineage: Gershon, Kohath, and Merari; and the span of Levi's life was 137 years.

6.17 The sons of Gershon: Libni and Shimei, by their families.

6.18 The sons of Kohath: Amram, Izhar, Hebron, and Uzziel; and the span of Kohath's life was 133 years.

6.19 The sons of Merari: Mahli and Mushi. These are the families of the Levites by their lineage.

> Verses 14 to 19 present the family background of Moses (through his father Amram). I believe it gives the Torah historical credibility.

6.20 Amram took to wife his father's sister Jochebed, and she bore him Aaron and Moses; and the span of Amram's life was 137 years.

> Torah law forbids a man from marrying his aunt (Leviticus 18:12-13), but obviously such a law was not applicable before the Torah.[2]

Though Amram's daughter, Miriam—Moses's older sister—plays a prominent role in the Torah, her birth is not recorded here, only the birth of sons, as was the norm in societies throughout much of history. Nevertheless, Miriam is regularly designated by name in the Torah, and is even regarded as a prophet (see, for example, Exodus 2:4-9, and 15:20-21).

6.21 The sons of Izhar: Korah, Nepheg, and Zichri.

6.22 The sons of Uzziel: Mishael, Elzaphan, and Sithri.

ESSAY: PROMINENT PARENTS AND THEIR CHILDREN

6.23 Aaron took to wife Elisheba, daughter of Amminadab and sister of Nahshon, and she bore him Nadab and Abihu, Eleazar and Ithamar.

Aaron's sons are mentioned but not Moses's. The lack of attention to Moses's sons here and elsewhere in the Torah—essentially nothing is said about them—needs to be explained. And the explanation is probably this: They did not amount to much.[3]

This raises the interesting issue of the difficulty many children of great people face in leading successful and satisfying lives. In a book about Moses, *Overcoming Life's Disappointments*, Rabbi Harold Kushner writes about this:

> Sometimes the father casts so large a shadow that he makes it hard for his children to find the sunshine they need to grow and flourish. Sometimes, the father's achievements are so intimidating that the child just gives up any hope of equaling him. But mostly, I suspect, it takes so much of a man's [the father's] time and energy to be a great man—great in some ways but not in all— that he has too little time left to be a father.

As the South African leader Nelson Mandela's daughter was quoted as saying to him, "You are the father of all our people but you never had time to be a father to me."[4]

Kushner relates a remarkable story he read in a magazine geared toward clergy, a fictional account of a pastor in a mid-sized church who had a dream one night in which a voice said to him, "There are fifty teenagers in your church, and you have the ability to lead forty-nine of them to God and lose out on only one."

Energized by the dream, the minister throws all his energy into youth work, organizing special classes and trips for the church's teens. He eventually develops a national reputation in his denomination for his work with young people.

"And then one night he discovers his sixteen-year-old son has been arrested for dealing drugs. The boy turned bitterly against the church and its teachings, resenting his father for having had time for every sixteen-year-old in town except him, and the father never noticed. His son was the fiftieth teenager, the one who got away."

Of course, this was not necessarily true of Moses's children, but the silence of the Torah concerning his children (which is not the case with the children of Abraham, Isaac, Jacob, and Aaron) serves as an important reminder to parents who have achieved success to be sure to make time for their children. They need to try to ensure their children feel they occupy a special place in their parents' hearts and no matter how pressing the parent's responsibilities, he or she will always find time for them.

6.24 The sons of Korah: Assir, Elkanah, and Abiasaph. Those are the families of the Korahites.

6.25 And Aaron's son Eleazar took to wife one of Putiel's daughters, and she bore him Phinehas. Those are the heads of the fathers' houses of the Levites by their families.

6.26 It is the same Aaron and Moses to whom the Lord said, "Bring forth the Israelites from the land of Egypt, troop by troop."

The Torah uses a military expression to highlight the force with which God will deliver the Israelites from Egyptian bondage.

6.27 It was they who spoke to Pharaoh king of Egypt to free the Israelites from the Egyptians; these are the same Moses and Aaron.

6.28 For when the Lord spoke to Moses in the land of Egypt

6.29 and the Lord said to Moses, "I am the Lord; speak to Pharaoh king of Egypt all that I will tell you,"

6.30 Moses appealed to the Lord, saying, "See, I am of impeded speech; how then should Pharaoh heed me!"

Regarding Moses's issues of speech and public speaking, see the commentary to Exodus 4:10-12.

CHAPTER 7

7.1 The Lord replied to Moses, "See, I place you in the role of God to Pharaoh,

Moses will have such command over Pharaoh he will in effect be playing the role of God in Pharaoh's life. This is particularly significant because Pharaoh sees himself—and his people see him—as a god.

7.1 (cont.) with your brother Aaron as your prophet.

The Hebrew word *navi* is commonly translated as "prophet," but it actually means "spokesman." The primary role of Aaron and of the later prophets in the Hebrew Bible, such as Amos, Isaiah, and Jeremiah, is not to predict the future, but to serve as God's spokesman (or spokeswoman). Aaron has precisely that role: to convey God's words to Pharaoh as they are transmitted to Moses.

7.2 You shall repeat all that I command you, and your brother Aaron shall speak to Pharaoh to let the Israelites depart from his land.

7.3 But I will harden Pharaoh's heart, that I may multiply My signs and marvels in the land of Egypt.

Once again, God reassures Moses that he should not grow dismayed when Pharaoh refuses to release the Israelites, because God will have strengthened Pharaoh's heart. Moses, therefore, should not feel that had he delivered his message more effectively, Pharaoh might have released the Israelites.

THE PLAGUES HAD THREE MAJOR PURPOSES

7.4 When Pharaoh does not heed you, I will lay My hand upon Egypt and deliver My ranks, My people the Israelites, from the land of Egypt with extraordinary chastisements.

There are three major purposes for the Ten Plagues.

The first and most obvious is to force Pharaoh and the Egyptians to release the Hebrews.

The second is to punish Pharaoh and the Egyptians for the terrible suffering they inflicted on the Israelites over hundreds of years—including for a time the mass murder of newborn Hebrew boys. God and the Torah believe in punishment when appropriate, because God and the Torah are preoccupied with justice. Thank God. While the world needs compassion and other good traits, they must all be rooted in justice or we end up with neither justice nor compassion.

The plagues were specifically directed against Egypt's nature gods.

The third purpose of the plagues is to demonstrate to the Israelites (and to the Egyptians) that God, not the gods of Egypt (including Pharaoh), is the real God. That is why, as we shall see, the plagues were specifically directed against Egypt's gods.

ESSAY: IS THERE SUCH A THING AS COLLECTIVE GUILT?

The punishments inflicted on Egypt raise the difficult issue of what is known as "collective guilt." Specifically, was it right to punish the Egyptian people for decisions made by their Pharaoh? (I will address the unique moral problem of the tenth plague, God's killing of the firstborn throughout Egypt, in the commentary on that plague.)

The Torah's answer is, yes—because the evils inflicted by the Egyptians on the Hebrews were not inflicted by a few individuals, but by the Egyptian people (though presumably not by every single Egyptian) over the course of centuries. The Torah made the collective nature of Egyptian participation in the enslavement, torment, and murder of Israelites clear in the first chapter of Exodus (verse 22).

The Torah also makes it clear when it comes to individual crimes, as opposed to national crimes, evil is to be punished only on an individual level. Thus, if a member of a family or clan murders a member of another family or clan, it is expressly forbidden to punish the murderer's family or clan. That is one of the great moral advances inherent in the much-misunderstood Torah law of an "eye for an eye…a life for a life." Every punishment must be equivalent to the crime, not more, and must only be inflicted on the perpetrator, not his family (except for capital punishment for murderers, the other punishments are all financial, not physical—see the commentary to Exodus 21:24-25).

But when it comes to mass evil committed by a nation, there can indeed be collective guilt. We cannot deny national evil just because not every member of a nation was guilty.

Take slavery in America. The whole American nation paid a terrible price—as the whole Egyptian nation did—because of the national crime of African slavery. America fought its Civil War because of slavery[1]—a war in which as many Americans died as in all the other American wars combined (a list that includes World Wars I and II, the Korean War, and the Vietnamese War—over 700,000—a statistic particularly striking given America's population in 1860 was only 31 million).

Of course, as in all wars, many of those most deserving of punishment, such as, in the case of American slavery, the slave kidnappers and traders, often got away with their crimes. In fact, according to the Torah (Exodus 21:16), those individuals deserved the death penalty. At the same time, many innocents suffered and many died. The only perfect justice is in the world to come.

Statements on slavery by two of America's greatest presidents affirm the notion of collective guilt. Thomas Jefferson, the third American president and the author of America's Declaration of Independence, warned that Americans will one day collectively pay for the sin of slavery: "I tremble for my country when I reflect that God is just: that his justice cannot sleep forever."[2]

During the American Civil War, Abraham Lincoln, too, affirmed America's collective guilt for slavery:

> Fondly do we hope, fervently do we pray, that this mighty scourge of war may speedily pass away. Yet, if God wills that it continue until…every drop of blood drawn with the lash shall be paid by another drawn with the sword, as was said three thousand years ago, so it must be said, 'the judgments of the Lord are true and righteous altogether'" (Psalm 19:10).[3]

To deny this, Lincoln told friends a week later, "is to deny that there is a God governing the world."[4] (Lincoln knew his Bible. While he did not regularly attend church, he constantly studied the Scriptures. As he put it: "In regard to this Great book, I have but to say, it is the best gift God has given to man…. But for it we could not know right from wrong."[5])

Slavery was a universally practiced evil. But the crimes of Germany during World War II, such as the bombing of civilian centers in England, Poland, Russia, and elsewhere, and the carefully engineered annihilation of two-thirds of Europe's Jews and millions of other innocents—the Holocaust—were unique. And given the knowledge and/or active support of most Germans for Hitler's invasions of countries and bombings of civilian centers, and given the active or tacit support for slave labor, and for mass deportations of Jews and others (even if not every German knew nearly all these people would be murdered), the Western democracies did not deem it immoral to bomb German cities.

Whereas God is preoccupied with good and evil and with justice, nature has no interest in any of them.

There was a general sense that the German people, not just a handful of Nazis, were responsible for Nazi evil, and therefore deserved punishment.

Among the first orders General Dwight D. Eisenhower, the head of the Allied war effort, issued after victory over Germany, was one compelling local

German populations to view the horrors committed in the concentration and death camps in their vicinity, and to provide a proper burial for the mounds of corpses piled high by the Nazis. Eisenhower obviously believed Germans as a whole were guilty.

Likewise, Japanese citizens overwhelmingly supported the Nazi-like Japanese regime during the 1930s and 1940s. That regime engaged in mass murder, mass rape, mass torture, mass enslavement, and grotesque medical experiments on fully conscious human beings in subjugated Asian countries such as Korea and China—and the evidence of internal resistance to the government is small, if not nil. As with Nazi Germany, the Japanese were deemed to be collectively guilty.

SPECIFIC EGYPTIAN GODS TARGETED BY THE PLAGUES

7.5 And the Egyptians shall know that I am the Lord, when I stretch out My hand over Egypt and bring out the Israelites from their midst."

As noted, the third purpose of the plagues was to demonstrate to the Israelites and to the Egyptians that God is God—most importantly God, *not nature*, is the only divinity. Therefore, the plagues were directed at the nature gods of Egypt.

Here is a list of some of the Egyptian nature gods against which the plagues were directed:[6]

- First plague (water turned to blood): The gods attached to the Nile River
- Second plague (frogs): The frog god and goddess
- Third plague (lice): The earth god
- Fourth plague (flies/insects): The fly-god and/or the beetle god
- Fifth plague (diseased cattle): Gods associated with bulls and cows

- Sixth plague (boils): Gods of healing
- Seventh plague (hail): Gods of the sky, atmosphere, and agriculture
- Eighth plague (locusts): The gods who protected against locusts and human disease
- Ninth plague (darkness): The sun god and moon god
- Tenth plague (deaths of firstborn): All of Egypt's gods, including Pharaoh; and a response to the mass killing of the Hebrews' sons

One of the Torah's primary purposes in Genesis 1—its opening chapter—is to disassociate God from nature, and to make it clear God is outside of nature and rules it. Here in Exodus, the plagues are all directed against the nature gods of Egypt, reinforcing Genesis 1 and demonstrating the One True God who created nature rules over it.

WORSHIP OF NATURE VS. WORSHIP OF GOD

It is thoroughly understandable that human beings would worship nature. In this world, nature, after all, is everything. But nature, unlike the God of the Torah, is amoral, and therefore unworthy of worship. Whereas God is preoccupied with good and evil and with justice, nature has no interest in any of them. Nature is governed by blind forces and the amoral law of the survival of the fittest; it is, in Tennyson's famous description, "red in tooth and claw."[7]

7.6 This Moses and Aaron did; as the Lord commanded them, so they did.

7.7 Moses was eighty years old and Aaron eighty-three, when they made their demand on Pharaoh.

7.8 The Lord said to Moses and Aaron,

7.9 "When Pharaoh speaks to you and says, 'Produce your marvel,' you shall say to Aaron, 'Take your rod and cast it down before Pharaoh.' It shall turn into a serpent."

7.10 So Moses and Aaron came before Pharaoh and did just as the Lord had commanded: Aaron cast down his rod in the presence of Pharaoh and his courtiers, and it turned into a serpent.

7.11 Then Pharaoh, for his part, summoned the wise men and the sorcerers; and the Egyptian magicians, in turn, did the same with their spells;

God begins with a startling act, albeit one the Egyptian magicians would be able to replicate. Perhaps this was to build up Pharaoh's confidence that he had nothing to fear from Moses and his God.

The tone of the Torah implies the Egyptian magicians performed real magic "with their spells," but it soon becomes clear this is magic only in the modern sense of the word—illusions that fool an audience. The fact Pharaoh later pleads with Moses, and not with his own magicians, to rid Egypt of frogs (Exodus 8:4) suggests Pharaoh regarded—or came to regard—his magicians as illusionists rather than as authentic magicians.

WHY THE TORAH SO OPPOSES MAGIC

7.12 each cast down his rod, and they turned into serpents. But Aaron's rod swallowed their rods.

The Torah radically opposes belief in magic (as opposed to magic tricks and illusions presented as entertainment) because magic implies forces other than God control the world. The swallowing of the Egyptian rods is therefore intended to demonstrate that a trick performed by illusionists through sleight of hand cannot stand up to a miracle of God. Hence, the Egyptian magicians cannot replicate what Aaron, acting at God's behest, does.

7.13 Yet Pharaoh's heart stiffened and he did not heed them, as the Lord had said.

7.14 And the Lord said to Moses, "Pharaoh is stubborn; he refuses to let the people go.

THE PLAGUES FOLLOW A PATTERN

7.15 Go to Pharaoh in the morning, as he is coming out to the water, and station yourself before him at the edge of the Nile, taking with you the rod that turned into a snake.

Pharaoh would go to the Nile every morning. Perhaps he went there to bathe, or perhaps to pray to the river god Hapi—who, the Egyptians believed, oversaw the annual flooding of the Nile, which deposited fertile soil on its banks.

In any event, Pharaoh's apparently daily visit to the Nile plays an important role in the way the plagues unfold. The events preceding each of the first nine plagues follow a pattern.

The first nine plagues are divided into three groups of three.

Before the first, fourth, and seventh plagues (blood, insects, hail), Moses is instructed to go in the morning and station himself where Pharaoh will be.

Before the second, fifth, and eighth plagues (frogs, pestilence, locusts), Moses is instructed to go to Pharaoh's palace and confront him there; and each of these plagues is executed by Aaron rather than Moses.

The third, sixth, and ninth plagues (lice, boils, darkness) strike without any warning.

This is yet another of the innumerable patterns in the Torah that seem to demonstrate a divine order in unfolding events. At the very least, great thought was put into how the plagues were executed. Nothing was random.

7.16 And say to him, 'The Lord, the God of the Hebrews, sent me to you to say, "Let My people go that they may worship Me in the wilderness." But you have paid no heed until now.

7.17 Thus says the Lord, "By this you shall know that I am the Lord." See, I shall strike the water in the Nile with the rod that is in my hand, and it will be turned into blood;

The contamination of the river served to discredit Egyptian polytheism. The Egyptians deified the Nile as the god Hapi.

This first plague may be considered a fitting retribution for Pharaoh's decree that all newborn Hebrew males had to be cast into the Nile. Since so much blood was shed in this river it would now turn to blood. Israeli Bible scholar Uriel Simon has noted the first plague's powerful symbolism. There were presumably many Egyptians who denied or ignored the evil done in their name; this plague, in bringing their crime to the surface so to speak, made such denial impossible.

7.18 and the fish in the Nile will die. The Nile will stink so that the Egyptians will find it impossible to drink the water of the Nile."

7.19 And the Lord said to Moses, "Say to Aaron: Take your rod and hold out your arm over the waters of Egypt—its rivers, its canals, its ponds, all its bodies of water—that they may turn to blood; there shall be blood throughout the land of Egypt, even in vessels of wood and stone."

7.20 Moses and Aaron did just as the Lord commanded: he lifted up the rod and struck the water in the Nile in the sight of Pharaoh and his courtiers,

> Aaron could not, of course, hold out his arm over "all [of Egypt's] bodies of water," as God commanded in the previous verse. And Aaron obviously did not assume the command was meant literally. Thus, the verse says Aaron "did just as the Lord had commanded," even though he lifted his rod only over the water in the Nile, not over all the waters of Egypt.
>
> As a result, there is still some uncontaminated water left for the Egyptian magicians to turn to blood when they replicate this seeming trick (see verse 22).

7.20 (cont.) and all the water in the Nile was turned into blood

7.21 and the fish in the Nile died. The Nile stank so that the Egyptians could not drink water from the Nile; and there was blood throughout the land of Egypt.

> For those seeking natural, as opposed to miraculous, explanations for the plagues, Sarna explains that one way of viewing the plagues is as an extreme intensification of natural phenomena. In this plague, a period of heavy rainfall caused the river to become so full of purple bacteria and eroded red sediment

that it appeared blood-like. The purple bacteria that washed down into the river disturbed the oxygen balance and killed off the fish, which in turn produced a foul stench. Of course, if the Nile turned into actual blood, as the literal reading of the text suggests, that, too, would have killed off the fish.

Since so much Hebrew blood was shed in this river, the river itself would now turn to blood.

All these explanations notwithstanding, "an extreme intensification of natural phenomena"—given its perfect timing—is also a miracle. In any event, I see no need to try to explain the plagues or any miracles as natural phenomena. If they are *only* natural phenomena, they aren't miracles.

7.22 But when the Egyptian magicians did the same with their spells,

In those directions toward which Aaron did not stretch forth his hand, pure water remained. Moses and Aaron must have found it rather humorous, if not absurd, that the Egyptian magicians were so eager to outdo Moses and Aaron they intensified the plague on their own country: "Look, Pharaoh, we, too, can ruin our water supply!"

7.22 (cont.) Pharaoh's heart stiffened and he did not heed them—as the Lord had spoken.

This time Moses does not panic or grow angry upon hearing Pharaoh's response, since God forewarned him Pharaoh would continue to refuse to set the Israelites free.

7.23 Pharaoh turned and went into his palace, paying no regard even to this.

7.24 And all the Egyptians had to dig round about the Nile for drinking water, because they could not drink the water of the Nile.

7.25 When seven days had passed after the Lord struck the Nile,

The number seven and its multiples figure prominently throughout the Torah. (See the commentary on the number seven in Exodus 6:6.) In this chapter, the word "Nile" is mentioned fourteen times (twice seven). These encoded patterns happen too often to be coincidence. They are there to suggest a single Author, or, for those who prefer, a single Editor.

7.26 the Lord said to Moses, "Go to Pharaoh and say to him, 'Thus says the Lord: Let My people go that they may worship Me.

7.27 If you refuse to let them go, then I will plague your whole country with frogs.

The god that this plague discredited was the frog-headed goddess Hekt, the consort of the god Khnoum. Given that Hekt was thought to assist in childbirth, this plague may be considered a second instance of retribution for the killing of the Hebrew male newborns.

7.28 The Nile shall swarm with frogs, and they shall come up and enter your palace, your bed-chamber and your bed, the houses of your courtiers and your people, and your ovens and your kneading bowls.

7.29 The frogs shall come up on you and on your people and on all your courtiers.'"

CHAPTER

8

8.1 And the Lord said to Moses, "Say to Aaron: Hold out your arm with the rod over the rivers, the canals, and the ponds, and bring up the frogs on the land of Egypt."

8.2 Aaron held out his arm over the waters of Egypt, and the frogs came up and covered the land of Egypt.

Of all of the plagues, frogs were the least destructive. This plague, in addition to being directed against the frog god of Egypt (Hekt), may have been designed simply to annoy and humiliate Pharaoh and the Egyptians. Even Pharaoh's bed (Exodus 7:28) was infested with frogs.

There is a song about this humiliation, commonly sung by Jewish children at the Passover Seder:

> One morning when Pharaoh woke in his bed
> There were frogs on his head and frogs in his bed
> Frogs on his nose and frogs on his toes
> Frogs—here!
> Frogs—there!
> Frogs were jumping everywhere![1]

8.3 But the magicians did the same with their spells, and brought frogs upon the land of Egypt.

As with the previous plague (water turned into blood), the Egyptians are so eager to outdo Moses and Aaron they bring further damage upon their own land. Pharaoh must have grown outraged with his magicians. He wanted them to rid the land of the frogs, not multiply them.

8.4 Then Pharaoh summoned Moses and Aaron and said, "Plead with the Lord to remove the frogs from me and my people. And I will let the people go to sacrifice to the Lord."

A significant change occurs here: Pharaoh directs his plea to rid the land of frogs not to his own magicians, but to Moses and his God. On some level, he must have understood his magicians relied on tricks, while what the God of Moses was doing was real.

The God introduced by the Torah is the first god in history to have been entirely above and beyond nature.

Now, Pharaoh uses God's name (as previously noted, when referring to God, all English translations use "Lord" when the Hebrew uses God's name, YHVH). He even asks Moses to pray to YHVH on his behalf. Evidently, Pharaoh is being converted, albeit slowly and reluctantly, into a believer in God—though not into an ethical monotheist; he is not a monotheist, since he probably still believes in Egyptian gods *in addition* to YHVH, and he certainly doesn't believe God demands ethical behavior.

8.5 And Moses said to Pharaoh, "You may have this triumph over me: for what time shall I plead in behalf of you and your courtiers and your people, that the frogs be cut off from you and your houses, to remain only in the Nile?"

In order to more fully convince Pharaoh of God's power, Moses lets Pharaoh select the time when he would like the frogs to be removed. Moses is acting like the magician who invites a member of his audience to "pick a card—any card." Were the magician to pick a card, the trick would impress no one.

8.6 "For tomorrow," he replied. And [Moses] said, "As you say—that you may know that there is none like the Lord our God;

This phrase, "that you may know that there is none like the Lord our God," appears four times during the plague stories (another deliberate pattern). It recurs with such frequency because the purpose of the plagues is, in large part, to reveal the one true God to humanity. This is the primary purpose of the Torah and of the Jewish people. And making God known has been the most important contribution to humanity ever made.

Here are fifteen reasons why this contribution has been so significant. Many of them are discussed at greater length at different points throughout this commentary.

ESSAY: THE GOD OF THE TORAH: THE MOST IMPORTANT IDEA IN WORLD HISTORY

1. The God introduced by the Torah is the first god in history to have been entirely above and beyond nature. And one of the first things God tells humans is to exercise dominion over nature (Genesis 1:26-28). This liberated humanity from believing it was controlled by nature, a revolution that made moral and scientific progress possible.

A second consequence of God being above nature is humans are not part of nature—meaning that just as we are to control the natural world outside us, we are to control our own human nature within us as well. We are to govern our lives by moral law, not by human nature.

2. The God introduced by the Torah brought universal morality into the world. Only if a moral God is universal, is morality universal. Morality was no longer local or individual. Cultures do not need to be universal; the world is enriched by multiple cultures. But morality must be universal.

3. The moral God introduced by the Torah means morality is real. "Good" and "evil" are not merely individual or societal opinions, but objectively real.

4. The God introduced by the Torah morally judges every human being. There had never been a concept like this. And it became a major reason for Jew-hatred. People do not like to be judged, and the people who introduced the idea of a God who morally judges people have paid a terrible price for

bringing the idea into the world. The social psychologist Ernest van den Haag wrote:

> Fundamental to [anti-Semitism] though seldom explicit and conscious is hostility to the Jewish belief in one God.... [The Jews'] invisible God not only insisted on being the one and only and all-powerful God—creator and lord of everything, and the only rightful claimant to worship—He also developed into a moral God.... No wonder [the Jews] are the target of all those who resent His domination.[2]

Having dialogued with atheists for decades, I have come to believe at least some of the current aggressive atheism is due to an animosity toward the idea there is a God Who will judge all of us (another reason is all the evil done in the name of God by radical Islamists—the worst sin according to the Ten Commandments [see Commandment 3 in Exodus 20]).

5. The just and good God introduced by the Torah gives humanity hope. One of those hopes is there is ultimate justice. The belief that God judges humans means both the good and the evil will get what they ultimately deserve. Even though justice is rarely served in this world, there is a good God who will ultimately set things right.

6. The God introduced by the Torah introduced holiness—the elevation of human beings from animals to creatures created in the divine image (see commentary to Leviticus 19:2).

7. The God introduced by the Torah gives every individual unprecedented self-worth. Since all humans are created in God's image, each of us is infinitely valuable. Every person has the right to say, as the Talmud put it, "For my sake was the world created."[3]

The nineteenth-century Hasidic master, Rabbi Simcha Bunim, suggested that every person carry in his or her pockets two pieces of paper. On one should be written, "For my sake was the world created," while the other should contain the words "I am but dust and ashes" (the words Abraham said when he argued with God in Genesis 18:27). Each paper should be consulted at the appropriate time. When you feel arrogant and proud of how much more you have achieved than others, remind yourself you are "but dust and ashes." And when you are feeling despair, remind yourself, "For my sake was the world created." There is some special mission and task only you can accomplish.

8. The God introduced by the Torah is necessary for human brotherhood. Since we all have the same Father, we are all brothers and sisters. As the Prophet Malachi asked: "Have we not all one Father? Did not one God create us?" (Malachi 2:10)

9. The God introduced by the Torah began the long journey to belief in human equality—solely as a result of the Torah statement that each of us is created in God's image. Slavery was abolished on a wide scale first in the Western world—by Christians who were rooted in the Torah and the rest of the Hebrew Bible and who specifically cited the Torah doctrine that all humans are created in God's image.

10. The God introduced by the Torah is incorporeal (no body; not physical). This opened the human mind to abstract thought by enabling humans to think in terms of a reality beyond that which is accessible to our senses.

11. The God introduced by the Torah teaches us the physical is not the only reality. Consequently, there can be non-physical realities such as a soul, an afterlife, and morality.

12. The God introduced by the Torah means there is ultimate meaning to existence and to each of our lives. Without this Creator, existence is random and purposeless.

That people make up meanings for their lives is a fine thing (at least, when that meaning is moral; many things—evil ideologies are the most obvious example—that give people meaning are not moral), but these meanings are nothing more than artificial constructs.

As one atheist professor expressed it, in summarizing the work of another atheist philosopher:

Ultimately, our lives are meaningless. Evolution is blind and serves no intrinsic purpose; in a cosmic sense, we each live for an insignificant amount of time....

[David] Benatar, a professor of philosophy at the University of Cape Town, argues that humans can enjoy "terrestrial" meanings—nurturing children, fighting for the rights of refugees, composing a symphony or making a delicious breakfast, for example.... Nevertheless, we are each but a "blip in cosmic time and space." Mr. Benatar insists that most of us are terminally anxious about this lack of cosmic meaning....

I did a very unscientific poll of my friends. None of them believe that there is some wider purpose to human existence.[4]

13. The God introduced by the Torah gives human beings free will. If we are only material beings (like the stellar dust of which we are composed), everything we do is determined by our genes and by our environment. Only if we have a non-material soul can we rise above our genes and our environment and act autonomously. The secular denial of anything beyond the physical deprives human beings of free will. That is why Clarence Darrow, the most famous criminal defense lawyer in American history (as well as America's most famous religious skeptic), opposed all punishment of criminals: "All people are products of two things, and two things only—their heredity and environment. And they act in exact accord with the heredity which they took from all the past and for which they are in no wise responsible, and the environment."[5]

14. The God introduced by the Torah teaches might is not right. It is God Who determines what is right, not displays of strength and force.

> *The just and good God introduced by the Torah gave humanity hope that there is ultimate justice.*

15. Finally, the God introduced by the Torah made human moral progress possible. Indeed, the Torah invented human moral progress. In the words of New York University historian Henry Bamford Parkes, "Judaism [starting with the Torah] repudiated the cyclic view of history *held by all other ancient peoples* and affirmed that it was a meaningful process leading to the gradual regeneration of humanity. *This was the origin of the Western belief in progress...*" (emphases added).[6]

What was "the cyclic view of history" referred to by Professor Parkes? In ancient civilizations, life was a cycle, meaning nothing changed from generation to generation. Every generation essentially repeated what came before it. There was therefore no such thing as moral progress—indeed, the word "progress" would have been meaningless. Then came the Torah and its God and life was no longer to be a cycle, but a line—a line moving forward toward a moral goal.

8.7 the frogs shall retreat from you and your courtiers and your people; they shall remain only in the Nile."

8.8 Then Moses and Aaron left Pharaoh's presence, and Moses cried out to the Lord in the matter of the frogs which He had inflicted upon Pharaoh.

Moses does not just speak to God or pray to Him; he cries out. Furthermore, he does so immediately upon leaving Pharaoh. Moses's response seems to imply he is anxious to relieve the suffering of the innocent Egyptians who were plagued by the frogs. Just as Abraham pleaded for those in Sodom who might be innocent (Genesis 18:23-32), Moses pleads for those Egyptians he believes are not full-fledged evildoers.

If this is an accurate read of the words "cried out," Moses was an almost perfect embodiment of justice and compassion. The man who killed an Egyptian taskmaster is now crying out for innocent Egyptians. In both cases, justice and compassion determined Moses's actions. In the first, justice demanded the taskmaster stop beating the slave, an innocent man; and compassion for the slave demanded the beating stop. In the second case, justice demanded Pharaoh be forced to release the Israelites; and compassion for the Israelites demanded the same thing.

Why Moses did not similarly cry out before and after later plagues, especially the tenth—the killing of the firstborn—is a question worth posing. We can only surmise that, for whatever reason, by the time of the last plague, Moses fully trusted in God and His judgments.

8.9 And the Lord did as Moses asked; the frogs died out in the houses, the courtyards, and the fields.

Moses was not instructed by God to let Pharaoh predict the time when the frogs should be removed. Moses determined the time, apparently confident God would act on his request.

8:10 And they piled them up in heaps, till the land stank.

8.11 But when Pharaoh saw that there was relief, he became stubborn and would not heed them, as the Lord had spoken.

God told Moses Pharaoh would stubbornly refuse to set the Israelites free, and amazingly, given the plague he just experienced, and while he could still smell the stench from the piles of decaying frogs, Pharaoh indeed refused.

8.12 Then the Lord said to Moses, "Say to Aaron: Hold out your rod and strike the dust of the earth, and it shall turn to lice throughout the land of Egypt."

8.13 And they did so. Aaron held out his arm with the rod and struck the dust of the earth, and vermin came upon man and beast; All the dust of the earth turned to lice throughout the land of Egypt.

8.14 The magicians did the like with their spells to produce lice, but they could not. The vermin remained upon man and beast;

This plague represents an escalation in intensity because, unlike the blood and frogs, Pharaoh's magicians are unable to bring about the lice. The magicians' failed attempt demonstrates a key theme of the Torah and of the plagues: God alone controls the universe.

8.15 and the magicians said to Pharaoh, "This is the finger of God!"

The magicians do not use God's proper name, YHVH, because they are not acknowledging the God of the Israelites caused the plague; they are simply informing Pharaoh that some divine power is responsible.

Slavery was abolished on a wide scale first in the Western world—by Christians who were rooted in the Torah and the rest of the Hebrew Bible.

8.15 (cont.) But Pharaoh's heart stiffened and he would not heed them, as the Lord had spoken.

The Torah here does not state that God makes Pharaoh's heart strong, but rather that Pharaoh does so himself. Only with the later plagues does the Torah claim God is directly responsible. This shift in language seems to signify that if Pharaoh really wanted to change his mind after one of the early plagues, God would have allowed him to; but by the time the later plagues strike and Pharaoh has already refused to free the Israelites several times, he loses his chance.

8.16 And the Lord said to Moses, "Early in the morning present yourself to Pharaoh, as he is coming out to the water, and say to him, 'Thus says the Lord: Let My people go that they may worship Me.

The purpose of the liberation from Egypt is not only liberation but the service of God—living according to His rules, and spreading ethical monotheism to the world's nations.

8.17 For if you do not let My people go, I will let loose swarms of insects against you

In the Hebrew, this verse contains a play on the word "send." A literal translation would read: "If you don't *send* My people, I will *send* a swarm of insects…." God is telling Pharaoh something will be sent: Either Pharaoh will "send" the Israelites, or God will "send" another plague.

8.17 (cont.) and your courtiers and your people and your houses; the houses of the Egyptians, and the very ground they stand on, shall be filled with swarms of insects.

8.18 But on that day I will set apart the region of Goshen, where My people dwell, so that no swarms of insects shall be there,

God adds another miraculous element to the impression He is making upon Pharaoh: He ensures the Israelites alone are not affected by the plague.

> *The Egyptian people might have thought that their enemy was the God of Israel, but the real enemy of the Egyptian people was Pharaoh.*

8.18 (cont.) that you may know that I the Lord am in the midst of the land.

Sarna comments that "for the first time a clear distinction is made between the Egyptians and the Israelites, and the time of the onset of the plague is fixed, both particulars leaving no doubt the source of the plague is not just any god, but YHVH, God of Israel." God therefore wants Pharaoh to realize He is God everywhere, not just in the wilderness where the Israelites have been seeking permission to go worship Him.

8.19 And I will make a distinction between My people and your people. Tomorrow this sign shall come to pass.'"

8.20 And the Lord did so. Heavy swarms of insects invaded Pharaoh's palace and the houses of his courtiers; throughout the country of Egypt the land was ruined because of the swarms of insects.

8.21 Then Pharaoh summoned Moses and Aaron and said,

This time, Moses and Aaron do not come before Pharaoh on their own initiative; they wait for him to call them.

8.21 (cont.) "Go and sacrifice to your Lord within the land."

Now Pharaoh concedes even less than he did before. Whereas he earlier granted the Israelites permission to leave Egypt for a brief period—a permission he later revoked—he now tells them they can worship their God, but only while remaining in Egypt.

8.22 But Moses replied, "It would not be right to do this, for what we sacrifice to the Lord our God is untouchable to the Egyptians. If we sacrifice that which is untouchable to the Egyptians before their very eyes, will they not stone us!

Moses provides a brilliant refutation of Pharaoh's offer of a week-long vacation to worship in Egypt: He tells Pharaoh the animals the Israelites wish to slaughter are worshipped in the Egyptian religion. Therefore, performing their sacrifices in the presence of the Egyptians might cause pandemonium and incite violence from the Egyptians. Moses seems to be speaking considerately to Pharaoh, but he is effectively deriding Pharaoh's religion by stating the Israelites need to slaughter and sacrifice Egyptian gods in order to serve their God. Moses has clearly become a shrewd negotiator.

8.23 So we must go a distance of three days into the wilderness and sacrifice to the Lord our God as He may command us."

8.24 Pharaoh said, "I will let you go to sacrifice to the Lord your God in the wilderness; but do not go very far. Plead, then, for me."

8.25 And Moses said, "When I leave your presence, I will plead with the Lord that the swarms of insects depart tomorrow from Pharaoh and his courtiers and his people; let not Pharaoh again act deceitfully, not letting the people go to sacrifice to the Lord.

Instead of leaving immediately to go plead with God, as he did the last time Pharaoh made this request, Moses first takes the time to rebuke Pharaoh for playing games with the Israelites. Moses increasingly feels free to speak to Pharaoh from a position of superiority.

8.26 So Moses left Pharaoh's presence and pleaded with the Lord.

Whereas Moses cried out to God during the plague of the frogs because he was concerned about the welfare of innocent Egyptians, Moses now merely pleads with God to fulfill His assurance to Pharaoh that He would do so. He is likely and understandably losing patience.

8.27 And the Lord did as Moses asked: He removed the swarms of insects from Pharaoh, from his courtiers, and from his people; not one remained.

8.28 But Pharaoh became stubborn this time also, and would not let the people go.

As with the other early plagues, it is Pharaoh who steels his own heart once the insects have been removed. Everett Fox, who has made the most literal English-language translation of the Torah, translates this verse: "But Pharaoh made his heart heavy-with-stubbornness this time as well, and he did not send the people free."

There is a lesson here for any of us who have stubbornly clung to a cause that is not only wrong, but is failing. The Japanese leaders knew they were losing World War II, but the stubbornness of their military leaders brought down upon them the atom bomb, as the stubbornness of Pharaoh soon brought down upon his people the death of their firstborn. The Egyptian people might have thought their enemy was the God of Israel, but just as the real enemies of the Japanese people were their own leaders, the real enemy of the Egyptian people was Pharaoh.

CHAPTER

9

9.1 The Lord said to Moses, "Go to Pharaoh and say to him, 'Thus says the Lord, the God of the Hebrews: Let My people go to worship Me.

9.2 For if you refuse to let them go, and continue to hold them,

9.3 then the hand of the Lord will strike your livestock in the fields—the horses, the asses, the camels, the cattle, and the sheep—with a very severe pestilence.

> Following Moses's allusion to the importance of sacred animals in Egypt (see 8:22), God now strikes those animals with pestilence, exposing the impotence of those gods and reaffirming only God is divine—and nothing in nature is.

9.4 But the Lord will make a distinction between the livestock of Israel and the livestock of the Egyptians, so that nothing shall die of all that belongs to the Israelites.

> This plague is even more striking because it affects only the Egyptian livestock, a particularly dramatic demonstration of God's control over the natural world.

9.5 The Lord has fixed the time: tomorrow the Lord will do this thing in the land.'"

> With each plague, God adds more miracles to make an even greater impression on Pharaoh. This time, God does not just announce the plague in advance; He also announces the time the plague will strike.

9.6 And the Lord did so the next day: all the livestock of the Egyptians died, but of the livestock of the Israelites not a beast died.

9.7 When Pharaoh inquired, he found that not a head of the livestock of Israel had died;

> Pharaoh makes inquiries, presumably sending aides, to verify this miracle has indeed taken place just as Moses said it would.

9.7 (cont.) Yet Pharaoh remained stubborn, and he would not let the people go.

9.8 Then the Lord said to Moses and Aaron, "Each of you take handfuls of soot from the kiln, and let Moses throw it toward the sky in the sight of Pharaoh.

> Following the pattern, Pharaoh does not receive any advance warning about the third plague of the second trio. See the description of the three sets of plagues in the commentary to Exodus 7:15.

9.9 It shall become a fine dust all over the land of Egypt, and cause an inflammation breaking out in boils on man and beast throughout the land of Egypt."

9.10 So they took soot of the kiln and appeared before Pharaoh; Moses threw it toward the sky, and it caused an inflammation breaking out in boils on man and beast.

9.11 The magicians were unable to confront Moses because of the inflammation, for the inflammation afflicted the magicians as well as all the other Egyptians.

9.12 But the Lord stiffened the heart of Pharaoh,

> After each of the first five plagues, the Torah says Pharaoh strengthened his heart. But for the first time, it is not Pharaoh, but God, who "strengthens" (translated here as "stiffened") Pharaoh's heart.
>
> Pharaoh's heart being strengthened means Pharaoh now has the strength to decide what to do with the Israelites of his own volition—not due to the weakening of his heart brought on by the plagues and fear of more plagues.

9.12 (cont.) and he would not heed them, just as the Lord had told Moses.

> Pharaoh does not listen to his advisors, who, we shall soon see, have become eager to get rid of the Israelites and their terrible plagues (10:7). The magicians

in particular are troubled by the plagues. They suffer from them as do all other Egyptians, but they suffer the added humiliation of being exposed as impotent before the God of Israel.

Meanwhile, Pharaoh is an example of an evil leader bringing destruction on the very people he claims to love. Quite often, tyrants who claim to love their people—Stalin, Hitler, and Mao are modern examples—eventually bring immeasurable suffering onto those very people. Likewise, Islamist terrorists have wreaked havoc not only on Jews and Christians and other non-Muslims, but even more so on Muslims, the group on whose behalf they murder non-Muslims.

> *Pharaoh is an example of the evil leader who brings destruction on the very people he claims to love.*

9.13 The Lord said to Moses, "Early in the morning present yourself to Pharaoh and say to him, 'Thus says the Lord, the God of the Hebrews: Let My people go to worship Me.

9.14 For this time I will send all My plagues upon your person, and your courtiers, and your people, in order that you may know that there is none like Me in all the world.

9.15 I could have stretched forth My hand and stricken you and your people with pestilence, and you would have been effaced from the earth.

God informs Pharaoh that just as He killed all the livestock in the plague of pestilence, so too could He have killed Pharaoh and all the Egyptians had He desired to do so.

9.16 Nevertheless I have spared you for this purpose; in order to show you My power, and in order that My fame may resound throughout the world.

The plagues mark the first time God has revealed Himself to large groups of people rather than to isolated individuals such as Abraham and Moses.

9.17 Yet you continue to thwart My people, and do not let them go!

9.18 This time tomorrow I will rain down a very heavy hail, such as has not been in Egypt from the day it was founded until now.

9.19 Therefore, order your livestock and everything you have in the open brought under shelter;

God wants Pharaoh to announce this plague to the Egyptians—to humble Pharaoh by having him be the one to relay the word of his slaves' God to his people.

As regards the Israelite slaves, with their debased self-image, it must have been gratifying (if not surreal) to them to hear the Egyptian Pharaoh making pronouncements to his people as instructed by the Israelite God.

Both the punishment of Pharaoh and his nation and of the Jews in sixth-century BCE Judea were in response to the mistreatment of slaves.

This verse poses an obvious dilemma: What livestock is it referring to? Didn't the Torah already state in verse 6, "all the livestock of the Egyptians died"? Any number of answers have been given, but I have not found them entirely persuasive. Either the word "all" in verse 6 was not meant literally or there is another explanation of which I am not aware. Given the Torah's general historicity and honesty, I am not troubled by the handful of verses I cannot explain.

9.19 (cont.) every man and beast that is found outside, not having been brought indoors, shall perish when the hail comes down upon them!'"

God does not want to kill all the Egyptians; He simply wants to free the Israelites and in the process to demonstrate His might. God therefore provides an advance warning to allow the Egyptians to protect themselves from the hail.

9.20 Those among Pharaoh's courtiers who feared the Lord's word brought their slaves and livestock indoors to safety;

9.21 but those who paid no regard to the word of the Lord left their slaves and livestock in the open.

Here is a sad instance where people—in this case, slaves of Egyptians—suffered not because of any wrongs they committed but because they had the misfortune to live among evildoers.

One might say almost all human suffering caused by people (rather than by nature) is done by those "who paid no regard to the word of the Lord." In biblical language, such people are synonymous with those who mistreat others—because to "pay regard to the word of God" is synonymous with treating other people decently. That is what ethical monotheism is all about.

9.22 The Lord said to Moses, "Hold out your arm toward the sky that hail may fall on all the grasses of the field in the land of Egypt."

9.23 So Moses held out his rod toward the sky, and the Lord sent thunder and hail, and fire streamed down to the ground, as the Lord rained down hail upon the land of Egypt.

9.24 The hail was very heavy—fire flashing in the midst of the hail—such as had not fallen on the land of Egypt since it had become a nation.

9.25 Throughout the land of Egypt the hail struck down all that were in the open, both man and beast; the hail also struck down all the grasses of the field and shattered all the trees of the field.

9.26 Only in the region of Goshen, where the Israelites were, there was no hail.

9.27 Thereupon Pharaoh sent for Moses and Aaron and said to them, "I stand guilty this time. The Lord is in the right, and I and my people are in the wrong.

Pharaoh has grown accustomed to referring to God by His proper name YHVH ("The Lord"). He has become increasingly convinced of the power of the Israelites' God, especially after witnessing those who stayed indoors survive the hail as God predicted.

It is interesting Pharaoh says not only he but "I and my people" are in the wrong. Either he is deflecting moral blame from himself or he is acknowledging the enslavement of the Israelites was a national effort. The fact the plagues are inflicted on all the Egyptian people, and not just Pharaoh and the royal court, would seem to support the latter view.

9.28 Plead with the Lord that there may be an end of God's thunder and of hail. I will let you go; you need stay no longer."

9.29 Moses said to him, "As I go out of the city, I shall spread out my hands to the Lord; the thunder will cease and the hail will fall no more, so that you may know that the earth is the Lord's.

Unlike the plague of frogs, when Moses promised to accommodate Pharaoh's every wish, even regarding the time when the frogs would disappear, this time Moses simply informs Pharaoh he will take care of the hail. Moses has clearly become more confident in his dealings with Pharaoh.

9.30 But I know that you and your courtiers do not yet fear the Lord God."

9.31 Now the flax and barley were ruined, for the barley was in the ear and the flax was in the bud;

9.32 but the wheat and the emmer were not hurt, for they ripen late.

9.33 Leaving Pharaoh, Moses went outside the city and spread out his hands to the Lord: the thunder and the hail ceased, and no rain came pouring down upon the earth.

9.34 But when Pharaoh saw that the rain and the hail and the thunder had ceased, he became stubborn and reverted to his guilty ways,

Although Pharaoh just confessed to Moses he was "in the wrong," he reverts to his wrongful behavior. This is typical of evildoers: They plead to be forgiven and then resume their bad behavior as soon as they are forgiven, or as soon as their punishment is ended. Abusive spouses are a classic example. They promise to change their behavior when their actions are exposed, or when they are threatened with punishment, or when the abused spouse threatens to leave them—and then revert to their abusive behavior after being forgiven or as soon as they believe they can get away with it.

A biblical example:

The Book of Jeremiah records that during a period of great peril to the citizens of Judea (around 586 BCE), when the Babylonian King Nebuchadnezzar and his troops were about to invade Jerusalem, the Jews freed all their Hebrew slaves (indentured servants), many of whom were held in violation of Torah law for longer than the permitted six years. Then, as soon as the danger seemed to pass, they "turned about and brought back the men and women they had set free and forced them into slavery again" (Jeremiah 34:11). This act of cruelty caused God to declare, through Jeremiah, that the Judeans would now suffer the worst sorts of suffering, involving famine, pestilence, and death. Further, in addition to being killed by their enemies as punishment for their wickedness, their carcasses would "become food for the birds of the sky and the beasts of the earth" (Jeremiah 34:20).

It is of great importance to note that both the punishment of Pharaoh and his nation and of the Jews in sixth-century BCE Judea—as described in this episode—are in response to the mistreatment of slaves. God holds His own people and the Egyptians accountable to the same basic standard—a unique concept in religious history up to that time.

The Torah does not legally ban slavery outright—3,000 years ago, any writing that did so would not have been taken seriously—but it morally condemns it. In general, though not always, the moral precedes the legal. First you teach people what is right and wrong, then they eventually put the teaching into law. First you teach people "all men are created equal" and "created in the image of God"—then eventually they end slavery.

9.34 (cont.) as did his courtiers.

9.35 So Pharaoh's heart stiffened and he would not let the Israelites go, just as the Lord had foretold through Moses.

CHAPTER 10

10.1 Then the Lord said to Moses, "Go to Pharaoh. For I have hardened his heart and the hearts of his courtiers, in order that I may display these My signs among them,

THE UNIQUE SIGNIFICANCE OF REMEMBERING

10.2 and that you may recount in the hearing of your sons and of your sons' sons how I made a mockery of the Egyptians and how I displayed My signs among them—in order that you may know that I am the Lord."

Through Moses, God instructs the Jews to tell generation after generation about God's miracles when taking the Jews out of Egypt. Remembering is an important value in the Torah.

Without remembering, there is no gratitude, no wisdom, and no faith.

Gratitude: Only when people remember the good others have done for them will they have gratitude. Unfortunately, however, most people remember the bad people have done to them far longer than the good. Or to put it another way, gratitude takes effort; resentment is effortless.

Wisdom: People attain wisdom in large part by remembering what happened in the past. No generation can attain wisdom without studying and remembering the past. None of those who believed in the 1960s aphorism, "Never trust anyone over thirty," became a wise person.

Without wisdom, all the good intentions in the world amount to nothing. Intending to do good without having wisdom is like intending to fly an airplane with no knowledge of airplanes or the laws of aerodynamics.

Faith: This verse speaks of the need to recount to every generation what God did to the Egyptians in liberating the Israelites. If we do not remember the

---
Gratitude takes effort.
Resentment is effortless.

---

good God did in the past, we are likely to lose faith in Him. Without remembering the miracles God has done for others, people are likely to ask, "Why should I trust in God—what has God done for *me*?" And without remembering what God may have done for us in the past, we are likely to ask, "What has God done for me *lately*?"

10.3 So Moses and Aaron went to Pharaoh and said to him, "Thus says the Lord, the God of the Hebrews, 'How long will you refuse to humble yourself before Me? Let My people go that they may worship Me.

10.4 For if you refuse to let My people go, tomorrow I will bring locusts on your territory.

10.5 They shall cover the surface of the land, so that no one will be able to see the land. They shall devour the surviving remnant that was left to you after the hail; and they shall eat away all your trees that grow in the field.

10.6 Moreover, they shall fill your palaces and the houses of all your courtiers and of all the Egyptians—something that neither your fathers nor fathers' fathers have seen from the day they appeared on earth to this day.'" With that he turned and left Pharaoh's presence.

Moses grows bolder with each plague. This time he does not wait for Pharaoh's response; he simply makes his pronouncement and leaves.

10.7 Pharaoh's courtiers said to him, "How long shall this one be a snare to us? Let the men go to worship the Lord their God! Are you not yet aware that Egypt is lost?"

The Torah documents the disagreement between Pharaoh and his advisors in order to emphasize Pharaoh's stubbornness. Even when his most trusted advisors tell him "Egypt is lost" and beg him to release his slaves, Pharaoh still insists on keeping the Israelites in bondage (though the following verse depicts him as making a minor, but ultimately irrelevant, concession). The advisors see what Pharaoh refuses to see: the Egyptian king is no match for the God of Israel.

But the advisors, too, are victims of their own false beliefs. Believing Pharaoh to be a divine figure, they either don't have the courage or the ability to overthrow him, release the Israelites and thereby save themselves, their families, and the Egyptian people from terrible suffering.

This verse proves that God's "hardening" Pharaoh's heart did not deprive Pharaoh of free will. God also hardened the courtiers' hearts (Exodus 10.1), yet, unlike Pharaoh, they decided the Israelites should be allowed to leave Egypt.

10.8 So Moses and Aaron were brought back to Pharaoh and he said to them, "Go, worship the Lord your God! Who are the ones to go?"

Pharaoh's question, "Who are the ones to go?" indicates he intends to keep some Israelites hostage in Egypt. Keeping some, or many, of the Israelites in Egypt will ensure that those who leave in order to worship God will return.

ON TAKING CARE OF YOUR OWN PEOPLE

10.9 Moses replied, "We will all go, young and old: we will go with our sons and daughters, our flocks and herds; for we must observe the Lord's festival."

This expression, "We will all go, young and old" (*b'ne'a'reinu u'z-kai'neinu nai'lekh*) has entered the Hebrew language as an expression of a Jew's commitment to not abandon other Jews in times of need or persecution.

This may be the first expression of the power of Jewish peoplehood. No one—not the old not the children, and not the women, the three most vulnerable groups—will be left behind. Jewish peoplehood is one of Judaism's three components. Though the term is not used, one may speak of a "Jewish trinity" consisting of God, Torah, and Israel (peoplehood).

Jews taking care of one another has aroused both admiration and hatred among non-Jews. Regarding the former, I recall a powerful moment when I was in my twenties and visiting then-communist Bulgaria. I was taken in by a

Bulgarian family with whom I could converse as we all spoke Russian. One night, they invited friends and relatives from more rural parts of Bulgaria to meet the young American staying with them.

At one point I mentioned I was a Jew, which created a momentary silence. None of them had ever met a Jew, and no one said anything until one of them asked me, "Are they the people who all take care of each other?"

That is all this Bulgarian knew about Jews. And he found it very admirable.

On the other hand, anti-Semites have often accused Jews of only taking care of one another and not caring about anyone else. Given the role of Jews in building hospitals and universities in America and elsewhere, the tremendous contributions Israel and individual Jews around the world have made to medical and other scientific research, and the great amount of charity Jews give to general charities, the accusation is not only unfounded, it's pernicious.

While taking care *only* of one's own is morally wrong, before you can love the world, you have to love your neighbor (see discussion of Leviticus 19:18). And you have to love (in the sense of taking care of) yourself and your family before you love and take care of your neighbor.

As the Talmud put it, when giving charity, "the poor of your own town come first."[1]

One very positive consequence of groups taking care of their own is not relying on others to take care of you. For the first generations of Jewish immigrants in America—though perhaps less so today—it was regarded as "shameful" (a *shandeh*, as Yiddish-speaking Jews put it) for a Jew to rely on non-Jewish institutions for support. Mormons, too, take care of fellow Mormons, and they have developed particularly admirable communities.

10.10 But he said to them, "The Lord be with you the same as I mean to let your children go with you!

His advisors had rightly challenged Pharaoh, "Are you not yet aware that Egypt is lost?" but instead of trying to ingratiate himself with Moses and Aaron,

Pharaoh speaks to them rudely and sarcastically. And despite example after example of God's power and support for the Israelites' cause, he tells Moses he will not let all the people leave any more than he believes the God of the Israelites will actually be with Moses's people. In essence, Pharaoh's rudeness to Moses and his sarcasm about God are a challenge to God to do His worst. God, as Pharaoh will soon see (Exodus 12:29), is up to the challenge.

10.10 (cont.) Clearly, you are bent on mischief.

The word translated here as "mischief" literally means evil— "You are bent on evil." Like slave-owners throughout history, Pharaoh regards slaves who want to be free as bent on evil. He is thereby notifying Moses he knows the Israelites intend to be free—forever—and he will not allow it. The moral hypocrisy of slave-owners' contempt for slaves who desire to be free was perfectly described some 3,000 years later by Abraham Lincoln: "Whenever I hear anyone arguing for slavery, I feel a strong impulse to see it tried on him personally."

10.11 No! You menfolk go and worship the Lord, since that is what you want." And they were expelled from Pharaoh's presence.

Pharaoh rejects Moses's demand; he will allow only the Israelite men to leave to worship.

10.12 Then the Lord said to Moses, "Hold out your arm over the land of Egypt for the locusts, that they may come upon the land of Egypt and eat up all the grasses in the land, whatever the hail has left."

WAS THE PLAGUE NATURAL OR MIRACULOUS?

10.13 So Moses held out his rod over the land of Egypt, and the Lord drove an east wind over the land all that day and all night; and when morning came, the east wind had brought the locusts.

God could have simply declared "Let there be locusts." Instead, He uses a wind to bring the locusts. As in each of the plagues except the tenth (and probably the ninth), God draws upon natural forces to bring devastation upon Egypt. God thus gives the Egyptians the option of attributing the plagues either to nature acting wildly or to the hand of God. In either case, the Egyptians, who believed in nature gods, would have had to conclude something had gone awry with their gods.

The choice the Egyptians had to make—coincidence or God?—is the same choice we all have to make. Do we regard everything that happens, even existence itself, as a coincidence, or is God involved?

10.14 Locusts invaded all the land of Egypt and settled within all the territory of Egypt in a thick mass; never before had there been so many, nor will there ever be so many again.

10.15 They hid all the land from view, and the land was darkened; and they ate up all the grasses of the field and all the fruit of the trees which the hail had left, so that nothing green was left, of tree or grass of the field, in all the land of Egypt.

There was precious little green in Egypt to begin with; the only vegetation is along the banks of the Nile, forming a narrow green strip running through Egypt. After the locusts, even that was gone.

WHY PHARAOH ADMITTING HE SINNED MEANS LITTLE

Polytheists such as Pharaoh believed a person could sin before one god while doing nothing wrong in the eyes of another god.

10.16 Pharaoh hurriedly summoned Moses and Aaron and said, "I stand guilty before the Lord your God and before you.

Pharaoh's statement that he sinned before Moses's God highlights a radical difference between biblical monotheism and other worldviews. Monotheists hold there is a single moral God of the universe before Whom we sin and can repent. Polytheists such as Pharaoh, however, believed a person could sin before one god while doing nothing wrong in the eyes of another. Though Pharaoh recognizes he has sinned before Moses's God, he cannot be truly contrite and repent because he does not believe he has done anything objectively wrong. He doesn't believe in objective morality; he thinks in terms of power (similar to the fifth-century BCE Athenians who destroyed the Melians during the Peloponnesian War, though Melos did them no wrong: "the strong do what they have the power to do and the weak accept what they have to accept"). Pharaoh sees that Moses's God is prevailing over him and concludes he must have done something offensive in the eyes of *this* god.

10.17 Forgive my offense just this once, and plead with the Lord your God that He but remove this death from me."

Like the abuser who asks for forgiveness and pretends the offense won't happen again, Pharaoh asks for forgiveness "just this once"—as if to convey to Moses he'll be good from then on.

10.18 So he left Pharaoh's presence and pleaded with the Lord.

10.19 The Lord caused a shift to a very strong west wind, which lifted the locusts and hurled them into the Sea of Reeds; not a single locust remained in all the territory of Egypt.

10.20 But the Lord stiffened Pharaoh's heart, and he would not let the Israelites go.

After removing the plague of locusts, God restores Pharaoh to his state of fearlessness so he can choose how he really wants to deal with the Israelites.

WAS THE PLAGUE OF DARKNESS A SOLAR ECLIPSE?

10.21 Then the Lord said to Moses, "Hold out your arm toward the sky that there may be darkness upon the land of Egypt,

Moses was usually commanded to extend his arm in the direction of the source of the plague. Since, in this instance, Moses was told to hold his arm out toward the sky, it is likely this plague involved the heavenly bodies. Some scholars therefore maintain the plague of darkness was caused by a solar eclipse that darkened Egypt, but not the land of Goshen, where the Israelites lived. It is very hard to believe, however, that this could have been caused by a solar eclipse, since eclipses last for hours, not days. Nor would an eclipse have completely spared nearby Goshen. It makes more sense to regard this as a miracle, meaning it was an event with no natural explanation.

The choice the Egyptians had to make—coincidence or God?—is the same choice we all have to make. Do we regard everything that happens, even existence itself, as a coincidence, or is God involved?

10.21 (cont.) a darkness that can be touched."
This further argues against an eclipse. An eclipse does not create total darkness, let alone darkness that can be touched.

Some commentators who reject the possibility of miracles have suggested that since darkness can be "touched" only if there is a substance making up that darkness, the ninth plague was caused by a thick sandstorm that swept over Egypt. That is not persuasive, however. A sandstorm would not have spared Goshen. This was a miracle. Period.

10.22 Moses held out his arm toward the sky and thick darkness descended upon all the land of Egypt for three days.

10.23 People could not see one another, and for three days no one could get up from where he was; but all the Israelites enjoyed light in their dwellings.

10.24 Pharaoh then summoned Moses and said, "Go, worship the Lord! Only your flocks and your herds shall be left behind; even your children may go with you."

Pharaoh, like the Japanese generals who did not want Japan to surrender even after the Americans dropped the atom bomb on Hiroshima, remained too prideful and stubborn to concede all of Moses's terms. After all, Moses just told him (verse 9) that they needed their flocks and herds to go with them.

10.25 But Moses said, "You yourself must provide us with sacrifices and burnt offerings to offer up to the Lord our God;

> Moses humiliates Pharaoh by insisting the Egyptians, who worship the animals the Israelites intend to slaughter, must provide those very animals for their slaves to sacrifice to *their* God.

10.26 our own livestock, too, shall go along with us—not a hoof shall remain behind: for we must select from it for the worship of the Lord our God; and we shall not know with what we are to worship the Lord until we arrive there."

> Moses is now as rude and sarcastic to Pharaoh as Pharaoh earlier was to him (10:10). Essentially, Moses is saying, "We'll decide exactly what we wish to sacrifice when we get there!" Alternatively, Moses is simply informing Pharaoh that until they arrive at the place of worship and receive God's instructions for which animals to slaughter, they won't know which ones they need.

10.27 But the Lord stiffened Pharaoh's heart and he would not agree to let them go.

10.28 Pharaoh said to him, "Be gone from me! Take care not to see me again, for the moment you look upon my face you shall die."

> The Hebrew for "take care" literally means "Watch yourself" (*hishamer lecha*), but here it is uttered more in the nature of a threat ("watch your step").

10.29 And Moses replied, "You have spoken rightly. I shall not see your face again!"

> There is no point—there never really was—to more negotiating. All that is left is for God to take His people out of Egypt once and for all.

CHAPTER

11

11.1 And the Lord said to Moses, "I will bring but one more plague upon Pharaoh and upon Egypt; after that he shall let you go from here; indeed, when he lets you go, he will drive you out of here one and all.

11.2 Tell the people

Though not apparent in this translation, in the Hebrew, God says to Moses, "*Please* tell the people. . ." There is a lesson here for those who have authority over others. Even though both God and Moses know Moses has to obey Him, God says "please" when issuing this directive. This preserves Moses's dignity— as it preserves the dignity of those in an inferior position, enabling them to feel they are partners, not only servants.

11.2 (cont.) to borrow, each man from his neighbor and each woman from hers, objects of silver and gold."

The JPS translation reads, "Tell the people to borrow." But "borrow" is an odd term, since the Israelites were about to permanently depart from Egypt and clearly would never return what they borrowed. The answer, however, lies in the Hebrew original, which literally reads, "Tell the people to *ask*," a rendering that makes more sense. The Israelites felt compensation was due to them for the centuries of servitude, and the Egyptians, traumatized by the plagues, would probably willingly give them what they asked for, if only to hasten their departure.

Since few, if any, Israelites were likely to have valuables after hundreds of years of slavery, "neighbor" can only refer to their Egyptian neighbors. Likewise, we read elsewhere the Israelites requested silver and gold from the Egyptians before they left Egypt (Exodus 3:22 and 12:35).

This is noted because it may have important implications. The Hebrew word used here for "neighbor," *ray'a*, is the same word used in the commandment "Love your neighbor as yourself" (Leviticus 19:18).

> *In the tenth plague, God does all the killing. No Israelite was ordered by God to kill a single Egyptian.*

Therefore "neighbor," in that central moral commandment, may similarly refer to the non-Jewish neighbor, not only to a Jewish neighbor—in other words to all people. Many commentators have argued that "neighbor" in Leviticus 19:18 refers only to one's Jewish neighbor. And given the context in which that commandment is ordained, both views may have legitimacy; but, given the Torah injunction to love the non-Jew living in the Jews' midst (Leviticus 19:34) and the use of the word *ray'a* here—meaning non-Jewish as well as Jewish neighbor—it is hard to believe the Torah only commands love of one's Jewish neighbors.

11.3 The Lord disposed the Egyptians favorably toward the people.

There are a number of possible explanations for this verse.

One is that the Egyptians, at least for a brief period, recognized there was a powerful God behind the Israelites, more powerful than their gods, and this disposed them to view the Israelites more favorably. In the ancient world, the gods of the winners elicited great respect. Might made right.

A second possible explanation is God intervened so the Egyptians would peacefully surrender their silver and gold to the Israelites as deserved compensation for all the years of unpaid slavery. In light of all the plagues, culminating in the killing of the firstborn, it may well indeed have necessitated divine intervention for the Egyptians to be favorably disposed toward the Israelites.

A third explanation was that of the first-century Jewish historian, Josephus, who offered the plausible view that the Egyptians were willing to give the Israelites anything they requested, including their most valuable possessions, just to finally get rid of them. But, of course, that doesn't quite explain the Torah's assertion that "The Lord disposed the Egyptians favorably toward the people."

As I mentioned before, the irony is profound as this silver and gold is quite likely the very silver and gold with which the Israelites later built the Golden Calf (Exodus 32:2-4).

11.3 (cont.) Moreover, Moses himself was much esteemed in the land of Egypt, among Pharaoh's courtiers and among the people.

The Hebrew literally states "the man Moses was very great in the land of Egypt." This verse, which interrupts the description of the eve of the Exodus, is one of the rare laudatory descriptions of Moses in the Torah. (The most famous is Numbers 12:3, which describes Moses as "a very humble man, more so than any other man on earth.")

The compliment registered here clearly relates to the first half of the verse: The Israelites were viewed favorably by the Egyptians, and Moses was particularly highly esteemed.

One reason the Egyptians may have so esteemed Moses is that in the ancient world—and in the Middle East to this day—the powerful leader is highly respected. And Moses was clearly quite powerful.

11.4 Moses said, "Thus says the Lord: Toward midnight I will go forth among the Egyptians,

Though the end of chapter 10 suggests Moses would not see Pharaoh again, it appears Moses is now speaking to Pharaoh.

This final plague, which Moses announces, differed from all the others because it was not brought about by anything Moses or Aaron did. Nor, unlike the earlier plagues, was there any way to explain this as having been brought about by natural means. God did not bring a great wind or have Moses and Aaron throw soot to the heavens. Moses did not even have to lift his rod.

Instead, God did everything—which, given it involved such widespread killing, is how it should have been.

11.5 and every first-born in the land of Egypt shall die, from the first-born of Pharaoh who sits on his throne to the first-born of the slave girl who is behind the millstones; and all the first-born of the cattle.

Throughout history, perhaps the cruelest indignity suffered by slaves was the inability of slave parents to protect their children—such as when slave parents in the American South could not protect their children from being sold to other owners by their masters. Here, the Israelites could not protect their newborn male babies from being drowned. Now, in an act of measure-for-measure, Egyptians will experience what it is like to be unable to protect their children.

Many people, myself included, are morally troubled by the tenth plague. My way of dealing with it is as follows:

As noted, God does all the killing. No Israelite was ordered by God to kill a single Egyptian. Therefore, even for those who believe the killing of the first-born was immoral, it is God alone Who does it; God would not instruct anyone to do something immoral.

> *There is not a hint in the Torah that Jews are to believe they can kill non-believers, let alone that they are directed to do so.*

Therefore, there is no issue here of a holy text depicting people being ordered by their God to kill infidels or innocents. Later there will be instructions to kill various Canaanite nations, and I deal with the moral issue of those instructions there. Suffice it to say, here those instructions were specific to one group of people and at one time. There is not a hint in the Torah that Jews are to believe they can kill non-believers, let alone that they are directed to do so.

We are then left with morally assessing God's actions. And here one must be intellectually honest. If God is good, God cannot do anything morally wrong. If God does something morally wrong, then God is not good. Intellectual honesty therefore demands that those of us who believe God is good assume He had moral reasons to do what He did, though the Torah certainly allows us to question those actions.

But it is one thing to question God, and it is another to reject God because of our questions. The God of the Torah—the book that furthered human morality more than any other; the book containing the Ten Commandments; the first book to ever command love and protection of the stranger (and does so more often than any other commandment)—has more than earned the benefit of any doubts we may have.

In this verse, Moses finally tells Pharaoh what God revealed to him much earlier, even before the first plague, while traveling through the desert from Midian back to Egypt, and which He instructed him to tell Pharaoh: "Thus says the Lord: Israel is my first-born son. I have said to you, 'Let my son go, that he may worship Me,' yet you refuse to let him go. Now I will slay your first-born son" (Exodus 4:22-23).

11.6 And there shall be a loud cry in all the land of Egypt, such as has never been or will ever be again;

11.7 but not a dog shall snarl at any of the Israelites, at man or beast—in order that you may know that the Lord makes a distinction between Egypt and Israel.

11.8 Then all these courtiers of yours shall come down to me and bow low to me, saying, 'Depart, you and all the people who follow you!' After that, I will depart." And he left Pharaoh's presence in hot anger.

The chronology of this final encounter with Pharaoh is problematic, because Moses's response to Pharaoh's threat to kill him if he ever again came into Pharaoh's presence (Exodus 10:29) was to declare he would never again see Pharaoh's face.

11.9 Now the Lord had said to Moses, "Pharaoh will not heed you, in order that My marvels may be multiplied in the land of Egypt."

11.10 Moses and Aaron had performed all these marvels before Pharaoh, but the Lord had stiffened the heart of Pharaoh so that he would not let the Israelites go from his land.

The final plague must be so awesome and terrible because none of the earlier plagues successfully persuaded Pharaoh to release the Israelites.

CHAPTER

~❦ 12 ❦~

12.1 The Lord said to Moses and Aaron

The Torah interrupts the narrative of the plagues to list the laws the Israelites must follow on the eve of the Exodus. From a dramatic perspective, this is poorly situated, since the suspense is now at its peak—God is about to bring the final and most devastating plague upon Egypt. Perhaps these laws are inserted here because God will not take the Israelites out of Egypt until they first reaffirm their connection with Him. After all, the purpose of the Exodus is not only freedom. Freedom alone gives license and results in anarchy. That's why, in God's name, Moses repeatedly demanded freedom for the Israelites so "that they may worship Me" (Exodus 9:1, 10:3; see also 5:1).

WHAT DOES IT MEAN TO WORSHIP GOD?

And how exactly does one worship God? Ritually, of course. But especially ethically. That God is primarily worshipped through moral conduct is emphasized repeatedly throughout the Bible:

"Do what is right and good in the sight of the Lord" (Deuteronomy 6:18).

"The holy God is made holy through righteousness" (Isaiah 5:16).

"He has told you, O Man, what is good, and what the Lord requires of you: Only to do justice, and to love goodness, and to walk humbly with your God" (Micah 6:8).

"Thus said the Lord: Let not the wise man glory in his wisdom; Let not the strong man glory in his strength; Let not the rich man glory in his riches. But only in this should one glory: In his earnest devotion to Me. For I the Lord act with kindness, justice and equity in the world; for in these I delight" (Jeremiah 9:22-23).

This listing of laws directing the Israelites on how to worship God is, therefore, intended to remind the Israelites they are being liberated from Egypt to serve God.

12.1 (cont.) in the land of Egypt:

Almost all of the laws of the Torah are given in the wilderness. These laws are unique in that they are given in Egypt.

12.2 This month shall mark for you the beginning of the months; it shall be the first of the months of the year for you.

The Torah is referring to the Hebrew month of Nisan. The Jewish calendar has two different first months. One is Tishrei, the autumn month that includes Rosh Hashanah (New Year) and Yom Kippur (Day of Atonement). It is celebrated as a time of repentance, new beginnings, and the creation of the world. The other is this month of Nisan, the spring month that includes Passover. It is celebrated as a time of rebirth, renewal, and the beginning of the Jewish nation. Virtually every nation celebrates both the beginning of the New Year and the beginning of its country. In the Torah they are both New Years.

SACRIFICING AN EGYPTIAN GOD

12.3 Speak to the whole community of Israel and say that on the tenth of this month each of them shall take a lamb to a family, a lamb to a household.

In verses 3–13, God outlines the laws of the paschal sacrifice ("Paschal" is from *Pesach*, the Hebrew word for Passover) offered on the eve of the Exodus. A purpose of this sacrifice, like the purpose of the plagues, is to teach the Israelites—and the Egyptians—about God. The lamb was one of many animals worshipped as gods by the Egyptians. The Israelites are therefore instructed to slaughter a god of their oppressors as a way of serving their own God, which was exactly what Moses warned Pharaoh would so infuriate him and the Egyptians (see 8:22).

The Israelites were told to sacrifice the gods of their Egyptian oppressors— before their oppressors' eyes.

The question of the morality of animal sacrifice is discussed in detail in the commentaries in Leviticus. Suffice it to say here the paschal sacrifice, like most of the animal sacrifices in the Torah, was eaten. Unless one holds that all meat eating is immoral, there is no moral problem in animal sacrifice. It was simply ritual slaughter for food as opposed to secular animal slaughter for food.

12.4 But if the household is too small for a lamb, let him share one with a neighbor who dwells nearby, in proportion to the number of persons: you shall contribute for the lamb according to what each household will eat.

If a household was too small to consume an entire lamb, it would join other small households to sacrifice a lamb together in order not to waste the sacrifice. In the words of Joseph Hertz (chief rabbi of the United Kingdom, 1913–1946) in his commentary on the Torah: "Had a family of two or three been compelled to take a [whole lamb], a considerable quantity would have been wasted."

12.5 Your lamb shall be without blemish, a yearling male; you may take it from the sheep or from the goats.

All animals sacrificed to God had to be perfect. People were not allowed to sacrifice their least desirable animals. Then it would not be a "sacrifice."

THE VIRTUE OF DELAYED GRATIFICATION

12.6 You shall keep watch over it until the fourteenth day of this month;

The Israelites have to acquire the lamb on the tenth day of the month, but they are not allowed to slaughter it until twilight on the eve of the fourteenth day, four days later. The lamb was to be slaughtered at the end of the daylight hours of the fourteenth day, immediately used for marking the doors, and then roasted for the meal that night. This waiting period might have been intended to test the Israelites' faith: Could they maintain a faith in God that was stronger than their fear of the Egyptians, who could attack them at any moment for preparing to slaughter one of their gods? [1]

The statement "I believe in God," tells us nothing about a person's beliefs or about the god in whom the person believes.

Another possible purpose of the waiting period between acquiring and slaughtering the lamb was to teach the Israelites the value of delayed gratification. Ordinarily, people slaughter an animal just before they eat it. However, the Israelites were also performing this slaughter for the sake of God, and thus their bodily hunger had to be subordinated to God's commandment. In addition, given that slaves are generally underfed and usually served the cheapest and least tasty food, any delay in consuming a roasted lamb required genuine self-discipline.

This delayed gratification is emulated at the Passover Seder, which commemorates the Exodus in the order of the events described in these chapters. One of the Seder's components is an elaborate meal, which is not eaten until the first half of the book, the Haggadah, that contains the Seder prayers and the story of the Exodus is read and discussed. At traditional Seders this process before the meal lasts at least one-and-a-half hours.

12.6 (cont.) and all the assembled congregation of the Israelites shall slaughter it at twilight.

Sarna writes that the slaughtering of an animal sacred to the Egyptians was intended to undermine the fear imposed by hundreds of years of Egyptian bondage and thereby remove an important psychological barrier to liberation: Only when the Israelites could bring themselves to sacrifice the gods of their oppressors—before their oppressors' eyes—would the Israelites truly be ready to embrace freedom. It would be analogous to people in totalitarian states gathering to publicly smash statues of the dictator.

The Hebrew phrase *bein ha-arbayim* (translated here as "twilight") literally means "between the evenings." As the period between the onset and completion of sunset, it is what we refer to as dusk.

12.7 They shall take some of the blood and put it on the two doorposts

Maimonides comments that the purpose of putting the blood on the doorposts is to let the world know the Israelites reject Egyptian ideas of the holy to such an extent they will even sacrifice an Egyptian god. Along similar lines, a nineteenth-century commentary by Rabbi Ya'akov Tzvi Mecklenburg, *Ha'Ktav Ve'haKabbalah*, notes that placing the blood on the doorposts was a way of publicizing the Israelites' offense against the Egyptians, thereby "braving the vengeance of their former persecutors," and forcing them to endanger their lives and demonstrate their faith in God.

12.7 (cont.) and the lintel of the houses in which they are to eat it.

The lintel is the board above the door that serves as the upper part of the doorframe.

12.8 They shall eat the flesh that same night; they shall eat it roasted over the fire,

Sarna explains that roasting may have been the quickest way to prepare meat at the time (see verse 11). Alternatively, roasting may have been the best way of removing all the blood, which is forbidden to eat (see Genesis 9:4).

12.8 (cont.) with unleavened bread and with bitter herbs.

12.9 Do not eat any of it raw, or cooked in any way with water, but roasted—head, legs, and entrails—over the fire.

God may be teaching the Israelites that they must be different from animals, who kill other creatures and immediately eat the meat. *Elevating human conduct above that of animals is one of the primary aims of Torah law,* and should be the aim of every civilization. Indeed, humans have often acted worse than animals (in inflicting pain on other humans solely for the sake of seeing them suffer).

12.10 You shall not leave any of it over until morning; if any of it is left until morning, you shall burn it.

12.11 This is how you shall eat it: your loins girded, your sandals on your feet, and your staff in your hand; and you shall eat it hurriedly: it is a Passover offering to the Lord.

God instructs the Israelites to be ready to leave because the Egyptians are about to throw them out of Egypt.

12.12 For that night I will go through the land of Egypt and strike down every first-born in the land of Egypt, both man and beast; and I will mete out punishments to all the gods of Egypt, I the Lord.

This plague serves to once again reinforce that only God is God and other gods are false.

ESSAY: DO ALL BELIEVERS IN ONE GOD BELIEVE IN THE SAME GOD?

This affirmation of God as the only God—the central theological tenet of the Torah—raises a vitally important question: Do all people who believe in one god believe in the same god? More specifically, do they all believe in this God the Torah introduced to the world?

The answer—and to many this may come as a surprise—is, no.

The reason this is so important is the God of the Torah (and the rest of the Bible) is often blamed by anti-religious people for any terrible actions committed by anyone who claims to believe in God.

When Jews, Christians, and Muslims—let alone people who identify with no specific religion—say, "I believe in God," they are not necessarily talking about the same God, and certainly not necessarily talking about the God of the

Torah. In fact, the statement, "I believe in God," tells us nothing about a person's beliefs or about the god in whom he or she believes.

To cite an obvious example, a god in whose name believers cut innocent people's throats, behead them, burn them alive, and rape girls and women—as is being done at the time of this writing by Islamist terrorists in the name of "the one God"—cannot be the same god as the God of the Torah, the God who gave the Ten Commandments, who commanded His people to "Love the stranger," and demanded holy and ethical conduct at all times. Likewise, those Christians who in the Middle Ages slaughtered entire Jewish communities in the name of Christ also clearly did not believe in the God of the Bible (let alone in those Church leaders who condemned such atrocities)—as virtually every Christian today would acknowledge.

Yet, there are many people who argue that all those who say they believe in God believe in the same God.

Why do people make this argument? Because all too often they have an anti-religious agenda. They say all those who claim to believe in God believe in the same God in order to discredit God and religion, especially religions rooted in the Bible.

So, then, how are we to know whether any two people who say they believe in God believe in the same God, specifically the God of the Torah?

We can find out by asking three questions:

1. *Do you believe in the God known as the "God of Israel"?*

Before responding, some people might need to have the term defined. The "God of Israel" is the God introduced to the world by the Jews and their Bible. This is the God Who created the world, Who revealed Himself to the Jews, and Who made His moral will known through the Ten Commandments and the Hebrew prophets. Obviously, all believing Jews would answer in the affirmative. The great majority of religious Christians would as well.

If, after having "God of Israel" defined, a person cannot answer the question in the affirmative, it is fair to say the individual does not believe in the God of the Torah. He or she believes in another god.

2. Does the god you believe in judge the moral behavior of every human being—and by the same moral standard?

There are many people today who say they believe in God, but not in a God who judges people's actions. These people are generally to be found among those who affirm no specific religion. For them, "God" is an entirely personal thing. Often, they will say "God is within me." But, of course, if God is only within them, who outside of them will ever judge them?

People who believe in a god who does not morally judge them and all other people do not believe in the God of the Torah.

They can be fine people. But the question here is not whether there are any good people who do not believe in the God of the Torah. Of course there are. The question is whether all people who say they believe in God believe in the *same* God, and specifically in the God introduced by the Torah.

People who believe in a god who does not morally judge them and all other people do not believe in the God of the Torah. In fact, a god indifferent to the moral behavior of human beings is so different from the God of the Torah that these believers might as well use a word other than "God."

Now, one might argue Islamist terrorists also believe in a judging God, as did Tomas de Torquemada, the infamous Catholic head of the Spanish Inquisition. But this argument is not pertinent, because such individuals believe God judges people by their faith alone, not by their moral behavior—and believers can therefore torture and kill non-believers. That is not the God of the Torah.

It should be clear, but in case it is not, it needs to be emphatically emphasized that one need not be a Jew—or a Christian, or a member of any faith—to believe in the God of the Torah. While it is the Torah's aim that all humanity believe in the God revealed in the Torah, there is not the slightest suggestion anyone needs to become a Jew to do so. Indeed the purpose of the Jewish people—the purpose of being Chosen—is to bring humanity to the God of the Torah, which, by definition, also means accepting God's moral demands (such as the "Noahide Laws" or the Ten Commandments).

The great Benjamin Franklin, one of America's founders, was one such example: He did not affirm the Christian Trinity, and he was not a Jew. But he believed in the God introduced by the Hebrew Bible, in its moral teachings, and that this God morally judges all human beings. As Franklin wrote in his autobiography: "I never doubted, for instance, the existence of the Deity, that he made the world and governed it by his Providence, that the most acceptable service of God was the doing of good to man, that our souls are immortal, and that *all crime will be punished and virtue rewarded either here or hereafter*" (emphasis added).

Franklin and many of America's founders were examples of ethical monotheists. They were the type of people the Torah wants all people to be.

3. *Do you believe in the God who gave the Ten Commandments?*

This question also needs to be asked even though it is included in the first question.

The reason it needs to be asked is if God never revealed His moral will, how would we know what behaviors He demands from us and what acts He judges as wrong?

None of these comments are a judgment of individuals; they are a judgment of the statement, "I believe in God." There are people who do not believe in the God of the Torah, and, for that matter, people who believe in no God, who are fine, upstanding individuals—just as there are people who believe in the God of the Torah who are not decent people. But for reasons made clear throughout this commentary, the best moral hope for mankind is to bring as many people as possible to belief in the God introduced by the Torah, though not necessarily to Judaism or any other religion. (While it is usually best to affiliate with a Torah-based religion, one can believe in the God of the Torah and in the Ten Commandments without being a member of a religion.)

12.13 And the blood on the houses where you are staying shall be a sign for you:

The sign is for "you," the Israelites, not for God, Who does not need signs. The sign functions to assure the Israelites that they will be spared in spite of all the death that will be taking place around them.

12.13 (cont.) when I see the blood I will pass over you, so that no plague will destroy you when I strike the land of Egypt.

The Hebrew word *pasachti* means "I will pass over." Obviously, the English name of the holiday, Passover, comes from this word.

ESSAY: THE SIX COMMANDMENTS OF REMEMBRANCE IN THE TORAH

12.14 This day shall be to you one of remembrance:

The Torah affirms the central importance of remembering. It may be credited with the invention of collective memory.

There are six commandments of remembrance in the Torah:

1. The Sabbath

"Remember the Sabbath day and keep it holy" (Exodus 20:8).

2. The Exodus

"You shall not eat anything leavened with it...so that you may remember the day of your departure from the land of Egypt as long as you live" (Deuteronomy 16:3).

3. Receiving the Law at Sinai

"So that you do not forget the things that you saw with your own eyes...and make them known to your children and your children's children, the day you stood before the Lord your God at Horeb...." (Deuteronomy 4:9-10)

4. Amalek

"Remember what Amalek did to you on your journey after you left Egypt, how, undeterred by fear of God he...cut down all the stragglers in your rear" (Deuteronomy 25:17-19).

5. The Golden Calf and other incidents in which the Israelites angered God

"Remember, never forget, how you provoked the Lord your God to anger in the wilderness" (Deuteronomy 9:7).

6. God's punishment of Miriam for speaking ill of Moses

"Remember what the Lord your God did to Miriam on the journey after you left Egypt" (Deuteronomy 24:9—the verse alludes to Miriam and Aaron's negative comments against Moses in Numbers 12:1-9).

Why is remembering so important?

Here are nine reasons.

1. *Remembering endows history with meaning and significance.*

If we do not remember an event, then, as far as we are concerned, it is as if it never occurred.

2. *Remembering enables us to learn from history.*

Though it may be difficult to know exactly what we should learn from any given historical event, some historical lessons are pretty obvious. For example, it is clear from the Exodus story that freedom is the desired human condition and should be fought for. Indeed, one of its great lessons is God wants humans to be free (this was the essential belief underlying the American Revolution). That is why oppressed groups in the West have so often used the Israelites' liberation from Egypt as their model for liberation. In *Exodus and Revolution*, the Princeton political philosopher Michael Walzer has made the case that the story of the Exodus has inspired more movements of social change than any other story in literature.

3. *Remembering leads to wisdom.*

Without remembering, wisdom is impossible (see comments on Exodus 10:2). Wisdom is learning from our own lives and from the lives of others.

Wisdom matters because good cannot be achieved without it. Good intentions without wisdom lead to either nothing or to actual evil. However much evil movements have appealed to the bad side of people's natures, almost every one of them, communism being the most obvious example, also appealed to people's good intentions.

4. *Remembering makes the moral progress of civilization possible.*

We remember where we came from to know what moral progress—or regress—we have made. The Torah essentially invented both history and progress. Prior to the Torah, virtually every civilization had what is known as a cyclical worldview. The cyclical worldview is well explained in the book *The Gifts of the Jews* by Thomas Cahill, a widely noted Catholic scholar of religion.

Cahill quotes Henri-Charles Puech, author of *Man and Time*: "[In the cyclical worldview], no event is unique, nothing is enacted but once...; every event has been enacted, is enacted, and will be enacted perpetually; the same individuals have appeared, appear, and will appear at every turn of the circle"

Nothing, therefore, progresses—not scientifically, not culturally, and most important, not morally. The Jews, specifically and only because of the Torah, differed.

As Cahill writes, "The Jews were the first people to break out of this circle .... It may be said with some justice that theirs is the only new idea that human beings had ever had."

5. *Remembering links us with those who came before us and reminds us we are part of an ongoing people and/or ideal.*

6. *Remembering ensures that those who have suffered and perished are not forgotten.*

7. *Remembering ensures that evil is not forgotten and allowed to disappear into the "ash heap of history."*

8. *Remembering is the only way to avoid repeating the mistakes of the past.*

9. *Remembering—by ensuring that goodness and good people are not forgotten—makes enduring gratitude possible.*

Without remembrance, there is no way to stay grateful.

12.14 (cont.) you shall celebrate it as a festival to the Lord throughout the ages; you shall celebrate it as an institution for all time.

The obligation to remember the Exodus is a permanent law; it applies to every subsequent generation.

This verse is the first of the many laws that will characterize the distinctive Jewish way of life throughout history.

12.15 Seven days

Once again, seven—the number of the days of creation—is the most important and recurrent number in the Torah. It reaffirms that God created the world (and therefore the world has purpose, meaning, design, moral standards, etc.).

The seven days of Passover can be understood as a replica of the seven days of creation, because the Exodus from Egypt signifies the start of a new world for the Jews and therefore for humanity, given the influence the Jews and their Bible have had on history.

12.15 (cont.) you shall eat unleavened bread;

Because we live in a physical world and need physical signs to concretize our values, major concepts in Judaism have accompanying ritual expressions. Thus, the commandment to remember the Exodus is accompanied by the ritual obligation to eat unleavened bread for seven days, which still symbolizes for those who observe this holiday it is better to eat the poor man's bread in freedom than to eat richer food as a slave.

> *Good intentions without wisdom lead to either nothing or to actual evil.*

This concept is quite relevant to modern times. Many intellectuals in the Western world defended the half-century (1959–2008) dictatorship of Fidel Castro of Cuba by noting, for example, under Castro's rule the literacy rate in Cuba rose to a hundred percent. However, Cubans were not allowed to read anything forbidden by the communist regime. In the view of Castro's defenders, it is better to be unfree and literate than to be free and illiterate. The Torah's view, however, would seem to be the opposite; it is better to be free and illiterate, just as it is better to eat a poor man's food and be free than to eat a rich man's food as a slave.

Furthermore, the very concept of freedom carries with it the possibility of improvement of one's circumstances. The illiterate are free to learn to read; the poor are free to work, retain the fruits of their labors, and improve their lot in life—perhaps even become wealthy, as so many have in the freedom of the Western, Bible-based world.

LEAVENING REPRESENTS DEATH

12.15 (cont.) on the very first day you shall remove leaven from your houses,

Leavening, a process believed to have been invented in Egypt about five hundred years before the Exodus, involves the fermentation of dough. Fermentation is a form of decomposition, and therefore represents decay and death. Egypt was known for its obsession with death: The greatest symbols of ancient Egypt are the pyramids, which are tombs. The Torah, in contrast, is rooted in the affirmation of life.

As discussed in detail in Leviticus, the Torah regards that which represents death as *tameh*, a word usually translated (imprecisely) as "unclean" or "impure." Perhaps it should be translated as "death-related." The Torah and later Judaism, therefore, enacted numerous ritual laws to separate that which represents death from that which represents life.

Examples include the separation of milk and meat (milk comes from a living creature and represents life, meat comes from a carcass and represents death); the separation of sexual intercourse (life) from menstruation (which represents the death of an egg that would be life had it been fertilized); the draining of the blood from an animal before it is eaten ("For the life of all flesh is its blood"; Leviticus 17:14; see also Genesis 9:4); and the prohibition on Jewish priests from coming into contact with the dead, as they are to be preoccupied only with life.

Thus, the avoidance of leaven on Passover may be seen as a symbolic rejection of the Egyptian preoccupation with death. Much Torah law and teaching is a rejection of the values of Egypt, most particularly the emphasis on death and the worship of nature.

WHAT DOES *KARET*—"CUT OFF"—MEAN?

12.15 (cont.) for whoever eats leavened bread from the first day to the seventh day, that person shall be cut off from Israel.

The Hebrew term for "cut off" is *karet*, one of the most severe punishments in the Torah. The Torah never makes fully clear what *karet* means, and there are three different ways in which the Talmud explains this term.

First, *karet* may refer to premature death. However, this understanding is problematic. For one thing, it could lead people to think—or at least suspect—the premature death of a Jew was punishment for some grave sin. And, on the other hand, many Jews who violated prohibitions entailing *karet* went on to live long lives. For these reasons, it is difficult to understand *karet* as meaning premature death.

Second, *karet* may refer to the eventual ending of the sinner's family line. This explanation has similar problems to the first. It can lead people to erroneously suspect a Jew whose family line ended (such as countless Jews in the Holocaust) was being punished by God, while many Jews who deserved *karet* nevertheless had many progeny. On the other hand, this explanation may refer to the ending of a family's Jewish line, and in that sense the punishment of *karet* has empirical validity. Jews who raise children without Passover and without ritual circumcision, both of which are punished with *karet* (regarding circumcision, see Genesis 17:14), tend not to have progeny who remain identifying Jews and who eventually assimilate into the larger population and disappear as Jews.

> *The Torah frequently specifies punishments primarily for the sake of indicating the severity of the sin.*

The third Talmudic explanation for the *karet* punishment is being "cut off" from life in the world to come.

In my view, the literal definition of *karet* may well be the best. Those who do not observe laws for which the punishment is *karet* do indeed "cut themselves off" from God and from their people. One may therefore explain the person who is punished with *karet* as "cut off from his God and his people."

Many of the Torah's most severe punishments, like *karet*, exist to teach the severity of the offense and to deter people from engaging in the particular sin.

That *karet* is a punishment/consequence of eating leaven on Passover shows how important the Torah considers refraining from eating leaven on Passover. Jews who believe in the moral and intellectual greatness of the Torah, not to mention its divine origins, will therefore honor this prohibition. Others will regard the prohibition as a quaint ritual or as simply pointless. But for such people, that is true of most of the Torah. Hopefully, one upshot of this commentary is to show people the Torah is so uniquely wise that when it specifies a law to be observed forever, one ought—at the very least—to consider doing so.

12.16 You shall celebrate a sacred occasion on the first day, and a sacred occasion on the seventh day;

THERE ARE SEVEN HOLIDAYS DESIGNATED AS HOLY DAYS IN THE TORAH

The Torah prescribes seven holidays—six annual holidays plus the weekly Sabbath:

1. Rosh Hashanah (in the Torah, the name for this holiday is *Yom Tru'ah*, the "Day of the Shofar Sound")
2. Yom Kippur (Day of Atonement)
3. Pesach (Passover)
4. Shavuot (Pentecost)
5. Sukkot (Tabernacles)
6. Shemini Atzeret (Eighth Day of Assembly)
7. Shabbat (Sabbath)

Regarding the other Torah-ordained holidays, Jews are commanded, with one important exception (to be explained), to observe the same laws as the Sabbath on the first day (and the last day, if there is more than one day) of that holiday. Yom Kippur is the one holy day that maintains all the Sabbath prohibitions (along with the additional prohibition against eating). Three of these holidays—Pesach, Sukkot, and Shavuot—are known as pilgrimage festivals, because the Jews traveled on foot to worship at the Temple in Jerusalem on these days.

12.16 (cont.) no work at all shall be done on them; only what every person is to eat, that alone may be prepared for you.

CHAPTER 12 | 143

Based on this verse, Jewish law held that Jews are allowed to cook on the festivals (using a pre-existing fire), unlike on the Sabbath: "The festival [laws] differ from the Sabbath only in respect to the preparation of food."[2]

12.17 You shall observe the [Feast of] Unleavened Bread, for on this very day I brought your ranks out of the land of Egypt; you shall observe this day throughout the ages as an institution for all time.

12.18 In the first month, from the fourteenth day of the month at evening, you shall eat unleavened bread until the twenty-first day of the month at evening.

Here is the number seven again. All of these dates are multiples of seven.

12.19 No leaven shall be found in your houses for seven days. For whoever eats what is leavened, that person shall be cut off from the community of Israel, whether he is a stranger or a citizen of the country.

12.20 You shall eat nothing leavened; in all your settlements you shall eat unleavened bread.

12.21 Moses then summoned all the elders of Israel and said to them, "Go, pick out lambs for your families, and slaughter the Passover offering.

12.22 Take a bunch of hyssop, dip it in the blood that is in the basin, and apply some of the blood that is in the basin to the lintel and to the two doorposts.

The hyssop plant has sponge-like branches that absorb liquid, and it was therefore well-suited to soaking up the sacrificial blood spread on the lintels and doorposts of the Israelite homes.

12.22 (cont.) None of you shall go outside the door of his house until morning.

We are not told in this verse why the Israelites are instructed to stay indoors, but the reason is most likely safety. As the next verse makes clear, it was only in a home with blood on the doorposts where they were assured protection from the plague that would kill all the firstborn of Egypt.

12.23 For when the Lord goes through to smite the Egyptians, He will see the blood on the lintel and the two doorposts, and the Lord will pass over the door and not let the Destroyer enter and smite your home.

12.24 "You shall observe this as an institution for all time, for you and for your descendants.

12.25 And when you enter the land that the Lord will give you, as He has promised, you shall observe this rite.

EDUCATING ONE'S CHILDREN IS A DIVINE LAW

12.26 And when your children ask you, 'What do you mean by this rite?'

The education of children is prescribed in the Torah (see also Deuteronomy 6:7), and children are encouraged to ask questions. To this day, children raised in traditional—and many non-traditional—Jewish homes publicly recite "The Four Questions" (the *Mah Nishtana)* at the Passover Seder. It constitutes most children's first act of public speaking (i.e., speaking before a group of adults) and it is not done by affirming a religious credo, but by asking questions.

This is one of four verses in the Torah dealing with the commandment to educate children about the Exodus. The Talmud associates each verse with a different type of child: a wise child, a bad child, a simple child, and "one who does not know how to ask." The question in this verse is associated with the "bad child" because he asks "what do *you* mean" instead of "what do *we* mean," or "what does *it* mean?" He is implicitly excluding himself from the community, as if he is above it all.

12.27 you shall say, 'It is the Passover sacrifice to the Lord, because He passed over the houses of the Israelites in Egypt when He smote the Egyptians, but saved our houses.'" The people then bowed low in homage.

This answer, which focuses on God's power both to destroy and save, is intended to make an impression on the child by instilling fear of God in him. Fear of a good and moral God is the basis of morality and a moral education. As the Bible states, "Wisdom begins with fear of God" (Psalms 111:10; Proverbs 9:10). Children should also have a degree—and I emphasize *a degree*—of fear of parents (Leviticus 19:3). I have asked many young people why they didn't use illicit drugs, and the single most common response has been, "Because my mother would have killed me."

12.28 And the Israelites went and did so; just as the Lord had commanded Moses and Aaron, so they did.

12.29 In the middle of the night the Lord struck down all the first-born in the land of Egypt, from the first-born of Pharaoh who sat on the throne to the first-born of the captive who was in the dungeon, and all the first-born of the cattle.

The Torah spends several verses on the paschal sacrifice and the commandment to eat unleavened bread, but only one verse on the killing of the first-born. It is as if the tenth plague is too painful to relate, as the Egyptians, too, are God's creatures, and many of the firstborn are innocents. The Torah in no way revels in the Egyptians' punishment (any more, for example, than the Americans who made the decision to drop the atom bomb reveled in the suffering of the Japanese people). In fact, one of the Torah's 613 laws actually prohibits hating the Egyptians (Deuteronomy 23:8). If only the Jews' enemies had such a law regarding Jews (though if they had such a law, the Jews wouldn't be their enemies).

Despite centuries of Egyptian oppression, one of the Torah's 613 laws actually prohibits hating Egyptians.

12.30 And Pharaoh arose in the night, with all his courtiers and all the Egyptians—because there was a loud cry in Egypt; for there was no house where there was not someone dead.

12.31 He summoned Moses and Aaron in the night and said, "Up, depart from among my people, you and the Israelites with you! Go, worship the Lord as you said!

12.32 Take also your flocks and your herds, as you said, and be gone! And may you bring a blessing upon me also!"

> Pharaoh, a little too late in the game, finally grants the Israelites everything they previously requested. He also asks Moses and Aaron to save him, because now he believes his life might be in danger as well.

12.33 The Egyptians urged the people on, impatient to have them leave the country, for they said, "We shall all be dead."

12.34 So the people took their dough before it was leavened, their kneading bowls wrapped in their cloaks upon their shoulders.

> The Torah has already taught that Jews are obligated to eat unleavened bread on Passover, but this commandment is now infused with national symbolic significance: Eating unleavened bread is a reenactment of the time during the Exodus when the Israelites fled Egypt in haste.

12.35 The Israelites had done Moses' bidding and borrowed from the Egyptians objects of silver and gold, and clothing.

> Again, what is translated here as "borrowed" actually means "asked."

12.36 And the Lord had disposed the Egyptians favorably toward the people, and they let them have their request; thus they stripped the Egyptians.

> It is hard to believe the Egyptians felt warmly toward the Israelites, whose God did to some of their children what the Egyptian Pharaoh earlier instructed them to do to all the male Israelite babies. On the other hand, that may be precisely why God's intervention was necessary.

HOW MANY ISRAELITES LEFT EGYPT?

12.37 The Israelites journeyed from Raamses to Succoth, about six hundred thousand men on foot, aside from children.

If 600,000 men left Egypt, the large majority of whom presumably had wives and children, then a minimum of two or more likely three million people would have left Egypt. The number 600,000 is based on the Hebrew word *eleph*, which means "thousand."

This term may have an additional meaning, such as "clan" or "tribal unit." Therefore, "600 *eleph*" may mean 600 clans or some large tribal grouping, but less than a thousand. As Boyd Seevers, Professor of Old Testament Studies at Northwestern College (Minnesota), wrote:

> One may also understand the numbers literally, but dif-
> ferently than as usually translated.... Though '*eleph*'
> usually means 'thousand(s),' the word could also mean a
> part of a tribe (perhaps best translated 'clan') that was
> smaller than the tribe but larger than an extended fam-
> ily.... [eds. note: and all these usages are contained else-
> where in the Bible]. For example, Gideon protested to the
> divine messenger who had called him to leadership, say-
> ing 'my clan ('*eleph*') is the weakest in [the tribe of]
> Manasseh, and I am the youngest in my family' (Judges
> 6:15). In a later event, Saul sought the fugitive David
> among all the "clans ['*elephs*'] of Judah" (*alphay Yehuda*;
> 1 Samuel 23:23).[3]

In other words, the Hebrew Bible later uses *eleph* to mean something other than "thousand." (I should note there are scholars who reject any definition of *eleph* other than "thousand.")

If *eleph* always means "thousand," that would mean approximately two million Israelites left Egypt (600,000 males plus an equal number of females plus children). But the Torah itself suggests that may not be a literal number. For example, Deuteronomy 7:1 states "When the LORD your God brings you to the land that you are about to enter and possess, and He dislodges many nations before you—the Hittites, Girgashites, Amorites, Canaanites, Perizzites, Hivites, and Jebusites, *seven nations much larger than you....*"

Now, I think the meaning of that verse is each one of the seven nations is "much larger" than the Israelites. That would mean at least fourteen million people (seven times two million-plus) lived in Canaan. And that is most unlikely: today, more than 3,000 years later, there aren't fourteen million people in the area known as Canaan. Furthermore, in the same chapter in Deuteronomy, Moses says, "It is not because you are the most numerous of peoples that the LORD set His heart on you and chose you—indeed, *you are the smallest of peoples.*" A nation of some two million is not "the smallest of people."

> *The law, "There shall be one law for the citizen and for the stranger who dwells among you," was probably unique in the ancient world.*

Nevertheless, the Torah may well intend that we take *eleph* literally as "thousand." I can live with either understanding of the word because whatever number of Israelites left Egypt and travelled through the desert for forty years, it was all a miracle.

12.38 Moreover, a mixed multitude went up with them, and very much livestock, both flocks and herds.

The Israelites left Egypt along with members of several other nations who comprised the lowest classes of Egyptian society. God could have easily instructed the Israelites not to let the "mixed multitude" of non-Jews join them. But neither God nor Moses raised any objection to rescuing other nations and having them join the Israelites. These people were also made in God's image, and therefore equally valuable, and wanted to be free of their Egyptian oppressors. *The Torah is not interested in blood lines nearly as much as it is in values.* This is exemplified by the Jewish tradition that holds whoever becomes a Jew at any time is considered to have stood at Sinai.

12.39 And they baked unleavened cakes of the dough that they had taken out of Egypt, for it was not leavened, since they had been driven out of Egypt and could not delay; nor had they prepared any provisions for themselves.

12.40 The length of time that the Israelites lived in Egypt was four hundred and thirty years;

12.41 at the end of the four hundred and thirtieth year, to the very day, all the ranks of the Lord departed from the land of Egypt.

12.42 That was for the Lord a night of vigil to bring them out of the land of Egypt; that same night is the Lord's, one of vigil for all the children of Israel throughout the ages.

12.43 The Lord said to Moses and Aaron: This is the law of the Passover offering: No foreigner shall eat of it.

12.44 But any slave a man has bought may eat of it once he has been circumcised.

12.45 No bound or hired laborer shall eat of it.

12.46 It shall be eaten in one house: you shall not take any of the flesh outside the house; nor shall you break a bone of it.

12.47 The whole community of Israel shall offer it.

12.48 If a stranger who dwells with you would offer the Passover to the Lord, all his males must be circumcised; then he shall be admitted to offer it; he shall then be as a citizen of the country. But no uncircumcised person may eat of it.

> Any non-Israelite could join with the Jewish people and eat of the Passover sacrifice by becoming circumcised.

12.49 There shall be one law for the citizen and for the stranger who dwells among you.

> This is one of the most important and morally sublime laws in the Torah, given to the Israelites as soon as they left Egypt, a society in which there wasn't "one law for the citizen and for the stranger." As in many contemporary societies, in the ancient world there was no legal protection at all for the stranger. This Torah law, to the best of our knowledge, was unique in the ancient Near East—and, one presumes, in the world.

12.50 And all the Israelites did so; as the Lord had commanded Moses and Aaron, so they did.

12.51 That very day the Lord freed the Israelites from the land of Egypt, troop by troop.

CHAPTER 13

13.1 The Lord spoke further to Moses, saying,

13.2 "Consecrate to Me every first-born; man and beast, the first issue of every womb among the Israelites is Mine."

Originally, before the Levites—and a sub-group within the Levites, the priests (*kohanim*) who carried out all the rituals involving animal sacrifice—were designated for temple service, firstborns of all tribes were consecrated to working for God.

A son who was his mother's first child was supposed to be dedicated to God's service, and to perform the religious rites subsequently assigned to the priests.

In remembrance and recognition of this earlier tradition that firstborn children were consecrated to working for God, a later Torah law designates that thirty-one days after the child is born, the father can pay a priest five silver shekels (Numbers 18:16) to "redeem" the child from temple work. (The ceremony of redeeming the firstborn is still practiced among observant Jews; it is known in Hebrew as *pidyon ha-ben*, redemption of the [firstborn] son.) Today, a father gives the priest five silver dollars, indicating it was never intended to be a large sum of money, and therefore a burden for poor people.

13.3 And Moses said to the people, "Remember this day, on which you went free from Egypt, the house of bondage, how the Lord freed you from it with a mighty hand: no leavened bread shall be eaten.

The Torah refers again and again to the importance of remembering the Exodus. As previously noted (see commentary to Exodus 10:2), memory perpetuates gratitude (no memory, no gratitude); it perpetuates faith (no memory, no faith); and it perpetuates the Jewish people (no national memory, no nation).

But there may be a fourth reason, which is related to the second one (faith). The Exodus—a time when God intervened forcefully and unequivocally on behalf of the entire Jewish people (or on behalf of any national entity, for that matter)—may have been a unique moment in history.

> *Memory perpetuates gratitude—no memory, no gratitude. It perpetuates faith— no memory, no faith. And it perpetuates the nation—no national memory, no nation.*

Clearly, there have been many times since the Exodus when Jews wished God had intervened on their behalf as He did in Egypt. But that was not to be; therefore, for the sake of keeping alive trust in God, it has been critical to recall the Exodus—and for every Jew throughout the generations to identify with the Exodus as if he or she actually experienced it. As is written in the Passover Seder service: "In every generation a person is obligated to see himself as if he himself has come out of Egypt."

Something powerful can happen when people assemble to express gratitude for something that happened—not to *them* or to their parents, or grandparents, or great-grandparents—but to ancestors who lived thousands of years earlier. By maintaining and expressing their gratitude, Jews have kept their faith and national identity alive.

If people are only grateful when something good happens to *them*, they may never be grateful (or will be grateful only for the briefest of times). Alternatively, they will be grateful only if such good is done to them repeatedly, as epitomized by the question long associated with ingrates: "What have you done for me *lately*?"

In sum, Jews are commanded to remember and celebrate the Exodus both as a statement of their faith and in order to maintain their faith.

13.4 You go free on this day, in the month of Abib.

Abib is the Hebrew word for spring (in modern Hebrew it is pronounced *Aviv*). The Jewish calendar is a lunar calendar, and therefore a year has 354 days, not 365, as does the solar calendar. The Hebrew lunar calendar is therefore adjusted by adding a leap month seven years out of every nineteen (as opposed to a leap day every four years in the solar calendar). Otherwise, Passover would fall eleven days earlier each year, and within a few years, Passover would become a winter holiday, then a fall one and then a summer one—and cease being a spring holiday as the Torah directs it to be.

The Muslim calendar is also lunar, but since there is no specification as to the season in which a holiday must fall, the holiday of Ramadan, for example, falls in different seasons over the course of the years.

13.5 So, when the Lord has brought you into the land of the Canaanites, the Hittites, the Amorites, the Hivites, and the Jebusites, which He swore to your fathers to give you, a land flowing with milk and honey, you shall observe in this month the following practice:

13.6 "Seven days you shall eat unleavened bread, and on the seventh day there shall be a festival of the Lord.

13.7 Throughout the seven days unleavened bread shall be eaten; no leavened bread shall be found with you, and no leaven shall be found in all your territory.

13.8 And you shall explain to your son on that day, 'It is because of what the Lord did for me when I went free from Egypt.'

This is one of four verses in the Torah dealing with the commandment to educate children about the Exodus. The Talmud associated each of these verses with a different type of child (see comment on Exodus 12:26).

In this verse, the Torah states only the parent's answer. As no question is cited, this child came to be known as "the child who does not know how to ask."

The parent's answer is given in the first person because some children—and adults, for that matter—are only able to relate to a self-centered explanation.

13.9 And this shall serve you as a sign on your hand and as a reminder on your forehead—in order that the Teaching of the Lord may be in your mouth—that with a mighty hand the Lord freed you from Egypt.

This verse is one of the primary sources for the Jewish practice of wearing *tefillin,* two leather boxes (one on the forehead and one on the upper arm) that contain words from the Torah (see also Deuteronomy 6:8). The word *tefillin* is usually translated as "phylacteries," which is Greek for "amulet" or "charm," neither of which properly describes *tefillin.* The word "tefillin" is etymologically related to the word "tefilla," the Hebrew word for prayer.

The Torah does not mention the word *tefillin* nor does it specify that this "sign" must be an actual physical object, let alone what that object should be. Nevertheless, as archaeological evidence has documented, *tefillin* have been physical objects for thousands of years.

Regarding the words, "on your forehead," the Hebrew literally states "between your eyes" (yet another indication they were intended to be tangible objects). In practice, the head *tefillin* are placed in the center of the forehead, above and between the two eyes.

13.10 You shall keep this institution at its set time from year to year.

13.11 "And when the Lord has brought you into the land of the Canaanites, as He swore to you and to your fathers, and has given it to you,

13.12 you shall set apart for the Lord every first issue of the womb: every male firstling that your cattle drop shall be the Lord's.

13.13 But every firstling ass you shall redeem with a sheep;

According to the medieval commentator Ibn Ezra, "since this [the donkey] was the only Israelite animal unfit for sacrifice [it was a non-kosher animal; therefore bringing a donkey for a sacrifice would have been like bringing a pig for sacrifice], no other species had to be redeemed in this way." Therefore, given that the priest had no use for an animal unfit for sacrifice, the owner of the donkey had to give the priest a sheep instead.

13.13 (cont.) if you do not redeem it, you must break its neck.

Only if the owner gives the priest a sheep in place of the donkey, is he permitted to keep the donkey. But if the owner does not bring a sheep, the donkey had to be killed so as not to be used. This law guaranteed Israelites paid their dues to the priests.

13.13 (cont.) And you must redeem every first-born male among your children.

See the commentary to verse 2.

13.14 And when, in time to come, your son asks you, saying, 'What does this mean?'

This question is associated with the simple child, because it is brief, straightforward, and unsophisticated (see comment on Exodus 12:26).

The answer given to the simple child is different from the answer given to the child who does not know how to ask because no two children are the same. Families almost always include different types of children, and parents must come up with the most appropriate answers for each of them. This notion is best expressed in Proverbs 22:6: "Educate a child, each according to *his* way...."

In general, children should not be raised in precisely the same way as their siblings (i.e., have the same achievements expected of them, automatically be sent to the same school, disciplined in the same way, etc.).

> *It is Moses, presumably the busiest of the departing Israelites, who remembers his people's promise: We have debts to the dead as well as the living.*

13.14 (cont.) you shall say to him, 'It was with a mighty hand that the Lord brought us out from Egypt, the house of bondage.

The purpose of this answer is to impress the simple child with God's strength, since this child is unlikely to be able to appreciate the nuances of the Exodus story.

13.15 When Pharaoh stubbornly refused to let us go, the Lord slew every first-born in the land of Egypt, the first-born of both man and beast. Therefore I sacrifice to the Lord every first male issue of the womb, but redeem every first-born among my sons.'

13.16 "And so it shall be as a sign upon your hand and as a symbol on your forehead that with a mighty hand the Lord freed us from Egypt."

13.17 Now when Pharaoh let the people go, God did not lead them by way of the land of the Philistines, although it was nearer; for God said, "The people may have a change of heart when they see war, and return to Egypt."

God knows that as ex-slaves who were in bondage for generations, the Israelites were not prepared to wage war against the Philistines (or presumably anyone else).

13.18 So God led the people roundabout, by way of the wilderness at the Sea of Reeds. Now the Israelites went up armed out of the land of Egypt.

This is the sea God will split so the Israelites can pass through safely.

13.19 And Moses took with him the bones of Joseph, who had exacted an oath from the children of Israel, saying, "God will be sure to take notice of you: then you shall carry up my bones from here with you."

As we read in Genesis 50:25, "So Joseph made the sons of Israel swear, saying, 'When God has taken notice of you, you shall carry up my bones from here.' It is Moses, presumably the busiest of the departing Israelites, who remembers this promise: We have debts to the dead as well as the living.

13.20 They set out from Succoth, and encamped at Etham, at the edge of the wilderness.

13.21 The Lord went before them in a pillar of cloud by day, to guide them along the way, and in a pillar of fire by night, to give them light, that they might travel day and night.

13.22 The pillar of cloud by day and the pillar of fire by night did not depart from before the people.

CHAPTER 14

14.1 The Lord said to Moses:

14.2 Tell the Israelites to turn back and encamp before Pi-hahiroth, between Migdol and the sea, before Baal-zephon;

> The next verse explains that God wants the Israelites to change their course so Pharaoh will think they have lost their way.

14.2 (cont.) you shall encamp facing it, by the sea.

> The "sea" refers to the sea God will split and the Israelites will cross.

14.3 Pharaoh will say of the Israelites, "They are astray in the land; the wilderness has closed in on them."

14.4 Then I will stiffen Pharaoh's heart and he will pursue them,

GOD IS GLORIFIED WHEN HE IS PERCEIVED AS JUST

14.4 (cont.) that I may gain glory through Pharaoh and all his host;

> When God inflicts or exacts just revenge (which is really just another term for punishment) on evildoers such as Pharaoh, His name is glorified. In other words: *God gains glory by rewarding good and punishing evil.*
>
> This can be shown by answering this question: What is it that causes many thinking and decent people not to believe in God, let alone glorify Him?

The answer is the amount of injustice in the world. That being the case, when God deals with injustice, He is most likely to be universally affirmed and glorified.

Justice is indeed God's glory—thus, the centrality of abolishing evil, punishing those who commit it, and, of course, doing good in the Torah.

Ironically, however, this is also a major reason many people reject the Torah and God. Many people are uncomfortable with being morally judged, and especially uncomfortable with a God who judges them (i.e., a God who might punish them). That is why, for example, surveys indicate far more people reject the concept of hell (afterlife punishment) than the concept of heaven (afterlife reward).

God hates evil and instructs us to do likewise: "You who love God [must] hate evil" (Psalms 97:10). Then we humans, too, can be glorified.

14.4 (cont). and the Egyptians shall know that I am the Lord. And they did so.

In spite of the Ten Plagues and all the other miracles, the Egyptians still do not recognize God as the God of the world; hence, they continue to monitor the Israelites' movements, thinking they can outwit the Israelites' God. Sarna argues that the words "And the Egyptians shall know that I am the Lord," means the Egyptians will finally realize the world is governed by a moral order that must ultimately prevail.

14.5 When the king of Egypt was told that the people had fled, Pharaoh and his courtiers had a change of heart about the people and said, "What is this we have done, releasing Israel from our service?"

14.6 He ordered his chariot and took his men with him;

The Hebrew literally states Pharaoh "hitched," not "ordered," his chariot. The traditional commentators noted Pharaoh was so anxious to pursue the Israelites that he prepared his chariot rather than taking the time to order a servant to do it for him.

Archeological evidence documents chariots were invented shortly before Pharaoh's time. Thus, they would have been seen as among the most, if not the most, advanced military weapons of the time.

14.7 he took six hundred of his picked chariots, and the rest of the chariots of Egypt, with officers in all of them.

14.8 The Lord stiffened the heart of Pharaoh king of Egypt, and he gave chase to the Israelites. As the Israelites were departing defiantly,

14.9 the Egyptians gave chase to them, and all the chariot horses of Pharaoh, his horsemen, and his warriors overtook them encamped by the sea, near Pi-hahiroth, before Baal-zephon.

14.10 As Pharaoh drew near, the Israelites caught sight of the Egyptians advancing upon them. Greatly frightened, the Israelites cried out to the Lord.

Only two verses earlier, the Israelites were described as leaving Egypt "defiantly." But the moment they see the Egyptians pursuing them, they cower. Understandably, given their centuries of servitude, the Israelites still have a slave mentality, not the mentality necessary to wage war—despite the fact they are armed (Exodus 13:18). That is why God, Ibn Ezra writes, subsequently "arranged for that whole generation of males to die in the wilderness—for

Many people are uncomfortable with being morally judged and especially uncomfortable with a God who judges them.

they would not have had the gumption to fight the Canaanites—to be replaced by a generation that had not known exile [and slavery]...."[1]

The Israelites welcomed their liberation from Egypt with joy, but soon found themselves filled with fear and depression when they considered the burdens and responsibilities of their newfound freedom (including self-defense and self-reliance). The Israelites will later entertain the possibility of returning to Egypt.

14.11 And they said to Moses, "Was it for want of graves in Egypt that you brought us to die in the wilderness? What have you done to us, taking us out of Egypt?

The Israelites' complaint is sarcastic; if any nation had enough graves, it was Egypt, whose religion revolved around death.

IS IT WORTH DYING TO BE FREE?

14.12 Is this not the very thing we told you in Egypt, saying, 'Let us be, and we will serve the Egyptians, for it is better for us to serve the Egyptians than to die in the wilderness'?"

The Israelites claim they would rather return to slavery than confront the Egyptians in battle. This, to be fair, is understandable. Most people would rather be enslaved than dead. Most, but not all. One of the most famous statements of the American War of Independence was that of the American patriot Patrick Henry: "Give me liberty, or give me death."

Henry's attitude, the antithesis of what the Israelites are saying here, helped make the founding of America possible—as well as the liberation of Europe, and the independence of South Korea and many other free countries. But it is hardly a universal sentiment. During the Cold War between the democratic West and the Soviet Union, there were, of course, many in the West who said, "Better dead than Red [communist]"; but many others subscribed to the slogan associated with Bertrand Russell, the twentieth century's leading atheist philosopher: "Better Red than dead."

Russell's slogan was consistent with that of much of the well-educated class in Britain. On February 8, 1933, right after Hitler came to power in Germany, the Oxford Union Debating Society held a debate on the resolution, "This House will in no circumstances fight for its King and Country." The resolution passed 275–153. The vote made an impression on Hitler and Mussolini, as it revealed that many of England's best educated would prefer to live under Nazism or Fascism than to fight for freedom and risk death.

The Israelites' statement made it clear to Moses they so valued life they would be willing to return to everything they endured in captivity—even the Egyptians' seeking to murder all of their newborn males—in order to avoid doing battle with the Egyptians.

14.13 But Moses said to the people, "Have no fear! Stand by, and witness the deliverance which the Lord will work for you today; for the Egyptians whom you see today you will never see again.

14.14 The Lord will battle for you; you hold your peace!"

This is perhaps the one time in Jewish history in which the Jews did not have to stand up for themselves and could simply rely on God. This is one of many ways the Exodus was a unique event.

14.15 Then the Lord said to Moses, "Why do you cry out to Me? Tell the Israelites to go forward.

Nevertheless, even in this singular instance, God does not want the Israelites to be utterly passive. Crying out to God is fine, but it never precludes taking action to the extent we're able. Words attributed to St. Augustine—but probably not actually said by him—are a good guideline: "Pray as if everything depends on God. Work as if everything depends on you."

14.16 And you lift up your rod and hold out your arm over the sea and split it, so that the Israelites may march into the sea on dry ground.

14.17 And I will stiffen the hearts of the Egyptians so that they go in after them; and I will gain glory through Pharaoh and all his warriors, his chariots and his horsemen.

14.18 Let the Egyptians know that I am Lord, when I gain glory through Pharaoh, his chariots, and his horsemen."

14.19 The angel of God,

In the Torah, angels of God are messengers who may take any form, human or otherwise.

14.19 (cont.) who had been going ahead of the Israelite army, now moved and followed behind them; and the pillar of cloud shifted from in front of them and took up a place behind them,

14.20 and it came between the army of the Egyptians and the army of Israel.

The cloud rests here to temporarily halt the advance of the Egyptian army.

14.20 (cont.) Thus there was the cloud with the darkness, and it cast a spell upon the night,

> The NIV provides a more helpful translation: "Throughout the night the cloud brought darkness to the one side and light to the other side; so neither went near the other all night long."

14.20 (cont.) so that the one could not come near the other all through the night.

WHY DID GOD USE WINDS TO SPLIT THE SEA?

14.21 Then Moses held out his arm over the sea and the Lord drove back the sea with a strong east wind all that night, and turned the sea into dry ground. The waters were split,

> God could have split the sea at any time or in any way. He did not need winds to do it when, for example, Moses would lift his arm. But instead, God sends strong winds to part the waters. Like most of the miracles, the splitting of the sea was achieved through God's manipulation of nature.
>
> There are two likely reasons for this. The first, and probably the most likely, was to reinforce in the minds of the Israelites that God controls nature; nature is not a god. The other possible reason for His use of nature to achieve this miracle (and nearly all the other miracles of the Exodus) was to enable the skeptic to deny the splitting of the sea was in fact a divine miracle: "It wasn't God; fortuitous winds did it!"
>
> This seems to be God's approach in general. Much like God wanted Pharaoh to have the strength to exercise his own will with regard to letting the Israelites go rather than be coerced into it by God, He apparently wants human beings to be free to choose to believe in Him rather than to compel them to believe in Him by making His existence incontrovertible. Just as the skeptic at the sea could claim winds coming at just the right moment split the sea, so, too, we are all free to argue that all of life, indeed all of the universe, came about by coincidence. God could have easily made us as certain of His existence as we are of anything material. But He didn't. He wants

God could have easily made us as certain of His existence as we are of anything material that exists. But He didn't.

humans to have free will, and that must include the freedom to choose or reject God.

14.22 and the Israelites went into the sea on dry ground, the waters forming a wall for them on their right and on their left.

14.23 The Egyptians came in pursuit after them into the sea, all of Pharaoh's horses, chariots, and horsemen.

> The Egyptians follow the Israelites into the sea in accordance with God's prediction to Moses in verse 17.

14.24 At the morning watch,

> Each night had three watches. The morning watch lasted from about 2:00 a.m. to 6:00 a.m.

14.24 (cont.) the Lord looked down upon the Egyptian army from a pillar of fire and cloud, and threw the Egyptian army into panic.

14.25 He locked the wheels of their chariots so that they moved forward with difficulty. And the Egyptians said, "Let us flee from the Israelites, for the Lord is fighting for them against Egypt."

> In accord with the famous statement, "Hell is truth seen too late," the Egyptians finally recognize the Lord (YHVH) as God. But it was too late; they drowned with that knowledge.

14.26 Then the Lord said to Moses, "Hold out your arm over the sea, that the waters may come back upon the Egyptians and upon their chariots and upon their horsemen."

14.27 Moses held out his arm over the sea, and at daybreak the sea returned to its normal state, and the Egyptians fled at its approach. But the Lord hurled the Egyptians into the sea.

> God had the Egyptians drown at a time of day when the Israelites would be able to see it happen. The Israelites, who so feared the Egyptians, needed to see their oppressors destroyed.

14.28 The waters turned back and covered the chariots and the horsemen—Pharaoh's entire army that followed them into the sea; not one of them remained.

The miraculous drowning of the Egyptians is narrated without literary flourish. Indeed, the Torah offers a rather mundane description of what was surely one of the most remarkable events in history.

14.29 But the Israelites had marched through the sea on dry ground, the waters forming a wall for them on their right and on their left.

14.30 Thus the Lord delivered Israel that day from the Egyptians. Israel saw the Egyptians dead on the shore of the sea.

Presumably, the waves washed the Egyptian corpses onto the shore (*Bekhor Shor*).

THE DIFFERENCE BETWEEN BELIEF IN GOD AND TRUST IN GOD

14.31 And when Israel saw the wondrous power which the Lord had wielded against the Egyptians, the people feared the Lord; they had faith in the Lord and His servant Moses.

Although this verse has become famous in Jewish liturgy and tradition, depending on how one translates the Hebrew word *va'ya'aminu*, the word can be viewed as reflecting either positively or negatively on the Israelites.

The normal translation of *va'ya'aminu* is "believed in." And if the verse means "they believed in the Lord" as "believe in" is usually understood, it would reflect negatively on the Israelites. It would imply that, despite all the miracles they already witnessed, they didn't believe that God existed until the splitting of the sea and the drowning of the Egyptians. And it would imply they also came to believe in Moses as a god-like figure.

Those problems are resolved, however, if the Hebrew word *va'ya'aminu* is interpreted as "they trusted in," or, as it is rendered here, "had faith in." In Hebrew, as in English, when we say to someone, "I believe in you," what we are really saying is "I trust you," not "I believe you exist." Thus, the drowning of the Egyptians did not convince the Israelites to believe in God's existence, but to trust in God—that He fulfills His promises. And just as the people learned to trust in God, they also learned to trust in Moses as a reliable servant of God.

Regarding the phrase "servant of God," it is worth noting again that the Hebrew word for "servant" is the same word for "slave" (*eved*). In this verse, it is obvious *eved* means "servant" —Moses was not the "slave of God." But in other places in the Torah, whether *eved* means slave or servant is not always clear—which complicates some of the discussion about slavery in the Torah.

CHAPTER

15

THE FOLLOWING SONG (VERSES 1-19) IS WRITTEN IN BEAUTIFUL HEBREW POETRY which cannot be fully captured in translation (in the widely-viewed English-language animated film about the Exodus, *The Prince of Egypt*, this is the one section from the Bible sung in Hebrew).

ESSAY: IS IT MORAL TO CELEBRATE THE DEATH OF EVILDOERS?

15.1 Then Moses and the Israelites sang this song to the Lord.

According to a well-known passage in the Talmud, the angels, too, broke out in song when the Egyptians were drowning in the sea. But, the Talmud states, God rebuked them: "My creatures [the Egyptians] are drowning, and you sing songs?"[1]

This Talmudic passage is often cited by Jews who believe it is wrong for people to rejoice at the fall of an enemy, no matter how evil. But the story does not support that view. God does not rebuke Moses and the Israelites. He only rebukes the angels.

Why? Because God does not hold people to the same standards as He does angels. When people see their—or even others'—would-be murderers drowning, it is both natural and moral to express relief followed by joy. Furthermore, the angels' lives were not in danger; the Israelites' were.

This is a fascinating passage, fraught with moral questions. One doesn't have to take the Talmudic passage literally to appreciate its moral insight—and its moral difficulty.

The morality of the passage is quite admirable. That ancient Jews would describe God as rebuking angels for celebrating the demise of those seeking to kill and enslave Jews is a remarkable moral achievement.

Nevertheless, there are moral grounds for challenging the passage. Was it really wrong for the angels to rejoice? One can understand why God might not be depicted as having rejoiced; every human being is His child, and remains so even when doing evil. But angels are not parents of all mankind. Why shouldn't they rejoice over the fact the Israelites—or any other innocents—were spared death and slavery? Why would that be wrong?

> *When people see their would-be murderers drowning, it is both natural and moral to express relief followed by joy.*

Furthermore, if we are to be honest, the Talmudic passage does imply criticism of the Israelites. If humans are supposed to aspire to be God-like, they are surely supposed to aspire to be angel-like; and if the angels were wrong in rejoicing, then on some level so were the Israelites.

It is also critical to note the angels' celebration is not necessarily about a victory for Jews, but a victory for morality. People intent on doing evil were prevented from doing so, thereby sparing the innocent suffering and death. That's a moral achievement and should therefore be rejoiced over. Yes, one can always acknowledge the death of those doing evil is ultimately a human tragedy. But it is infinitely less tragic than the alternative.

Similarly, when people pose the question as, "Should one celebrate the fall of one's enemy?" they are not posing a moral question. The issue is not whether one should celebrate the fall of one's enemy; it is whether one should celebrate the fall of evil people and the consequent saving of the innocent.

When I watch World War II films and see Nazi soldiers killed, I am mindful of the fact those soldiers were drafted, and they left behind grieving mothers, fathers, girlfriends, wives, and children. But I am happy they were killed because either the Nazi soldier or the soldier of a decent country was going to die; and the death of every Nazi soldier hastened the end of the Nazi regime and the closing of the Nazis' death and concentration camps. Would it be more noble not to be happy about all those facts? If one should not be happy the soldier fighting against the Nazi regime was spared and the life of the Nazi regime was shortened, what should one feel?

Some might say the proper response is happiness over the sparing of the Allied soldiers and the weakening of the Nazi regime, but not over the death of Nazi soldiers. But that avoids confronting the moral reality that the only way to have saved the lives of Allied soldiers and hasten the end of the Nazi regime was to kill Nazi soldiers. If no Nazi soldiers were killed, the Nazis would never have surrendered.

Whatever one concludes about the morality of celebrating the downfall of evil, this Talmudic story achieves two important purposes: It reminds us that even one's enemies, and even those who do evil, are still human beings created in God's image. And it forces us to ask moral questions.

15.1 (cont.) They said: I will sing to the Lord, for He has triumphed gloriously;

Horse and driver He has hurled into the sea.

This entire song is about God; Moses plays no active role. And there is no mention of the angel of death, the cloud, or the darkness. It is God alone Who is celebrated here (Sarna). The desire to keep attention focused on God and not on a human being (great as Moses was) likewise characterizes the Passover Seder Book, the Haggadah, in which Moses's name is mentioned only once, and only in passing.

15.2 The Lord is my strength and might;

He is become my deliverance.

This is my God and I will enshrine Him;

The God of my father, and I will exalt Him.

TO BE A "GOD OF LOVE," GOD MUST ALSO
BE A "GOD OF WAR"

15.3 The Lord, the Warrior—

The Hebrew literally says, "The Lord is a Man of War."

This strikes those moderns for whom war is by definition immoral as a morally primitive way of describing God. Many people are much more comfortable saying "God is Love." But sometimes the only way to stop evil and increase love is through war. God must therefore be both Love and Warrior. In this case, when the Israelites are fleeing heavily-armed professional troops, God acts as a warrior on their behalf. That was the only thing a God of Love could do.

15.3 (cont.) Lord is His name!

15.4 Pharaoh's chariots and his army

He has cast into the sea;

And the pick of his officers

Are drowned in the Sea of Reeds.

15.5 The deeps covered them;

They went down into the depths like a stone.

15.6 Your right hand, O Lord, glorious in power,

Your right hand, O Lord, shatters the foe!

15.7 In Your great triumph You break Your opponents;

You send forth Your fury, it consumes them like straw.

15.8 At the blast of Your nostrils the waters piled up,

The floods stood straight like a wall;

The deeps froze in the heart of the sea.

15.9 The foe said,

"I will pursue, I will overtake,

I will divide the spoil;

My desire shall have its fill of them.

I will bare my sword—

My hand shall subdue them."

15.10 You made Your wind blow, the sea covered them;

They sank like lead in the majestic waters.

15.11 Who is like You, O Lord, among the gods;

> This verse, one of the most famous lines in Jewish liturgy, does not imply God is one among many gods; rather, it means none of the false gods who are worshipped by pagan nations can compare to the One True God.

15.11 (cont.) Who is like You, majestic in holiness,

Awesome in splendor, working wonders!

Sometimes the only way to stop evil and increase love is through war.

15.12 You put out Your right hand,

The earth swallowed them.

15.13 In Your love You lead the people You redeemed;

In Your strength You guide them to Your holy abode.

15.14 The peoples hear, they tremble;

Agony grips the dwellers in Philistia.

> Philistia refers to the Philistines. When, many centuries later, the Romans conquered Judea, they sought to obliterate all memory of it as a Jewish nation, and renamed it "Palestine," after the ancient Philistines.

15.15 Now are the clans of Edom dismayed;

The tribes of Moab—trembling grips them;

All the dwellers in Canaan are aghast.

15.16 Terror and dread descend upon them;

Through the might of Your arm they are still as stone—

Till Your people cross over, O Lord,

Till Your people cross whom You have ransomed.

15.17 You will bring them and plant them in Your own mountain,

The place You made to dwell in, O Lord,

The sanctuary, O Lord, which Your hands established.

15.18 The Lord will reign for ever and ever!

15.19 For the horses of Pharaoh, with his chariots and horsemen, went into the sea; and the Lord turned back on them the waters of the sea; but the Israelites marched on dry ground in the midst of the sea.

15.20 Then Miriam the prophetess, Aaron's sister, took a timbrel in her hand,

> This is the first time Moses's sister is described as a prophetess (curiously, she is only identified as Aaron's sister, not as Moses's as well), which is among the highest accolades a person can receive in the Hebrew Bible. A prophet or prophetess is a spokesperson for God. Miriam is the only woman designated as such in the Torah, though later biblical books speak of other women prophets, such as Deborah (Judges 4:4), Hulda (II Kings 22:14), and Noadiah (Nehemiah 6:14). Also, the prophet Isaiah writes that his wife was a prophetess (Isaiah 8:3). Genesis records the matriarch Rebecca receiving a direct revelation from God (Genesis 25:22-23).

15.20 (cont.) and all the women went out after her in dance with timbrels.

> Rashi comments that the women of that generation had such great faith in God they took timbrels with them when they left Egypt, confident they would use them to celebrate God's miracles on the Israelites' behalf.

15.21 And Miriam chanted for them:

Sing to the Lord, for He has triumphed gloriously;

Horse and driver He has hurled into the sea.

15.22 Then Moses caused Israel to set out from the Sea of Reeds. They went on into the wilderness of Shur;

The Israelites' First of Four Crises in the Desert

15.22 (cont.) they traveled three days in the wilderness and found no water.

The lack of drinking water described in verses 22–26 is the first in a series of four crises that befall the Jewish people on their way to Mount Sinai. Each of these crises (the second involved a lack of food, the third a lack of water again, and the fourth an attack by a desert tribe) illustrated both the precarious nature of Israel's survival and God's providential care.

Despite all that has been done on their behalf, during three of these crises the Israelites complain bitterly to Moses and to God. Although God does not get angry with the people in any of these situations, the Torah's account is an implied critique of the people's repeated ingratitude and lack of faith. No matter what God does for the Israelites, their implicit or explicit response is, "What have you done for me lately?"

It took the Israelites a mere three days to lose sight of all the miracles God performed and to start complaining.

Most people, like the Israelites, complain far more often than they express gratitude. People frequently register a complaint with a manufacturer or service provider, but they rarely write a note of thanks for a job well done. We would all do well to consider writing a thank you note each time we write a letter of complaint. Similarly, and more importantly, too many people criticize their spouses more often than they compliment them. That is the road to an unappy marriage.

15.23 They came to Marah, but they could not drink the water of Marah because it was bitter; that is why it was named Marah.

The Hebrew word *marah* means bitter. Jews eat a bitter herb at the Passover Seder to identify with the suffering of the slaves; it is called *maror.*

15.24 And the people grumbled against Moses, saying, "What shall we drink?"

15.25 So he cried out to the Lord, and the Lord showed him a piece of wood; he threw it into the water and the water became sweet.

While it has been noted this can be explained as a natural phenomenon in which porous wood filters out impurities in the water and renders it drinkable, what renders this a miracle is that a piece of wood can sweeten the water for so large a number of people.

15.25 (cont.) There He made for them a statute and a law, and there He put it to the test.

15.26 He said, "If you will heed the Lord your God diligently, doing what is upright in His sight, giving ear to His commandments and keeping all His laws, then I will not bring upon you any of the diseases that I brought upon the Egyptians, for I the Lord am your healer."

This verse does not say that if the Israelites observe all of God's laws they will never suffer any disease. It only says God will not bring upon them any of the diseases He brought upon the Egyptians.

The Israelites could easily have thought, given all God did on their behalf, they would be treated by God in a special way, that God would not apply the same standards to them as to all other nations. Ironically, if that is what they thought, they were right. God did not judge them by the standards by which He judged other nations. He judged them by a higher standard.

ESSAY: GOD DOESN'T PROTECT RELIGIOUS PEOPLE FROM ILLNESS

Understanding this verse properly—with its assertion that if Jews observe God's laws, He will not inflict on them the diseases He inflicted on Egypt—is important for another reason.

There are many religious people who believe if they act or believe in accordance with God's will, God should and will protect them from calamities such as bad health and early death.

At a speech in an Orthodox Jewish synagogue in London, I was asked how I explain that observant Jews—Jews who strictly observe the laws of Shabbat and Kashrut, for example—get struck with cancer or a heart attack at an early age. I was taken aback by the question, as I never associated keeping God's commandments with protection from illness. So I asked those present to raise their hands if they believed God protected the observant from disease. About half the audience raised their hands.

Likewise, there are Christians who believe that with enough faith, one will not get seriously ill.

There are many problems with that belief.

First, it is obviously not true. Many pious people have been afflicted with disease and many non-religious and evil people have lived long and healthy lives. It should be obvious to anyone there is simply no correlation between religiosity and being protected from illness. (There are measurable health benefits to leading the purposeful, family-centered, and community-centered life healthy religious practices provide, but that is another matter.)

How could there be such a correlation? As Harold Kushner has observed, does the belief God protects the righteous mean a good religious person can go out in freezing weather without a coat and never get sick?

Second, if God really did protect religious people from all illness, why would any rational person not be religious?

Moreover, faith would no longer be faith. It wouldn't take any faith to believe in God and to lead a religious life. It would be a completely empirically based decision: Observe x and you will never get cancer; believe y and you will never get heart disease. That's not faith, it's a health care decision.

Third, the belief God protects those with proper observance or faith from all disease must ultimately lead to an unsympathetic, even judgmental, response to people who get sick: "If only they were more observant [or] if only they had a deeper faith—they wouldn't have gotten cancer or had that heart attack." The victim of cancer or a heart attack is then doubly victimized.

So, are there rewards for being a good person, or, specifically, for being a faithful religious person?

Yes, there are, and they fall into two categories—this-world rewards and rewards in the afterlife.

Regarding the afterlife, any belief in a just God must mean the good are rewarded and the evil are punished. It is axiomatic that if there is a God and if that God is just, there is ultimate justice. And since such justice rarely exists in this world—just think of young children murdered in terrorist attacks or mistreated by abusive parents—ultimate justice must take place in the next world.

A Talmudic passage teaches, "There is no reward for the commandments [*mitzvot*] in this world," meaning God does not reward the faithful in this world.[2]

There are many religious people who believe if they act or believe in accordance with God's will, God will protect them from calamities such as bad health and early death. But God never promises to do that.

That does not mean there aren't rewards for leading a religious life in this world. There certainly are. But they differ from rewards in the next world in that they are not dispensed by God; they are intrinsic to leading a good religious life.

The reward for keeping God's laws is in the keeping of the laws. Again, as the Talmud puts it: "The reward for [observing] a commandment is the [observing of the] commandment" (*s'char mitzvah mitzvah*).[3]

In other words, performing that *mitzvah* (commandment) is the reward. The clearest example is the Shabbat. Taking one day every week off from work, away from business and commerce, and spending it with friends, family, and community is so beneficial to one's life that asking to be rewarded further is asking too much. It would be like asking for a reward for driving sober. The reward of driving without drinking is (usually) getting to one's destination alive and well.

In fact, if one wants additional, divine, rewards for keeping one, some, or all of God's laws, it can only mean that individual finds little, or nothing, intrinsically rewarding in the keeping of the law(s).

15.27 And they came to Elim, where there were twelve springs of water and seventy palm trees; and they encamped there beside the water.

CHAPTER
~ 16 ~

16.1 Setting out from Elim, the whole Israelite community came to the wilderness of Sin, which is between Elim and Sinai, on the fifteenth day of the second month after their departure from the land of Egypt.

MIRACLES BRING PEOPLE TO FAITH IN GOD— FOR A VERY SHORT TIME

16.2 In the wilderness, the whole Israelite community grumbled against Moses and Aaron.

By supplying an exact date, the Torah is reminding us it was only a little over a month since the Israelites sang a song of gratitude at their triumph over the Egyptians. Yet, as we will now see, they are already complaining that they would rather be back in Egypt.

The ingratitude of the Israelites so soon after the miracles they witnessed is not only a statement about the Israelites. More importantly, it demonstrates a truism that is by no means self-evident: Despite what almost all of us may think, miracles do not necessarily lead to faith.

In this regard, the witty American filmmaker Woody Allen was wrong when he insisted he would come to believe in God, "if only God would give me a clear sign, like making a large deposit in my name in a Swiss bank."

He was wrong because if a miracle is what gives people faith, such faith won't last long. Shortly after a miracle, people begin to demand another miracle. Let's imagine a large deposit was made in Woody Allen's name in a Swiss bank account. For how long would he continue to believe in God? Until the money was depleted? Until he contracted a severe illness and demanded a miraculous cure? Until he came to believe some anonymous human donor made the deposit? Besides, there are miracles surrounding us every single day of our lives.

Why isn't the universe a miracle? Why isn't biological life a miracle? Intelligent life? Love? Music? The workings of the cell?

When you think about it, any of these things dwarf one split sea in terms of the miraculous. A human being is created from one sperm cell entering an egg: Why isn't that miraculous? Because it happens so frequently? So what? Why isn't that a miracle, too? Indeed the most rational explanation for the existence of anything is that it is a miracle. Why is "everything came about on its own, by chance," more rational than "everything is a miracle" —meaning divine intervention made the otherwise improbable (if not impossible) happen?

> *If a miracle is what gives people faith, such faith won't last long.*

DO PEOPLE PREFER LIBERTY—OR TO BE TAKEN CARE OF?

16.3 The Israelites said to them, "If only we had died by the hand of the Lord in the land of Egypt, when we sat by the fleshpots, when we ate our fill of bread!

The Israelites draw an exaggerated, idealized picture of the past. They long to return to Egypt not because the food was really as plentiful as they claim, but because as slaves they did not have to provide for themselves. It is a myth people yearn most for freedom. Some people, thank God, do. But many, if not most, people prefer to be taken care of—even at the price of a loss of freedoms—rather than to have to take care of themselves. That is why people almost everywhere in the world prefer a big state to a limited one, even though, by definition, the bigger the state, the less the individual's freedom. That is why the American experiment in limited government was unique in world history and therefore produced the freest country in world history. It is not coincidental it was founded by people who revered the Hebrew Bible. As noted, the words on the Liberty Bell, the symbol of the American Revolution, are from the Torah, and they are about liberty (Leviticus 25:10).

16.3 (cont.) For you have brought us out into this wilderness to starve this whole congregation to death."

> Complainers are masters of exaggeration. Did they really believe God's and Moses's motivation in confronting Pharaoh and bringing the Ten Plagues down upon Egypt was to free the Israelites and then starve them to death?

16.4 And the Lord said to Moses, "I will rain down bread for you from the sky, and the people shall go out and gather each day that day's portion—

> Although it is not yet referred to as such, this is the beginning of the manna God provides the Israelites throughout their forty years of wandering in the desert.

16.4 (cont.) that I may thus test them, to see whether they will follow My instructions or not.

> Most people understand this to mean God is testing the people's faith to see if they will trust God to provide them with enough food to eat every day. But the opposite may also be true: God may be testing the people's faith by giving them food every day to see if they will still believe in Him even when they are well fed. We are tested in our faith regardless of our material circumstances. If we are poor, we have to be able to affirm God in spite of our privation; if we are rich, we have to keep God in our lives even though we might be tempted to think we don't really "need" Him.
>
> Both the poor and the rich have reasons to doubt and reasons to believe. Belief in God, like just about everything else in life, is a choice.

16.5 But on the sixth day, when they apportion what they have brought in, it shall prove to be double the amount they gather each day."

> The Israelites will receive a double portion of manna on Friday so they do not have to gather it on Shabbat Day. This double portion is the origin of the Jewish tradition of serving two Shabbat breads (*challot*) at Shabbat meals.

16.6 So Moses and Aaron said to all the Israelites, "By evening you shall know it was the Lord who brought you out from the land of Egypt;

This is quite a statement. Are Moses and Aaron really saying that only after receiving manna—as opposed to witnessing the Ten Plagues, the splitting of the sea, and the drowning of the Egyptian army—the Israelites will "know it was the Lord who brought you out from the land of Egypt"? This statement underscores yet again that miracles sustain faith for only a brief period.

16.7 and in the morning you shall behold the Presence of the Lord, because He has heard your grumblings against the Lord. For who are we that you should grumble against us?

16.8 Since it is the Lord," Moses continued, "who will give you flesh to eat in the evening and bread in the morning to the full, because the Lord has heard the grumblings you utter against Him, what is our part? Your grumbling is not against us, but against the Lord!"

Moses here is not merely absolving Aaron and himself from blame. He is reminding the Israelites that neither he nor Aaron is the source of miracles; God alone is. In the Book of Numbers, Moses does seem to (inadvertently) take credit for the miracle of extracting water from a rock, and for that reason he is not allowed to enter the Promised Land. (See the commentary on Numbers 20:20.)

16.9 Then Moses said to Aaron, "Say to the whole Israelite community: Advance toward the Lord, for He has heard your grumbling."

16.10 And as Aaron spoke to the whole Israelite community, they turned toward the wilderness, and there, in a cloud, appeared the Presence of the Lord.

16.11 The Lord spoke to Moses:

16.12 "I have heard the grumbling of the Israelites. Speak to them and say: By evening you shall eat flesh, and in the morning you shall have your fill of bread; and you shall know that I the Lord am your God."

16.13 In the evening quail appeared and covered the camp; in the morning there was a fall of dew about the camp.

16.14 When the fall of dew lifted, there, over the surface of the wilderness, lay a fine and flaky substance, as fine as frost on the ground.

16.15 When the Israelites saw it, they said to one another, "What is it?" —for they did not know what it was. And Moses said to them, "That is the bread which the Lord has given you to eat.

Both the poor and the rich have reasons to doubt and reasons to believe. Belief in God, like just about everything else in life, is a choice.

16.16 This is what the Lord has commanded: Gather as much of it as each of you requires to eat, an *omer* to a person for as many of you as there are; each of you shall fetch for those in his tent."

16.17 The Israelites did so, some gathering much, some little.

16.18 But when they measured it by the *omer*, he who had gathered much had no excess, and he who had gathered little had no deficiency: they had gathered as much as they needed to eat.

An *omer* is approximately 3.5 lbs. or 1.6 kilograms. The people were permitted to gather this amount of manna per day. No matter how much they gathered, it would always miraculously amount to exactly the measure needed to feed each of them. If this miracle did not take place, Israelites would likely compete and even fight with one another to gather more manna for themselves.

16.19 And Moses said to them, "Let no one leave any of it over until morning."

God wanted the people to learn they could rely on Him to provide food for the next day.

16.20 But they paid no attention to Moses; some of them left some of it until morning, and it became infested with maggots and stank.

The Torah reports that right after the drowning of the Egyptians, the people "believed [i.e., trusted] in the Lord and Moses, His servant" (Exodus 14.31). Now, a month later, they disregard Moses's instructions out of a lack of faith in him. The point is made again and again: A faith based on miracles will quickly fade, dependent on the next miracle. Such an attitude cannot even be called faith.

16.20 (cont.) And Moses was angry with them.

Moses will become angry with his people often in the Torah; usually appropriately, sometimes not. It is another example of the Torah showing the flaws of either its greatest hero or of the Jews—and an important argument for believing in the veracity of the Torah.

16.21 So they gathered it every morning, each as much as he needed to eat; for when the sun grew hot, it would melt.

16.22 On the sixth day they gathered double the amount of food, two *omers* for each; and when all the chieftains of the community came and told Moses,

16.23 he said to them, "This is what the Lord meant: Tomorrow is a day of rest, a holy sabbath of the Lord. Bake what you would bake and boil what you would boil; and all that is left put aside to be kept until morning."

16.24 So they put it aside until morning, as Moses had ordered; and it did not turn foul, and there were no maggots in it.

16.25 Then Moses said, "Eat it today, for today is a sabbath of the Lord; you will not find it today on the plain.

Here is the establishment of the Shabbat (Sabbath) by God—a holy day each week, set apart from the other days for rest and spiritual rejuvenation. God had not yet given the Ten Commandments, in which He will command the Israelites to observe the Shabbat. God's provision of manna for Shabbat on the day before—the only day of the week on which the excess food provision they gathered wouldn't spoil—caused the Israelites to instantly regard the Shabbat as a day distinct from other days of the week.

16.26 Six days you shall gather it; on the seventh day, the sabbath, there will be none."

One of the miraculous aspects of the manna is it does not conform to the natural order. Unlike the sun, for example, which rises every morning, the manna falls only six days out of seven.

16.27 Yet some of the people went out on the seventh day to gather, but they found nothing.

16.28 And the Lord said to Moses, "How long will you men refuse to obey My commandments and My teachings?

The Torah has specified very few commandments and teachings at this point. Examples would include circumcision (Genesis 17:12-14), Passover and its rituals (Exodus 12:14 and 17-20), and the Sabbath in the preceding verses.

But the larger point here is despite all God has done for them in the last few months—providing for them and saving them with one miracle after another—they still didn't follow God's ways.

16.29 Mark that the Lord has given you the sabbath; therefore He gives you two days' food on the sixth day. Let everyone remain where he is: let no one leave his place on the seventh day."

By emphasizing God is giving "you two days' food on the sixth day," this was likely and specifically a prohibition on the Israelites going out and seeking manna on the Shabbat.

16.30 So the people remained inactive on the seventh day.

Finally the people obey God's commandment.

16.31 The house of Israel named it manna; it was like coriander seed, white, and it tasted like wafers in honey.

This description of the manna is included in the Torah for the sake of later generations of readers who would not have any idea what manna was or how it tasted.

16.32 Moses said, "This is what the Lord has commanded: Let one *omer* of it be kept throughout the ages, in order that they may see the bread that I fed you in the wilderness when I brought you out from the land of Egypt."

16.33 And Moses said to Aaron, "Take a jar, put one *omer* of manna in it, and place it before the Lord, to be kept throughout the ages."

Again, memory is the key to gratitude. The Jews are to preserve an *omer* of manna as a reminder of the manna, one of God's early acts of kindness to them.

It was a major challenge to convert the slaves of Pharaoh—or any other people then or later— into ethical monotheists.

16.34 As the Lord had commanded Moses, Aaron placed it before the Pact, to be kept.

As has been noted, the Torah is not always written in chronological order, and this is another example. "The Pact" refers to the Ark in which the Ten Commandments were kept, yet the giving of the Ten Commandments isn't described until chapter 20.

16.35 And the Israelites ate manna forty years, until they came to a settled land; they ate the manna until they came to the border of the land of Canaan.

For forty years, God nursed the Israelite nation like a mother would an infant, providing the Israelites' food and water, hoping they would eventually mature as a people. Forty years is a long weaning period, but it was a major challenge to convert the slaves of Pharaoh—or their children, or any other people then or later—into ethical monotheists.

The daily portion of manna continued until after the death of Moses, and only stopped during the time of Moses's successor, Joshua (Joshua 5:12).

16.36 The *omer* is a tenth of an *ephah*.

An *ephah* equals about thirty-five liters.

CHAPTER 17

17.1 From the wilderness of Sin the whole Israelite community continued by stages as the Lord would command. They encamped at Rephidim, and there was no water for the people to drink.

This is the third of four crises to befall the Israelites between their departure from Egypt and arrival at Sinai.

THE ISRAELITES DO NOT SEEM TO DIFFERENTIATE BETWEEN GOD AND MOSES

17.2 The people quarreled with Moses. "Give us water to drink," they said; and Moses replied to them, "Why do you quarrel with me? Why do you try the Lord?"

The Israelites do not seem to differentiate between God and Moses; they demand that Moses, not God, provide them with water. This is understandable given how visible Moses was as opposed to the invisible God, given the miracles God performed through him, and given their previous life in a society in which the Pharaoh was a man-god.

In his responses, Moses made the differentiation clear and argued against their testing a demonstrably trustworthy God:

a) "Why do you quarrel with me?" I, Moses, am not the source of the water.

b) "Why do you try (literally, "test") the Lord?" After all God has done for you, why do you continue to test Him?

17.3 But the people thirsted there for water; and the people grumbled against Moses and said, "Why did you bring us up from Egypt, to kill us and our children and livestock with thirst?"

Again, the Israelites seem to attribute miracles—this time the Exodus itself—to Moses. This confusion of Moses with God will loom as a major theme in the Torah. It is ultimately, as I will show, the reason Moses is not allowed to enter the Promised Land.

The Israelites do not seem to differentiate between God and Moses. This will have fateful consequences for Moses.

We have here more of the exaggerations and distortions that so often characterize chronic malcontents and complainers. Did these people really believe Moses took them out of Egypt to kill them? Of course not. But when complainers get angry they often exercise no restraint over their tongues and say whatever mean-spirited thoughts come into their heads.

EVEN THE MOST DEVOUT HAVE DOUBTS ABOUT GOD INTERVENING ON THEIR BEHALF

17.4 Moses cried out to the Lord, saying, "What shall I do with this people? Before long they will be stoning me!"

Moses seems to be genuinely afraid of the people. The throwing of rocks has apparently characterized Middle Eastern political protests from time immemorial.

Moses, too, may be expressing a lack, or at least a lapse, of trust in God. Does he really think God will allow him to be killed?

This point is made not to cast blame on Moses, a true giant among men, but only to illustrate how normal it is for anyone—even Moses, for whom God has already done so much—to have doubts about whether God will again intervene on his behalf.

17.5 Then the Lord said to Moses, "Pass before the people;

In Rashi's view, God is annoyed with Moses for suggesting the Israelites are threatening his life. "Why have you uttered slander against My children?" Rashi imagines God saying. God, therefore, tells Moses to walk in front of the people so he will realize they are not going to stone him after all.

17.5 (cont.) take with you some of the elders of Israel, and take along the rod with which you struck the Nile, and set out.

> Previously, Moses used this rod to turn the Nile to blood. God wants the people to realize He can do whatever He wants with Moses's rod. Whereas it once functioned to deprive the Egyptians of drinking water (by turning the Nile into blood), it will now serve to provide water for the Israelites (Sarna).

17.6 I will be standing there before you on the rock at Horeb. Strike the rock and water will issue from it, and the people will drink." And Moses did so in the sight of the elders of Israel.

We Should Relate to God as Adults Relate to Parents— Not as Children Do

17.7 The place was named Massah and Meribah, because the Israelites quarreled and because they tried the Lord, saying, "Is the Lord present among us or not?"

> The Hebrew words *Massah* and *Meribah* mean "test" and "quarrel."
>
> The people defined whether or not God was in their presence by whether or not they got what they needed. Like children, the Israelites were only able to trust in God when He was directly and obviously providing for their welfare. That is an understandable view of God for the first generation of monotheists, who, moreover, were led out into the wilderness with no way to supply their own basic needs. But we who live thousands of years later should no longer be like children in our attitudes toward God. We should relate to God as adults; and just as adults can no longer rely on their parents to provide for their every need, religious people should not rely on God to provide for their every need.
>
> God provided for all the needs of the people in the desert because the people of Israel were still in their infancy, and because they were unable in their circumstances to provide for themselves.
>
> According to developmental psychology, we need our parents to take care of us when we are young in order to develop the emotional maturity sufficient to take care of ourselves as adults. Jews (and all others who believe in God) should do the same. So long as we remember the Exodus and God's caring for

the Israelites in the desert, we should develop the emotional and theological maturity not to demand ongoing divine intervention—just as mature adults do not demand this of their parents—and to know God exists and loves us even when we do not perceive or receive direct intervention. There is no other choice. If faith in God and leading a religious life were dependent on constant and obvious divine intervention on our behalf, no one would believe in God.

17.8 Amalek came and fought with Israel at Rephidim.

The sudden, unprovoked aggression of the nation of Amalek is the fourth crisis to befall the Israelites in their journey from Egypt to Sinai.

17.9 Moses said to Joshua, "Pick some men for us, and go out and do battle with Amalek. Tomorrow I will station myself on the top of the hill, with the rod of God in my hand."

17.10 Joshua did as Moses told him and fought with Amalek, while Moses, Aaron, and Hur went up to the top of the hill.

17.11 Then, whenever Moses held up his hand, Israel prevailed; but whenever he let down his hand, Amalek prevailed.

17.12 But Moses' hands grew heavy; so they took a stone and put it under him and he sat on it, while Aaron and Hur, one on each side, supported his hands; thus his hands remained steady until the sun set.

Obviously, connecting Israel's fortunes in the battle to whether or not Moses's hands were upraised suggests this can only be explained as yet another divine miracle. A less miraculous interpretation is offered by the Talmud: "Did the hands of Moses make or break [the course of the war]? Rather, the text implies that whenever the Israelites looked up and dedicated their hearts to their Father in heaven, they prevailed, but otherwise they fell."[1]

17.13 And Joshua overwhelmed the people of Amalek with the sword.

17.14 Then the Lord said to Moses, "Inscribe this in a document as a reminder, and read it aloud to Joshua: I will utterly blot out the memory of Amalek from under heaven!"

This verse seems to contain a contradiction: We are supposed to remember the nation of Amalek, yet God will blot out Amalek's memory. Which is it?

Perhaps the point is that we are to remember great evil, but ideally the perpetrators of the evil are forgotten. Those who do evil—from the mass murderers in our societies to the monsters of genocide—all want to make a name for themselves. They should not be rewarded in this way (perhaps that is why the Torah leaves out the name of the Pharaoh who ordered the murder of the Israelite babies in order to ensure his acts are remembered, but not his name).

If faith in God were dependent on constant and obvious divine intervention on our behalf, no one would believe in God.

To this day, when Jews speak of a particularly evil figure—in the modern period, generally Hitler—they will often follow the mention of the person's name with the words, "May his name and memory be blotted out" (*ye-mach she-mo ve-zichrono*).

As to the reason for the particular animosity against Amalek, see the commentary on Deuteronomy 25:17–18.

17.15 And Moses built an altar and named it Adonai-nissi.

"Nissi" means my *nes*, which in biblical Hebrew means a banner or a standard. So the name of the altar is "YHVH is my banner."

17.16 He said, "It means, 'Hand upon the throne of the Lord!' The Lord will be at war with Amalek throughout the ages."

CHAPTER

18

ANOTHER NON-JEWISH HERO IN THE TORAH

18.1 Jethro priest of Midian,

In order to read through the Torah in its entirety in synagogue each year, Jews long ago divided the Torah into weekly portions. Each portion is named for the first major word appearing in the portion. The first major word in this verse is Jethro, so Jethro is the name of this portion.

Jethro is one of three portions in the Torah named for non-Jews (or more precisely, non-Israelites); the two others are *Noah* and *Balak*. Both Noah and Jethro are outstanding people: Noah was renowned for his righteousness, and Jethro for his wisdom. Balak was the villainous king of Moab. The same number of Torah portions are named for Jews: Sarah, Korach, and Pinchas. Sarah is the first matriarch, Korach was a malevolent demagogue, and Pinchas was a zealous defender of the faith, but not one to be emulated (see commentary on Numbers 25:6-8).

This distribution of names underscores yet again the Torah is not a provincial document concerned only with Jews; its concern is all humanity, and its primary concern is goodness. That's why it doesn't begin with Jews, but with the creation of the world. So, too, although the Jews are the Chosen People, they are never accorded special rights; on the contrary, they are held to higher standards than other people, and punished accordingly. As the Prophet Amos cites God saying to the Jews: "You alone have I singled out of all the families of the earth; that is why I will call you to account for all your iniquities" (Amos

3:2). And, as noted previously, the Torah often depicts Jews acting badly, and non-Jews as moral heroes. In this portion, for instance, Jethro is the hero, even though he is a Midianite (i.e., pagan) priest.

In keeping with the Torah's universal and moral concerns, the medieval Jewish commentator Radak made a powerful point: The story of Jethro follows right after the story of Amalek lest any Jew conclude that all non-Jews are enemies of the Jewish people. Similarly, Yad Vashem, the museum in Israel that documents the Holocaust, has an extensive forest of trees planted to honor non-Jews who risked their lives to save Jews during the Holocaust, those known as "The Righteous Among the Nations." This grove plays a comparable role to the placement of the Jethro story here, a reminder that even during the Holocaust, not all non-Jewish Europeans were Jew-haters.

> *Perhaps the story of Jethro follows right after the story of Amalek lest any Jew conclude that all non-Jews are enemies of the Jewish people.*

The Torah mentions Jethro is a Midianite priest completely matter-of-factly. He is not only a non-Jew, but a priest who serves what the Torah regards as false gods. But the Torah mentions him without even a hint of opprobrium. What matters is he is a good man, he is Moses's father-in-law, and he does not deny the God of the Jews (he even believes, as we shall see, in the supremacy of God while still serving Midianite gods).

Neither the Torah nor later Judaism demand everyone in the world be Jewish. God wants, more than anything, that people be good. And the best way to achieve that end is to have the world believe in God and His moral law, specifically the Ten Commandments or the ancient Talmudic formulation "the Seven Noahide Laws," seven basic moral laws the Rabbis deduced from Genesis ("Noahide" refers to "the sons of Noah"—meaning all humanity).

THE TORAH REPEATEDLY IDENTIFIES JETHRO—A MIDIANITE PRIEST—AS "MOSES'S FATHER-IN-LAW"

18.1 (cont.) Moses's father-in-law,

Importantly, Jethro is *always* described as Moses's father-in-law. Such a repetition of a person's relationship to another is unique in the Torah. One obvious reason is his significance (at least at this point in the story) emanates from his relationship to Moses. But whatever the reason, it is noteworthy the Torah constantly emphasizes Jethro's familial relationship to Moses. It is noteworthy because later Jewish law, which, due to its strong opposition to intermarriage (primarily to prevent an assimilation that could lead to the disappearance of the small Jewish people), would certainly not go out of its way to mention a familial connection between a Jew and a non-Jew related through marriage.

18.1 (cont.) Heard all that God had done for Moses and for Israel His people, how the Lord had brought Israel out from Egypt.

The Hebrew is ambiguous here. It is not clear whether the Israelites are being described as God's people or as Moses's people. The truth is both would be accurate in this context, but it is uniformly understood in Jewish sources as meaning God's people (hence the capitalized "H" in the word "His").

18.2 So Jethro, Moses' father-in-law, took Zipporah, Moses' wife, after she had been sent home,

Like Jethro, Zipporah is always identified in terms of her relationship to Moses. (And she, too, was not born a Jew, though it is generally assumed she converted in some way or another—evidence for which is suggested by her punctiliousness about circumcising their son.)

This verse suggests Moses had earlier sent his wife and children back to Midian so his father-in-law could take care of them while Moses was dealing with Pharaoh and leading the Israelites out of Egypt. Moses's considerable responsibilities and consequent absence from his family must have taken a toll on him and his family. Throughout history, great missions undertaken by individuals have often come at the expense of the person's family life. For example, the Torah strongly implies Abraham and his wife Sarah permanently separated after Abraham nearly sacrificed their son Isaac (see comment on Genesis 22:19); and the Torah never makes any reference to what became of Moses's two sons (see commentary to Exodus 6:23).

18.3 and her two sons—of whom one was named Gershom, that is to say, "I have been a stranger in a foreign land";

18.4 and the other was named Eliezer, meaning, "The God of my father was my help, and He delivered me from the sword of Pharaoh."

Baruch Hashem ("Blessed be the Lord") is said three times in the Torah, in each case by a non-Jew.

Moses's second son's name refers to the time when Pharaoh wanted to kill Moses for killing the Egyptian overseer (see 2:15). Moses fled to Midian, where God protected him from Pharaoh's wrath (4:19), and where he married Zipporah. Gershom's birth was recorded in Exodus 2:22, while Eliezer is mentioned here for the first time.

18.5 Jethro, Moses' father-in-law, brought Moses' sons and wife to him in the wilderness, where he was encamped at the mountain of God.

This is Sinai, where the Israelites will receive the Ten Commandments.

18.6 He sent word to Moses, "I, your father-in-law Jethro, am coming to you, with your wife and her two sons."

Jethro refers to Gershom and Eliezer as Zipporah's two sons rather than as "your [Moses's and Zipporah's] two sons." It seems an odd way to describe a man's children. Perhaps in that culture at that time this was a common way for a father to refer to the children of his daughter, or perhaps Jethro intended to convey some message. We cannot know.

18.7 Moses went out to meet his father-in-law; he bowed low and kissed him; each asked after the other's welfare, and they went into the tent.

18.8 Moses then recounted to his father-in-law everything that the Lord had done to Pharaoh and to the Egyptians for Israel's sake, all the hardships that had befallen them on the way, and how the Lord had delivered them.

It must also have been a great pleasure for Moses, as it is for any leader, to have someone with whom he could talk freely and unselfconsciously.

18.9 And Jethro rejoiced over all the kindness that the Lord had shown Israel when He delivered them from the Egyptians.

THE ORIGINS OF THE EXPRESSION *BARUCH HASHEM* ("BLESSED BE THE LORD")

18.10 "Blessed be the Lord," Jethro said,

In Hebrew, the words for "Blessed be the Lord" are *Baruch Hashem*, which to this day remains one of the most commonly used expressions among religious Jews. Religious Jews almost always answer the question "How are you?" with "*Baruch Hashem*." The phrase has come to mean God is deserving of blessing regardless of one's situation at any given moment.

Few Jews realize, however, it was a Midianite priest who most famously uttered these traditional words of praise for God. In fact, the term *Baruch Hashem* is said three times in the Torah, and, remarkably, always by a non-Jew—by Jethro in this verse, by Noah (Genesis 9:26), and by Abraham's servant, presumably Eliezer (Genesis 24:27).

Rabbi J. J. Schacter notes what is also striking is that while people normally use the expression "Blessed be the Lord" to refer to God's treatment of them, Jethro expresses his gratitude to God for God's kind treatment of others, in this case Moses and the Israelites.

ON CARING ABOUT LOVED ONES BEFORE STRANGERS

18.10 (cont.) "who delivered you from the Egyptians and from Pharaoh, and who delivered the people from under the hand of the Egyptians.

Jethro's first concern is for his son-in-law. He praises God for saving Moses, and then for saving the people. Jethro's statement is a reminder that though it is not appropriate to care only about our loved ones, it is appropriate to care about our loved ones first. Anyone who does not feel the suffering or death of a loved one more acutely than the suffering or death of a stranger is not emotionally normal. But anyone who feels nothing about the suffering or death of strangers is not a mensch (i.e., is not a good person).

NOT BY MIGHT: GOD IS NOT GOD BECAUSE HE WINS BATTLES

18.11 Now I know that the Lord is greater than all gods,

Jethro believes in God because of God's show of force against Egypt. His theology would seem to square with the prevailing attitude at that time—gods, like nature, are governed by the law of survival of the fittest. Whichever god proves strongest is the god that commands belief (or at least, the most belief).

The Bible, in contrast, holds that God is not God because He wins battles, but because of His superior morality and the power of His spirit. As the Hebrew prophet famously expressed it: "Not by might and not by power, but by My spirit, says the Lord" (Zechariah 4:6).

Thus, many centuries later when the Temple in Jerusalem was destroyed and the Jews taken into captivity and dispersed by the Babylonian King Nebuchadnezzar, the Jews did not presume the Babylonian gods were stronger than the God of Israel, but that the God of Israel sent Nebuchadnezzar to punish the Israelites for their sinfulness. The Jewish belief, rooted in the Torah, was that God was God whether the Jews won or lost any given war. That is a major reason Judaism survived, while all the other religions of antiquity (whose adherents, unlike Jews, adopted the religion of their conquerors) did not.

8.11 (cont.) yes, by the result of their very schemes against [the people]."

According to Onkelos, the late first-century to early second-century translator-commentator, Jethro, in referring to the Egyptians' "schemes," is saying he believes God is greater than the Egyptian gods because God was able to use the schemes employed by the Egyptians to save His people. For example, the

Egyptians drowned newly born Israelite males in the Nile—and God, in turn, drowned the pursuing Egyptian troops.

18.12 And Jethro, Moses' father-in-law, brought a burnt offering and sacrifices for God; and Aaron came with all the elders of Israel to partake of the meal before God with Moses' father-in-law.

> The Torah here uses the universal name for God, *Elohim*. The use of this name probably signifies that although Jethro is bringing an offering to the one God, he is not relating to God as if he were a believing Israelite (in which case, the Torah would most likely have used the name YHVH). He never became an Israelite, but remained a Midianite priest, albeit one who recognized the universal God of the Israelites. To repeat (because of the importance of this point), that is what the Torah and Judaism want of non-Jews—to adopt the God and moral values of the Torah, but not necessarily to become Jews (though converts are welcomed and loved).

18.13 Next day, Moses sat as magistrate among the people, while the people stood about Moses from morning until evening.

18.14 But when Moses's father-in-law saw how much he had to do for the people, he said, "What is this thing that you are doing to the people? Why do you act alone, while all the people stand about you from morning until evening?"

18.15 Moses replied to his father-in-law, "It is because the people come to me to inquire of God.

18.16 When they have a dispute, it comes before me, and I decide between one person and another, and I make known the laws and teachings of God."

> Most of God's laws and teachings were not known until after the people received the Ten Commandments and whatever else God revealed to Moses at Sinai. It is therefore likely this story actually takes place after the revelation at Sinai. Even the traditional commentators note the Torah does not always unfold in chronological order. As the Talmud stated, *ain mukdam u'mi'uchar baTorah*—"There is no early or late in the Torah."[1]

Moses's statement, "I make known the laws and teachings of God," makes clear he recognizes he is merely the conduit of God's laws and teachings, and not their author.

AN EXAMPLE OF THE ANTIQUITY AND HISTORICITY OF THE TORAH NARRATIVE

18.17 But Moses' father-in-law said to him, "The thing you are doing is not right;

18.18 you will surely wear yourself out, and these people as well. For the task is too heavy for you; you cannot do it alone.

18.19 Now listen to me. I will give you counsel, and God be with you! You represent the people before God: you bring the disputes before God,

Jethro has observed the Israelite camp from the perspective of an outsider, and he sees the procedure employed by Moses in judging the people is exhausting and inefficient (Sarna).

The Torah ascribes the Israelite judicial system to the initiative and advice of a Midianite priest. This is truly remarkable given the hostility later characterizing the relationship between the Midianites and the Israelites (see, for example, Numbers 25 and Judges 6:1-6).

A characteristic that is valued perhaps more than any other in our time is absent from the list of a leader's necessary qualities—compassion.

It is highly unlikely later generations of Israelites would have wanted to give one of their worst enemies credit for developing this central Israelite institution. That the Torah does so serves as another indication the Torah was written in ancient times, contemporaneous or virtually contemporaneous with the events it chronicles.

It thereby also challenges the notion, almost universally accepted in the academic world, that the Torah consists of four documents (the Documentary Hypothesis) put together many centuries later by an editor or editors (known as the Redactor). Why would a later Jewish editor choose to keep in a story depicting a Midianite as so influential in forming Jewish law (and setting down the characteristics required of judges; see verse 21)—and in this significant way, the most influential man after Moses himself? (This story also conveys the message that even if a group, in this case, the Midianites, subsequently becomes your enemy, you must remember there were or are some very righteous people in that group, and people from whom you can learn.)

18.20 and enjoin upon them the laws and the teachings, and make known to them the way they are to go and the practices they are to follow.

18.21 You shall also seek out from among all the people capable men who fear God, trustworthy men who spurn ill-gotten gain. Set these over them as chiefs of thousands, hundreds, fifties, and tens, and

The Hebrew phrase *anshei chayil*, translated here "capable men," literally means "men of valor," and connotes not just capability but also courage and strength.

The characteristics in this verse describe the ideal characteristics of good leaders and judges:

1) "Strong men" (translated here, I believe less accurately, as "capable men")
2) "Fearing God" (and therefore not fearing other men)
3) "Men of truth"
4) "Hating ill-gotten gain" (i.e., incorruptible)

It is worth noting that a characteristic valued perhaps more than any other in our time is absent—compassion. It is not mentioned for good reason. Although compassion is a beautiful human trait and we need to be most compassionate in our personal lives, judges (and other leaders) cannot be guided solely by compassion because compassion often subverts justice. If a poor man and a rich man wind up in a dispute, a judge who acts compassionately by ruling in the poor man's favor despite evidence showing the rich man is in the right has subverted justice. That is why the Torah expressly prohibits judges from favoring the poor in judgment (and, of course, the rich as well—see Leviticus 19:15).

18.22 let them judge the people at all times. Have them bring every major dispute to you, but let them decide every minor dispute themselves. Make it easier for yourself by letting them share the burden with you.

18.23 If you do this—and God so commands you—you will be able to bear up; and all these people too will go home unwearied."

ESSAY: HOW TO RESPOND TO ADVICE AND CRITICISM

18.24 Moses heeded his father-in-law and did just as he had said.

Moses is apparently not the slightest bit resentful of, or even annoyed with, his father-in-law. On the contrary, he appreciates Jethro's criticism and advice, and immediately acts on his father-in-law's recommendations. This is the intelligent and mature way to respond to criticism and advice, but it is far from common. People are frequently offended when they receive advice, let alone criticism. This is especially true, as in this instance, when the advice and criticism seem to be unsolicited.

So, then, let's answer this question first: When receiving advice or criticism, how does one know when to be offended and when to be thankful?

One way is to assess the intentions of the person giving the advice and criticism. Does the person have your best interests in mind or is he/she giving the advice or criticism to hurt you in some way?

This, in turn, raises a second question: How do you assess the advice-giver's intentions? There is no perfect answer. Intentions—even our own—are not always clearly discernible. But we can usually arrive at a correct answer by pondering these questions: Is this a good and honorable person? How well do I know this person? Does he/she have a history of having my best interests in mind?

And what do we do when we do not know the motives of the advice/criticism giver?

The ideal answer is to focus not on the person, but solely on the criticism or advice: Does it seem valid? Even a person who does not have our best interests in mind can accurately critique a situation and give valid advice and criticism. As a public person who has often taken strong positions, I have received a great deal of criticism from people who wish me ill. I know they wish me ill because they have actually said so (usually in anonymous correspondence). Yet, I have trained myself to read the criticisms while ignoring the animosity. And on occasion the criticism, even when accompanied by expletives, was something I could learn from.

Moses took the criticism and advice from his father-in-law—not someone from whom many people easily take advice or criticism—and acted upon everything Jethro suggested. Moses obviously trusted him. But, perhaps even more importantly, Moses rationally concluded the criticism and advice were valid.

While Moses could take criticism and advice from Jethro because he respected and trusted him, there was an even more important reason he could do so: Moses cared more about the welfare of the Israelite people than he did about his ego. This is one of the reasons the Torah could write that Moses was the most humble man on earth (Numbers 12:3—see the commentary there on how, if, as tradition holds, Moses wrote the Torah, he could write such a verse.)

When it comes to national and rational leadership, it is nothing less than catastrophic to have a leader who not only does not listen to criticism, but who forbids and punishes it. Such is the case with every tyrant.

Take, for example, Mao Zedong, the communist dictator of China from communist China's founding in 1947 until his death in 1976—a tyrant responsible for the death of more innocent people than any person in recorded history.

During the late 1950s, there were widespread food shortages in China. Mao insisted that no such shortages existed, claiming rich peasants who refused to hand over their grain were maliciously spreading those reports. In truth, the 1959 grain harvest was at least thirty million tons less than the preceding year's, but Chinese Communist officials, knowing how Mao would react to news that would reflect poorly on his decisions, instead issued a report claiming large increases.

Finally, one courageous man, Peng Dehuai, the minister of defense, sent Mao accurate reports about widespread starvation. He even wrote a personal letter to Mao, amplifying on his reports about the effects of Mao's "Great Leap Forward." Mao ignored the criticism, and denounced Peng as "an anti-Party element." Peng was placed under house arrest, and forced to write debasing "self-criticism." Several years later, Mao had Peng tortured and murdered.

> *"If no one feels comfortable criticizing you, the likelihood that you will be better tomorrow is most probably nonexistent."*
> —Joseph Telushkin

Just as Peng predicted, scores of millions of Chinese died of government-induced starvation. Philosopher and historian Jonathan Glover observed: "Mao's policies needed corrective feedback, but most people were too frightened to give it."

The Hasidic Rabbi Nachman of Bratslav (1772–1810) taught, "If you are not going to be better tomorrow than you were today, then what need do you have for tomorrow?" To which Telushkin has added: "And if no one feels comfortable criticizing you, the likelihood that you will be better tomorrow is most probably nonexistent."

18.25 Moses chose capable men out of all Israel, and appointed them heads over the people—chiefs of thousands, hundreds, fifties, and tens;

The Torah uses military terminology to describe these judicial positions, suggesting the Israelites are going to be a nation ruled by law in much the same way other nations are ruled by generals, sergeants, and captains in the military.

18.26 and they judged the people at all times: the difficult matters they would bring to Moses, and all the minor matters they would decide themselves.

18.27 Then Moses bade his father-in-law farewell, and he went his way to his own land.

CHAPTER

19

19.1 On the third new moon after the Israelites had gone forth from the land of Egypt, on that very day, they entered the wilderness of Sinai.

19.2 Having journeyed from Rephidim, they entered the wilderness of Sinai and encamped in the wilderness. Israel encamped there in front of the mountain,

19.3 and Moses went up to God. The Lord called to him from the mountain, saying, "Thus shall you say to the house of Jacob and declare to the children of Israel:

THE TWO TYPES OF FAITH—IN GOD'S EXISTENCE
AND IN GOD'S GOODNESS

19.4 'You have seen what I did to the Egyptians, how I bore you on eagles' wings

In alluding to the Ten Plagues, the splitting of the sea, and to His protection of the Israelites, God is reminding the people of what He has done for them. This is a prelude to a demand He will now make of them.

This is a rare instance in the Torah in which God speaks in poetic language. According to Rashi, God compares Himself to the eagle that carries its young on its wings because other birds put their young between their feet—they are afraid of birds that can fly above them and snatch their young. But the eagle knows no other bird can fly higher and it can protect its young by putting them on its wings. This image expresses God's protective love for His people.

The two parts of this verse—"what I did to the Egyptians" and "how I bore you on eagle's wings"—reflect the duality of faith in God. By seeing what God did to the Egyptians, the Israelites "saw" God's existence in action; by hearing God carries them on eagles' wings, they hear of God's love. Belief in God means more than believing God exists; it also means believing God cares about us. After all, if God exists but doesn't care about us, what difference does it make to us whether God exists? For all intents and purposes, there is no difference between atheism and the existence of a God who doesn't care about us.

> *It is less rational to believe there is no Creator than it is to believe creation created itself.*

For many people, however, the first belief, that God exists, is much easier to affirm than the second. Many of us find God's existence to be rationally self-evident. We find it more rational to believe there is a Creator than to believe creation created itself; more rational to infer a Designer than no Designer when we look at the world with all its design. But given all the tragedy and unjust suffering in the world, the belief that God cares for us is not as rationally compelling. Unlike belief in God's existence, belief in God's goodness and concern for each human life usually involves what the Danish theologian Søren Kierkegaard called a "leap of faith."

I understand the need for that leap of faith, but I contend it is more rational to assume God cares about His creation than to believe He doesn't. *Why would an uncaring Creator create a caring being?* But in any event, it is one of the great achievements of the Torah that it identifies the Creator with the moral and the good.

19.4 (cont.) and brought you to Me.

God says He brought the people "to Me," not as one might suppose, "out of Egypt" or "out of bondage." The reason is the primary purpose of the Exodus was more than rescuing a people from bondage; it was to bring the Israelites to God and His moral law. This is in line with God's repeated instruction to Moses to tell Pharaoh, "Let My people go that they may worship Me" (see, for example, Exodus 9:1). The point is *while liberty is necessary, it is not sufficient for a good life*. As the brilliant French observer of early American democracy, Alexis de Tocqueville (*Democracy In America*), wrote, "Whoever seeks in liberty anything other than liberty itself is born for servitude."[1] In other words, while liberty is magnificent, the only thing liberty guarantees is liberty, not goodness, not morality, not integrity, etc. Liberty must be accompanied by higher values, because liberty alone will lead to moral chaos, and ultimately, de Tocqueville prophesizes, servitude.

IS GOD'S LOVE UNCONDITIONAL?

19.5 Now then, if you will obey Me faithfully and keep My covenant, you shall be My treasured possession

God is establishing with the Israelites the terms by which He will be their God and they will be His people.

The "if" in this verse is often overlooked, yet it is of immense significance. It means Israel's being God's "treasured possession" is conditional: Only if the Jews obey God's laws will they be a treasure to God.

Now, the Prophet Hosea teaches later in the Bible that God will always be prepared to take back a penitent Israel. But that does not contradict God's admonition here. (Thus, in Exodus 32, when the people break God's covenant and worship a golden calf, God's first instinct is to destroy them and make a great nation for Moses with another people—verses 9-10.)

There are many people who find the notion of being loved conditionally upsetting and therefore unacceptable. We live in an age of belief in "unconditional love," in which the idea that anyone, even God's people, would have to continually earn God's esteem and affection violates many people's desire to believe in unconditional love and acceptance. But the Bible—and the God of the Bible—is interested first and foremost in people behaving lovingly, decently, justly, and mercifully: "He has told you, O Man, what is good and what the

Lord demands of you: Just to act justly, love mercy, and walk humbly with your God" (Micah 6:8). That's why even the special status of God's Chosen People as His treasured people is conditional upon their living God-centered, moral lives.

Furthermore, the good behavior God demands from us is rendered much less likely when people think there is literally nothing they could do, no matter how heinous, that will stop them from being treasured or loved. Precisely because God is a loving God, He will show His displeasure toward those who engage in evil. It is not loving to love mass murderers and others who dedicate their lives to cruelty. The notion that God loves people no matter how cruelly they act toward other human beings—who are, let us remember, God's other children—is neither loving nor moral. The Torah links God's love—as it does everything else—to morality.

This is a lesson that applies equally to human love. If we love those who do extraordinary evil as much as we love those who are extraordinarily good to people, we are saying love is unrelated to morality. And in that case, *love ends up being the one thing we decouple from good and evil.*

"CHOSEN" DOES NOT MEAN SUPERIOR

The verse says, "you shall be My treasured possession among the peoples."

The Jews are not chosen to be God's treasure because they are inherently superior to other nations. The Hebrew Bible's repeated critical portrayal of the Israelites and of Jews later should make that abundantly clear. Israel is chosen to spread knowledge of God and His moral law to all of humanity.

Nor do the Jews become inherently superior because they are chosen. To the extent Jews have ever lived more moral lives than their neighbors (and in many societies they did) or had a disproportionate impact on humanity (which they have), it is entirely due to the impact of the Torah on them. And to the extent any other people wish to lead good lives and positively impact the world, they, too, would do well to follow the Torah.

GOD CHOOSES WHOM HE CHOOSES

19.5 (cont.) Indeed, all the earth is Mine,

People may question why God chose the Jews from all other people. One answer is God declares the world belongs to Him, and He can do whatever He wants with it. We don't know why God chose Abraham, of all the people then living, to be the father of a nation assigned the special burden of acting as His emissary to humanity. But we can be fairly certain, given the imperfect nature of every human being, we wouldn't understand why any particular person was chosen, no matter who it was.

This idea was put forth as directly as possible by a Roman Catholic priest on a radio show I moderated for many years. The show, "Religion on the Line," featured a Protestant minister, a Catholic priest, and a rabbi; there were different ones each week. On one occasion, a listener called in to berate the rabbi on the panel over the Jews' belief in being the Chosen People.

The caller charged that Chosenness is a chauvinistic and dangerous belief, and Jews should drop it. The rabbi, obviously somewhat uncomfortable with the doctrine, was unable to effectively respond to the caller. Finally, the Catholic priest asked if he might respond to the caller, and said: "Sir, this is the Roman Catholic priest. God chose the Jews. Get a life."

19.6 but you shall be to Me a kingdom of priests

The task of a priest is to minister to individuals and bring them closer to God. The task of the Jewish people is to minister to humanity and bring as much of it as possible closer to God.

THE MEANING OF THE WORD "HOLY"

19.6 (cont.) and a holy nation.'

The Hebrew word for holy, *kadosh*, also means "separate" or "distinct." In the time of the Torah, when the Jews were surrounded by pagan nations, it was particularly important to remain separate in order to preserve their distinct religious/moral identity. This has been the view of believing Jews ever since.

Therein lies a tension between the command to be a holy nation and the fulfillment of the purpose of Chosenness. There is no question maintaining holiness demands separation. But too much separation makes the Jews' task of spreading belief in the God of the Torah and obedience to God's will as expressed in the Ten Commandments (or the Seven Noahide Laws) almost impossible. It is difficult to influence people if you have virtually no contact with them.

> The notion that God loves people no matter how cruelly they act toward other human beings—who are, after all, God's children—is neither loving nor moral. The Torah links God's love—as it does everything else—to morality.

The call to holiness has additional significance. Throughout the world, virtually throughout history, human beings have generally been confined to the social and/or economic class into which they were born; the ideal of social mobility was utterly foreign to ancient, and virtually all other, societies. Certainly, that was the case in the Egyptian society from which the Israelites were just freed. Now God offers a very different vision for His people and ultimately for all humanity: we can elevate our lives by our own free will.

This option of God calling men to be holy was another world-changing innovation of the Torah. In the words of Walter Kaufmann, the Princeton philosopher and self-described heretic: "Every man [not just one class of people] is called upon to make something of himself. *Perhaps this was the most revolutionary idea of world history*" (emphasis added). In those countries in which the Hebrew Bible has made an impact, Kauffman continued, "this idea may appear to be a commonplace..." but everywhere else, "one can appreciate the revolutionary impact of these words."[2]

19.6 (cont.) These are the words that you shall speak to the children of Israel."

19.7 Moses came and summoned the elders of the people and put before them all that the Lord had commanded him.

19.8 All the people answered as one, saying, "All that the Lord has spoken we will do!" And Moses brought back the people's words to the Lord.

> Of course, God already knows what the people have said to Moses, since God is all-knowing. Nevertheless, Moses relates the people's words to God. Given all the complaints earlier offered by the Israelites, it must have felt good to Moses to be able to bring such a report to God.

19.9 And the Lord said to Moses, "I will come to you in a thick cloud,

> God appears in a thick cloud because He can never be seen directly (see, for example, Exodus 33:20).

19.9 (cont.) in order that the people may hear when I speak with you and so trust you ever after." Then Moses reported the people's words to the Lord,

19.10 and the Lord said to Moses, "Go to the people and warn them to stay pure today and tomorrow.

THE IMPORTANCE OF CLOTHING

19.10 (cont.) Let them wash their clothes.

> The first way in which the Israelites must make themselves holy is by cleaning their clothes, something that seems surprisingly mundane. However, the Torah recognizes we are physical beings, and therefore acknowledges how much the physical affects us morally, spiritually, and in just about every other way. Studies of school dress codes show when students must dress somewhat formally for school, and are not allowed to wear anything they want, the schools have fewer discipline problems and the students achieve higher grades. The impact of clothing on the individual is profound. People take themselves and what they

are doing more seriously when they wear clothes that befit the circumstance. Just ask people who wear uniforms—police, military, security guards—how donning their uniform makes them feel, as well as how others react to them.

The clothing people wear also reflects their level of respect for the situation and the people involved. Given the unique level of holiness the Israelites were about to experience, it would be, to say the least, unworthy of the magnitude of the event to wear dirty clothes. When God appears before you, you should wear the best clothes you own. In this situation, the Israelites' best clothes were their regular clothes, but at least that clothing had to be clean.

The Talmud later said God held the mountain over the heads of the people and threatened to drop it on them if they did not accept the Law. People don't like moral rules.

If people should wear special clothing to school, how much more should they do so in a house of worship. When you enter a church or synagogue, for example, you should show deference in every way. Clothing is an important component of that. Throughout American history, for example, it was expected of Christians to attend church dressed in what was referred to as their "Sunday best." This commitment to wearing one's best to church has largely disappeared—hopefully not permanently—though it continues in other parts of the Christian world and among almost all Jews who attend synagogue.

To those who argue, "God doesn't care what you wear," this verse would seem to suggest otherwise. So does common sense. Taking one's time to dress more formally before appearing at any event is a statement of the esteem in which we hold that event. The American president Ronald Reagan never took off his jacket and tie when in the presidential office of the White House, not even when he was alone. Why should the place where we encounter God be less significant?

19.11 Let them be ready for the third day; for on the third day the Lord will come down, in the sight of all the people, on Mount Sinai.

Though God cannot be seen, in some way He will make Himself manifest on the third day.

19.12 You shall set bounds for the people round about, saying, 'Beware of going up the mountain or touching the border of it.

Echoing what God said to Moses at the burning bush—not to approach it because of its holiness—and given that no man can see God and live (Exodus 33:20), this directive is presumably about keeping the people from getting close enough to touch the area where God is present and being struck dead. This will also be the case with regard to entering the Temple's Holy of Holies, where the Ark rested.

9.12 (cont.) Whoever touches the mountain shall be put to death:

The consequences are very severe for disobeying God's word at this unique moment in human history—God's revelation of the Ten Commandments and of Himself to an entire nation. Like many other instances in the Torah, the threat of the death penalty is likely made in order to communicate the severity of the sin.

19.13 no hand shall touch him, but he shall be either stoned or shot; beast or man, he shall not live.' When the ram's horn sounds a long blast, they may go up on the mountain."

ANY PLACE CAN BE MADE HOLY (OR UNHOLY)

The people are free to ascend the mountain once God's presence has departed, since it will no longer be a holy place. No natural place is inherently holy; a holy place is where people are engaged in holy activity. When people honor God in a football stadium, the stadium becomes holy at that time.

For example, the most widely attended Chanukah menorah lighting in history (at least as of this writing) occurred at a 1987 Miami Dolphins football game during halftime when 75,000 spectators and players on both teams participated as a Chabad rabbi lit the candles and chanted the blessings. For those few minutes, that stadium became a sacred space. Minutes later, when players went back to tackling, yelling, and even cursing at each other, it didn't become a bad place; it just ceased to be a holy place.

19.14 Moses came down from the mountain to the people and warned the people to stay pure, and they washed their clothes.

19.15 And he said to the people, "Be ready for the third day: do not go near a woman."

Although sex as such is not considered unholy in the Torah, the Israelites are instructed to refrain from intercourse during the three days preceding the revelation. The days immediately preceding this unique divine revelation were not a time for sex. The Israelites were to have loftier matters on their minds.

19.16 On the third day, as morning dawned, there was thunder, and lightning, and a dense cloud upon the mountain, and a very loud blast of the horn; and all the people who were in the camp trembled.

Fear Is Part of Relating to God...

God frightened the people with unusually terrifying natural phenomena.

In the Talmud there is a legend that depicts God holding the mountain over the heads of the people and threatening to drop it on them if they did not accept the Law.[3] This is quite a powerful statement, a sober take on what was happening at Sinai—and more generally, on human nature. The Talmud recognized few people want to be bound by rules, but that is precisely what the Ten Commandments do. Indeed, the revelation at Sinai—specifically, the giving of the Ten Commandments—is regarded by many Jewish and non-Jewish thinkers as the root cause of Jew-hatred.

This combination of love and fear is a model for how people should strive to relate to God (and to parents, who are regarded as God's agents on earth).

Hitler, for example, acknowledged this. "We are fighting," he said, "against the most ancient curse that humanity has brought upon itself. Against the so-called Ten Commandments, against them we are fighting." His life's mission, he said, was to destroy "the tyrannical God of the Jews [and His] life denying Ten Commandments."[4]

With the Ten Commandments, the Jews introduced into the world moral absolutes to live by—backed by a judging God.

...AND SO IS LOVE

This verse clearly suggests the aforementioned Talmudic text made a valid point: the Israelites accepted the covenant out of fear.

While fear is the only component mentioned here, God wanted the Israelites to accept the revelation, the covenant, and the Ten Commandments out of love as well. Thus, God preceded the Sinai revelation with His poetic description of His love for and protection of His people. Terrified as the Israelites were of God's power, they hopefully also recognized God lovingly carried them out of Egypt on eagles' wings.

This combination of love and fear is a model for how people should strive to relate to God (and to parents, who are regarded as God's agents on earth).

19.17 Moses led the people out of the camp toward God, and they took their places at the foot of the mountain.

19.18 Now Mount Sinai was all in smoke, for the Lord had come down upon it in fire; the smoke rose like the smoke of a kiln, and the whole mountain trembled violently.

Sarna explains this image is intended to convey that God is wholly independent of His creation, and even nature trembles before Him. The Torah constantly repeats that nature is subservient to God because Torah monotheism came to, among other things, eradicate nature worship.

19.19 The blare of the horn grew louder and louder. As Moses spoke, God answered him in thunder.

19.20 The Lord came down upon Mount Sinai, on the top of the mountain, and the Lord called Moses to the top of the mountain and Moses went up.

19.21 The Lord said to Moses, "Go down, warn the people not to break through to the Lord to gaze, lest many of them perish.

> Like drivers slowing down to see an accident on a highway, the Israelites are eager to see as much as possible.

19.22 The priests also, who come near the Lord, must stay pure, lest the Lord break out against them."

19.23 But Moses said to the Lord, "The people cannot come up to Mount Sinai, for You warned us saying, 'Set bounds about the mountain and sanctify it.'"

> Moses believes that since he warned the people once, they will surely not try to come too close to the mountain. But God repeats this injunction because He has a better understanding of human nature. One warning won't suffice to hold the people back from getting closer to this once-in-a-lifetime spectacle.

19.24 So the Lord said to him, "Go down, and come back together with Aaron; but let not the priests or the people break through to come up to the Lord, lest He break out against them."

> Even the priests are still not allowed to come close enough to touch the mountain (as noted in verse 22).

19.25 And Moses went down to the people and spoke to them.

CHAPTER
~❧20❧~

GOD, NOT MOSES OR ANYONE ELSE, GAVE THE TEN COMMANDMENTS

20.1 God spoke all these words, saying:

This chapter begins with a critically important statement: It is God Who spoke all the following words. Lest there be any question, at any time, the Torah is making it unequivocally clear that God—not Moses, nor any other human being—is the sole source of *all* the words in the document that becomes known as the Ten Commandments.

The Torah describes the laws in this chapter not as the "Ten Commandments," but as the "Ten Statements" (*Aseret Hadevarim*: Exodus 34:28). In fact, the alternative English name of the Ten Commandments, "the Decalogue," means the "Ten Words" —from the Greek words *deca* (ten) and *logos* (word). The best-known term, the "Ten Commandments," while not used in the Torah, is nevertheless thoroughly accurate. Therefore, I use this term here and elsewhere.

THE TEN COMMANDMENTS ARE UNIQUE

Nahum Sarna identifies at least four ways in which the Ten Commandments are unique, original, and unparalleled:

1. The Ten Commandments are the first and only example of a covenantal relationship between a deity and an entire people. Or, as Yechezkel Kaufman, professor of Bible at the Hebrew University, put it prior to Sarna: "The Ten

Commandments are unique in that God revealed His will not just to a single prophet or to a privileged class, but to an entire people, all of whom became answerable to its terms."

2. Unlike other ancient treaties between a ruler and his people, the Ten Commandments focus not only on the people's relationship with the ruler, but also on each individual's behavior toward every other individual.

3. The Ten Commandments treat both religious and social obligations as expressions of divine will. In doing so, the religious conscience is expanded to include matters of interpersonal morality, thereby ensuring a person who is unethical could not, and should not, be regarded as religious.

4. Unlike other legal codes, the Ten Commandments are laws that are simple, absolute, and devoid of qualification.

THE TEN COMMANDMENTS WERE DELIBERATELY NOT GIVEN IN THE LAND OF ISRAEL

God chose to give the Ten Commandments in the no-man's land of a desert rather than in the land of Israel. I would offer three reasons for this:

First, the Ten Commandments are not just a one-nation guide to behavior, but applicable to all people. From their revelation until today, the Ten Commandments are the best guide to human behavior for Jews and non-Jews alike.

Second, by giving the Ten Commandments outside of Israel, God wanted the Israelites then and Jews forever to understand the Ten Commandments are binding on them not only when they are in their homeland, but everywhere they live.

Third, God did not want to privilege any one Israelite tribe's territory as the site of revelation, which would have likely been the case had the Ten Commandments been given in the Land of Israel.

THE TEN COMMANDMENTS CONSTITUTE A FORM OF ABSOLUTE MORALITY

Because the Ten Commandments are given by God, they are absolute. People can and should argue about how to apply any of these commandments in any given situation—such as what constitutes a violation of the Sabbath, what constitutes disrespect for a parent, or when taking a human life is to be defined as murder. But because they are decrees from God, only those types of debates make sense, not debates about whether they are binding.

> *God gave the Ten Commandments in the no-man's land of a desert rather than in the land of Israel, to signify these laws do not just belong to one people, but to all humanity.*

The Ten Commandments therefore stand in direct opposition to all relativistic approaches to morality—the notion that each individual or society determines what is right or wrong. The Ten Commandments are not relative. (The one exception is the Sabbath commandment, which one can deem as binding only on Jews. Historically, however, most Christians have viewed all Ten Commandments, including the Sabbath, as binding. Western civilization has paid a serious societal, psychological, and familial price for letting go of the Sabbath Day. And Jews who have transformed the Sabbath into just another day of the week have paid the highest price; it is doubtful whether Judaism could long survive the death of the Shabbat—see discussion of the Shabbat Commandment.)

FOUR DEFINING CHARACTERISTICS OF THE TEN COMMANDMENTS

1. They contain no abstract moral principles, such as "Be a good person."

One reason is the Torah recognizes human beings need specific laws in order to do the right thing and be good people. Telling people to be good without giving them specific directions on how to be good is as useless as telling a person, "Be a good pilot," without giving the person flying lessons.

A second reason is most people, even those who are not good, think they are good, and might easily conclude, therefore, they don't need the Ten Commandments—or any divine commandments, for that matter.

2. Nearly all the Ten Commandments are formulated as prohibitions: "You shall not…"

Only two commandments, the Fourth and Fifth, are explicitly positive, and these, too, have essential negative components. The commandment to observe the Sabbath is largely defined as a prohibition against doing work on that day; and the commandment to honor one's father and mother—in light of Exodus 21:15 and 17—seems to have as its main purpose the prohibition against offending the dignity of one's parents.

This emphasis on prohibitions reflects an awareness that the first prerequisite for a stable, decent society is for people to desist from wrongful behaviors. In the words of the famous rule for physicians: "First, do no harm."

A great deal of evil has been done by individuals who believe themselves preoccupied with doing good and by ideologies proclaiming good intentions (communism being the most obvious example)[1]—hence the famous motto, "the road to hell is paved with good intentions."

Telling people to be good without giving them specific directions on how to be good is as useless as telling a person, "Be a good pilot," without giving the person flying lessons.

Of course, we should be preoccupied with doing good, but because good intentions rarely guarantee good results, we must first ask whether the good we intend will do harm. This is as true in the personal realm as in the societal. For example, parents preoccupied with doing good things for their children while making few demands of them end up hurting them by spoiling them and producing ungrateful people (and ungrateful people are neither good nor happy).

3. The Ten Commandments are formulated in terms of obligations, not rights.

While the Torah obviously recognizes fundamental basic human rights, given that each person is created "in God's image," it makes clear such rights will more likely be secured if people first feel morally obligated to others rather than first feel they have rights. The most famous verse in the Torah, "Love your neighbor as yourself" (Leviticus 19:18), is written as a moral obligation to act lovingly toward your neighbor, not as a right ("You have the right to be loved by your neighbor").

4. Each one of the Ten Commandments is in the singular.

The word "you" (or "your") in Hebrew has both a plural and a singular form, and the word for "your God" (Elohecha) in this verse is in the singular. One would think the plural form would be used given that God is addressing many people. But the singular is used throughout the Ten Commandments to emphasize the words of the Ten Commandments are directed to each person individually.

Each commandment is directed to the individual—to "you" in the singular.

A good society is composed of individuals doing what is right. That is why the most important question any society must address is, "How can we make every individual as good a person as possible?" A society in which too many parents, for example, are more concerned with their children's happiness, intelligence, success, or popularity than with their character will sooner or later fail.

20.2 I the Lord am your God who brought you out of the land of Egypt,

Because this verse does not command or prohibit any specific action, Christians enumerate the Ten Commandments slightly differently than Jews always have. As noted above, the Torah's name for this document is the Ten Statements, not the Ten Commandments. Consequently, technically speaking, a Jew would regard this verse as the First Statement (followed by nine commandments), whereas Christians count the next verse, Exodus 20:3, as the First Commandment.

I have no quibble with Jews who regard this statement as commanding acceptance of God as God and as the God Who brought the Jews out of Egypt. Nor do I have a quibble with non-Jews who regard this document as consisting of ten commandments beginning with verse 3—"You shall have no other gods..."—which Jews enumerate as the Second Statement or Commandment. The point is that all are agreed on the number ten and all are agreed on the words. There is no difference between Jews and Christians regarding the wording of the Ten Commandments.

Having acknowledged this verse is written as a statement rather than as a commandment, I should note that some Jewish commentators, most famously the great Jewish philosopher Maimonides, did interpret this verse as a commandment: to believe God exists. The opening words of Maimonides' *The Book of the Commandments (Sefer Hamitzvot)*, an explication of the Torah's 613 laws, read: "By this injunction we are commanded to believe in God; that is, to believe there is a Supreme Cause who is the Creator of everything in existence. This commandment is contained in His words: 'I the Lord am your God who brought you out of the land of Egypt.'"

While I do believe we are all obligated to attempt to believe in God, the Supreme Cause and Creator of everything, I find it difficult to believe the First Statement of the Ten Statements is a commandment to believe—because it is God Who is speaking here. If Moses were speaking, it would make sense for him to tell the Israelites to believe in God. But given that the people believe they are hearing God, it seems illogical God would command people who believe they are listening to Him to believe He exists.

Therefore, as I understand it, this verse is concerned not with the question, "Is there a God?" but with the question, "Who is God?" And the answer is the Lord (YHVH) is God; and it is He Who is responsible for the Exodus.

I am not alone in interpreting the First Statement/Commandment differently from Maimonides. Two medieval Jewish thinkers, Hasdai ibn Crescas and Don Isaac Abarbanel, also disagreed with Maimonides' position that this verse constitutes a command to believe in God. They argued that if you don't believe in God, you certainly won't believe God commands you to believe in Him.

WHY GOD MENTIONS THE EXODUS AT THE BEGINNING OF THE TEN COMMANDMENTS

This opening statement, that God freed the Israelites from Egyptian slavery, establishes God's "right" to demand observance of the commandments that follow. In effect, God is saying, "I took you out of bondage, I saved your very existence both as individuals and as a people; and now, in return, here is what I want from you...."

And yet, God asks nothing for Himself. This fact perfectly encapsulates the essence of the Torah's values—what God demands in the Ten Commandments in exchange for what He has done for Israel is (God-based) moral behavior. (As we shall see, the commandments against false gods and taking God's name in vain are also ultimately about morality.)

WHY GOD DIDN'T INTRODUCE HIMSELF AS THE CREATOR OF THE WORLD

Wouldn't "I am the Lord your God who created the Heavens and the Earth" be more impressive than "I am the Lord your God who took you out of the land of Egypt...."?

Three possible reasons occur to me as to why God chose the latter way:

1. God identified Himself to the Israelites in terms most relevant to them. The Israelites were far more likely to relate to, feel indebted to, and feel obligated to the God Who had just liberated them from slavery than to the God Who created the universe. Wouldn't you?

2. That God is the Creator of the world is certainly awesome and inspiring. But it doesn't necessarily mean He cares about His creations. Such is Aristotle's Unmoved Mover—the creator who sets things in motion and then abandons his creation. God, therefore, wanted to establish immediately that He cares about His creation, and He acts in history. Even for us today, who did not directly benefit from the Exodus, the fact God cares about us matters more to us than the fact God created the world.

Whatever achievements Jews attain—and they have achieved as much or more than any other people, and have had a unique influence on the course of human history—such achievements are ultimately due to God, the Ten Commandments, and this Torah.

3. God identifies Himself as the Israelites' liberator in order to state His desire that men be free. Why the Torah does not ban slavery outright—though it places enormous limitations upon it—is discussed in the chapters dealing with slavery (see, in particular, Exodus 21). But the fact God identifies Himself as the liberator of slaves—and in no other way—in His great revelation to humanity at Sinai and in His preamble to the great moral code known as the Ten Commandments makes His antipathy to slavery and love of freedom incontrovertibly clear. Millennia later, it was this understanding of God's will—He wants us to be free—that became the governing belief of the founders of the United States of America, the greatest experiment in human liberty ever devised. Thus, as noted in Chapter 4, the one inscription on the symbol of the American Revolution, the Liberty Bell, is from the Torah (Leviticus 25:5): "Proclaim Liberty Throughout All The Land Unto All The Inhabitants Thereof."

WHY ARE THE WORDS "HOUSE OF BONDAGE" ADDED TO DESCRIBE EGYPT?

20.2 (cont.) The house of bondage:

Why are the words "house of bondage" (the Hebrew literally says "house of slaves") used to describe Egypt? Did the Israelites need to be reminded Egypt was a house of slaves?

I would argue the reason is to prevent the Israelites from ever romanticizing Egypt, which is precisely what they did (see, for example, Exodus 16:3 and Numbers 11:5) as they traveled through the desert and encountered difficulties. They need to always remember Egypt was a house of slaves.

People who live in liberty have a tendency to forget such things when the going gets rough. For example, there are many people who lived under communism, and who hated its totalitarian suppression of all individual freedom, who eventually came to romanticize it (Stalin, the killer of tens of millions of Russians and other Soviet citizens, remains a popular figure among many

Russians)—just as the Israelites came to romanticize Egypt. To prevent this, God appends the words, "house of bondage."

Finally, and this point is relevant to all humanity, God doesn't want later generations to marvel at the glories of Egypt (such as the pyramids) without remembering those accomplishments were achieved on the tortured backs of slaves. When people look at these spectacular feats of human engineering, they need to also see inhuman slavery. The Greek historian Herodotus noted that in the reign of Pharaoh Necho II (610–595 BCE) some 120,000 laborers were worked to death trying to construct a canal connecting the Nile and the Red Sea.

God also wants the Israelites to forever remember their humble origin; they started out as slaves, on the lowest rung of human society. This is to keep them humble despite any achievement they might eventually attain as a people. But, more important, it is to make clear to the Israelites that whatever achievements they ultimately attain—and the Jews have achieved as much or more than any other people and have had a unique influence on the course of human history— such achievements are ultimately due to God, the Ten Commandments, and this Torah.

ESSAY: FALSE GODS

20.3 You shall have no other gods besides Me.

Most people, when they think of this commandment and ancient worship of gods, understandably think primarily of idols. But, significantly, the commandment not only refers to "idols"; it says "other gods" (other gods being, by definition, false gods).

And even when people think of false gods that are not idols, they think of ancient deities such as gods of the sun and the moon, of rain and fertility, other nature gods, and chief gods such as the Roman Jupiter and the Greek Zeus.

As a result, most people in modern times think of this commandment as essentially irrelevant to the modern age. Who in our time worships idols or rain gods?

The truth is, however, this commandment is not only relevant to modern life; it is in many ways the mother of all the other commandments. Today we have as many false gods as the ancients did. And it is the mother of the other commandments because by identifying false gods, we will eliminate one of the greatest barriers to a good world.

Let's begin by defining a false god. The point of the Torah's monotheism is there is only one god and only this God—the Creator of the universe Who demands we keep these Ten Commandments—is to be worshipped.

One God means one human race. Only if we all have the same Creator, a Father in Heaven, are we all brothers and sisters. Nothing else makes all of us brothers and sisters—not shared DNA, not a similar human form. Nothing.

And one God means one moral standard for all people. If God declares murder wrong, it is wrong for everyone, and you can't go to another god for another moral standard.

When anything else is worshipped, it is a false god. In other words, *when anything is made an end in itself, rather than as a means to God and goodness* (as defined, most especially, by the Ten Commandments), *it is a false god.*

What are examples of false gods—things people regard as ends in and of themselves rather than as means to God and goodness? When asked, many people respond by naming money. But while a lot of people do regard money as an end in and of itself, and devote their lives to acquiring it, money is not really a false god. Even people who live for money rarely claim money is worth living for, or that they live for it, let alone that it is the highest value in life (as people would say of education or art, for example—see below).

Therefore, in order for a thing or an idea to truly be a false god, people must not only make it an end in itself, *they must believe it is a worthy and noble thing* to live for. Genuine false gods are therefore often beautiful things people come to venerate as ends in and of themselves—things such as education, art, and even love and religion.

All of these things are noble when pursued in the service of God and goodness, but when removed from God and goodness, they can lead to evil.

One almost universally worshipped false god of the modern era has been education. Vast numbers of people sincerely believe education makes people better. But that is simply false, and often the opposite is truer. Education, when divorced from the higher ends of God and goodness, has either had no moral impact or has actually made people worse.

Many of the best-educated people in Germany supported Hitler and the Nazis. Professor Peter Merkl of the University of California at Santa Barbara studied 581 Nazis and found that Germans with a high school education "or even university study" (at a time when a much smaller percentage of the population attended university) were more likely to be anti-Semitic than those with less education.[2]

Immediately after World War II, in 1946, the Russian-Jewish linguist and historian Max Weinreich wrote a book detailing how extensive the support for Hitler and the Nazis was among German professors. The book, *Hitler's Professors*, was republished in 1999 by Yale University.

So, too, the large majority of the Western world's supporters of the genocidal regimes of Stalin in the Soviet Union and Mao in China were highly educated. And at the time of this writing, universities are at the center of Israel-hatred in the Western world.

Nearly every American university was founded to teach young people theology and other subjects. Moral education was deemed the most important form of education, and knowledge of the Bible was assumed to be part of that moral curriculum. By the early-to-mid twentieth century, education, first at universities, then at high schools and elementary schools, was divorced from God and the Bible, and a disproportionately high percentage of secular intellectuals adhered to immoral ideologies and intellectually foolish beliefs. (See, for example, British historian Paul Johnson's book on the subject, *Intellectuals*, and Paul Hollander's book, *Political Pilgrims*).

Nowhere is the belief in education as the road to a moral society more apparent than in some of the later writings of the father of psychoanalysis, Sigmund Freud. In 1927, Freud, an atheist who was deeply committed to moral behavior, published a critique of religion, *The Future of an Illusion* (the illusion being God and religion). Freud did not fear the breakdown of belief in God would have any moral implications among intellectuals: "Civilization has little to fear from educated people and brain-workers. In them, the replacement of religious motives for civilized behavior by other secular motives, would proceed unobtrusively."

As Dr. Freud was to witness within ten years of his statement, civilization has as much, if not more, to fear from educated people as from the uneducated. Freud's fellow Austrian and German intellectuals showed no more moral insight or strength than any other group of Germans and Austrians. What Germany lacked during World War II was not enough educated people or, for that matter, artistically sophisticated people (see following paragraphs), but enough good people.

The moral failure of German Christians is almost universally acknowledged. But the moral failure of German secular education and intellectuals is almost universally ignored.

Many would counter here that Germany lacked enough good people among the religiously educated as well. They would be entirely right. The failure of German Christianity was horrific. But the moral failure of German Christians (with noble exceptions such as Dietrich Bonhoeffer) is almost universally acknowledged—even by virtually all Christians.[3]

On the other hand, *the moral failure of secular education and secular intellectuals in Germany is almost universally ignored.*

ART

Art can uplift the spirit, elevate the human being, and illuminate the human condition. And it has done all that primarily during religious periods in Western history and/or by God-centered artists.

For example, the man widely considered to be the greatest composer of music was Johann Sebastian Bach. This is not a "Euro-centric" assessment; it is a view held by Japanese, Koreans, Chinese, and other non-Westerners just as much as it is by Westerners. In Bach's view, "The aim and final reason…of all music…should be none else but the Glory of God and the recreation of the mind."[4]

Another musical giant, Franz Josef Haydn—the father of the symphony and of the string quartet—began the manuscript of his compositions with the Latin words *in nomine Domini* ("In the name of the Lord") and ended his manuscripts with *Lauds Deo* ("Praise be to God").[5]

Probably the most widely known of the greatest composers, Ludwig van Beethoven, though not as overtly religious as Bach or Haydn, thought the greatest work he ever composed was his music to the Catholic Mass, the *Missa Solemnis.*

As belief in God and Christianity declined in Europe in the late nineteenth century—and especially after World War I—classical music deteriorated, as did the other arts.

The "death of God" (pronounced by Friedrich Nietzsche in 1882) and the near-death of great art are related. I asked one of the preeminent orchestral conductors of the late twentieth and early twenty-first centuries, Sir John Eliot Gardiner, if he agreed with this assessment. I assumed he, not known to me as a religious man, would respectfully disagree. But he completely agreed.

In fact, Gardiner often notes the words *Soli Deo Gloria* ("To God alone the Glory") are the words Bach wrote on every manuscript of every one of his more than two hundred cantatas.

Much of post-modern, post-Christian, classical music and art came to celebrate the ugly and the meaningless. More and more art has even celebrated the scatological:

In 1987, a photograph by the American artist and photographer Andres Serrano showing a crucifix submerged in a jar of the artist's urine (titled *Piss Christ*) was an award-winning work of "art" shown in museums and galleries throughout America.

In 2011, a German sculpture depicting a lifelike policewoman squatting and urinating—even the puddle is sculpted—received an award from a prestigious German foundation, the Leinemann Foundation for Fine Art.

In 2013, the Orange County Museum of Art in California placed a huge twenty-eight-foot sculpture of a dog outside the museum, where it periodically "urinates" a yellow fluid onto a museum wall.

In 2016, one of the most prestigious art museums in the world, the Guggenheim in New York, featured a pure gold, working, toilet bowl, which visitors to the museum were invited to use. The name of the exhibit was "America"—so one could literally relieve oneself on America.

These are but a few examples of prestigious museums in the Western world showing scatological art. There are hundreds, likely thousands, of works of "art" composed of urine, fecal matter, menstrual blood, or depicting scatological acts.

And there are an immeasurable number of works of "art" depicting nothing—paint droppings, blank canvasses, unidentifiable objects, and the like.

All these works are the antitheses of art produced by Leonardo da Vinci and other God-centered artists who made most of the greatest works of art.

> The "death of God" (announced by Friedrich Nietzsche in 1882) and the near-death of great art are related.

There were great works of art—certainly great for their time—prior to Western civilization and its affirmation of God. But those pre-Western artists—such as the Greeks—also believed in gods higher than themselves, if not in God. The same holds true for the beautiful works of art in many non-Western civilizations.

Although not all art needs to be God-centered—and some great and/or beloved art, from Claude Monet's *Water Lilies* to Pablo Picasso's *Guernica*, have not been—the overall trajectory of the art world since the bohemian, often anti-God, era of the nineteenth century to today has been a dramatic diminution in the quality and transformative power of art. In the West, when God dies, so does higher culture. And in the many other countries where secularization has become the norm, there has been a similar decline in the arts.

Moreover, even great art and music produced by God-centered artists and composers doesn't necessarily elevate those who appreciate and love it. When art is not a vehicle to God and God-centered morality, it often becomes a morally worthless false god. That explains how cruel human beings could love beautiful music and art. Hollywood director Stanley Kubrick vividly made this point in his classic 1971 film based on the Anthony Burgess novel, *A Clockwork Orange*. In it, men rape and murder while classical music plays in the background. This was all too real. The Nazis forced death camp prisoners to play classical music while Jews were led to gas chambers. Rudolf Hoess, the commandant of Auschwitz, the largest Nazi concentration and death camp, played classical music in his house after gassing up to 10,000 people, mostly Jews, each day.

As one who deeply loves and appreciates classical music (I have periodically conducted orchestras much of my adult life), it has been painful to realize people could cry at Mozart and then support or even commit murder. But the realization that art, when valued as an end in itself, does nothing to make a person good and may even enable bad people to think they are good—because many people equate being cultured with being good—was one of the most important, and depressing, realizations of my life.

As we shall see in the chapters regarding the building of the Tabernacle, the Torah clearly maintains aesthetic beauty in the service of God (such as the art of Leonardo da Vinci) is magnificent and important. But not otherwise.

As the early twentieth-century American rabbi Emil Hirsch put it: "To the Greeks, the beautiful was holy; to the Jews, the holy was beautiful."

LOVE

Even love can become a false god. When morally directed, love is incomparably beautiful. But it is not a moral guide in and of itself, any more than art or education.

In the twentieth century, tens of millions of people put love of country (which can be a good thing) or of race (which can never be a good thing) or of an ideology above moral considerations, and evil resulted.

Over the course of forty years, I have asked young people in America if they would first save their pet or a stranger if both were drowning. A smaller and smaller minority have said they would save the stranger. Why would the majority save their pet before a human being? Because, they say, they love their pet and they don't love the stranger. In other words, they follow the dictates of love. That is one reason the Torah and other books of the Bible warn us against trusting our hearts (see, for example, Numbers 15:39).

And why stop at a pet? If love is the sole criterion, why not save your family photos or your beloved car before a stranger? Surely most of us love many things more than we love a stranger.

Love, like education and art, must be morally directed, or it, too, can be a false god.

Even love of fellow human beings needs to be measured by moral standards. Since we cannot love everyone, what type of people do we choose to love? Do we love evil people? Nobel Prize-winning novelist Saul Bellow put it this way: "A man is only as good as what he loves." Joseph Telushkin makes the point that Bellow's words should be kept in mind when we hear of people who love vicious individuals: The women who loved monsters such as Hitler, Stalin, Mao and, for that matter, mass murderers in prison, and myriad other men like them (albeit on a smaller level of destruction) put love above morality.

This commandment against false gods made the ethical revolution of the Bible and of the Ten Commandments—what is known as ethical monotheism—possible. Worship the God of the Ten Commandments and you will make a good world. Worship anything else—no matter how noble-sounding—and you can too easily end up with evil.

REASON

Reason, too, can become a false god. Like love, we cannot live without it; but we need more than reason to lead a good life and make a better world.

Many people believe reason, without faith, is all we need to be moral and to make a moral world. In the words of the prominent American secular humanist and Yale professor of philosophy Brand Blandshard: "Rationality, or the attempt at it, takes the place of faith... Take reason seriously.... Let it shape belief and conduct freely. It will shape them aright if anything can."[6]

Blandshard was wrong. The belief that reason automatically leads to moral behavior is itself unreasonable—because *reason is only a tool*. Once you know what end you wish to achieve, reason becomes indispensable. If you want to build hospitals, you need reason; and if you want to build concentration camps, you need reason.

But reason doesn't tell you for what ends you should be aiming. If you want to live completely for yourself, reason will help you do that. If you want to live a life of kindness to others, reason will help you do that. But reason doesn't tell you whether to be kind or to be self-centered. Reason just as easily argues for immoral actions as it does for moral actions.

If you are a student who wants to get into a prestigious university, it is entirely reasonable to cheat on tests in order to do so. It is morally wrong, but it is reasonable because:

a) Cheating can help you get into a more prestigious university.

b) If you believe "everyone else cheats," you will be at a clear disadvantage if you don't cheat.

When the average German citizen remained silent while his Jewish neighbors were deported, he was acting entirely according to reason. Reason suggested not endangering one's life by aiding a Jew. In fact, it may be argued the only people in Nazi Germany who acted morally acted *against* reason.

Similarly, it may be rational to kill infirmed babies, which is precisely what the ancient Greeks, the fathers of reason, did. But according to the God of this Torah, that is immoral.

Not only does reason alone fail the morality test; it fails in determining a right response to almost every question involving values. For example, is it rational to have children? Yes and no. Reason argues both ways. Whether people—at least, people who do not need children for economic reasons—have children is far more a values question than a rational question. One proof is in industrialized societies, secular people have considerably fewer children than religious people of the same economic means. If you believe God wants you to have children, you are more likely to have children than if you care more about personal freedom, the ability to eat out, opportunities to travel, or, for that matter, more time for reading and reflection.

Is it rational to adopt a child who suffers from severe physical or emotional problems? Not really. Yet, I have personally met many religious Christians who have done so. And when asked why they do this, they never respond, "It was the rational thing to do." They always respond with a religious reason.

> *Is reason the best guide to good behavior? It may be argued the only people in Nazi Germany who acted morally acted against reason.*

Simply put, reason without God-based moral values—beginning with the Ten Commandments —can become a false god. Reason is exactly like a map. No map shows where you should go; only how to get there. So, too, reason tells you how to get to the place you want to go. But, whether you want to use reason to get to a moral place, or even know what a moral place is, is determined by your values.

Nevertheless, it must be stressed that reason is a glory of the human mind. Anti-rational beliefs have often led to terrible evils. If you put reason first, you need God; and if you put God first, you need reason. Nothing guarantees goodness, but that combination offers the best hope for a moral world.

RELIGION AND FAITH

Even religion and faith can be false gods when they hold that something other than goodness is God's primary demand. Neither faith nor ritual observance must be an end in and of itself; both must be a means of making us better people by living according to God's moral will.

The danger of religious false gods resides in every religion, even the most ethically demanding ones.

In Judaism, there is the danger that preoccupation with ritual law (the "Laws between Man and God") can overshadow the Torah's and the rest of the Hebrew Bible's demands of moral behavior above all. This is a major theme of the Hebrew Prophets, who, speaking in God's name, repeatedly admonished the Jews to remember moral behavior—meaning proper treatment of fellow human beings—is God's foremost demand. Indeed, other than the Sabbath

Commandment and the ban on worshipping false gods (both of which are filled with ethical content), the Ten Commandments are all about moral behavior.

In Christianity, there is also a danger. It is not posed by ritual law becoming more important than moral behavior, but by faith becoming more important than moral behavior. In the New Testament, James warns "Faith without works is dead" (James 2:20).

But for much of Christian history, James's view did not prevail. It was a dangerous overemphasis on faith that allowed medieval Christian Crusaders to murder entire Jewish communities in Germany on their way to the Holy Land. Their rationale for doing so was the Jews refused to accept Christian belief, and in the Crusaders' minds should therefore convert or be killed. To the Crusaders, right faith, not right conduct, was what mattered.

Martin Luther, the father of the Protestant Reformation, broke with the Catholic Church on many issues. But on the issue of faith Luther was even more extreme, insisting faith was incomparably more important than morality. As Luther expressed it: "Be a sinner and sin vigorously, but even more vigorously believe and delight in Christ who is victor over sin, death and the world .... It is sufficient that we recognize through the wealth of God's glory the lamb who bears the sin of the world; from this, sin does not sever us, even if thousands, thousands of times in one day we should fornicate or murder."

It is not surprising Luther even held the New Testament Book of James in contempt. He described it as "mere straw" and without "merit." Why? Because it attributes "righteousness to works."[7] Nor is it surprising Hitler and the Nazis idolized Luther because of the anti-Semitic sentiments that characterized his final years—a hatred emanating entirely from his placing faith above morality.

Nevertheless, Luther made something much better than himself. What he helped to create—Protestant Christianity—ultimately became a gift to mankind. Among their other moral achievements, Protestants led the modern world's abolition of slavery, and they created the United States of America. One might say Protestants created much of the modern world.

In Islam, both dangers exist, since both faith and ritual can overwhelm the moral. And for much of Islamic history they have. One reason is the Quran has no prophets analogous to those of the Hebrew Bible repeatedly berating Muslims for unethical behavior. Another is the Quran's division of humanity between believers (Muslims) and non-believers (non-Muslims and non-monotheists), rather than between good and evil.

MONEY

As already noted, while there have always been people who live for acquiring money and material items, money is not a false god because—unlike art, education, reason, religion, and faith—almost no one, even among those who do live for money, argues money is the highest good. So, while it may function as a god, it is not believed in as a god.

This commandment against other gods reflects one of the most important and pervasive themes in the Torah: the obliteration of false gods. It is so important that the Talmud states, with only a little exaggeration, "Whoever denies idolatry is considered to have fulfilled the whole Torah."[8]

This is why the seven basic laws Judaism traditionally has deemed obligatory on all people (the Seven Noahide Laws) do not obligate people to worship God. They demand the denial of all other gods.[9]

20.4 You shall not make for yourself a sculptured image, or any likeness of what is in the heavens above, or on the earth below, or in the waters under the earth.

The primary purpose of this commandment is to prohibit images intended to be representations of God. As people tend to confuse image with essence, there is a danger that if God is depicted visually, people will confuse the depiction with God. In addition, they could come to believe God is a material being. By forbidding the making of images of God, the Ten Commandments prevents people from thinking of God as having a physical form (e.g., "You saw no shape when the Lord your God spoke to you at Horeb [Mount Sinai]" (Deuteronomy 4:15).

The invisibility and incorporeality (no bodily form) of God are essential characteristics of the God of the Torah. If God were a physical being, He would be part of nature, not above and beyond it. And if God were material, there would be no immaterial reality. That, in turn, would mean there could not be an immaterial part of the human being—that is, the human soul. And if the human being has no soul, humans are merely material beings, not intrinsically more valuable than a pebble. Finally, if there is no soul, there is no afterlife.

This commandment relates to the previous one in that both can be understood as warnings against the potential dangers of art—art as a false god and using art to render God physical.

This commandment, however, is not a prohibition against all art: The Torah is explicit about the importance of art and beauty in the construction of the Tabernacle. But, of course, that is art for the sake of bringing us closer to God. Indeed, there is room for all art—including the not explicitly religious—that elevates people.

Neither the Torah nor later Judaism is anti-art or material aesthetic beauty. The Torah does not prohibit people from building beautiful houses of prayer such as synagogues and cathedrals—or, for that matter, other beautiful buildings (that are not devoted to false gods). As anyone who enters a beautiful house of prayer knows, the power of aesthetic magnificence to elevate the individual to contemplate the divine and experience the holy is considerable. We are physical beings and we are moved by physical beauty. Clearly, then, that should be part of a God-centered life.

Moreover, if we are going to spend money on the secular, we should also spend money on the religious. Many people who oppose spending money on beautiful houses of prayer are quite open to spending great amounts of money on art museums and concert halls, and, for that matter, on sports stadiums. But a society that spends large sums on the latter and minimal sums on houses of worship is not one I would wish to live in. That is precisely what is happening in Europe at this time; expensive new museums and concert halls are regularly built, but virtually no new church is—reflecting the godless nature of most European societies. This does not bode well for Europe's future.[10]

Nevertheless, it is true to say that while the Torah places emphasis on using the visual—and aural (i.e., music)—to bring people closer to God, Judaism has not been famous for its frescoes, figurines, or great art. According to Rabbi Gunther Plaut, prayer assumed the place of eminence denied to the visual arts. As he put it, because visual depictions of God were viewed as idolatrous, Jews developed beautiful ways of *addressing* God instead of beautiful ways of *portraying* God.[11]

As true as that is, some Jews, myself included, believe many synagogues built after the 1950s—compared to synagogues built before then—have been physically uninspiring. The same may be said of many modern churches; the larger secular culture often has an impact on religions.

For reasons noted in detail in this commentary, the assertion that God is spiritual and non-physical is of particular importance. Maimonides included the belief in God's incorporeality as the third of his Thirteen Principles of the Jewish Faith.

Of course, Christianity later held that God appeared in human form. From a Jewish perspective, this compromised the doctrine of an incorporeal God; but this unquestionably enabled many people to more easily relate to the divine. And by doing so, Christianity played a seminal role in bringing knowledge of the Torah and God to the world. Maimonides, who had profound disagreements with Christian theology, wrote it was through Christianity that the Torah, the Messianic hope, and the commandments "have become familiar topics of conversation among the inhabitants of the far isles and many peoples."[12]

This commandment relates only to the visual arts. The Torah has no analogous limitation on music. Indeed, the Psalms are filled with accounts of praising God through musical instruments—e.g., "Praise Him with timbrel and dance, praise Him with lute and pipe" (Psalms 150:4).

The Torah is far more suspicious of the eye than of the ear, and rightly so: People are often led to sin when something glittering catches their eye or when they are seduced by someone who is irresistibly attractive to the eye. This commandment reflects this understanding that, of all our senses, the eye has the greatest power to lead us astray. Numbers 15:39, when translated literally, enjoins people, "Do not follow your hearts and eyes after which you prostitute yourselves" (asher atem zonim acharei-hem).

20.5 You shall not bow down to them or serve them.

One reason the Torah forbids bowing to other gods is it recognizes behavior deeply influences the mind and the heart. Act kind and you'll feel kinder; act happy and you'll feel happier; bow down to idols and you'll start believing in them.

DOES GOD REALLY GET "JEALOUS"?

20.5 (cont.) For I the Lord your God am an impassioned God,

The word translated here as "impassioned" literally means "jealous," and in many Bible translations it is indeed rendered "jealous."

This statement is fodder for those who wish to mock the Bible. They ask: How impressive is a God Who is jealous?

A first response is that God, of necessity, must speak in terms understandable to human beings. This was recognized thousands of years ago by the rabbis of the Talmud who said, "the Torah speaks in the language of human beings" (dibra Torah bilshon bnei adam).[13] The moment God speaks to human beings, He is, in effect, compromising His godliness. If God spoke pure "God-talk," we humans would presumably understand nothing. The notion of God being a "jealous God" is a powerful message delivered in human terms.

And what is this powerful message?

God's "jealousy" is a statement of His love. That men and women who love their spouses occasionally feel—or at least are capable of feeling—jealousy means they love their spouses. Love does not exist where there is no possibility of jealousy. (Of course, spouses should not too easily feel jealous; a perpetually jealous spouse will ruin a marriage.)

God wants His people to be faithful to Him. God, therefore, likens His reaction to Israelite infidelity to that of a spouse whose husband or wife is unfaithful. This is neither foolish nor primitive. God is speaking in terms we can emotionally relate to, and He is humbling Himself in order to describe as powerfully and humanly possible how much He loves His people.

And, of course, God knows the evils that ensue when people abandon Him and worship false gods (see above).

DOES GOD PUNISH THE CHILDREN OF BAD PEOPLE?–I

20.5 (cont.) visiting the guilt of the parents upon the children, upon the third and upon the fourth generations of those who reject Me,

This statement is often understood to mean God will punish the children, grandchildren, and great-grandchildren of those who "hate" God (the word translated above as "reject" literally means "hate"). The reason is so many translations, including the JPS translation used here, say God "will visit the sins of the fathers unto the children...."

It is true that one meaning of the Hebrew verb *po-ked* is "visit." But I believe the most accurate translation in this context is "take account of," which is how the verb is often used in the Bible. See, for example, Exodus 3:16, I Samuel 17:18, and other biblical verses where the meaning is not "visit," but "take account of," and where the word has nothing to do with punishment.

It is therefore very unlikely, from a moral perspective (and the Ten Commandments form, after all, a moral document) the intent of the verse is God punishes the decent children and grandchildren of grievous sinners.

First, the Torah has already established God is just—beginning with Abraham's argument with God over the destruction of Sodom (Genesis 18).

Second, if the verse really meant to say God punishes four generations of offspring for the sins of their ancestors, it would not only be unjust, it would be utterly counterproductive. It would be announcing that no matter how good a person you become, no matter how different a person you are from your God-hating father or grandfather, you will still be punished. And that alone would make someone hate God. Legitimately.

Third, the Torah itself expressly bans punishing children for the sins of their parents: "Parents shall not be put to death for children, nor children be put to death for parents: a person shall be put to death only for his own crime" (Deuteronomy 24:16). (In contrast, the ancient Babylonian Code of Hammurabi ruled that if a man, acting negligently, causes the death of his neighbor's son or daughter, the son or daughter of that man should be put to death; [paragraph 230].)

And the Prophet Ezekiel announced: "The one who sins is the one who will die. The child will not share the guilt of the parent, nor will the parent share the guilt of the child. The righteousness of the righteous will be credited to them, and the wickedness of the wicked will be charged against them" (Ezekiel 18:20).

What we probably have here are divine scare tactics. The Torah may be warning parents that if they are really bad and seek to undermine ethical monotheism ("hate God" is pretty severe), the chances are their children will suffer for what they have done—both because children suffer when their parents are bad people, and because they are more likely to follow in their parents' footsteps. Examples are legion. To cite but one example of each consequence, a son of Bernie Madoff, one of the greatest crooks in American history, committed suicide owing to the shame he felt over his father's crimes. And the worst mass shooting in American history as of this writing—leaving fifty-eight people at an outdoor concert in Las Vegas dead and over five hundred injured—was committed by a man whose father was a lifelong criminal and on the FBI's "Ten Most Wanted Fugitives List."

Fathers need to think about how they act. Their actions have enormous impact on their children.

DOES GOD PUNISH THE CHILDREN OF BAD PEOPLE?–II

20.6 but showing kindness to the thousandth generation of those who love Me and keep My commandments.

This part of the commandment would seem to prove God's previous statement about the third and fourth generation is not to be taken literally. If one takes the first part literally—that God punishes the children of evildoers to the fourth generation—then one must take the second part literally as well: God rewards the descendants of those who obey God for a thousand generations. But that is as morally impossible as the first part. Does it mean that no matter how badly one behaves, he is shown kindness if his great-great-great-great-grandfather obeyed God? Of course not. Furthermore, how can it be decided which grandparent is the determinant of how his descendant is treated? If you go back just ten generations—let alone a hundred—we all have slightly more than a thousand grandparents, some of whom were wonderful human beings and some of whom were awful.

Again, the point is didactic. In this case, God wants to contrast His desire to reward good with His need to punish bad.

Regarding the words, "of those who love Me," love of God, like hatred of God, refers not to feelings but to actions. The defining characteristic of loving God is keeping God's commandments, which means acting justly and treating people with decency and kindness.

20.7 You shall not swear falsely by the name of the Lord your God; for the Lord will not clear one who swears falsely by His name.

While the translation being used in this Torah commentary is that of the Jewish Publication Society (1962), and one with which I sometimes disagree (though I hold it in very high regard), in this instance, I believe the JPS translation is far off the mark. Indeed, I greatly prefer the older version of the 1917 JPS translation: "Thou shall not take the name of the Lord thy God in vain; for the Lord will not hold him guiltless that taketh His name in vain."

"Swearing falsely in God's name"—this translation—is much more narrow an understanding of this commandment than "taking the name of the Lord in vain." Moreover, the word "swear" is not used.

So what, then, does this commandment prohibit?

ESSAY: THE WORST SIN IS COMMITTING EVIL IN GOD'S NAME

Is there such a thing as the worst sin?

Apparently, there is. And this is it.

How do we know? Because it is the only one of the Ten Commandments whose violation God says He will not forgive—"the Lord will not hold him guiltless" (literally, "God will not cleanse" the one who violates this commandment).

But this immediately raises a question as obvious as it is troubling: Why, of all sins, would a moral and just God say the only person He will not forgive is one who takes His name in vain? What kind of God is prepared to potentially forgive stealing, giving false testimony, possibly even murder but not forgive saying God's name for no important reason? Is murder potentially forgivable, but saying, "Oh God, did I have a tough day today" not forgivable?

Obviously, this cannot be.

And, indeed, it is not.

For one thing, the word "God" is not God's name. So, saying something like "God, did I have a tough day today" does not violate this commandment. "God" is God's title. But God's name is YHVH (we do not know exactly how it is pronounced, and Jews refrain from pronouncing it). It is *this* name (in the Hebrew original) we are forbidden to say in vain.

But the ultimate, and far more important, reason this sin is unforgiveable is due to something else, which can only be understood if we translate the verb of this commandment literally. Do not "take" is not what the commandment actually says. The Hebrew verb in the commandment, *tisa*, means "carry." The commandment therefore reads, "Do not *carry* God's name in vain."

And who carries God's name in vain? Any person who claims to be acting in God's name while doing the opposite of what God wants—evil. Obvious modern examples would include Islamist terrorists who shout, *Allahu Akbar* ("God Is the Greatest") when they murder innocent people; or a priest or any other clergy who, utilizing the respect engendered by his clerical status, molests a child. There is little question Islamist terrorists and molesting clergy have both played a role in the rise of atheism in our time.

When any person commits evil, it reflects badly on the person. But when a person commits evil in God's name, it reflects badly on God as well. The result is the only solution to evil—God-based morality—is thoroughly undermined. When associated with evil, God and ethical monotheism are thoroughly discredited. And *that* is unforgivable, as it dramatically reduces the chances of creating a good world.

No atheist activist is nearly as effective in alienating people from God and religion as are evil "religious" people.

As noted, the Hebrew word *y'nakeh* ("hold guiltless") literally means "cleanse." Essentially God is saying if anyone dirties God's name, God will never cleanse that person's name.

20.8 Remember the sabbath day and keep it holy.

"Remember" may refer to the fact the Israelites have already been made aware of the Sabbath. They already knew about the Sabbath from the cycle of the manna, which fell daily except for Shabbat (a double portion fell on Friday to provide food for Shabbat; see Exodus 16:21-30). More likely, however, "Remember" means "Never forget to" keep the Sabbath day.

The careful reader will note this commandment does not say, "Remember the sabbath day to rest." While work is prohibited on Shabbat, our primary aim on the Shabbat should not be to rest. It should be to make it holy.

Is there such a thing as the worst sin? Apparently, there is—doing evil in God's name.

"Holy" in Hebrew (*kadosh*) means "separate" or "distinct" —in this case, separate and distinct from the other six days of the week. Those six days are, one could say, the secular days of the week, while the Shabbat is the holy day. It is a day elevated, as the commandment goes on to say, "to God." Therefore, we cannot just rest on the Sabbath; if we were to stay in bed from Friday night until Saturday night, though we would have certainly rested, we would not have kept the Shabbat. In fact, holy work *is* permitted, even though it is still work. For example, rabbis and cantors not only work on the Shabbat, it is the day of the week on which they work the hardest. But their work is related to making the Shabbat holy, and therefore permitted. Conversely, while shopping is hardly work, it is not related to making Shabbat holy, and therefore would violate the command to make the Sabbath Day holy.

Essay: Why the Sabbath Commandment Is Unique

The Shabbat Commandment is unique for at least three reasons, all of which underscore how important it is.

First, it is one of only two of the Ten Commandments that ordain positive action. Other than honoring one's parents and the Shabbat, all the commandments are stated in the negative ("You shall not…").

Second, and even more remarkably, it is the only ritual commandment in the Ten Commandments. This almost surely means the Shabbat is the most important ritual in the Torah and therefore in the Jewish religion.

Why the Shabbat is so important—for both the individual and the community—will be explained. But it is worth noting here, more than any other Jewish ritual, the Shabbat preserved the Jewish people. As one major Jewish writer of the early twentieth century, Ahad Ha'am (1856–1927), put it, "More than the Jews have kept the Shabbat, the Shabbat has kept the Jews."

There is yet another unique aspect to the Shabbat. It is not only the one ritual in the Ten Commandments, it is the one major ritual of the Torah and Judaism that is universally applicable. As ethically rooted as most Torah rituals are, including the laws of kosher food (as we shall see in Leviticus), there is no compelling reason for non-Jews to eat only kosher food. But there are very compelling reasons for non-Jews to observe the Shabbat. The world would be a better place, and people of every background would enjoy a higher of quality of life, if the Shabbat were widely observed.

This further reinforces the belief that undergirds this commentary—the Ten Commandments are universally applicable. Traditionally, Judaism has not demanded the world embrace all Ten Commandments, but rather what it calls the "Seven Laws of the Children of Noah" (the "Seven Noahide Laws")—and the Shabbat is not one of them, the obvious reason being God did not prescribe the Shabbat to Noah or his descendants. But if one believes, as I do, the Ten Commandments should serve as the basic moral code for every civilization, it would include some form of the Sabbath.

> *The Christian world is thus far the only non-Jewish civilization to have adopted the Ten Commandments, and societies that did so benefited immeasurably.*

The Christian world is thus far the only non-Jewish civilization to have adopted the Ten Commandments, and societies that did so benefited immeasurably. The best example is the United States, the non-Jewish society that took the Ten Commandments the most seriously—as illustrated by the many sculptures of Moses holding the Ten Commandments throughout America, including on sculpted friezes inside and outside of the United States Supreme Court. Throughout their history, Americans widely observed the Sabbath (on Sunday) until the radical secularization of America that began after World War II.

The third reason the Shabbat Commandment is unique is it is the only one of the Ten Commandments for which a reason is given. This is not a coincidence. Obviously, the only way to ensure people understand the theological point of the commandment—to affirm God as the Creator—is to say so.

But there may be another reason for offering an explanation. The Torah recognizes a ritual is more compelling to many people when a reason is given for it. Sometimes, it is true, the reason for a ritual commandment is inscrutable, and we obey it solely because we believe God commanded it. But the human being is supposed to be a rational creature, and the Torah is overwhelmingly a rational document—meaning, a document that accords with reason.

God could have simply said "Keep the Sabbath" without giving any reason to do so. But it would not have had the cosmic and universal meaning it has. While the Shabbat has a great deal of intrinsic meaning—the power of a day of rest, a day of sacred time, a day to connect with family and friends—God wanted us to know there is a monumental reason for the Shabbat.

That reason is to affirm each week that God created the world, and just as He ceased from work on the Seventh Day, so do we.

This is another reason the Sabbath is applicable to non-Jews. The reason God gives for the Sabbath is a universal one, not a specifically Jewish one. When Moses restates the Ten Commandments in the book of Deuteronomy, he provides a specifically Jewish reason for the Shabbat: The Israelites are to observe it because God released them from slavery in Egypt, and free people, unlike slaves, can choose not to work one day a week. (I explain there why, I believe, Moses made that change—see commentary to Deuteronomy 5:12-15).

WORK IS NOBLE

20.9 Six days you shall labor and do all your work,

There are those who take this as an obligation to work six days a week. Others regard it as a statement that one should do all one's work six days of the week so as to be able to desist from work on Shabbat.

Whichever interpretation one subscribes to, one clear implication of these words is the Torah values labor. In the Torah, there are no negative associations with either labor or money. Like everything else, work and money can be directed toward noble or ignoble ends. But the Torah wants us to observe a day without work or monetary concerns. God matters, too.

20.10 but the seventh day is a Sabbath of the Lord your God:

In his book *The Sabbath*, Rabbi Abraham Joshua Heschel writes that we do not rest on the Sabbath so we can work during the week; rather, we work during the week so we can rest and refresh our souls on the Sabbath: "Man is not a beast of burden, and the Sabbath is not for the purpose of enhancing the efficiency of his work."

The Seventh Day is the purpose and the culmination of the rest of the week, so much so that in Hebrew until this day, the days of the week are named in reference to their proximity to the Shabbat. Sunday is known as *yom rishon*, the "first day" (toward the Sabbath), Monday is *yom sheni*, the "second day" (toward the Sabbath), etc.

20.10 (cont.) You shall not do any work—

Only free people—not slaves, as the Israelites were in Egypt and as so many other human beings were (and are) all over the world—can take a day off from work every week. By refraining from work on Shabbat, a person affirms his status as a free human being. Therefore, from the Torah's perspective, a person who works seven days a week is a slave, even if he does so voluntarily. And if he earns a great deal of money by working seven days a week, he would then simply be deemed a wealthy slave.

The division of time into seven days is not rooted in the natural; it is rooted in the supernatural—in God's creation of the world.

The Sabbath is a time to reflect on the meaning of the work we did during the other six days. In this sense, Shabbat functions as a monastery, providing a weekly retreat from the world.

SLAVES, ANIMALS, AND STRANGERS MUST ALSO HAVE A SABBATH

20.10 (cont.) You, your son or daughter, your male or female slave, or your cattle, or the stranger who is within your settlements.

This is one of the least quoted, yet most ethically revolutionary, commandments in history.

The Ten Commandments became the first and, as far as is known, the only legal code to grant slaves a weekly day of rest (see also Exodus 23:12). While the Bible did not universally abolish slavery, the Sabbath commandment was one of numerous commandments in the Torah that greatly humanized that terrible institution and eventually helped make slavery untenable to any society that venerated the Bible.

By definition, slave owners throughout the world were under no obligation to allow a slave to ever rest, let alone to rest one day every week. Yet, that is exactly what this commandment commanded. And by asserting a slave has fundamental human rights, the Torah began the arduous task of teaching people that slaves, too, are human beings.

As regards animals not working on the Sabbath, one can accurately say the Ten Commandments were not only thousands of years ahead of their time, but ahead of their time today in almost every society that still uses animals for work.

The Torah was also unique with regard to the stranger. In the ancient world, and much of the world until today, the stranger has been regarded as outside the protection of the law. But not so in the case of the Torah. Exodus 23:12 makes clear the concern with the stranger, "in order…that your bond-man and the stranger be refreshed."

In these three ways, then, it is inaccurate to describe the Shabbat command-ment as only "ritual." It is profoundly and uniquely moral.

THE SABBATH: THE RITUAL THAT AFFIRMS THE CREATOR

20.11 For in six days the Lord made heaven and earth and sea, and all that is in them, and He rested on the seventh day; therefore the Lord blessed the Sabbath day and hallowed it.

Sarna makes the important point that the division of time into seven days is not rooted in the natural; it is rooted in the supernatural, in God's creation of the world. The day corresponds to one complete rotation of the earth on its axis, and the month corresponds to one cycle of the moon's phases, but the week is completely disassociated from the movement of the celestial bodies. It is an unnatural and arbitrary measurement of time.

Therefore, by observing the Shabbat every seven days, one is worshipping the Creator of nature, not nature—affirming the existence of a God Who is above nature and Who created it.

That is the ultimate significance of Shabbat. It is a weekly public announce-ment that God created the world. *There is no other ritual or ethical law in the Bible whose purpose is to affirm God as the Creator of the world.* As noted in the commentary to Genesis 1:1, that verse, "In the beginning, God created the heavens and the earth," is arguably the most important verse in the Bible. The entire Bible rests on that claim. Life having ultimate meaning rests on it. If there is no Creator, there is no design and no purpose. All is random and ultimately meaningless, including right and wrong.

Every time a person observes the Shabbat—especially in the presence of people who do not believe in the God of the Bible—that person is affirming God created the world, and all is not random.

I experienced this when I was a university student in England. One Saturday afternoon, I was lying on my bed reading a book when my non-Jewish roommate happened to stop by the apartment. Seeing me lying down midday, he asked if I was feeling alright. I told him I felt perfectly fine.

"So," he asked me, "why are you lying down?"

"It's my Sabbath," I responded. "and I'm resting."

He was obviously taken aback. A physics major and an atheist, it is doubtful he ever encountered a believer, let alone one living out his faith.

"You believe in God?" he asked incredulously.

"I do."

"What's God?" he immediately asked with more than a hint of disdain.

Knowing he was a scientist, I answered—as matter-of-factly as I could— "God is the only absolute in a universe of relativity."

"Oh."

It was apparent he was surprised that a religious person could utter an intellectual-sounding sentence, especially about God.

But what made the biggest impact on me was I had lived out the mandate of the Sabbath commandment—publicly affirming the Creator.

We affirm the Creator by not working on the Seventh Day. For that reason alone, our increasingly godless world needs people who will observe the Sabbath—and invite others to celebrate it with them.

THE PERSONAL IMPACT OF THE SABBATH

As if all the above achievements of the Sabbath were not enough, there is one other as important as any of them—the impact on your life if you have a Sabbath in it.

When a person takes off from work one day every week to keep the Sabbath, that day almost inevitably becomes a day spent with people—which means family and/or friends. The biggest reason people are not generally with family and friends is work. Therefore, with no work allowed, what else is one going to do, if not spend much of the day with people?

People inevitably spend the Sabbath with friends and family. For many Jews throughout history, Shabbat has meant family-day more than anything else—especially the hours-long Friday night and Saturday afternoon meals. In my parents' home, Shabbat—particularly Friday evening—was more or less the only time I engaged in protracted conversation with my parents.

Shabbat has similar positive effects on marriages. Ask anyone married to a workaholic how good it would be for his or her marriage if the workaholic would not work for one day each week and you can appreciate the power of the Sabbath Day.

THE UNIQUENESS OF THE COMMANDMENT TO HONOR OUR PARENTS

20.12 Honor your father and your mother

This is the first of the Ten Commandments addressing only human-to-human relations. As such, it would seem to belong to the second of the two tablets, all five of whose commandments likewise only address human-to-human behavior. Yet, it is listed among the first five, immediately following the commandment to observe the Sabbath.

Both of these commandments serve as a bridge between relating to God and relating to people. The Sabbath begins with acknowledging God as the Creator and leads to proper treatment of servants, animals, and strangers. As for parents, they are, along with God, our co-creators (biologically and non-biologically) and honoring parents is a building block of civilization; societies in which parents are honored will long survive (which is precisely what the commandment soon says).

There is another way in which this commandment is a bridge between God and man. If a child does not honor parental authority, he is less likely to honor divine authority (and the converse is also true). There is a hierarchy in life without which moral order is unlikely: God, parent, child.

As noted, this commandment and the one for the Sabbath are the only two of the ten rendered in the positive. The other commandments tell us what not to do (remember, the first, even in the original Jewish enumeration, is a statement, not a commandment ordaining behavior).

If there is no Creator, there is no design, and no purpose. All is random and ultimately meaningless, including right and wrong.

This fact alone tells us how important God deems honoring parents. In effect, the Ten Commandments tell us to *do* only two things: remember the Sabbath and honor our father and mother.

The unique importance of this commandment is further underscored by the fact there is no other commandment in the Torah—not just in the Ten Commandments—demanding we honor someone or something.

ESSAY: WE ARE NOT COMMANDED TO LOVE OUR PARENTS

The Torah commands us to love God (Deuteronomy 6:5), to love our neighbor (Leviticus 19:18), and to love the stranger who dwells among us (Leviticus 19:34). But, in a particularly compelling example of the Torah's psychological sophistication, it does not command us to love our parents.

Why?

One reason is such a command would either be superfluous or impossible to obey. Those who already love their parents don't need to be commanded to do so, while those who do not love their parents could not be commanded to do the impossible; the Torah understands how often child-parent relations are emotionally troubled.

Another reason—and the more essential one—is it is more important to honor parents than to love them. It is a beautiful thing when children love their parents. But many, perhaps most, people experience a variety of emotions toward their parents throughout their lifetimes, sometimes dependent on the parents' behavior, and sometimes dependent on the child's own emotional evolution and psychological makeup.

The moral success of a society does not depend on children loving parents; it does depend on children honoring their parents.

An analogy might help here. It would be very nice if everyone in a society loved their city's police and their country's president. But that is utopian. What matters much more to a functioning society is that citizens honor the police and their president. And just as people who did not vote for or even vigorously opposed a president stand when he enters a room, so, too, children who do not love a parent must still honor their parent.

Yes, there are parents who are so evil—not just annoying, obnoxious, or ill-tempered, but actually evil—it is impossible for their child to relate to, let alone honor, them. But in the overwhelming majority of cases a parent's failings do not amount to evil.

Moreover, the Torah does not command us to always obey our parents, but to honor them. The distinction between honor and obedience is highlighted in a later Torah verse: "You shall each revere his mother and father, and keep My Sabbaths" (Leviticus 19:3).

The Talmud explains the juxtaposition of these two laws this way: We must obey our parents, but not if they tell us to violate the Sabbath. In Biblical Hebrew, the word "and" (which is actually just a single letter [*vav*] attached to the beginning of a word) often means "but" (see, for example, Psalms 96:5). Thus, the Leviticus verse would be more accurately translated: "You shall each revere his mother and father, *but* keep My Sabbaths."

In other words, there is a moral authority higher than one's parents: God. Accordingly, if our parents tell us to do something that violates God's will, we are to respectfully decline to obey. The Talmud offers an example of a father who instructs his child not to return a lost item: the child is not to obey (though admittedly that is a lot to ask of a young child).[14]

Though we do not owe our parents control of our conscience, we do still owe them honor. Maimonides writes: "If one sees his father violating a Torah law, he should not say, 'Father, you have violated the Torah'; rather, he should say, 'Father, is it not written in the Torah?' as if he were asking a question, not delivering a warning."[15]

As much as parents may want to be honored, children need to honor their parents for their sake, not only the parents'.

Those who find it difficult to honor a parent (and find themselves often arguing with, or even shouting at, a parent) should nevertheless attempt to find a way to observe this commandment. For example, sometimes it might be easier to honor one's parents by not living near them. In other instances, it might be best to avoid prolonged stays with one's parents. Whatever it takes to keep this commandment is worth pursuing.

Additional points:

- Implicit in the commandment to honor parents is the expectation for parents to act in ways that elicit their children's respect. This means, first and foremost, parents must act honorably. It is difficult to honor parents who act dishonorably (such as parents who act criminally, who are dysfunctional due to drug or alcohol addiction, or who treat the other parent with contempt). It also means parents must act as their children's parents, not as their peers.

- As much as parents may want to be honored—and they should want to be—children need to honor their parents for their sake, not only the parents'. It is difficult to become a decent and happy adult if an individual does not honor his or her parents while growing up.

- We also honor our parents in the ways we behave toward all other people (even after our parents have passed on). Our actions, good and bad, reflect on our parents (sometimes undeservedly). Thus, we do not honor our parents only through how we treat them, but how we treat others throughout our lives. When a person acts well toward others, people generally assume the person was raised by good parents.

- If we honor our parents, our children will see how we act toward them and are more likely to treat us similarly. This is not just a selfish reason to observe this commandment, but a socially important one as well: By honoring our parents, we promote a value the younger generation is likely to emulate.

- The selfish reason is also valid. Whenever I see middle-aged people who ignore their parents or act disrespectfully toward them, I wonder if they have ever considered the behavior they are modeling for their own children. In contrast, I recall my father Max Prager's behavior toward his mother, my grandmother. She was a difficult woman, the sort who would frequently yell at him on the telephone. In all my years of overhearing those conversations, I do not recall my father ever yelling back, but rather saying every minute or two, "Yes, Ma; Yes, Ma." Moreover, he called his mother every night and brought her to our home every Sunday. That made a profound impression on me and on my behavior toward my parents when I grew up.

> *The Torah commands us to love God, to love our neighbor, and to love the stranger. But, in a particularly compelling example of the Torah's psychological sophistication, it does not command us to love our parents.*

- The Hebrew does not state "Honor your father and mother." It states, "Honor your father and *your* mother" to emphasize the equal importance of both parents. There is no difference in God's eyes between father and mother; they are equals. To underscore this, elsewhere the Torah lists the mother first: "You shall each revere his mother and father" (Leviticus 19:3).

HONORING PARENTS: THE ONLY ONE OF THE TEN COMMANDMENTS THAT SPECIFIES A REWARD

20.12 (cont.) that you may long endure on the land that the Lord your God is assigning to you.

The Fifth Commandment is the only one of the Ten Commandments that specifies a reward. But this reward is not to be understood as a promise that the individual who honors his or her parents will live a long life. The commandment promises the nation collectively that if its members honor their parents, the family will be preserved, its religious traditions and beliefs will be preserved, and the civilization will therefore long endure. The breakdown of the family is a guarantor of the breakdown of a civilization. One reason is "a society in which children do not honor parents will lose the means through which the society's culture, religion, and ethics are transmitted" (Telushkin).

Yet another reason why honoring parents and a long enduring civilization are connected is strong families form a major bulwark against totalitarian regimes. A standard feature of totalitarian regimes is the shifting of children's loyalty and obedience from their parents to the state. One of the first things totalitarian regimes seek to do is weaken parental authority and replace it with the party or state. In such countries, children are encouraged to inform on their parents if they make critical comments—or even tell jokes—about government leaders or about the dominant ideology (in the modern period, that would almost always refer to communism, Nazism, or radical Islamism). Consequently, parents would often fear to speak openly in front of their children.

ESSAY: ONLY IF THERE IS A GOD, IS MURDER WRONG

20.13 You shall not murder.

Although none of the second five of the Ten Commandments mention God's name, they all relate to God because God is the giver of these commandments. Indeed, ultimately God is the reason to observe them. One does not have to be religious to acknowledge this. As Bertrand Russell, perhaps the twentieth-century's most eloquent atheist, put it: "*I cannot see how to refute the argument for the subjectivity of all ethical values*, but I refuse to accept that the only thing wrong with wanton cruelty is that I don't like it" (emphasis added).[16] Though Russell lived well into his nineties, he was never able to produce a stronger argument against wanton cruelty than "I don't like it."

To state the case as clearly as possible: If there is no God who says, "Do not murder," there is no way of saying murder is objectively wrong. One can say, "I don't like it," or "I think it is wrong," or "I feel it is wrong," or "My society says it is wrong," but not "It is wrong." For that, you need God.

The commonly offered utilitarian argument—we don't murder others because we don't want others to murder us—is not a coherent argument.

First, it is not even an argument that murder is morally wrong. It is only an argument that for reasons of self-interest, people should want to see murder outlawed.

Second, it is terribly naïve. Of the vast number of individuals and groups who have committed murder, very few wanted to be murdered. Yet, that fact stopped none of them from murdering. They murder because they believe they will get away with it; they don't think they will be murdered.

Third, in those rare cases in which people do not care if they are killed—such as Islamist suicide bombers who believe they will receive heavenly rewards for murdering people they deem heretical—the utilitarian argument is completely useless.

Fourth, as Yale Professor Timothy Snyder wrote regarding Hitler, "Rejecting the biblical commandments, said Hitler, was what human beings must do. 'If I can accept a divine commandment,' he wrote, 'it's this one: "Thou shalt preserve the species."'"[17] In other words, murderous ideologies are far more likely to be guided by "survival of the fittest" than the argument, "Well, since I don't want to be murdered, I won't murder."

In sum, it is unlikely there has been even one would-be murderer in history who decided not to murder because of the argument, "We don't murder others because we don't want others to murder us."

There are no qualifiers whatsoever in the Sixth Commandment. It prohibits the murder of any human being, regardless of race, religion, class, gender, or any other distinction. The murder of a non-Jew is as heinous in God's eyes as the murder of a Jew, as is the murder of a person of a different race, a baby, a centenarian, or any other innocent human being.

ESSAY: THE SIXTH COMMANDMENT PROHIBITS MURDER, NOT KILLING

As important as the Sixth Commandment is, it is also one of the most misunderstood and frequently misquoted commandments. The reason is the Sixth Commandment *does not forbid killing; it forbids murder.* Murder is the immoral killing of a human being. There is moral killing and immoral killing. If the Ten Commandments forbade killing, the taking of human life under any circumstance would be forbidden. There would be no such thing as a just killing. Killing in self-defense would be forbidden, as would killing in the defense of another person, and no war would ever be justified.

If the commandment said "Do not kill," it would be forbidden to kill someone who was in the process of shooting a hundred schoolchildren; it would be forbidden to kill a man who had entered your home and was about to murder your spouse and your children; it would have been forbidden to fight the Nazis, thereby allowing them to take over as much of the world as they wished, and to then murder, torture, and enslave hundreds of millions of people. (Jehovah's Witnesses, who do understand this commandment as forbidding all killing, did not fight *against* Hitler or *for* him. Some Jehovah's Witnesses, specifically because of their pacifism, were incarcerated in Nazi concentration camps where the Nazis employed them as barbers; they were the only inmates the Nazi murderers were confident would not slit their throats.)

"Do not kill" is the position known as pacifism, the belief it is always wrong to take a human life. Such a position is morally untenable, as the above examples should make abundantly clear—and it has nothing to do with the Sixth Commandment, which prohibits murder, not killing. Hebrew, like English, has two words for taking a life: *harog* ("kill") and *ratzach* ("murder"). The Sixth Commandment uses *ratzach*.

The prohibition of murder is reserved for taking the life of innocent humans, not people who deserve to be killed (such as the person murdering the schoolchildren). That is why we say, "A terrorist *murdered* five people," but we say, "The police *killed* the terrorist." That is why we say, "I killed a fly," not "I murdered a fly"—because "murder" is reserved for taking human life. And that is why we say, "I killed him in self-defense," not "I murdered him in self-defense."

> *If there is no God who says, "Do not murder," murder is not objectively wrong. One can say, "I don't like it," or "I think it is wrong," or "My society says it is wrong," but not "It is wrong." For that, you need God.*

Unfortunately, most English-language Bibles, going back to the King James translation, have translated this verse as "Thou shalt not kill." This has led to many people using this commandment to defend pacifism and to oppose capital punishment for murder. (There may be valid reasons to oppose the death penalty for murder, but the Sixth Commandment is not one of them.)

Why did the King James translation of the Bible use the word "kill" rather than "murder"? Probably because four hundred years ago, when the translation was made, "kill" was synonymous with "murder." Whatever the reason, it is inconceivable the brilliant translators of the King James Bible thought the Ten Commandments forbade killing in self-defense, killing in defense of one's family or of an innocent stranger, or conducting a just war.

Nor do you have to know how the English language has evolved in order to understand the Ten Commandments could not have prohibited all killing. The very same part of the Bible that contains the Ten Commandments—the

Torah—commands the death penalty for premeditated murder (to cite one of many examples, see Exodus 21:12-14), and allows killing in war and in self-defense (see commentary to Exodus 22:1).

ESSAY: WHY IS ADULTERY IN THE TEN COMMANDMENTS?

20.13 (cont.) You shall not commit adultery.

The prohibition on a married person having sexual relations with anyone other than his or her spouse is probably, for many people, the most consistently difficult of the Ten Commandments to observe. The reasons are not hard to guess. One is the enormous power of the sex drive. It can be very hard to keep it in check for the entirety of one's marriage, especially when an attractive outsider makes him or herself sexually and/or emotionally available. Another reason is the human desire to love and be loved. For most people, there is no more powerful emotion than love. If one falls in love with someone other than one's spouse while married, it takes great effort not to commit adultery. And if we add the unfortunate but all too common circumstance of a troubled marriage, adultery becomes even more difficult to resist.

> *The Sixth Commandment does not prohibit killing. It prohibits murder.*

Why is adultery prohibited in the Ten Commandments? Because, like the other nine commandments, it is indispensable to forming and maintaining higher civilization. Adultery threatens the building block of the civilization the Ten Commandments seek to create. That building block is the family—a married father and mother and their children (this does not mean no other forms of families exist, but this is the Torah ideal). Anything that threatens the family unit is prohibited in the Bible. Adultery is one example. Other examples include not honoring one's father and mother and the prohibitions against injecting any sexuality into the family unit.

Why is the family so important? Because without it, social stability is impossible. Because without it, the passing on of society's values from generation to generation is impossible. Because commitment to a spouse and children makes men and women more responsible and mature. Because the family meets most people's deepest emotional needs. Because it is the best provider of economic security to women, children, and even men (studies repeatedly show how much more money married men earn and save, how much less time they spend on non-productive pursuits, etc.).[18] And because nothing comes close to the family in giving children a secure and stable childhood.

Why does adultery threaten the family? The most obvious reason is sex with someone other than one's spouse can all too easily lead to the spouses separating. Adultery does not automatically lead to divorce, but it often does. There is another reason adultery is inimical to family life: It can lead to pregnancy and then to the birth of a child who will, in almost all cases, start out life without a married father and mother (or even otherwise committed to each other and to the child).

Even if adultery doesn't destroy a family, it can do serious harm—particularly when it is ongoing—to a marriage. Aside from the sense of betrayal and loss of trust it causes, it means the partner having an affair lives a fraudulent life. When a husband or wife is having an affair, his or her thoughts are almost constantly about that other person and/or about how to deceive one's spouse. The life of deception an affair necessarily entails damages a marriage even if the betrayed spouse remains unaware of the affair—because when you deceive someone daily, that person is not relating to the real you, but to an actor.

Finally, the commandment prohibiting adultery doesn't come with an asterisk saying adultery is okay if both spouses agree to it (a so-called "open marriage"). Spouses who have extramarital sex with the permission of their husband or wife may not be hurting their spouse's feelings, but they are harming the institution of marriage and their children, if they have any. Protecting the family, more than protecting spouses from emotional pain, is the reason for the commandment.

Moreover, the Torah considers adultery to be an offense against three parties: the spouse, the family/community, and God. For this reason, too, even if a couple agrees to have an "open marriage," an adulterous affair is still forbidden by this commandment.

No one knows what goes on in anyone else's marriage. And if we did, we might often well understand why one or the other sought love outside the marriage. But no higher civilization can be created or can endure that condones adultery—thus, the importance of this commandment. It is intended to preserve the sanctity of the family, which is the essential structure of civilization. Indeed, Commandments Six through Ten are each intended to safeguard a foundation of civilization: life, family, property, truth, and justice; and the Tenth Commandment, as we shall see, protects all of them.

Adultery is considered a capital offense in the Torah. However, in my view, in virtually all cases of capital punishment in the Torah except for murder, the punishment is prescribed primarily to communicate the severity of the offense and to serve as a deterrent—as opposed to being carried out. We have no record in Jewish history of which I am aware when a person was executed (except for murder) for a capital offense listed in the Torah. In the case of adultery, for example, according to ancient Jewish law, capital punishment for adultery was only possible if two witnesses had warned the couple of the consequences of their behavior, if the couple acknowledged the warning and essentially said that they didn't care, and the couple then closed themselves in a room to which others could not gain access. In other words, it was virtually impossible for the death penalty to be meted out for adultery.

Finally, in the Torah, both the man and the woman are held responsible for committing adultery, and therefore receive the same punishment (Leviticus 20:10).

ESSAY: THE UNIQUE IMPORTANCE OF THE COMMANDMENT AGAINST STEALING

20.13 (cont.) You shall not steal.

The Eighth Commandment, "Do not Steal," is unique in that *it encompasses all the other commandments on the second tablet*:

Murder is the stealing of another person's life.

Adultery is the stealing of another person's spouse.

Giving false testimony is stealing justice.

And coveting is the desire to steal what belongs to another person.

This commandment is unique in another way: It is the only completely open-ended commandment. All the other commandments are specific. The Fifth Commandment, for example, states whom one must honor—one's parents. The Sixth Commandment, prohibiting murder, is only about taking the life of an innocent human being. The Seventh Commandment, prohibiting adultery, is also specific to a married person; two unmarried people cannot commit adultery.

But the commandment against stealing doesn't even hint at what it is we are forbidden to steal. It means we cannot take *anything* that belongs to another person.

STEALING HUMAN BEINGS

This commandment was always understood to mean, before anything, we are not allowed to steal human beings. The early rabbinic tradition interpreted this commandment as specifically referring to kidnapping.[19]

That is one reason no one with even an elementary understanding of the Eighth Commandment could ever use the Bible to justify the most common manner by which people became enslaved: kidnapping. Kidnapping people and selling them into slavery, as was done to Africans and others throughout history, is forbidden by the Eighth Commandment. Critics of the Bible who argue the Bible allowed such slavery, and defenders of such slavery who used the Bible, were both wrong.

And lest there be any confusion about this issue, the very next chapter of the Torah specifies a person who kidnaps another—particularly when done with the intention of selling the victim into slavery—"shall be put to death" (Exodus 21:16).

STEALING PROPERTY

Of course, the most obvious meaning of the Eighth Commandment is a prohibition against stealing property—and that, in turn, means God sanctifies personal property. Just as we are forbidden to steal people, we are forbidden to steal what people own.

It has been shown over and over that private property, beginning with land ownership, is indispensable to creating a free and decent society. Virtually all tyrannies, especially totalitarian regimes, take away private property rights. And in the ancient and medieval worlds, almost no one had property rights: a few rich people owned all the land.

Then, in nineteenth-century Europe, many socialists argued for confiscating private property and giving it to the "people." Where that advice was followed, in what came to be known as the communist world, theft of property quickly resulted in a total theft of freedom, and ultimately a massive theft of life.

STEALING ANOTHER PERSON'S REPUTATION, DIGNITY, ETC.

Another enormously important meaning of the commandment against stealing concerns stealing the many non-material things each person owns: his or her reputation, dignity, trust, and intellectual property.

1. A person's reputation: Stealing a person's good name—whether through libel, slander, or gossip—is a particularly destructive form of theft. Unlike money or property, once a person's good name has been stolen, it can almost never be fully restored. As Shakespeare put it in *Othello*: "Who steals my purse steals trash; 'tis something, nothing, 'twas mine, 'tis his.... But he that filches from me my good name robs me of that which not enriches him and makes me poor indeed." In *Othello*, the theft of Desdemona's good name leads to her murder.

2. A person's dignity: The act of stealing a person's dignity is known as humiliation. And humiliating people, especially in public, can do permanent damage, given that dignity may be the most precious thing we own.

3. A person's trust: Stealing a person's trust is what we know as deceit. In fact, a Hebrew term for deceiving someone uses the term *stealing* (*g'neivat da'at*), which literally means "stealing knowledge," or "stealing another's mind." An example is the tricking of people into buying something, as when a real estate agent omits telling a prospective purchaser about the flaws in a home in order to make a sale.

Another example would be when someone deceives another person with insincere proclamations of love in order to obtain material or sexual favors. He or she has stolen from the person knowledge about their true intentions.

4. A person's intellectual property: This form of theft includes anything from copying software or films, to downloading music and movies without paying for them, to stealing a person's words (plagiarism).

In a major moral statement emphasizing how right and important it is to cite the source of an idea or a quote, the Mishna says, "A person who quotes a statement in the name of the person who stated it brings redemption to the world."[20]

Why would this act "bring redemption to the world"? Because when people cite the source of an idea or statement they quote, they are declaring they value truth over ego; and a world that values truth over ego would indeed be a redeemed world. Conversely, when we do not cite the source of a quote—or idea, or a humorous line—we are stealing that quote or idea from the person who came up with it. Amazingly, at least in America, people actually admit it. I have been told

> *Kidnapping people and selling them into slavery, as was done to Africans and others throughout history, is forbidden by the Eighth Commandment.*

any number of times after a speech, almost always by honorable people, "I'm going to steal that idea from you!" They don't realize how literally true their statement is.

Stealing a life, a person, a spouse, material property, intellectual property, a reputation, dignity, or trust: there is hardly any aspect of human life not harmed—sometimes irreparably—by stealing.

It is fair to say if everyone observed only one of the Ten Commandments, observing the commandment "Do Not Steal"—with all of its manifold implications—would, by itself, make an ethically decent world.

There is another reason why stealing may well be the ultimate root of most evil. That reason is: corruption.

Virtually every society in history, and most societies in the world today—certainly non-democratic ones—were and are filled with corruption. People pay government officials for favors; government officials get rich selling state companies and contracts; individuals pay police or government officials to avoid prosecution; judges are bribed to twist verdicts (a practice specifically banned in the Torah—Exodus 23:8); schools and officials are bribed to get a son or daughter into a prestigious university; and so on.

> *Stealing also applies to the non-material things each person owns: his or her reputation, dignity, trust, and intellectual property.*

More than anything else, it is widespread corruption that makes it impossible for a society to progress politically, morally, or economically.

THE NINTH COMMANDMENT: LIES CAUSE THE GREATEST EVILS

20.13 (cont.) You shall not bear false witness against your neighbor.

The Ninth Commandment prohibits lying (specifically in court, but, as we shall see, outside of a courtroom as well).

While goodness and compassion may be the most important values in the micro, or personal, realm, in the macro, or societal, realm, truth is even more important than compassion or kindness. Virtually all the great societal evils—whether African slavery, communism, Nazism, or anti-Semitism—have been based on lies. There were probably some slave traders, Nazis, communists, and anti-Semites who were compassionate to at least some people, but all of them told, and most of them believed, some great lie that made or allowed them to participate in great evil.

African slavery was made possible in large measure by the lie that blacks were inherently inferior to whites. Communist totalitarianism was entirely based on lies. That's why the Soviet Union's Communist Party newspaper was named *Pravda*, the Russian word for "truth"—because the Party, not objective reality, was the source of truth. (The other major Soviet newspaper was *Izvestia*, which means "news." Thus, the Soviet dissident witticism: "There is no *Pravda* in *Izvestia* and no *Izvestia* in *Pravda*.")

The Holocaust would have been impossible without tens of millions of people believing the lie that Jews were sub-human. But the Nazis' lies about Jews are just one example of the lies anti-Semitism has always been based on. Indeed, Jews have been the most consistent objects of lies in history. These lies have been so grotesque they led to the mass murder of Jews. In medieval Europe—and even later—Jews were accused of killing Christian children in order to use their blood to bake Passover matzos. Whole Jewish communities were annihilated or expelled because of lies. Jews in medieval Europe were accused of causing the great plague known as the Black Death, even though Jews also died in the plague.

And the one Jewish state, Israel, has likewise been the subject of enormous lies fueling the desire to annihilate it. One such example is "Israel does to the Palestinians what the Nazis did to the Jews." That was actually said by one of my debate opponents at the most prestigious debating forum in the world, the Oxford Union, in 2014. It would make sense that anyone who believes such a lie would want to see the Jewish state annihilated.

> *Virtually all the great societal evils—whether African slavery, communism, Nazism, or anti-Semitism—have been based on lies.*

There is only so much evil that can be done by individual sadists and sociopaths. In order to murder millions of people, vast numbers of normal, even otherwise decent, people must believe lies. Mass evil is committed not because a vast number of people seek to be cruel, but because they are fed convincing lies that what is evil is actually good.

WHAT THE NINTH COMMANDMENT PROHIBITS

The Ninth Commandment means two things:

1. Do not lie when testifying in court.

2. Do not lie outside of a courtroom.

The first is obvious, since the word "witness" appears in the commandment. But both the twelfth-century Jewish commentator, Abraham Ibn Ezra, and the influential twentieth-century biblical scholar, Brevard Childs of Yale University, wrote that the commandment was about truth-telling generally. As Childs pointed out, if the Ten Commandments were solely concerned with truth and falsehood in a courtroom, it would have added words such as "in court."

Regarding false testimony in court, it should be clear to anyone that when people testify falsely in a courtroom, there can be no justice. And without justice, there is no civilization.

In addition to prohibiting perjury in the Ten Commandments, other Torah laws ordain measures to discourage it.

First, two eyewitnesses are required in order for the evidence to be regarded as valid: "A person shall be put to death only on the testimony of two or more witnesses; he must not be put to death on the testimony of a single witness" (Deuteronomy 17:6). It is much more difficult to commit and get away with perjury with another person than alone.

Second, false witnesses were at risk of receiving the same punishment that would be meted out to the accused: "If the man who testified is a false witness...you shall do to him as he schemed to do to his fellow" (Deuteronomy 19:18-19). That would mean the false witnesses in a murder case, for example, would be put to death if their testimony led to the falsely accused being executed.

Third, in cases involving capital punishment, the witnesses had to initiate the execution (Deuteronomy 17:7).

This phrase "against your neighbor" must mean something not obvious; otherwise, the commandment would simply state, "Do not bear false witness." Why does it add "against your neighbor"?

The answer is the commandment prohibits lying "against" —that is, to the detriment of—your neighbor. The commandment is not against all lying. If one lies for moral reasons to aid one's neighbor, as did those non-Jews who hid Jews during the Holocaust, such lying is allowed. Lying is sometimes moral, just as killing is sometimes moral. Those who argue that lying is always wrong have to explain why killing is sometimes moral but lying is never moral. They also have to explain why the rape, torture, and murder of innocent men, women, and children is morally preferable to telling a lie in order to save them.

For reasons incomprehensible to me, there have been brilliant and universally admired religious figures who condemned all lies as equally evil. St. Augustine, perhaps the preeminent Church Father—certainly the most famous—believed lying to save a life is short-sighted and unjustifiable, since telling a lie costs a person eternal life: "Does he not speak most perversely who says that one person ought to die spiritually, so another may live?...Since then, eternal life is lost by lying, a lie may never be told for the preservation of the temporal life of another."[21]

One wonders what Augustine and other religious figures who condemn all lying thought of God's approval of Rahab the Canaanite lying to protect the Israelite spies (Joshua 2).

In the modern period, the most famous German philosopher, Immanuel Kant (1724–1804), echoed Augustine's view: If a would-be murderer asks whether "our friend who is pursued by him has taken refuge in our home," we cannot lie to save our friend's life.[22]

In later Judaism, lying to protect *shalom bayit*, "peace in the home," was also permitted.

Finally, the Hebrew words for "truth" and "lie" are illuminating: The word meaning "false," *shaker*, is a variant of *sheker*, the Hebrew word for "lie." Both words consist of three Hebrew letters: the next-to-last letter of the Hebrew alphabet (*shin*) and the two letters preceding it (*kuf, resh*). In contrast, the Hebrew word for "truth," *emet*, consists of the first (*aleph*), middle (*mem*), and last (*tav*) letters of the Hebrew alphabet. This may, of course, be mere coincidence. But I doubt it. Hebrew words in the Torah have a great deal of meaning beyond their literal definition. As Jewish tradition points out, the Hebrew word for "lie" encompasses a tiny percentage of the Hebrew alphabet—the three penultimate letters—while the word for truth encompasses the entire Hebrew alphabet. Lies are a tiny fraction of what is real, whereas truth encompasses everything.

THE MEANING OF THE TENTH AND LAST COMMANDMENT

20.14 You shall not covet your neighbor's house: you shall not covet your neighbor's wife, or his male or female slave, or his ox or his ass, or anything that is your neighbor's.

Commandments Six, Seven, Eight, and Nine prohibit murder, adultery, stealing, and perjury. What could be left for the final commandment to prohibit?

What remains is a prohibition of the primary reason people murder, commit adultery, steal, and lie—they covet something that belongs to others: their spouse, their house, their servants, their animals, etc.

The most obvious example, of course, is stealing. Thieves steal because they covet that which they stole. But coveting is also the reason for many murders; it is, of course, the reason for adultery—coveting the spouse of another person—and the reason for bearing false witness is to conceal all the crimes so often caused by coveting.

In fact, coveting not only leads to committing one of the preceding four actions—murder, adultery, theft, lying—but coveting often leads to committing *more* than one of them. The Bible later provides two such examples in the lives of two kings.

The first example is found in II Samuel 11–12, where King David covets Bathsheba, the beautiful wife of Uriah, an officer in David's army. He summons her to the royal palace and sleeps with her. When she becomes pregnant, and David realizes—after making strenuous efforts—he will not be able to keep the matter quiet, he arranges to have Uriah killed. What starts with coveting a married woman leads to both adultery and murder.

The second example, in I Kings 21, occurs a little over a century later, when King Ahab covets a field adjacent to the royal estates belonging for generations to a man named Navot, who refuses to sell the land to the king. (Israelite law seems to have protected a commoner's right to refuse a royal demand; in this case, the king's demand to sell to him Navot's family estate.) King Ahab is deeply disturbed, but feels there is nothing he can do. Then his wife, the Baal-worshipping Queen Jezebel, tells her husband she knows how to gain possession of the land for him. She arranges for two witnesses to give false testimony of Navot cursing God and King Ahab, an act regarded as treason, for which the punishment was death and confiscation of the guilty party's property.

That, indeed, is what Jezebel does. Navot is convicted on the basis of false testimony, put to death, and the state (meaning the king) confiscates Navot's land. In one of the Bible's most dramatic episodes, while Ahab is enjoying his new possession, the prophet Elijah, acting at God's behest, confronts him and says, "Have you murdered and also inherited?" (I Kings 21).

In this story, what began as coveting culminated in the violation of three other of the Ten Commandments: the prohibitions against bearing false witness, murder, and stealing.

The Only Commandment against Thought

Most remarkably, however, the Tenth Commandment does something highly atypical of Torah law: it legislates thought. Each of the other nine commandments legislates behavior. In fact, of the 613 laws in the Torah, virtually none prohibit thought. We therefore need to understand what coveting means and, equally importantly, what it doesn't mean.

To covet is much more than "to desire." The Hebrew verb *lachmod* means to desire to the point of seeking to take something that belongs to another person. Note there are two operative elements here: "seeking to take," and "belongs to another person."

"Seeking to take" does not mean "to desire"; nor does it mean envying or, in the case of your neighbor's spouse, lusting after. *Neither envy nor lust is prohibited in the Ten Commandments.* While uncontrolled envy and lust can surely lead to bad things and both can be psychologically and emotionally destructive, neither one is prohibited here.

Why? Because neither is the same as coveting. The Tenth Commandment does not prohibit people from thinking, "What a great house (or car or spouse) my neighbor has; I wish I had such a house (or car or spouse)." That may end up being destructive. But it may also end up being constructive because it can spur people to work harder and improve their lives so they can obtain a house, car, or spouse like the one their neighbor has.

It is when people want and seek to gain possession of the *specific* house, car, or spouse belonging to another that evil ensues. That is what the Tenth Commandment prohibits. Therefore, one of these Ten Commandments, these ten basic rules of life, must be that we simply cannot allow ourselves to covet what belongs to our neighbor. Whatever belongs to another person must be regarded as sacrosanct. We cannot seek to own anything that belongs to another.

Unlike desire, envy, or lust, coveting almost inevitably leads to evil, and is, therefore, the one forbidden thought. We are not prohibited from wanting similar items to what our neighbor has; we are prohibited from wanting *what* our neighbor has.

AT LEAST WITH REGARD TO COVETING, PEOPLE CAN CONTROL HOW THEY THINK

The prohibition against coveting anything belonging to another—like the commandment against stealing anything belonging to another—reflects the Torah's profound affirmation of private property. The Torah recognizes there is dignity in having possessions.

Finally, the prohibition against coveting means the Torah recognizes, at least with regard to coveting, people can control how they think. The medieval commentator Ibn Ezra offered a good lesson on training ourselves how not to covet: We should come to regard anything belonging to another as beyond the realm of possibility of ever attaining. He gives the example of a poor village man who would never think of coveting the royal princess because he knows she is simply unattainable. On the other hand, this peasant might be tempted to covet the wife of his poor neighbor. What he needs to do, therefore, is train himself to think of his neighbor's wife in the same way he thinks of the princess—unattainable.

An even more obvious, contemporary, example of controlling our thoughts in this regard is how we might view a person who marries our sibling. Imagine you are a twenty-year-old man, and your twenty-three-year-old brother is dating a woman to whom you are attracted. You may well have all sorts of thoughts regarding her. But now imagine your brother and his girlfriend marry. Though you will continue to regard her as an attractive woman, you will now (hopefully) regard her as entirely off limits to you.

> *Coveting—not envy or lust—is prohibited by the Tenth Commandment.*

20.15 All the people witnessed the thunder and the lightening, the blare of the horn and the mountain smoking;

> The Torah emphasizes that an entire nation was present at Sinai, and witnessed the revelation—not a small group of followers, and not one chosen individual. This means Israelite skeptics and deniers as well as believers, young and old, men and women, the highly intelligent and those of lesser intelligence, all encountered God. The revelation at Sinai is not presented as a statement of faith, but as an historical event.
>
> One upshot of this claim is God is accessible to everyone. As the Psalmist writes, "The Lord is near to all who call Him" (Psalms 145:18). The Torah, too, is accessible to everyone—as the Torah itself proclaims later in Deuteronomy: "It [the Torah] is not in Heaven" (Deuteronomy 30:12).

20.15 (cont.) and when the people saw it, they fell back and stood at a distance.

20.16 "You speak to us," they said to Moses, "and we will obey; but let not God speak to us, lest we die."

20.17 Moses answered the people, "Be not afraid; for God has come only in order to test you, and in order that the fear of Him may be ever with you, so that you do not go astray."

20.18 so the people remained at a distance, while Moses approached the thick cloud where God was.

20.19 The Lord said to Moses: Thus shall you say to the Israelites: You yourselves saw that I spoke to you from the very heavens:

> God emphasizes it was He who spoke with the Israelites, not Moses. Commandments without a Commander are not compelling.
>
> Sarna adds that God noted He spoke from the heavens in order to emphasize He is entirely removed from the physical world; His "abode," so to speak, is in the heavens.

20.20 With Me, therefore, you shall not make any god of silver, nor shall you make for yourselves any gods of gold.

> Now that the Israelites have encountered God, He instructs them on how to properly worship Him. They may not make material representations of God even for the sake of worshipping God: If God is physical, the physical world is all there is, and death means total and permanent annihilation. So long as God exists beyond the physical world, there exists a realm in which we will endure beyond the death of our bodies.
>
> Also, the idea God is real even though He cannot be seen liberated the human mind to entertain the notion that even that which cannot be visualized exists. In this sense, the incorporeality of God ultimately helped make modern scientific thought possible.

20.21 Make for Me an altar of earth and sacrifice on it your burnt offerings and your sacrifices of well-being, your sheep and your oxen; in every place where I cause My name to be mentioned I will come to you and bless you.

> God does not need altars of gold and silver; they can even use the dirt of the earth to worship Him.
>
> Cassuto explains God repeats the term "your" ("your burnt offerings," "your sacrifices," "your sheep," "your oxen") in order to emphasize the people, not God, need sacrifices. This is an extremely important point. At Sinai, God demanded

we not murder, not steal, and keep the Sabbath; but He did not demand we pray to Him, sacrifice to Him, or otherwise worship Him—except by keeping His laws.

This verse is a license to have multiple centers of worship— "in every place where I cause my Name to be blessed." The Israelites may be worried that once they leave Mount Sinai, they will no longer be able—or at least have a place—to worship God. Therefore, God told them He is not exclusively connected with Mount Sinai; they can pray to Him no matter where they find themselves (sacrifices, however, were subsequently confined to the Tabernacle and later to the Great Temple in Jerusalem).

> *The complete desexualization of religion and of the family are two of the greatest achievements of the Torah.*

20.22 And if you make for Me an altar of stones, do not build it of hewn stones; for by wielding your tool upon them you have profaned them.

Why were hewn stones prohibited in the making of an altar to God?

According to Maimonides, "the idolaters of that time built their altars of hewn stones, therefore God forbade it. Lest we should be like them…He commanded the altar to be made of earth…that we might not worship him in the same manner in which idolaters used to worship their fictitious deities."[23]

20.23 Do not ascend My altar by steps, that your nakedness may not be exposed upon it.

This verse may be understood as a reaction to the widespread mixing of sex and religion in the ancient world. Ancient worship often involved cult prostitution and sexual displays. The Torah, in its ongoing battle against pagan practices, insists nakedness has no place in worship because it defames God's sanctuary. The complete de-sexualization of religion and of the family are two of the greatest achievements of the Torah.

CHAPTER

~21~

21.1 These are the laws that you shall set before them:

Essay: Why Didn't the Torah Abolish Slavery?

21.2 When you acquire a Hebrew slave, he shall serve six years; in the seventh year he shall go free, without payment.

The first laws God gave the Israelites after giving them the Ten Commandments concern the proper treatment of slaves. Just as the Ten Commandments begin with God's declaration that He took the Israelites out of Egypt, out of the "house of slaves," God begins this additional set of laws with slavery—as if to say to the Israelites, "Though you will be allowed an institution called 'slavery,' it cannot be anything like what you experienced in Egypt."

Nevertheless, the fact the Torah does not entirely abolish the institution of slavery is troubling. Since it is nearly universally agreed today slavery is inherently evil, how could a document claiming to be a moral guide—which, moreover, claims it is of divine origin—not prohibit slavery?

Here are several reasons:

First, the Torah did indeed ban the type of slavery modern people think of when they picture slavery—kidnapping free human beings and selling them for use as slaves. As explained regarding the Eighth Commandment, "Do not steal," the commandment was understood from its inception as first and foremost prohibiting stealing human beings. And, as if that were not enough, verse 16 in this chapter makes kidnapping of *any* person—Israelite or non-Israelite—for the purpose of enslavement a *capital crime.*

It is therefore not true to say the Torah did not ban slavery. What is true is the Torah did not ban *every form* of slavery. It prohibited what became the African slave trade and all institutions of slavery based on kidnapping. That there were Jews and Christians who nevertheless engaged in the African slave trade no more denies the Torah's prohibition of it than the existence of Jewish and Christian adulterers denies the Torah's prohibition of adultery.

> *It is not true to say the Torah did not ban slavery. What is true is the Torah did not ban every form of slavery.*

To provide a clarifying contrast, Muslims who were involved in the equally large Muslim slave trade were not violating Quranic or later Islamic law. The Muslim trade in slaves—of individuals kidnapped in Africa, India, Central Asia, and Central and Eastern Europe—also involved millions of souls. But unlike the Christian world, Islam "never preached the abolition of slavery as a doctrine."[1] The reason the Christian world ultimately abolished it is, quite simply, the Torah and the rest of the Bible.

Second, given how entrenched it was in every human society, had the Torah banned every form of slavery, it is quite likely many Israelites would have simply opted out of the Torah system entirely. To provide an analogy, had the founders of the United States banned slavery at the outset—something many of them wished to do—there would never have been a United States of America; the Southern colonies would never have joined the Union.

Similarly, had the Israelites opted out of the Torah's legal system over the issue of slavery, that would have ended ethical monotheism.

Nor would a complete ban have necessarily been a morally unambiguous achievement. Most of the "slavery" discussed in the Torah is "indentured servitude," wherein a person worked off a debt over a set period, or the destitute found room and board working for no pay. Again, the American parallel is morally clarifying. "Between one-half and two-thirds of all white immigrants to the British colonies between the Puritan migration of the 1630s and the Revolution came under indenture."[2] The reason was indentured servitude was the only way out of abject poverty for vast numbers of people—and they were Europeans in seventeenth and eighteenth century, not Middle Easterners in the Late Bronze Age 3,000 years ago.

The Torah is revolutionary in many of its teachings, such as its outright ban on the universal practice of human sacrifice. It is quite possible the Torah was the first legal document we know of to completely ban the practice. But sometimes the Torah's approach is *evolutionary*. In addition to slavery, one example might be animal sacrifice. Allowing animal sacrifice might have served as a way of weaning people away from—by offering a substitute for—human sacrifice.

Another example is polygamy. While the Torah allowed polygamy, its ideal is monogamy (see Genesis 2:24), which is why every instance of polygamy described in the Torah is described in a negative way. And Torah narrative is as important a source of values as is Torah law.

Though it did not immediately abolish all forms of slavery, the Torah both demanded and legislated a radically new attitude toward slaves, one not only more humane than the laws that prevailed in the ancient world, but more humane than laws that prevailed until the abolition of slavery in the West thousands of years later (see commentary to verse 26 in this chapter).

While the Torah does not expect people to completely transform themselves and their society overnight, the Torah *is* revolutionary and transformative in its ethical monotheism. It is revolutionary in its presentation of God as universal (not tribal); as wholly above and beyond nature; as the judge of all mankind; and as non-physical. It is revolutionary in its removal of all sexuality from God and from religion; in its removal of all sexuality from the family (in contrast to Egypt, where Egyptian royalty preferred and practiced incest); in its demand to love one's neighbor as oneself; in demanding repeatedly that we love and safeguard the stranger who resides among us; and in forbidding the rape of women during wartime—just to cite some of the major revolutionary theological and moral teachings and commandments of the Torah.

Third, in the following discussion, with the exceptions of verses 21 and 26, slavery refers to the institution of indentured servitude, wherein people sell themselves into "slavery" in order to pay off debts—either debts they do not have the funds to repay or debts incurred as a result of criminal activity, such as a thief who lacks the means to pay back what he stole (see, for example, Exodus 22:2 and 22:6).

In the case of criminal activity, given how rare it is for people who cheat and steal from others to ever recompense their victims, the institution of indentured servitude is not necessarily morally inferior to a thief or embezzler spending time in prison and in no way compensating those from whom he stole. Moreover, given the lack of a mechanism to recompense victims of theft, and given the abysmal prison conditions throughout history (and often now as well), ancient Israelite society was actually quite progressive in its reliance on indentured servitude instead of prison. If *A* robs *B*, who benefits from *A* going to prison? Society doesn't—it has to pay for the robber's room, board, incarceration costs, medical attention, etc. And, of course, *B* is never compensated for his losses. Added to that, many, if not most, criminals do not leave prison morally transformed, if for no other reason than they spent years with other criminals.

Indentured servitude was the only way out of abject poverty for vast numbers of people throughout history.

21.2 (cont.) When you acquire a Hebrew slave

The Hebrew actually says, "if," not "when" you acquire a slave. The Torah does not encourage, let alone require, Israelites to own slaves; it simply states that if they do, these laws must be obeyed.

There were three types of people who could become Hebrew slaves: paupers, debtors, and thieves. A pauper who could not make a living worked for another person in exchange for room and board; a debtor who was unable to pay his debts worked without salary until he worked off his debts; and a thief who was unable to make restitution would have to work off his theft.[3]

Furthermore, Hebrew slavery, as we see, was not perpetual. After a debt was paid, or a certain amount of time elapsed, the indentured individual became a free person.

21.2 (cont.) he shall serve six years; in the seventh year he shall go free,

No matter how great the sum needed to be paid back, the Torah set a six-year limit on a Hebrew slave's term of service (and less, if a debt was worked off sooner). Once again, the Torah uses the number seven—the great reminder that God created the world. In this instance, just as God created the world in six days and rested on the seventh, the Hebrew slave had to work for a maximum of six years and went free in the seventh.

21.2 (cont.) without payment [to the master].

Once the six years of service are concluded, the slave does not have to ransom himself or pay any sort of restitution to his master; he simply goes free. In addition, Deuteronomy legislates the slave should not be sent out without any funds or possessions, understanding if he came in as a pauper or in debt and then left his years of servitude with nothing, he would be back where he started. Thus, Deuteronomy rules: "When you set him free, do not let him go empty-handed. Furnish him out of the flock, threshing floor and vat, with which the Lord your God has blessed you" (see Deuteronomy 15:13-14 and the commentary there).

21.3 If he came single, he shall leave single; If he had a wife, his wife shall leave with him.

If the slave brought his wife and children into slavery with him, following the completion of his term of service they leave with him. The master does not have a right to anything or to anyone the slave brought with him into his servitude.

21.4 If his master gave him a wife, and she has borne him children, the wife and her children shall belong to the master, and he shall leave alone.

It was common at the time for a master to mate a Hebrew slave with a non-Israelite bondswoman. Whatever the intention of the master (most likely to procure more slaves for himself), in this way, the foreign woman who had somehow fallen into Israelite hands could have some semblance of a normal life, including children. The Torah makes no allowance whatsoever for separating her from her children, as was done to slaves in the American South and wherever else there was chattel slavery.

The Torah is silent about the issue of the non-Israelite slave woman's wishes regarding marrying the Israelite slave. Presumably, she did not have this choice, and that is morally troubling. On the other hand, few *free* women in history had a choice regarding whom they married. Also, the Torah was unique in legislating humane treatment of a captured non-Israelite female (see Deuteronomy 21:10-14).

Of course, to us today, leaving one's family after being freed is morally troubling. However, it is important to note the man does not have to leave his family. He can choose to remain with his master and thereby remain with the wife given to him while he was in servitude (and with his children)—the proof being this option is discussed in the very next verse.

21.5 But if the slave declares, "I love my master, and my wife and children: I do not wish to go free,"

Four points may help us understand this law from a moral perspective.

1. The male indentured servant who wants to remain with the non-Israelite wife given to him can choose to remain with her and their children. (Also, as noted two verses earlier in 21:3, if he came into servitude with a wife, he does leave with his wife and children; they do not remain with the master.)

2. If the slave does not love his master—or, more likely, simply detests his master—but only loves his given wife and their children, after he completes his term of service, he can try to buy back his newly formed family.

3. That the slave/bondsman no longer works for his master while his non-Israelite wife does, does not necessarily mean he loses all contact with her and his children. It would depend, presumably, on the humanity of the master.

4. This verse implies Hebrew masters often treated their slaves/bondsmen quite well. Otherwise, the existence of this provision—"if he loves his

master"—would have been unrecognizable to ancient Israelites, who would have scoffed at it.

21.6 his master shall take him before God.

In this context, the word *Elohim*, which normally means "God," refers to the local judges, who are thought to be doing God's work. This is not the only example of this use of *Elohim* in the Torah.

A TORAH CONTRAST TO THE CODE OF HAMMURABI

21.6 (cont.) He shall be brought to the door or the doorpost, and his master shall pierce his ear with an awl; and he shall then remain his slave for life.

This unique piece of legislation is a dramatic example of how dissimilar Torah law was from the laws of surrounding societies. With its focus on the ear, this law was clearly a response to the final ruling in the older Babylonian Code of Hammurabi (number 282): "If a male slave has said to his master, 'You are not my master,' his master shall prove him to be his slave and cut off his ear."

In other words, under Babylonian law, which is widely regarded as morally advanced for its time, cutting off the ear was a punishment for the slave who wanted to be free. In contrast, the Torah rules that the slave's ear is only pierced— *for wanting to remain a slave*. As Walter Kaufman, the Princeton philosopher, noted, this law is a "deliberate echo of [Hammurabi's ruling]—an echo that seems designed to bring out the deep differences between the two legislations."

WERE DAUGHTERS REALLY SOLD INTO SLAVERY?

21.7 When a man sells his daughter as a slave, she shall not be freed as male slaves are.

As I will explain, parents could not sell their children into slavery. What is depicted here is not about slavery and certainly not about sexual slavery. It is about indentured servitude.

People understandably think of it as slavery, because the Hebrew word *eved* is almost always translated as "slave." But this word also means "servant."

Moses, for example, is called an "*eved* of God"; no one assumes he was a "slave" of God.

Furthermore, a girl could become a maidservant—not a slave—only if her family sold her. No one else could sell a girl into "slavery."

Of course, any notion of parents selling their children is disturbing. But thousands of years ago, it was done everywhere including—albeit rarely—in Israel in circumstances of abject poverty. As reported later in the Bible (Nehemiah 5:5): "Although we are of the same flesh and blood as our fellow Jews and though our children are as good as theirs, yet we have to subject our sons and daughters to slavery. *Some of our daughters have already been enslaved, but we are powerless, because our fields and our vineyards belong to others*" (emphasis added).

In the twelfth century, Maimonides, in his Code of Jewish law, ruled: "A man may not sell his daughter [as a maidservant] unless he became impoverished to the extent that he owns nothing, neither land nor other property, not even the clothing he is wearing."[4] As Maimonides' ruling makes clear, the Torah is therefore putting parameters around a tragic practice. But recognizing that it almost inevitably occurs under dire circumstances, as is clear from the next verse, the Torah assures the girl many protections.

Capital punishment for premeditated murder is the only law that appears in all five books of the Torah.

For example, the girl was sold to a man with the expectation either he or his son would marry her. Of course, to most people today, it is unacceptable that a woman's family (essentially meaning her father) would choose a daughter's spouse. But that has been the case in all societies throughout history and in many societies to this day. Women—and men—began to freely choose whom they would marry only in the relatively recent past, and almost exclusively in parts of the Western world. Furthermore, having one's family choose a woman's husband in no way meant sexual slavery; if it did, virtually every married woman in history was a sexual slave.

21.8 If she proves to be displeasing to her master, who designated her for himself, he must let her be redeemed; he shall not have the right to sell her to outsiders, since he broke faith with her.

The Hebrew, translated here as "outsiders," literally means "a foreign nation." That would imply the Torah may have originally allowed the maidservant to be sold to another Israelite—as opposed to a non-Israelite, in which case she would likely be used, abused, and resold. However, from very early times, it was understood as a prohibition to sell her to anyone, including another Israelite.[5]

If neither the master nor his son marries the young woman, the master is regarded as having acted deceitfully, a sin greatly magnified if he then sells her off to someone else, which is expressly forbidden here. Thus, if the master decides he does not wish her as a wife for himself or his son, since he is not allowed to sell her, he must let her be redeemed by her relatives.

21.9 And if he designated her for his son, he shall deal with her as is the practice with free maidens.

The maidservant is guaranteed protection as a wife of either the father or the son. The very fact she is to be treated as if she were a "free maiden" is yet another reason to believe the Torah is not referring to slavery when speaking about a family selling its daughter.

21.10 If he marries another, he must not withhold from this one her food, her clothing, or her conjugal rights.

If the master marries another woman in addition to his maidservant, the maidservant wife is not to be neglected in favor of the new wife. She retains the rights and privileges of a wife.

What is remarkable here is the concept of "conjugal rights." Sarna points out that of all the ancient Near Eastern law codes, the Torah was unique in asserting a woman is legally entitled to sexual gratification. And what "slave" has ever had conjugal—or any other—rights?

A sold daughter is not only not to be a sex slave, she is not to be a chattel slave either; she is not owned property. Therefore, it is not accurate to call a daughter who is sold by her parents a "slave." She is sold to a man who will eventually marry her; and if he doesn't want to marry her, his son can. If neither does, she goes free (see next verse). That is not slavery.

21.11 If he fails her in these three ways, she shall go free, without payment.

> The Torah restates that many obligations are owed to this daughter who was sold. The Torah delineates protection after protection of the girl involved. She has human rights; she has the dignity of marriage; she cannot be sold; she is to be redeemed by her family, if she is not to be a wife; and she even has conjugal rights.

21.12 He who fatally strikes a man shall be put to death.

> The prohibition against murder is the most important ethical commandment, and thus it is dealt with next in what is essentially a recapitulation and explication of the Ten Commandments.

> As Maimonides ruled: "There is no offense about which the Torah is so strict as it is about bloodshed, as it is said: 'You shall not pollute the land in which you live; for blood pollutes the land'" (Numbers 35:33).[6]

Since man was created in God's image, the last place a murderer could, or should, find refuge is in a house of the Creator.

> Capital punishment for premeditated murder is the only law that appears in all five books of the Torah (Genesis 9:6; this verse and verse 14 in this chapter; Leviticus 24:17; Numbers 35:16 ff.; and Deuteronomy 19:11-13). But the Torah makes it clear in the very next verse (and elsewhere) that when a homicide is unintentional or unpremeditated, capital punishment is not imposed.

UNINTENTIONAL HOMICIDE

21.13 If he did not do it by design, but it came about by an act of God, I will assign you a place to which he can flee.

> This verse refers to a killing that is not premeditated, what we would generally deem an accidental killing. The term "act of God" is used to this day (in insurance policies, for example) to denote such accidents. Three examples of such accidents are offered in Numbers 35:22-23: pushing someone without malice

aforethought, throwing an object that hits someone unintentionally, and inadvertently dropping a heavy object upon another person.

In the ancient world, if a member of one family killed a member of another, the family of the victim would feel compelled, or at the very least permitted, to defend its honor by either killing the killer or even other members of the killer's family. These blood feuds were entrenched in ancient society, so it would have been impossible to banish them altogether. The Torah instead provides a means of protecting the accidental killer from avengers.

The words, "I will assign you a place to which he can flee" refer to a city of refuge, a designated place in which a person who killed through accident or non-criminal negligence was guaranteed legal protection (see Numbers 35:9-15).

UNLIKE IN OTHER CULTURES, THERE IS NO SANCTUARY FOR MURDERERS

21.14 When a man schemes against another and kills him treacherously, you shall take him from My very altar to be put to death.

In societies as diverse as Phoenicia, Syria, Greece, and Rome, the altar of a temple provided protection to fugitives, including those guilty of premeditated murder. The Torah was the only legal code in the ancient world to declare there is no sanctuary for murderers.

Since man was created in God's image, the last place a murderer could, or should, find refuge is in a house of the Creator. A later biblical text confirms this Torah law was not just on the books, but was enforced. When the late King David's general, Joab, a man with much blood on his hands, tried to claim sanctuary by holding onto an altar, King Solomon ordered his leading general to kill Joab on the spot as punishment for "the blood of the innocent that Joab has shed" (I Kings 2:28-34).

The Torah wording, "you shall take him from My very altar to be put to death," also makes it clear people are not to rely on God to execute murderers. It is human beings who are responsible for executing one who deliberately takes the life of another—"Whoever sheds the blood of man, *by man* shall his blood be shed" (Genesis 9:6; emphasis added).

The Torah's view is in direct opposition to the frequently stated argument that only God has the right to take the life of a murderer. People may make this argument, but there is no basis in the Bible for it.

HITTING A PARENT IS A GRAVE OFFENSE

21.15 He who strikes his father or his mother shall be put to death.

A father or mother who is struck does not have to die in order for the child to deserve to be put to death. This law is a radical defense of the uniquely high status the Torah gives to parents. This is shown by the fact that only when one hits a parent—not hitting an offical, not even a king—is one punishable by death. Hitting a parent is a profound violation of the commandment to honor one's parents. A child (of almost any age) who hits a parent has not only dishonored but also humiliated the parent, and completely undermined the parent's authority.

While the Torah does not specify what exactly constitutes striking a parent, the Talmud ruled that to be subject to the death penalty, a person would have to hit his parent hard enough to draw blood.[7]

While the Torah forbids striking a parent, Talmudic law subsequently forbade a parent to hit a grown child. The Talmud even records the view that a parent who strikes an adult child should be excommunicated—lest that provoke the child to hit back and thereby violate this serious biblical prohibition.[8]

This law also protects the child: even if hit severely, the parent is not allowed to kill the child, only a court can ("will be put to death" means a court will do it). The Hebrew phrase *mot yu'mat* ("he shall be put to death") always refers to a court condemning a guilty party to death. Instead of allowing the parent to kill a violent child—which was permitted, for example, in Roman law—the parent must instead bring the child to court.

Since we have no record of an Israelite being executed for hitting a parent, we should infer Jews understood the punishment was meant to show how serious the offense was (see commentary to verse 17), rather than an injunction to actually be carried out.

Finally, and of particular significance, the Torah makes it clear hitting either a father or mother is an equally terrible act. Over and over, as in the Fifth Commandment, the Torah emphasizes the equal status of both parents. The father is not more important than the mother. If the Torah didn't hold both parents in equally high esteem, it would have made striking one's father a greater offense than striking one's mother.

21.16 He who kidnaps a man—whether he has sold him or is still holding him—shall be put to death.

In Deuteronomy 24:7, Moses speaks of punishing with death a slave-trading kidnapper who abducts a fellow Israelite. Here, the Torah is clearly referring to the kidnapping of any person (the Hebrew word is *ish*, the generic term for "person"). *The kidnapping of any human being, regardless of religion, race, or nationality, is a capital offense.*

The English translation here uses the word "kidnaps." But the Torah uses the word *gonev*, which means "steal." It is the same word used in the Eighth Commandment—one reason that commandment was always understood, first and foremost, as prohibiting kidnapping, i.e., stealing a person.

It therefore bears repeating the Eighth Commandment, as well as the explicit prohibition against stealing a human being in this verse, would have forbidden most forms of slavery, given that historically most slavery began with the stealing of human beings.

CURSING A PARENT IS ALSO A GRAVE OFFENSE

21.17 He who insults his father or his mother shall be put to death.

The Hebrew word *m'qalel*, translated here as "insults," is more accurately translated as "curses." The Torah is likely referring to cursing in which the name of God is invoked, thereby simultaneously showing contempt both for God and one's parents (see a related case in Leviticus 24:10-16 and 23, which does not involve a parent, but which involves the only instance in the Torah of cursing which results in a death sentence).

As we do not know of a case in which a child who cursed a parent was actually put to death, one surmises the death penalty is listed here in order to emphasize how terrible cursing a parent is.

21.18 If men quarrel and one strikes the other with stone or fist, and he does not die but has to take to his bed—

21.19 if he then gets up and walks outdoors upon his staff, the assailant shall go unpunished, except that he must pay for his idleness and his cure.

The assailant described here is engaged in a fight with the person he hit, and therefore is not regarded as necessarily more in the wrong than the person who was injured. Nonetheless, he still has to face the consequences of his actions, and must therefore compensate the victim for the time during which he was unable to work and for his medical expenses. The word *shivto*—translated here as "idleness," and which literally means "his sitting"—refers to the time the injured man is unable to work.

IF A SLAVE IS BEATEN AND DIES

21.20 When a man strikes his slave, male or female, with a rod, and he dies there and then, he must be avenged.

When a human life is taken by intent or by reckless endangerment, it must be avenged. Thus, like any murderer, a master who murders his slave is subject to the death penalty. Sarna points out that of all the ancient Near Eastern law codes, the Torah is unique in protecting slaves from homicide and other forms of maltreatment by their masters (Exodus 21:26-27).

21.21 But if he survives a day or two, he is not to be avenged, since he is the other's property.

This verse sounds troubling because in this translation (and many others), it appears to say if a master beats his slave, and the slave dies after a day or two, nothing happens to the master. But this may not be what the verse intends to say. Again, as always, we must first go to the Hebrew original:

"But if he stands for a day or two, he is not avenged...."

The Hebrew does not say "survives," it says "stands." This literal reading may imply that if the slave is not so injured as to be unable to get up, the master is not put to death if the slave dies some time later (of course, if a tooth or eye was knocked out, or a leg or arm permanently injured, the slave went free). In other words, if the slave is strong enough to get up and stand for a day or two, the master is not punished (with a death sentence—see previous verse).

> *The kidnapping of any human being, regardless of religion, race, or nationality, is a capital offense.*

Reinforcing this read is the highly regarded NIV (New International Version) translation: "But they (the master) are not to be punished if the slave recovers after a day or two ...."

Three thousand years ago, when "medicine" was usually worthless (and often harmful), people generally died from severe beatings, and if they recovered for a day or two, it was not assumed it was the beating that caused the person's death. Moreover, if the beaten slave did not "stand" for a day or two, and then died, the master was liable for the death penalty.

Regarding the seemingly callous statement that "he is the other's property," it is undoubtedly meant to convey the idea that no rational master would want to lose a slave, given how valuable a slave was.

Now, of course, one can imagine a very wealthy master who doesn't care about his monetary loss, or a sadistic master who would beat his slave to within an inch of his life.

Nevertheless, even a master who was so wealthy he didn't care about the freeing of any number of slaves (and one doubts there were many such people) would have to be concerned about causing the death of the slave (within a day) because he, the master, would not merely lose a slave; he would lose his own life.

As regards a sadistic master, he would have to be quite concerned about injuring (not to mention causing the death of) a slave, because merely knocking out one tooth of a slave meant the slave would go free. As verses 26–27 in this chapter state: "When a man strikes the eye of his slave, male or female, and destroys it, he shall let the slave go free because of his eye. If he knocks out the tooth of his slave, male or female, he shall let the slave go free because of his tooth."

And, further protecting every slave was the Torah law that no one may return a runaway slave to his master (Deuteronomy 23:15). That law alone afforded unparalleled rights to slaves, whether Israelite or non-Israelite.

In addition, the words, "he is the other's property," seem to suggest this verse does not apply to a Hebrew slave, since no Hebrew slave was "property." This narrows the verse's applicability to foreign slaves—usually procured in a war. And compared to the treatment of captured slaves in all other societies—where killing, torturing, or otherwise injuring a slave was in no way punishable—the Torah's many protections of the foreign slave are unique. Joachim Jeremias (1900–1979), a German Lutheran biblical scholar, and member of the British Academy, described the Jews' treatment of Gentile slaves as "a great deal more humane than elsewhere in the ancient world."[9]

That conclusion is not surprising given the previous verse's equation of a slave's life to that of all other human beings, the implicit prohibition of mistreating a slave because of the ban on returning a runaway slave, the automatic freeing of a slave if he lost an eye or a tooth at the master's hand, and the Ten Commandments' mandate that slaves rest every Sabbath.

ESSAY: THE ONE MENTION OF PREMATURE BIRTH IN THE TORAH

21.22 When men fight, and one of them pushes a pregnant woman and a miscarriage results, but no other damage [ason] ensues, the one responsible shall be fined according as the woman's husband may exact from him, the payment to be based on reckoning.

21.23 But if other damage [*ason*] ensues, the penalty shall be life for life,

21.24 eye for eye, tooth for tooth, hand for hand, foot for foot,

21.25 burn for burn, wound for wound, bruise for bruise.

The Torah now treats a third type of killing. Verse 12 refers to premeditated homicide; verse 13 to accidental killing; and these verses (22-25) to a type of killing that is unintentional yet not fully accidental, somewhat corresponding to what is known in the United States as "involuntary manslaughter."

The words in verse 22, *ve-yatzu ye-la-deh-ha*, translated here as "and a miscarriage results," literally mean, "and her children leave her" (see below). It is not at all clear why the verse speaks of "children" in the plural.

Many students of the Bible either find these verses less than entirely clear or even misunderstand them. One difficulty is: Why would the death penalty apply, given that the killing is neither premeditated nor intentional?

The Talmud offers a plausible answer: The two men were trying to kill one another. If the pregnant woman (and/or the children?—see below) was killed, the death(s) may be considered a form of premeditated murder.[10]

Regarding the plural word, "children," this probably referred to a specific case that prompted this ruling, given that the text goes out of its way to specify the woman was pregnant with more than one child.

There is, however, a more important difficulty: Does the word *ason*—translated as "damage" (or "harm")—refer to the pregnant woman, to the children she is carrying, or to either of them?

The answer, I believe, lies in a literal translation of the text:

"If men are fighting one another, and they hit a pregnant woman, *and her children leave her*, and if there is no harm (*ason*), he shall surely be punished according to what the woman's husband lays on him; he will give according to judgment. But if there is harm (*ason*), you shall give life for a life, eye for an eye...."

A literal reading of the text can *only* mean harm has come to either the pregnant woman or to the "children who leave her."

So, then, why is there confusion? It is due to the translation of the words *vi'yatzu yiladeha*, "and her children leave her," in this JPS translation and in other translations. I have consulted dozens of translations and few of them translate *vi'yatzu yiladeha* as "miscarriage"; virtually every translation is a variation on the King James translation, "her fruit depart." This includes even some Jewish translations, such as the earlier JPS translation (1917), which translates the words as "her fruit depart," as does the English translation provided by Bar-Ilan University, Israel's preeminent Orthodox university.[11]

In fact, we know in the Torah, a live birth, not a miscarriage, is described using the same verb ("to leave") as in this verse. See, for example, Genesis 25:25-26, when Rebecca gives birth to Esau and Jacob, both of whom are said to "leave" her—or are born alive. Likewise, the second word, *yiladeha* ("her children") is also used elsewhere to refer to the birth of children (e.g., Genesis 33:7, Exodus 21:4, and later in the Bible in Ruth 1:5).

The Hebrew verb *yatza*, meaning to "go forth" or "leave," is used over 500 times in the Hebrew Bible, and often refers to the emergence of a living being (see Genesis 1:24; Genesis 8:17; Genesis 15:4; 1 Kings 8:19; Jeremiah 1:5; 2 Kings 20:18). And as significantly, the verb never means "miscarriage" (except in Numbers 12:12 where the verse explicitly states the baby is born dead).

Further protecting every slave was the Torah law that no one may return a runaway slave to his master.

Moreover, there *are* two biblical words for "miscarriage," *shakal* and *nafal*, and neither is used here. *Shakal* is used four times (Genesis 31:38; Job 3:16, Ecclesiastes 6:3-4, and Psalms 58:9 [in the Jewish numbering; Psalms 58:8 in Christian numbering]), and it means "miscarriage" in each case. *Nafal* is used three times (Exodus 23:26, Hosea 9:14, and Job 21:10) and it means "miscarriage" in each case (or "abort" in the verse from Job).[12]

Now, let us return to the verse. If the words are translated as "miscarriage"—for which there is no Torah or later biblical basis—the text would read, "If there is a miscarriage and harm (*ason*) ensues...." it could only mean the

Torah does not consider the premature death or injury of the children as "harm." But when the words are literally translated as "her children leave her"—meaning the pregnant woman's children have been expelled from the woman's womb—the words, "If there is harm," apply to the children or to the mother or to both.

It therefore seems clear that what the verses are saying is this: If the mother gives birth and there is no harm to either her or to the children, the husband goes to the court, which fines the man who induced premature birth. But if there is harm (*ason*)—whether injury or death—to either the children or the mother, then punishment is life for a life, eye for an eye, etc.

I recognize this literal reading of the Torah passage contradicts a widespread Jewish understanding of these verses, which translates "her children leave her" as "miscarriage," and therefore regards the premature death of the "children" as only demanding monetary compensation. But I believe the only fair reading of the verses—given the other times the Torah and the Bible use either the verb "leave" or the noun "children"—describes the birth of a child, either healthy, or injured, or dead.

ESSAY: ABORTION

While I believe there is no valid reason to translate *vi'yatzu yiladeha* ("her children leave her") as a "miscarriage," that does not mean we can infer the Torah's view of all abortions from this verse. We can only infer the Torah views the value of a fetal life that is recognizably human (or perhaps viable, since "child" in the Torah refers to a viable child) to be equal to that of all other human beings.

(My own view, which plays no role in my explanation of these verses, is that most non-medical abortions—abortions undertaken solely as a form of birth control, or, for example, aborting a female fetus because one wants a male baby—are not morally defensible. I should add this position concerns the morality of abortion, not the question of its legality.)

What now follows is a brief summary of traditional Jewish and Christian views on abortion.

THE JEWISH VIEW

Jewish law has been somewhat ambiguous on this issue. For example, ancient Jewish law considered abortions performed by non-Jews a capital crime. This somewhat puzzling position was probably due to ancient rabbis' perceptions that the non-Jewish societies in which they lived had little regard for human life, whereas Jews would perform abortions only in the rarest of circumstances (such as rape or a threat to the life of the mother). Thus, Maimonides ruled, "A 'Son of Noah' [that is, a non-Jew] who killed a person, even a fetus in its mother's womb, is capitally liable."[13]

The ancient rabbis also ruled that prior to forty days, the fetus was not considered a human being.

However, Orthodox Jews generally regard abortions as forbidden in all but the most extenuating circumstances (almost always regarding the health of the mother and, on rare occasions, the emotional health of the woman, such as a woman who was raped or is carrying for example, a Tay-Sachs baby). The contemporary Orthodox Jewish position is summarized on the website of the Orthodox Jewish organization, Aish:

> The easiest way to conceptualize a fetus in halacha [Jewish law] is to imagine it as a full-fledged human being—but not quite. In most circumstances, the fetus is treated like any other 'person....' There is even disagreement regarding whether the prohibition of abortion is Biblical or Rabbinic. Nevertheless, it is universally agreed the fetus will become a full-fledged human being and there must be a very compelling reason to allow for abortion.... As a general rule, abortion in Judaism is permitted only if there is a direct threat to the life of the mother by carrying the fetus to term or through the act of childbirth....

The positions of non-Orthodox Jewish movements—specifically Conservative and Reform Judaism—generally allow for abortion in cases of endangerment to the pregnant woman's psychological and emotional well-being as well as her physical health. In the words of the Union for Reform Judaism, "any decision should be left up to the woman within whose body the fetus is growing." Nevertheless, the Reform movement adds that "abortion should never be used for birth control purposes."[14]

THE CHRISTIAN VIEW

Regarding the traditional Christian position, the Greek-language Septuagint—a very early, if not the earliest, translation of the Hebrew Bible, dating from the third century BCE—rendered the word *ason* as "form." Thus the verse would read, "But if there is form, then you will give a life for a life." While *ason* does not literally mean "form" —it always means "harm" in the Torah (see Genesis 42:4, 38; 44:29; and Exodus 21:22, 23)—the Septuagint was not necessarily wrong in its intent because "yiladeha" ("her children") does seem to refer only to born-children in Torah Hebrew. So, the verse may indeed refer only to "formed" children "coming forth" from the pregnant woman.

Some early Christians, relying on the Septuagint translation, held that if there is no form to the expelled fetus, the man who induced the pregnant woman to expel her fetus would be fined, but if there is form, then you will give "life for a life." The seminal Catholic thinker, Augustine (354–430), relying on the Greek Septuagint, drew a distinction between an embryo "informatus" ("unformed") and an embryo "formatus" ("formed"), with only the "formed" equivalent to full human being.

Even in his day, however, Augustine's view of *ason* as meaning "formed" was not the dominant Church view. Another Church Father, Jerome (347–420), who lived at the same time as Augustine, also translated the Bible, and did not translate *ason* as "formed."

The Catholic position on abortion is expressed thus in the *Catechism of the Catholic Church*:

Human life must be respected and protected absolutely from the moment of conception. From the first moment of his existence, a human being must be recognized as having the rights of a person—among which is the inviolable right of every innocent being to life.

"Before I formed you in the womb I knew you, and before you were born I consecrated you" (Jeremiah 1:5)....

Since the first century the Church has affirmed the moral evil of every procured abortion. This teaching has not changed and remains unchangeable. Direct abortion, that is to say, abortion willed either as an end or a means, is gravely contrary to the moral law....

From the beginning of Protestant Christianity in the sixteenth century, the Protestant position was the same. I will only cite John Calvin (1509–1564), one of the first and most important Protestant theologians. In his commentary on Exodus 21:22, he wrote:

...the unborn, though enclosed in the womb of his mother, is already a human being, and it is an almost monstrous crime to rob it of life which it has not yet begun to enjoy....

Liberal Protestant denominations do not condemn abortions, holding that each woman must decide what is right. The Presbyterian Church USA, for example, upholds "the ability and responsibility of women, guided by the Scriptures and the Holy Spirit, to make good moral choices in regard to problem pregnancies."

In sum, whatever one concludes from these verses, the first task of the intellectually honest is to know what they say.

ESSAY: "EYE FOR AN EYE"—ONE OF THE GREAT MORAL ADVANCES IN HISTORY

In Jewish history, this list of punishments— "eye for eye, tooth for tooth, hand for hand, foot for foot, burn for burn, wound for wound, bruise for bruise" —was never taken literally. Only "a life for a life" was taken literally, because the Torah meant it literally: The Torah repeatedly demands the taking of the life of one who commits premeditated murder (see, for example, Exodus 21:14). God Himself announces in Genesis that taking the life of a murderer is part of the moral foundation of civilization (Genesis 9:6).

However, none of the others—"an eye for an eye," "a tooth for a tooth," etc.—were ever meant to be taken literally because they could not possibly be taken literally. If you take a man's eye out, you may easily end up killing him. The same holds true regarding the taking of a hand or a foot. And it is certainly not possible to burn, wound, or bruise a person exactly as he burned, wounded, or bruised his victim. Any of these would upset the moral balance constituting the entire point of the *lex talionis* (Law of Retaliation, as these laws are known).[15]

Thus, throughout Jewish history, the assailant was required to pay monetary compensation for any limbs and organs he damaged.

Many people regard the *lex talionis* as morally primitive. Mahatma Gandhi's biographer Louis Fischer said, in summarizing Gandhi's views, "An eye for an eye will make the whole world blind." Fischer said this view emanated from Gandhi's commitment to pacifism and doctrine of non-violence. But this commitment also led Gandhi to recommend to the Jews of Nazi-occupied Europe they not engage in, or support, any violent resistance to Hitler, and to recommend to the British soldiers in the spring of 1940, when Hitler seemed poised to take over Europe, to lay down their arms, not fight the Nazis, and let the Nazis occupy England. In Gandhi's own words: "If these gentlemen [the Nazis!] choose to occupy your homes, you will vacate them. If they do not give you free passage out, you will allow yourselves, man woman and child to be slaughtered, but you will refuse to owe allegiance to them."[16]

Dismissing the *lex talionis* as primitive is simply wrong. This principle of equal punishment is a fundamental statement of the Torah's preoccupation with justice. It represents, on several levels, a revolutionary moral advance over other ancient cultures' morality.

First, *lex talionis* is the ultimate statement of human equality. No one's eye is worth more than the eye of anyone else. This was new in history. For example, the Babylonian Code of Hammurabi, considered one of the great moral advances of ancient civilization, legislated the eye of a noble was of much greater value than the eye of a commoner. It therefore imposed different fines, depending on the status of the person whose eye was taken.

Second, the principle of "an eye for an eye" ensured only the guilty party was punished for his crime. In contrast, to cite yet another example from Hammurabi's Code, if a builder erected a house for a client and the house collapsed, killing the client's daughter, the builder's daughter was to be executed (Law 229). Torah law differed from this law in two ways. First, the Torah made special provisions for accidental homicide, and did not allow for execution in such a case. Second, and most important, the biblical principle of "an eye for an eye" ensured no one other than the guilty party should suffer punishment. In Deuteronomy, the Torah formalized this prohibition: "Parents shall not be put to death for children nor children be put to death for parents; a person shall be put to death only for his own crime" (Deuteronomy 24:16).

> *Perfect justice, therefore, would dictate that what I deliberately did to an innocent person be done to me.*

Third, the *lex talionis* is based on justice and therefore prohibits unjust revenge. In the ancient Near East and elsewhere, if a man gouged out another man's eye, the victim would likely seek out a violent revenge—such as gouging out both the attacker's eyes, killing him, gouging out his children's eyes, etc. In contrast, this principle teaches that the victim receives the appropriate compensation for the damages he suffered, and is permitted to exact no more.

Fourth, the Torah is preoccupied with justice. And it recognizes it is profoundly unjust for a person who has deliberately and unjustly gouged out the eye of another person to keep his own eye. Perfect justice, therefore, would dictate that what I deliberately did to an innocent person be done to me. Of course, except for taking a murderer's life, this is not possible. As noted, no eye or foot can ever be damaged in precisely the same way one damaged the eye or foot of another. Therefore, the *lex talionis* was *always* understood to be a statement of ideal, though impracticable, justice—and justice is the Torah's paramount concern. The only doubled-noun commandment in the Torah is the repetition of the word "justice" in Deuteronomy 16:20; "Justice, justice you shall pursue."

Many people object to "an eye for an eye" on the grounds it calls for "revenge," not justice. But "revenge" is a loaded word; it invariably communicates a morally negative message. Yet, just as there is just and unjust violence, there is just and unjust revenge. After all, just about every punishment has an element of "revenge." The moment one seeks to inflict any form of pain on an evildoer, one is engaged in "revenge." Opponents of capital punishment for murderers often argue murderers should be given a life sentence in prison without the possibility of parole. But isn't that a form of revenge?

In fact, some societies do take the position punishment is essentially revenge and therefore do not sentence even the most sadistic murderers—or even mass murderers—to anything approaching a life sentence. To cite one well-known example, in 2011, a Norwegian named Anders Behring Breivik, a self-described fascist and National Socialist, murdered seventy-seven people, most of them young, at a summer camp in Norway. He was sentenced to twenty-one years in prison, the maximum sentence Norway permits for any crime. Norway is not alone in regarding the desire to see an evildoer suffer at least something analogous to the suffering he inflicted on his victim(s) as "revenge"—a primitive human impulse that must be expunged. I don't.

Nor, apparently, does the Torah. On the contrary, the desire to pluck out the eye of a person who deliberately plucked out the eye of an innocent person is actually very human in the best sense of the word. It seems to me anyone who does not want to see a person experience the suffering he deliberately inflicted on an innocent person lacks empathy as well as the most elementary sense of morality and justice. Therefore, even a monetary fine would seem insufficient punishment in many cases—a long prison sentence would seem far more just. However, we do not know of the existence of prisons, as such, in the Torah.

21.26 When a man strikes the eye of his slave, male or female, and destroys it, he shall let him go free on account of his eye.

As noted in verse 20, the Torah is unique in protecting slaves from homicide. It is similarly unique in protecting slaves from other forms of maltreatment by their masters.

Although verse 21 describes a slave as "property," verse 26 makes it clear this fact does not allow the owner of this human "property" to be abusive. A slave, too, is a human being. Job, in asserting his essential goodness as a human being, points to his treatment of his slaves: "Did I ever brush aside the case of my servants, man or maid, when they made a complaint against me?" (Job 31:13)

The principle of "an eye for an eye" ensured only the guilty party was punished for his crime.

Cassuto writes the Torah is the only ancient law code that includes a punishment for mistreating a slave. In all other codes, a man would not be punished for harming a slave any more than he would be punished for breaking some inanimate object he owned.

The Torah, in contrast, is concerned with the welfare of the mistreated slave, because the slave, though owned, is a human being, not an object.

In at least four ways, Torah laws' treatment of slaves was morally superior to what prevailed in, for example, the United States until the end of slavery in the 1860s.

1. A slave was freed if a master ruined the slave's eye or just knocked out a tooth (Exodus 21:26-27).

2. It was forbidden to return a runaway slave to his master (Deuteronomy 23:16).

3. Slave owners who killed a slave were to be executed (Exodus 21:20).

4. Slaves were to desist from work on the Sabbath just as their owners did (Exodus 20:12).

21.27 If he knocks out the tooth of his slave, male or female, he shall let him go free on account of his tooth.

Benno Jacob points out that although a master is not forbidden from hitting his slaves, he will have to pay dearly if a beating leads to so much as a lost tooth, not to mention a lost eye.

It is true a blind slave cannot work efficiently, but a slave's effectiveness is hardly impaired by a lost tooth. Clearly, then, the consequences suffered by an owner for injuring a slave have nothing to do with whether or not the slave is still fit for labor. The fact the loss of an eye and a tooth are equated—even though the former is an infinitely more serious loss—underscores the law's intention to protect a slave from permanent harm or cruel discipline.

WHY KILL AN OX THAT KILLED A PERSON?

21.28 When an ox gores a man or a woman to death, the ox shall be stoned

Usually the Torah uses the word "man" to refer to a man or woman. In these laws, however, the Torah constantly repeats the phrase "a man or a woman" to emphasize the lives of both are identical in value

As regards the stoning of the ox, Nahum Sarna comments on this verse at length and addresses the issue of just how seriously the Torah regards the killing of a human being:

"The killer ox is not destroyed solely because it is dangerous. This is clear from the fact it is not destroyed when the victim is another ox and from the prescribed mode of destruction—not ordinary slaughter but stoning. The execution of the ox was carried out in the presence, and with the participation, of the entire community—implying the killing of a human being is a source of mass pollution and the proceedings had an expiatory function. The killing of a homicidal beast is ordained in Genesis 9:5-6: 'For your own life-blood I will require a reckoning: I will require it of every beast.... Whoever sheds the blood of man, by man shall his blood be shed, for in His image did God make man.' The sanctity of human life is such as to make bloodshed the consummate offense, one viewed with unspeakable horror. Both man and beast that destroy human life are thereafter tainted by bloodguilt."

Sarna's explanation is undoubtedly correct. The stoning of the animal is society's way of demonstrating how terrible killing a human being is, whether done by man by choice or by an animal by instinct.

This was once brought home to me on my radio show. A woman whose family raised ostriches called to tell me her beloved father had been killed by one of their ostriches. I asked her what, if anything, was done to the ostrich.

She replied that nothing was done to the animal.

"So," I asked, "when people visit, you just point to the ostrich and say, 'that's the ostrich that killed my dad'"?

"Yes," she answered unhesitatingly.

I respectfully told her that unless her father was deliberately tormenting the ostrich, I thought that showed disrespect to her father, that it sort of made light of his killing.

Were it not for this Torah law, I don't know if I would have reacted as strongly as I did.

21.28 (cont.) and its flesh shall not be eaten,

There must be no benefit derived from an animal that kills a human being.

21.28 (cont.) but the owner of the ox is not to be punished.

The Hebrew word *naki* (translated as "not to be punished") literally means "clean," and signifies the owner of the ox is clean of moral blemish or fault; prior to this incident, he had no way of knowing his ox was dangerous.

21.29 If, however, that ox has been in the habit of goring, and its owner, though warned, had failed to guard it, and he kills a man or a woman—the ox shall be stoned and its owner, too, shall be put to death.

The Torah now refers to a case in which an ox is known to have gored people previously. This ox does not have to have killed anyone else already; a history of goring is sufficient to render the owner negligent. Though the owner has been warned of his ox's goring tendencies, he has failed to either lock up the animal or remove its horns. The owner may be compared to a judge who repeatedly lets drunk drivers get off easy; it is likely one of those drivers, like the goring ox, will go on to cause a fatal accident.

> *Anyone who does not want to see a person experience the suffering he deliberately inflicted on an innocent person lacks empathy.*

From the Torah's perspective, the owner who fails to take care of his goring ox is functionally equivalent to a murderer, since the ox is, in effect, a loaded weapon not kept under lock and key.

21.30 If ransom is laid upon him, he must pay whatever is laid upon him to redeem his life.

In general, the Torah does not permit a person to pay ransom for his life when he is deserving of capital punishment: "You may not accept a ransom for the life of a murderer who is guilty of a capital crime; he must be put to death" (Numbers 35:31). The owner of the ox is an exception because he is not morally equivalent to a man who's committed premeditated murder. Although he is responsible for the death of another human being, he has killed his ox's victim indirectly, and through negligence rather than intent. Therefore, in this exceptional instance, he is granted the option of paying a ransom for his life.

ANOTHER TORAH REJECTION OF THE LAWS OF ITS TIME

21.31 So, too, if it gores a minor, male or female, [the owner] shall be dealt with according to the same rule.

Until about 1900, this verse caused quite a bit of confusion; it read like a non sequitur. In assigning punishment to the goring ox's owner, what does it matter if the victim of the attack was someone's son or daughter?

However, with the discovery of related ancient Semitic legal codes at the turn of the twentieth century, it became clear this law was intended to distinguish Torah law from contemporaneous codes, which ruled that if a man's ox killed another man's son or daughter, then the son or daughter of the ox's owner would be killed. The Torah, therefore, expressly forbids such reciprocal vicarious punishment (see also Deuteronomy 24:16). No matter who is killed, it is the ox's owner alone who is punished, and not his son or daughter.

This is an extremely important point for an additional reason. There are undoubtedly other instances in the Torah that can seem odd or even objectionable to us but which would be understood if we were more conversant with the Near East 3,000 years ago. It is essential to remember the Torah, while eternal in its values, first had to be intelligible and create a moral revolution in the late Bronze Age.

21.32 But if the ox gores a slave, male or female, he shall pay thirty shekels of silver to the master, and the ox shall be stoned.

The ox is killed, just as it would be if the ox gored a free person.

21.33 When a man opens a pit, or digs a pit and does not cover it, and an ox or an ass falls into it,

21.34 the one responsible for the pit must make restitution; he shall pay the price to the owner,

Even though the digger of the pit did not hurt the other man's animal deliberately, he is nonetheless negligent.

21.34 (cont.) but shall keep the dead animal.

21.35 When a man's ox injures his neighbor's ox and it dies, they shall sell the live ox and divide its price; they shall also divide the dead animal.

In this context, "divide" means they shall divide the value of the dead animal.

WHEN BAD THINGS HAPPEN, THERE ISN'T ALWAYS A VILLAIN

In contrast to the previous case involving the pit, this verse refers not to a matter of negligence but to an accident. The owner of the ox has done nothing wrong; he had no way of preventing his ox from injuring his neighbor's animal.

While the owner of the goring ox is responsible for his animal, he need restore only half the value of an ox to his neighbor, since the incident is understood to be an accident.

This approach should be contrasted to contemporary societies, in which accidents are rarely recognized as such. People just want to assign blame.

The Torah, however, acknowledges a more nuanced reality: Sometimes things happen that are beyond people's control. True, an accident has occurred and a victim has suffered. But in a certain sense, the owner, too, having had no reason to anticipate such behavior from what might well have been an unaggressive, even mild-mannered, animal is also a victim. To hold him responsible for all payments would constitute a judgment of negligence against him. So, the Torah splits the payment between the ox's owner and the dead animal's owner.

Telushkin notes, "while this might not be a perfect solution, the alternatives offered in a litigious society are certainly not superior. A friend embarrassedly confessed to me that when a nanny tripped in his house (she simply lost her footing; there was no object on the floor), his first concern was that she would sue him. A litigious society causes people to view people they unintentionally hurt, or who are simply hurt on the owner's property—even when the owner is not at fault—as potential plaintiffs rather than simply as a fellow human who is hurt."

Consequently, many people even hesitate to say "I'm sorry," lest that be an admission of guilt in a lawsuit against them.

In short, the Torah understood sometimes sad things happen and injuries result, with no one really at fault. In other words, just because there is a victim doesn't mean there is a villain.

21.36 If, however, it is known that the ox was in the habit of goring, and its owner has failed to guard it, he must restore ox for ox, but shall keep the dead animal.

In this case, the owner of the ox is culpable because he failed to control an ox known for its goring tendencies. He must make full restitution.

21.37 When a man steals an ox or a sheep, and slaughters it or sells it, he shall pay five oxen for the ox, and four sheep for the sheep. —

Since the thief has deliberately stolen from another, he must pay that person not only restitution for the stolen goods, but an additional amount as punishment for his crime.

In addition to deserving punishment, there is another reason for the fine. If all the thief was required to do was restore what he stole, he would have no reason not to steal again, since the worst that could happen would be he had to return what he took.

Just because there is a victim doesn't mean there is a villain.

As regards the reason for the higher than normal fines imposed on the thief for stealing an ox, oxen were more essential to one's livelihood in ancient Israelite society, since they could perform hard labor. Therefore, the penalty for stealing an ox was greater than the penalty for stealing a sheep.

CHAPTER

22

Note to reader: There is a different enumeration of verses in this chapter between Jewish and Christian editions of the Bible. In the Christian enumeration, the first verse of this chapter is the last verse of the preceding chapter. Therefore, what is listed here as 22:1 is 22:2 in Christian editions—meaning that each verse in this chapter is one verse behind the Christian enumeration.

22.1 If the thief is seized while tunneling, and he is beaten to death,

> This chapter opens with a case in which an individual or a family is confronted with a thief clandestinely breaking into their home. This verse is understood as referring to a case in which the thief is intruding at night, at a time when the members of a household are expected to be home. It can be assumed, therefore, that such an intruder is prepared to encounter opposition and to kill if necessary.

22.1 (cont.) there is no bloodguilt in his case.

> One who kills a nighttime invader is assumed to have acted in self-defense, and is not charged with murder. As regards all instances in which a person has good reason to fear an assailant might kill him, the Talmud teaches a basic principle of Jewish jurisprudence: "If one comes to kill you, wake up early [i.e., anticipate him] and kill him first."[1]

22.2 If the sun has risen on him, there is bloodguilt in that case. —

> In the daytime, the members of a household are not expected to be at home. Consequently, a thief who intrudes at this time, particularly if not armed, is not assumed to have homicidal intent. One who is not in physical danger and who

311

kills such a thief is therefore charged with killing. As Sarna explains: "The biblical scales give priority to the protection of life, even the life of a burglar, over the protection of property."

As the Talmud later put it: "If it is as clear to you as the sun is shining that the burglar is not a physical threat to you, then you will bear guilt for killing him."[2]

All this of course is based on individual circumstance. A daytime intruder who is armed and obviously willing to murder should be confronted, and, if necessary, killed.

22.2 (cont.) He [the thief] must make restitution;

As a rule, the thief has to pay double the value of what he has stolen (see verses 3 and 6).

22.2 (cont.) if he lacks the means, he shall be sold for his theft.

The Torah recognizes a thief owes money to the person from whom he stole. Therefore, if he cannot pay it, he is sold (into indentured servitude—"slavery") and must work off his debt until he makes full restitution. Regarding the notion of indentured servitude/slavery, which strikes modern readers as morally disturbing, see commentary to Exodus 21:2.

In ancient Israel, the fear of God was so great an oath invoking God was regarded as sufficient proof of innocence.

22.3 But if what he stole—whether ox or ass or sheep—is found alive in his possession, he shall pay double.

The final verse in chapter 21 (the first verse of this chapter in the Christian enumeration) legislated that a thief must pay five oxen for every ox stolen and slaughtered, and four sheep for every sheep stolen and slaughtered. This verse legislates that a thief must pay only double if the stolen animal has not been slaughtered. There are two reasons (I find each plausible) for the difference in punishment depending on whether or not the stolen animal is found alive:

Nahum Sarna argues that if the animal is still alive, the owner's loss is only minimal and temporary: He gets the very same animal (plus an additional animal) restored to him and, presumably, he gets it back shortly after it was stolen. As a result, the owner is not entitled to as much compensation for the theft.

Another possible reason for imposing a heavy additional penalty is if the animal has been slaughtered, the thief has killed an animal that could still produce much through its labors, possibly producing offspring, and providing wool, milk, etc.

22.4 When a man lets his livestock loose to graze in another's land,

The Torah does not say "in one's neighbor's land," because neighbors often make arrangements in which they agree to allow their livestock to graze on one another's property. This verse is referring only to the land of those people who have not granted such permission.

22.4 (cont.) and so allows a field or a vineyard to be grazed bare, he must make restitution for the impairment of that field or vineyard.

The animal is, of course, not punished; animals cannot know where they shouldn't graze. But the owners of animals do know, and they are, therefore, punished for failing to control their livestock. An owner is, therefore, obligated to do more than just make restitution—because restitution alone would hardly discourage him from acting the same way in the future. Thus, an owner's punishment for not preventing his animal from grazing on another's land—even if his animal grazed only on the less valuable parts of the other person's land—is he must overcompensate for his violation. The verse, when rendered literally, reads, "he must pay from the best of his field or the best of his vineyard."

22.5 When a fire is started and spreads to thorns, so that stacked, standing, or growing grain is consumed, he who started the fire must make restitution.

This case, unlike the previous one, does not involve negligence; it is purely accidental. Therefore, the person on whose land the fire started is obligated only to make restitution; no additional fine is imposed.

The Torah is preoccupied with justice (and deterring injustice). One byproduct is the Torah's opposition to assessing blame where there is none.

22.6 When a man gives money or goods to another for safekeeping, and they are stolen from the man's house—if the thief is caught, he shall pay double;

22.7 If the thief is not caught, the owner of the house shall depose before God that he has not laid hands on the other's property.

The owner of the house, the guardian of the missing property, must swear in court before God that he neither used nor stole his neighbor's property, and he is then freed from making payment. If the guardian refuses to take such an oath, he has to make restitution for the stolen items.

In ancient Israel, the fear of God was so great an oath invoking God was regarded as sufficient to end a trial.

The words, "he has not laid hands on the other's property," make it clear the guardian is forbidden to make any use of the object he is guarding. If he does, he becomes responsible for any subsequent damage (including stealing) that befalls the object. Thus, he is required to swear he did not lay hands on the object (unless it was simply to move it to a more secure place for safekeeping). In modern terms, if I allow someone going on vacation to leave his car within my garage and I use the car while the person is gone, I am responsible for any mishap that happens to the car prior to the owner's return, including repayment if the car is stolen.

> *In general, the Torah legislates behavior rather than belief or thought. One reason is the Torah is not totalitarian—it leaves the mind free.*

22.8 In all charges of misappropriation—pertaining to an ox, an ass, a sheep, a garment, or any other loss, whereof one party alleges, "This is it" —the case of both parties shall come before God: he whom God declares guilty shall pay double to the other.

The verse is a bit confusing. Rashi explains: In the case described here, the guardian of an animal informs the owner the animal was stolen. Based on the later testimony of witnesses, it comes out the guardian stole it. He is therefore required, like any thief, to return the stolen animal and to give an additional animal as punishment. However, if the witnesses are found to have lied, they pay double to the guardian.

As explained earlier (Exodus 21:8), the word *Elohim* is translated here as "God"—understandably so, since *Elohim* and *Lord* (YHVH) are the two most common words for "God" in the Hebrew Bible. However, in this context, it actually means "judges (acting in God's name)."

22.9 When a man gives to another an ass, an ox, a sheep or any other animal to guard, and it dies or is injured or is carried off, with no witness about,

22.10 an oath before the Lord shall decide between the two of them that the one has not laid hands on the property of the other; the owner must acquiesce,

to the judgment of the court, which is based on the guardian's oath.

22.10 (cont.) and no restitution shall be made.

22.11 But if [the animal] was stolen from him, he shall make restitution to its owner.

The Talmud deduces that the guardian in this instance is a paid guardian who has a professional responsibility to guard the animal. However, if he is guarding the animal for free, as a favor to the owner (as the Talmud understands to have been the case in verse 7), he is not responsible in case of theft.

This ruling accords with common sense. If a friend is watching our car for free, as a favor, while we are out of town, we intuitively sense it would be unfair to hold him financially responsible if the car is stolen. However, if we are paying someone to watch our car, a parking garage, for example, we would deem it quite reasonable to demand the garage pay if the car is stolen.

22.12 If it was torn by beasts, he shall bring it as evidence;

The person who is watching over the animal has to bring the torn carcass as evidence.

22.12 (cont.) he need not replace what has been torn by beasts.

The guardian, even though he was paid, does not have to reimburse the owner because he is neither expected nor required to risk his life to fight off wild beasts.

22.13 When a man borrows [an animal] from another and it dies or is injured, its owner not being with it, he [the borrower] must make restitution.

This law concerns a borrower, not a guardian. Unlike a guardian—someone who is doing the owner a personal favor—a borrower, for whom the owner is doing a favor, is assumed to accept full responsibility for the animal's welfare. If anything happens to the animal while it is entrusted to his care, he must make restitution to the owner. In modern terms, if you borrow someone's car and it is damaged (even if it was not your fault and payment cannot be exacted from the person who damaged it) you, the borrower, are required to make restitution.

22.14 If its owner was with it, no restitution need be made; but if it was hired, he is entitled to the hire.

The owner is responsible for his animal so long as he is with it. The last part of the verse is not fully clear, though I understand it to mean the one who rented ("hired") the animal is not responsible to replace the animal, but he is responsible to pay for his usage of the animal up until the time the animal died or could no longer work.

ESSAY: THE TORAH AND PREMARITAL SEX

22.15 If a man seduces a virgin for whom the bride-price has not been paid, and lies with her, he must make her his wife by payment of a bride-price.

This is the only time the Torah deals in a legal context with consensual intercourse between two unmarried people. (Because polygamy was legal, the man in this instance may be a married man, but since the two people in this instance may both be unmarried, I am addressing the issue in that regard.)

This, in and of itself, may be a comment on the Torah's lack of preoccupation with the matter. And even this verse is not primarily concerned with premarital sex as such. It is primarily concerned with protecting the woman, specifically her ability to marry, by protecting the worth of her virginity, which was an extremely important consideration throughout history— and remains so in traditional societies. For

> *The Torah is emphatically behaviorist. It recognizes it is bad behavior, not bad thoughts, that does the most damage in life.*

this reason, the Torah does not deal with a man seducing an unmarried woman who is not a virgin. (The seduction of a married or betrothed woman would fall under the category of adultery.)

Regarding sexual matters, the Torah is preoccupied with:

1. Desexualizing God, desexualizing religion, and desexualizing family life.

2. Creating nuclear families and protecting them—from adultery and incest.

3. Channeling the male sex drive into marriage.

4. Sustaining the male-female distinction.

Assuming the family (and the woman in those cases where the family takes her desires into account) is in favor of the marriage, the man who seduced the virgin is obligated to marry her and to pay the bride-price. A man, therefore, must be very careful before sleeping with a virgin, even when the act is consensual, because she and her family can insist he marry her.

Though not preoccupied with the issue of sex between two unmarried people—which in Western society is often referred to as "fornication," but for which there is no equivalent term in the Hebrew Bible—the Torah nevertheless considers sexual intercourse to be an act of great significance whose only rightful place is within marriage. A man is therefore forbidden to seduce a woman if he has no intention of marrying her; and if he does seduce her without marital intentions, he can be compelled to marry her (and she, or at least her family, can refuse.)

In that sense, this law may be considered a version of a moral law in the Talmud, which I like to refer to as the Storekeeper Law. It forbids a person from going into a store and inquiring about the price of an item if he has no intention of buying it.[3] People are not allowed, the Talmud explains, to raise the hopes of a storekeeper for no good reason.

In this case, with its far higher psychological and emotional stakes, we can infer that just as a storekeeper has the right to assume a customer asking about an item is seriously considering buying it, so, too, in ancient Israel, a woman seduced by a man who is wooing her had the right to assume he wanted to marry her.

Today there are no legal consequences if a man seduces a virgin (assuming, of course, she is not a minor). However, at the very least, a decent man is sensitive to the emotional importance of the sex act to most women.

After World War II, Western society underwent what is known as the "Sexual Revolution." With the weakening of biblical values, and the ease in obtaining both contraception and, since the 1970s, abortion, more unmarried people have had sexual relations with more partners than ever before in Western—and perhaps world—history. However, in addition to creating more fatherless children than ever before, this revolution has harmed both sexes, especially women. But men, too, have paid a price in at least two ways.

One is fewer men seek to marry, and men benefit enormously from marriage. In the words of Nobel Prize-winning economist George Akerlof, "Men settle down when they get married; if they fail to get married they fail to settle down."[4] And in the words of the late University of Virginia sociologist Steven Nock, "Marriage is one of the last 'rite[s]' of passage into manhood" remaining in our society.[5]

The other is many men are less motivated to succeed in life. One of the primary reasons men always worked hard was to "earn" the commitment of a woman. But if women are readily available without having to achieve much, fewer men will seek to achieve much.

Women, for their part, were told they could enjoy emotionless and commitment-free sex as much as men could. But a host of academic studies and popular reports of sexually promiscuous women refute this notion. Indeed, among young women, high rates of depression often relate to casual sex.

For example, a major study of American college-aged women, published in *The Journal of Sex Research*, a publication of the United States National Institutes of Health, concluded "hookup behavior during college was positively correlated with experiencing clinically significant depression symptoms."[6]

Similarly, regarding teenagers generally, "A recent longitudinal study published in the *Journal of Abnormal Psychology* suggests that teenagers who engage in casual sex are more likely to suffer from depression than their peers who don't engage in casual sex.... Given that teens who practiced celibacy were rated lowest for clinical depression and depressive symptoms on the charts, promiscuity may be symptomatic of depression."[7]

One consequence of so many young women believing the message that they can—and should—enjoy sex with as many men as men can with women was summarized in this comment by a young woman cited in the American magazine *Vanity Fair*: "It's rare for a woman of our generation to meet a man who treats her like a priority instead of an option."[8]

Finally, it needs to be stressed the Torah's language here makes it unambiguously clear it is referring only to consensual sex, not anything approaching forced sex, i.e., rape. For example, in Genesis, when Shechem sleeps with Jacob's daughter Dinah, the Torah uses entirely different language: he "lay with her by force" (Genesis 34:2; see also II Samuel 13:14), making it clear this was an act of coercion. Here, the verb is *ye-fa-teh*, correctly translated as "seduced."

As regards rape, two eminent Bible scholars, Richard Elliott Friedman and Shawna Dolansky, summarized the Torah's views thus: "What should not be in doubt is the biblical view of rape: it is horrid. It is decried in the Bible's stories. It is not tolerated in the Bible's laws."[9]

22.16 If her father refuses to give her to him, he must still weigh out silver in accordance with the bride-price for virgins.

If the woman's family does not support the marriage, the man must still pay the bride-price as punishment. Lest the Torah be misinterpreted by a man thinking he could acquire a woman as a wife by simply seducing her to sleep with him, the Torah makes it clear that whether or not the woman's family allows her to marry the man, he still has to pay the very same price to her family he would pay if he did marry her.

Three Polytheistic Practices That Merited the Death Penalty (At Least in Theory)

1. Sorcery

22.17 You shall not tolerate a sorceress.

This verse and the two that follow contain prohibitions of three polytheistic practices the Torah regards as so destructive to moral civilization they merit the death penalty. (This verse, if translated literally, means, "You shall not keep a sorceress alive.")

The first is sorcery or magic.

Belief in, and the practice of, magic were universal in the ancient world. Although many societies had laws forbidding the use of magic for malevolent purposes, only the Torah outlawed magic altogether. Magic was the antithesis of the Torah's worldview: Whereas magic suggests mysterious supernatural forces control the universe—and select individuals are capable of acquiring those abilities and becoming God-like—the Torah maintains God alone has dominion over the world.

During periods when witchcraft was widespread, there is evidence the death penalty was—on rare occasions—enforced. But as previously noted, I am convinced the death penalty in the Torah almost always serves to emphasize the seriousness of the offense.

In case the point needs to be made, Torah law would in no way oppose magic shows that are presented as entertainment. What it opposes are people presenting themselves as able, through incantations or other occult practices, to control another person's destiny.

2. Bestiality

22.18 Whoever lies with a beast shall be put to death.

The second prohibition is bestiality.

Whoever lies (sexually) with an animal has reduced him or herself to the level of an animal and thereby blurred the distinction between humans and animals—just as sorcery blurs the distinction between humans and God. As we will see later in the Torah, blurring monotheism's distinctions—man and animal, God and man, good and evil, holy and profane, man and woman, life and death—undermines the order of the universe as designed by God.

> *"The stranger was to be protected, although he was not a member of one's family, clan, religion, community, or people, simply because he was a human being. In the stranger, therefore, man discovered the idea of humanity."*
> **–Hermann Cohen**

Of all the ancient Near East's legal systems, only the Hittite code contained prohibitions on the (widespread) practice of bestiality. But while this code punished (with death) intercourse with pigs, dogs, and sheep, it allowed human intercourse with mules and horses.[10] Presumably, the Torah wrote "a beast" in this verse so as to emphasize there is no such thing as acceptable and unacceptable bestiality; it is forbidden to sleep with any animal.

Although bestiality is no longer commonly practiced, it could experience a revival. In an increasingly secular world, indifferent to divine prohibitions, many people find themselves easily bored and seek ever-increasing excitement and novelty. Irving Kristol, the American godfather of the neo-conservative political movement, argued that given the contemporary secular mind-set even strictures against bestiality might, therefore, be at risk: "Pure reason cannot tell us that bestiality is wrong; indeed the only argument against bestiality these days is that since we cannot know whether animals enjoy it or not, it is a violation of 'animal rights.' The biblical prohibition, which is unequivocal, is no longer powerful enough to withstand the 'why not?' of secular humanist inquiry."[11]

3. Sacrifices to Other Gods
(The Torah Bans Behavior, Not Thought)

22.19 Whoever sacrifices to a god other than the Lord alone shall be destroyed.

The third capital prohibition is the bringing of sacrifices to other gods—even if the person also brings sacrifices to God.

This verse prohibits worshipping other gods, but it does not explicitly prohibit believing in them. Of course, the Ten Commandments state, "Do not have other gods besides me" (Exodus 20:3). But the prohibition here is specifically against *bringing sacrifices* to other gods. In general, the Torah legislates behavior rather than belief or thought. One reason is the Torah is not totalitarian—it leaves the mind free. The Torah is emphatically behaviorist. It recognizes it is bad behavior, not bad thoughts, that does the most damage in life. And it recognizes that once certain behaviors end, the thoughts leading people to engage in those behaviors will likely end as well. *If people stop bringing sacrifices to other gods, they will eventually stop believing in them.*

LAWS REGARDING THE MOST VULNERABLE

22.20 You shall not wrong a stranger or oppress him, for you were strangers in the land of Egypt.

Verses 20-24 consist of laws regulating the treatment of four categories of unprotected, vulnerable individuals: the stranger, the widow, the orphan, and the poor. We should not think we can get away with mistreating people who cannot protect themselves. God promises to be their protector: "If you do mistreat them, I will heed their outcry as soon as they cry out to Me" (verse 22).

These verses underscore the moral need for ethical monotheism, with the emphasis on *ethical* as much as on *monotheism*. Unless we recognize there is a God above us, and His primary demand of human beings is ethical behavior, and a moral God will judge us all, there is nothing to prevent us from oppressing those who are too weak to stop us.

A classic example of this amoral—and, as we shall see, immoral—nontheistic ethic is found in Thucydides' fifth-century BCE *History of the Peloponnesian War*. As Thucydides recounts, Athens and Sparta were at war, and the Athenians were pressuring the residents of the island of Melos to support their war effort and to pay them tribute. The Melians wished to remain neutral, insisting they had done and would do Athens no harm, and simply wished to be left alone. The Athenians countered that this was an unacceptable option, that Athens would appear weak to other nations if it let Melos remain neutral, and threatened the island with destruction.

"Is that your idea of fair play?" the Melians asked the Athenian delegates.

"So far as right and wrong are concerned," the Athenians answered, "there is no difference between the two." Rather, "the strong do what they have the power to do and the weak accept what they have to accept."

The Melians refused to pay tribute, and Athens besieged Melos. Once the Melians surrendered, the Athenians murdered the men and sold the women and children into slavery. Some twenty-four hundred years later, Friedrich Nietzsche, the nineteenth century's most famous atheist ("God is dead") wrote with great contempt of those who sympathized with the Melians' moral appeals.

It is precisely this belief of both the Athenians and Nietzsche— "the strong do what they have the power to do and the weak accept what they have to accept"—ethical monotheism came to combat.

THE NON-JEWISH RESIDENT MUST NOT BE OPPRESSED

Several modern commentators offer thoughts on the juxtaposition of this verse about the stranger with the previous three verses prohibiting sorcery, bestiality, and bringing sacrifices to false gods.

1. Nahum Sarna comments that the arrangement of these laws highlights the stark moral contrast between polytheism and monotheism: Whereas

polytheism is about sorcery, bestiality, and the worship of other gods, Torah monotheism is about protecting those who cannot protect themselves.

2. Benno Jacob makes the point that the Torah prohibits oppressing the non-Jew who resides among Jews immediately following the three verses about idolatrous practices in order to teach that the non-Israelite has to abandon those practices in order to be worthy of equal treatment in Israelite society.

3. Umberto Cassuto maintains the Torah's injunction to protect the stranger immediately follows the laws about pagan abominations to indicate the Torah's opposition is not to foreigners themselves, but to particular practices in which they engage.

The idea that we have moral obligations to those who are not part of our ethnic, religious, racial, or national group was another revolutionary innovation of the Torah. On this subject, it is worth repeating something the German-Jewish philosopher Hermann Cohen wrote (and quoted in the commentary on Genesis 12:12): "The stranger was to be protected, although he was not a member of one's family, clan, religion, community, or people, simply because he was a human being. In the stranger, therefore, man discovered the idea of humanity."

When people emerge from pain and oppression, they have two options: they can use their anger over their suffering to legitimize their oppression of others; or they can use the memory of their pain to empathize with others.

No other ancient Near Eastern culture, or any ancient culture with which I am familiar, had such a law.

The challenge of the Torah, however, is to treat the stranger morally while remaining true to the Torah's values and to Israelite identity, and to attempt to bring the stranger into the Torah's value system (though not necessarily into the Israelites' religion). Many Jews have forgotten this. Ever since the Jews were emancipated in the nineteenth century, they have been disproportionately involved in universalist movements; but, in their embrace of humanity, they often abandoned the Torah and Jewish identity. They did not wish to acknowledge that it is *specifically* because of the Torah's teachings that humanity came to view all people, including, of course, strangers, as created in God's image and therefore—in the words of the American Declaration of Independence— "endowed by their Creator with certain unalienable rights."

When Jews abandoned the Torah and ethical monotheism, these very values affirming the sanctity of all human life have often been abandoned as well—as was the case with those Jews who embraced communism (which made war on religion and God-based values) and ended up supporting the tyrannical and murderous Soviet Union and other communist regimes.

Essay: The Unique Moral Power of Empathy

The law against wronging the stranger ends with the words, "for you were strangers in the land of Egypt."

It is a fact of life we can only fully empathize with other people when we have experienced what they have experienced. That is why the Torah commands love of the stranger by reminding the Israelites about their own painful experience as strangers in Egypt.

I personally learned this truth about empathy after undergoing a period of serious, sometimes disabling, physical pain. I realized that when listening to, or reading about, people in pain, one can, and of course should, *sympathize* with them; but unless one has experienced similar pain, it is not possible to truly *empathize* with them. It is like telling people in Sub-Saharan Africa about the pain of freezing in the Russian winter. Or, telling men about the pain of childbirth; only women who have given birth can truly empathize with the pain another woman experiences while giving birth. As the list of examples is endless, I will give only one more illustration. A man whose twenty-one-year-old son died in a car accident told me his grief was so intense nothing brought him any comfort—not religion, not friends, not psychotherapy. Only when he finally discovered meetings of parents who lost children did he begin to heal at all—because, he explained, only people who lost their children could empathize with him.

The Torah so frequently repeats the injunction to love and to treat the stranger justly because empathy, like most other moral traits, does not come naturally to people; it needs to be constantly taught.

Given the unique power of empathy to lead to moral behavior, it is incumbent on all of us to aspire to empathy; and even though complete empathy is often impossible, we have to do everything we can as parents to instill empathy in our children. That is one reason parents should punish their children when they hurt others; only by experiencing the pain of punishment can many children begin to understand the pain they have inflicted. Moreover, a lack of empathy is a defining characteristic of the sociopath.

In fact, even those who have suffered often need to be taught empathy. Unfortunately, suffering is no guarantee of empathy and the decent behavior it engenders. When people emerge from pain and oppression, they have two options: they can use their anger over their suffering to legitimize their oppression of others; or they can use the memory of their pain to empathize with others. Suffering ennobles only those who want to be ennobled by it.

Empathy is so important it might well be the solution to the problem of human evil. If people identified with others, they would no longer find it easy to inflict suffering on them, or to ignore the suffering of others.

That is another reason it is not wrong for people to want to see people who do great evil suffer. We intuitively understand that unless evildoers experience some of the pain they have inflicted on another, they will never be able to empathize with their victim and therefore never understand the horror of what they have done.

22.21 You shall not ill-treat any widow or orphan.

22.22 If you do mistreat them, I will heed their outcry as soon as they cry out to Me,

In ancient society, the widow and the orphan had no one to protect them because in each instance the male figure who would ordinarily protect them—a husband or father—was dead. Therefore, people should know someone would indeed watch over them—God.

MEASURE-FOR-MEASURE: THE TORAH'S OBSESSION WITH JUSTICE

22.23 and My anger shall blaze forth and I will put you to the sword, and your own wives shall become widows and your children orphans.

Because the Torah is preoccupied—even obsessed—with justice, this verse reflects the Torah's theme of measure-for-measure: The way in which we treat others will in turn affect how we are treated. If we are not able to empathize with the vulnerability of the widow and the orphan, we will be forced to directly experience their plight.

In nineteenth-century America, it was not uncommon for slaveholders to break up families of black slaves by selling off their children, thereby separating parents from offspring. These slaveholders engaged in a whole host of behaviors for which they would have demanded the death penalty for anyone who engaged in such behaviors against their own wives and children. Then, sure enough, the Civil War came along and caused tens of thousands of slave-owners' wives and children to become widows and orphans. Abraham Lincoln said in his second inaugural

> *The idea we have moral obligations to those who are not part of our ethnic, religious, racial, or national group was another revolutionary innovation of the Torah.*

address he saw all this as God's judgment "until every drop of blood drawn with the lash shall be paid by another drawn with the sword." (For more on this address by Lincoln, see the commentary to Exodus 7:4.)

Sometimes, even the most irreligious of people can sense a divinely ordained retribution for the evil they have done. The philosopher and ethicist Jonathan Glover reports the story of Odilo Globocnik, the Nazi SS leader in Lublin, Poland, who recalled an incident in which he expressed to another Nazi officer, a Major Hofle, how much it bothered him to think about the Polish children freezing to death while being transported by the Nazis from Lublin to Warsaw. He could not look at these young children without thinking of his own three-year-old niece. Hofle, he recalled, looked at me "like [I was] an idiot." Sometime later, Hofle's own baby twins died of diphtheria and, at the cemetery, he cried out that it was heaven's punishment for his misdeeds.[12]

God addresses the Israelites in the plural rather than the singular; He is addressing the entire nation. If the Israelites oppress widows and orphans, they will become a nation of widows and orphans. Once again, the collective suffers because of the sins of some of its members. Another warning not to allow the bad people in our midst to get away with evil.

LOANS

22.24 If you lend money to My people, to the poor among you, do not act toward them as a creditor; exact no interest from them.

On two occasions, the Torah forbids charging interest on loans extended to the poor (here and Leviticus 25:35-37). Essentially, then, this law is just another way of enjoining us to act charitably to the poor, who borrow money to pay for necessities, and might otherwise have to sell themselves as bondservants until they can afford to pay off their debts, debts that will increase dramatically if they are obligated to pay interest. On the other hand, if someone wants to borrow money to expand his business, for example, there is no moral reason why one should be prohibited from taking interest, since the borrower intends to use the money to make money.

Having said that, Deuteronomy 23:20-21 forbids taking interest on any loans from fellow Israelites. To this day, Jewish communities worldwide have established "free-loan" societies to give loans to the poorest members of the community. However, as economies advanced, Jews devised legal fictions to enable them to make business loans.

This law in Exodus applies only to loans made to fellow Israelites in need. The Israelites were permitted to make loans to foreigners because they were almost always in Israel for business reasons.

God touchingly refers to the Israelites in this verse as "My people."

22.25 If you take your neighbor's garment in pledge, you must return it to him before the sun sets;

A pledge is an object offered as security to guarantee the payment of a debt. The term more commonly used today for pledge is "collateral."

22.26 it is his only clothing, the sole covering for his skin. In what else shall he sleep?

The Torah is referring to a person who has only one garment and would therefore have no other way of keeping warm at night.

GOD DECLARES HIMSELF COMPASSIONATE

22.26 (cont.) Therefore, if he cries out to Me, I will pay heed, for I am compassionate.

The Torah's preoccupation is with justice, but a good world also needs compassion. Once justice is secured in society, the society and its individual members can, and should, demonstrate compassion. But compassion only works in a just world. That is why the Torah warns in the next chapter (verse 3) against judges favoring the poor in rendering a judgment (obviously it also outlaws favoring the rich) because justice comes before compassion. However, in the personal, as opposed to the societal, realm, it is often appropriate for compassion to come first.

God declares Himself "compassionate." This is important for two reasons.

The first is we are supposed to imitate God.

The other is God's compassion is not something we would necessarily deduce from the world as is; neither nature nor humanity, both created by God, are particularly compassionate.

God's existence does not necessitate a big "leap of faith." There is an element of faith but, given the otherwise inexplicable existence of the world, of life, of intelligence, of order, and of design, belief in God the Creator, while not provable, is rational, even rationally compelling. However, given all the evil caused by human beings and all the suffering caused by nature, belief in God's goodness may necessitate a leap of faith. That's why God informs us, "I am compassionate."

RESPECT FOR JUDGES AND LEADERS

22.27 You shall not revile [curse] God, nor put a curse upon a chieftain among your people.

In this verse, the word normally reserved for God, *Elohim*, means "judges," as it does on a number of occasions (Exodus 21:6, for example). Consequently, the verse should read, "You shall not revile [curse] judges, nor put a curse upon a chieftain among your people." A second reason is it makes sense in this verse, as it connects both parts of the verse. And a third reason is God does not refer to Himself in the third person anywhere in this section.

God's compassion is not something we would necessarily deduce from the world as is; neither nature nor humanity, both created by God, are particularly compassionate.

The word *nasi* (chieftain) may also be translated as "ruler" or "leader" (in modern Hebrew, *nasi* means "president"). The Torah is commanding us to treat our leaders with respect. A certain degree of respect is due to individuals because of the office they hold, even if we disagree with the person currently holding it.

Of course, just as there are times when one must violate the commandment to honor one's parents (see commentary to Leviticus 19:3), there are times when one is expected to disobey the authorities. Certainly, in a tyranny, where leaders have attained authority and rule through violence, and where judges form an arm of those criminal leaders, one is not expected to honor or obey such people.

22.28 You shall not put off the skimming of the first yield of your vats.

This verse is explained by the NIV translation: "Do not hold back offerings from your granaries or your vats."

22.28 (cont.) You shall give Me the first-born among your sons.

Needless to say, the text is not commanding child sacrifice; child sacrifice is specifically listed as one of the Canaanite abominations (Deuteronomy 18:10), and is punished with a death sentence for Israelites and non-Israelites alike

(Leviticus 20:2). Rather, God is referring to the ritual of consecrating firstborn sons unto Him, which was described earlier in Exodus (see the commentary on the procedure of redeeming the firstborn in 13:2).

22.29 You shall do the same with your cattle and your flocks: seven days it shall remain with its mother; on the eighth day you shall give it to Me.

The straightforward way of understanding this verse is all firstborn permitted animals are to be ritually sacrificed to God on the eighth day. As Rashi explains, basing his comments on Leviticus 22:26 ("...and from the eighth day it shall be acceptable as an offering...") from the eighth day on, but not before, it is permitted to sacrifice the animal.

22.30 You shall be holy people to Me: you must not eat flesh torn by beasts in the field; you shall cast it to the dogs.

The Hebrew word for "torn," *treifah*, is related to the word *treif*, which ultimately came to describe anything non-kosher. However, in its original Torah context, the term means "torn," and refers to the torn flesh of animals.

A major purpose of the Torah is to teach people how to elevate themselves above animals. This may be one such example. Whereas animals will eat any dead flesh they find in a field, Israelites must slaughter any animal they plan to eat in accordance with particular rules. They are also expected to bless God when they eat (Deuteronomy 8:10; Joel 2:26). In such ways, they distance themselves from animal-like behavior, and bring themselves closer to godly behavior, which in turn brings them closer to God.

CHAPTER
23

A BAN ON SPREADING RUMORS

23.1 You must not carry false rumors;

The language of this verse echoes the language of the Third Commandment, which prohibits using God's name in vain. The literal translation of the Third Commandment reads, "Do not carry the name of your Lord God in vain." This verse uses the same words: "do not carry" (*lo tisah*), and "vain" (*shav*—translated here as "false").

The unusual similarity in wording suggests the Torah deems "carrying" false rumors as a serious sin, in some ways comparable to "carrying" God's name in vain.

Almost by definition, rumors are negative and often malicious. People don't make up nice "rumors" about people. And we would all react nervously if someone told us "there's a rumor going around about you."

Therefore, passing on rumors, even if they turn out to be true, is almost always morally wrong; and considerably worse, and what is prohibited here, is passing on false rumors.

People often do not realize the rumor they are spreading is false. When they finally learn what they said about someone wasn't true, they claim they shouldn't be blamed because they didn't know it was untrue. By then, however, it is too late. Great damage has been done to an innocent party. Once a person's good name is lost, it is very hard, if not impossible, to get it back.

23.1 (cont.) you shall not join hands with the guilty to act as a malicious witness:

> This statement prohibits testifying on behalf of a defendant or a litigant whom you know is in the wrong.

THE MAJORITY—THE "HERD"— IS TOO OFTEN MORALLY WRONG

23.2 You shall neither side with the mighty to do wrong—

> Translated literally this means, "Do not side with the many to do wrong."

> This law is a prohibition on people allowing themselves to be led astray by large groups or majority opinion. One of the saddest facts of the human condition is that most people follow the herd. Sometimes, of course, the herd is morally right. That, obviously, is the ideal. But most good is achieved by individuals who have the courage to part from the majority when it is morally wrong.

> In addition, people tend to act worse in groups than when alone. The herd, not to mention the mob, emboldens people to do bad things they would rarely do if they had no such support.

> Of course, people will also act better among morally good groups. But, again, that is relatively rare. So, the Torah is warning us that when dealing with groups, we have reason to be wary. The philosopher Bertrand Russell recalled these very words from the flyleaf of the Bible his beloved grandmother gave him on his twelfth birthday, words which he acknowledged continued to influence him even after he "had ceased to believe in God": "Thou shalt not follow a multitude to do evil" (the King James translation of this verse).[1]

> An American film classic, *Twelve Angry Men*, tells the story of a man who was the lone holdout on a jury whose other eleven members were certain the defendant was guilty of murder. Wanting to be done with the task and get home as quickly as possible, the other jurors put intense pressure on the holdout—who believed there was reasonable doubt as to whether the defendant committed murder—to

One of the saddest facts of the human condition is that most people follow the herd.

vote "guilty." During the film, the lone juror succeeded in convincing the others, one by one, that the evidence presented against the defendant was flawed, and the defendant might be innocent or, at the very least, not "guilty beyond a reasonable doubt." By the end of the film, it was clear the defendant was very likely innocent.

> *The role of a judge is not to undo society's ills, but to render justice in the particular case that has come before the court.*

People go along with the majority when it is wrong for at least two reasons:

First, people want to be well-liked, popular. And the desire to be liked can be very dangerous, since it may lead a person to prefer being liked to being morally right.

Second, it takes courage to dissent from the immoral majority. They may hurt you—physically, or financially, or hurt your reputation. It is a lot safer to side with an immoral majority.

23.2 (cont.) you shall not give perverse testimony in a dispute so as to pervert it in favor of the mighty—

JUDGES ARE TO ENFORCE JUSTICE, NOT COMPASSION

23.3 nor shall you show deference to a poor man in his dispute.

The role of a judge is not to undo society's ills, but to render justice in any particular case before the court. A judge is thus distorting his professional calling if he rules on behalf of a poor man who is in the wrong. If the judge so desires, he is, of course, free, once the case is resolved, to give the poor man money out of his own pocket.

The Torah is warning judges not to see the judge's role as repairing society. The judge's primary role is to render justice in the courtroom. That is how he will help repair society. When judges forsake that role, they actually harm society, not repair it, because a good society rests first and foremost on justice.

Essay: How to Treat One's Enemy

23.4 When you encounter your enemy's ox or ass wandering, you must take it back to him.

23.5 When you see the ass of your enemy lying under its burden and would refrain from raising it, you must nevertheless raise it with him.

Virtually every one of us has enemies, rivals, or people we simply dislike. This verse prohibits us from allowing hostile and vindictive emotions to override basic human decency. We cannot do the wrong thing— in this case, allow an animal to suffer—just because a personal enemy owns the animal.

By "enemy," the Torah is referring to personal enemies, not to enemies in the sense of evil people with whom one may be at war. The Torah is not a suicide document. If we are fighting a just war, we are not expected to return captured tanks to the enemy or to return a gun to a person who we have reason to believe will misuse it.

The law in 23:5 furthers the principle enunciated in the previous verse. It reflects the Torah's advocacy not only of acting decently toward all people, but toward animals as well— something legislated repeatedly in the Torah.

Again, the Torah was unique in its preoccupation with demanding humane treatment of animals—from the Ten Commandments to the present verse. But unlike many in our own time, it never equates human worth and animal worth. In the Torah's view, we owe animals decent treatment, but we are allowed to kill them for valid purposes—most notably for food and in biblical times for sacrifices that elevated human behavior (and which in the large majority of cases involved eating the sacrificed animal).

If we cannot mistreat an animal because we loathe its owner, how much more so must we act decently toward people related to those we personally dislike. Examples would be the spouse, sibling, child, parent, or friend of an enemy. Each is a person in his or her own right, who therefore cannot be mistreated because of his or her relationship to someone whom we dislike, perhaps with good reason.

A true story illustrates this point.

Abraham Isaac Kook, among the greatest rabbinic figures of the twentieth century, was often unfairly attacked by the Neturei Karta, a small ultra-Orthodox anti-Zionist group. On one occasion, the daughter of a Neturei Karta leader, a man who made some of the most extreme attacks on Rabbi Kook, fell ill with a serious and rare disease. This man learned that a doctor in another country was perhaps the only person who could treat her. However, there was little chance the exceptionally busy physician would have time to see and treat the daughter; and, in any case, his fees were far beyond anything the father could pay.

But the father learned the doctor was a great admirer of Rabbi Kook: If the rabbi asked the doctor to treat the girl, he would likely do so. The Neturei Karta leader was in a quandary. How could he, who hated and publicly attacked Rabbi Kook, now ask Kook to intervene? In desperation, the man sought out Rabbi Aryeh Levine, a well-known friend of Rabbi Kook, and asked him to speak to the rabbi. Rabbi Levine did so, and Rabbi Kook responded, "Of course I am prepared to give the man a letter to the doctor. What does this have to do with the difference of opinion between the girl's father and me?"

Rabbi Kook not only wrote the letter, but depicted the father in favorable terms. He explained to his friend, "I will let no personal bias influence me as I write this."

Rabbi Kook even wrote a letter to a shipping line with whose directors he had warm relations, asking them to offer the man and his daughter a substantial discount on their passage.[2]

In the same vein, the Midrash relates a story:

"Two ass drivers who hated each other were walking on the road when the ass of one lay down under its burden. His companion saw it, and at first he passed on. But then he reflected: Is it not written in the Torah, 'When you see the ass of your enemy lying under its burden and would refrain from raising it, you must nevertheless raise it with him.'

"So he returned, lent a hand, and helped his enemy in loading and unloading. He began talking to his enemy, 'Release a bit here, pull up over there, unload over here.'

"Thus peace came about between them, so that the driver of the overloaded ass said [to himself]: 'Did I not suppose that he hated me? But look how compassionate he was with me.'

"By and by, the two entered an inn, ate and drank together, and became close friends. What caused them to make peace and become friends? Because one of them kept what is written in the Torah, 'When you see the ass of your enemy lying under its burden and would refrain from raising it, you must nevertheless raise it with him.'"[3]

Treat a personal enemy with fairness and respect, and the person might well find it impossible to remain an enemy.

23.6 You shall not subvert the rights of your needy in their disputes.

Whereas verse 3 forbids favoring the poor in court, this verse forbids *dis*favoring the poor in court, historically a considerably more common occurrence. The purpose of courtroom justice is to determine which party is responsible in each situation. Period.

Neither the wealth nor the poverty of the parties in a legal dispute should matter in court. In the courtroom, the only thing that matters is determining who is legally in the right and who is legally in the wrong.

CORRUPT JUDGES DESTROY SOCIETIES

23.7 Keep far from a false charge;

This is a warning to judges, a warning that throughout history has too often gone unheeded by judges who knowingly did not "keep far from a false charge" (or, as the Torah literally says, "Stay far away from falsehood").

The Torah, preoccupied with justice as the foundation of a decent society, knows only too well corrupt judges destroy societies.

23.7 (cont.) do not bring death on those who are innocent and in the right, for I will not acquit the wrongdoer.

This is one of the most important declarations of the Torah.

First, God would prefer we spare a wrongdoer than sentence an innocent person to death. Second, God explains why: because He will ultimately punish the evil-doers whom we fail to punish.

Now, given the fact that is obvious to everyone, that many evildoers avoid punishment, this verse can only mean one thing—God punishes the evil in an afterlife. This verse, therefore, with its divine declaration, "I will not acquit the wrongdoer" is one of the clearest suggestions in the Torah there is an afterlife.

> *Nothing explains the success or failure of countries more than does the presence or absence of corruption.*

ESSAY: THE TERRIBLE POWER OF CORRUPTION

23.8 Do not take bribes, for bribes blind the clear-sighted and upset the pleas of those who are in the right.

I have discussed the terrible consequences of societal corruption in discussing the central importance of the Eighth Commandment—"Do not steal." But as the Torah now specifically addresses the subject—by prohibiting bribery—we shall return to it.

Bribery is the single most common form of corruption in society. It involves giving a person money in order to receive a favor in return. Obviously, giving people money for some goods or services is how all economies function. But a bribe is giving someone money, goods, or services *dishonestly* to gain an unfair advantage over others. It is a bribe when a judge is given money to provide the bribe-giver with a verdict in his favor. That bribe has subverted justice. If enough judges are bribed, a society has no justice, and cannot function.

When a policeman is given a bribe to look away, it is for the payer to get away with a criminal act or for the policeman to extort money from the innocent. When enough police take bribes, a society is overrun by criminality.

When enough government officials take bribes, the wheels of government grind to a halt (except for those who can muster the funds to pay the bribes), and the society ceases to function.

All of these types of bribes fall under the category of corruption.

Corruption is the primary reason societies fail to thrive; societies in which corruption is held in check prosper economically, socially, and morally. Nothing explains the success or failure of countries more than does the presence or absence of corruption.

For example, the failure at this time of most African and Latin American countries, and Russia, to lift themselves from poverty is due overwhelmingly to corruption. Both Africa and Latin America have an abundance of both natural resources and human talent. But neither can overcome the corruption that permeates those societies. I have learned of this firsthand in visits to twenty countries in Africa and almost as many in Latin America.

In Angola, for example, I saw rows of unfinished modern apartment buildings—unfinished because government officials were not offered sufficient bribes to allow completion of those buildings. (I saw this problem on a far larger scale in China.) In the West African country of Togo, the car I was in was stopped at a police blockade, a policeman walked over to the driver, took money, and only then allowed the car to proceed. The driver explained that this is routine. The same practice is common in Mexico and other Latin American countries.

African economists have argued that corruption—not Western colonialism, not lack of Western aid—is why Africa hasn't escaped poverty. These economists have begged Western countries to stop giving monetary aid to corrupt African countries because nearly all the money goes to corrupt government officials and thereby further increases their corrupt power.[4]

Meanwhile, in Europe, North America, Japan, Singapore, and a handful of other countries, corruption is far more likely to be prosecuted and therefore far less prevalent. That is a major reason for their continuing prosperity.

To most people, corruption sounds bad, but most people do not recognize how devastating it actually is. The Torah does.

The words translated here as "upset the pleas of those who are in the right" literally mean will "confuse the words of the righteous."

The Hebrew word for "the righteous" is *tzaddik*, a term generally considered a high appellation (only Noah is so described in the Torah). The use of this term here suggests even the most morally upright person is not free from the temptation of bribery. In light of this, the Talmud warns: "Don't trust yourself until the day you die."[5]

23.9 You shall not oppress a stranger, for you know the feelings of the stranger, having yourselves been strangers in the land of Egypt.

Nefesh, the word translated here as "the feelings of," more accurately means "soul" or "essence." These words can also be translated as "you know the soul of the stranger," underscoring that insofar as unjust suffering is concerned, the Jew and the stranger share the same soul. This verse can also be seen as the Torah's argument for the universality of the human soul and, consequently, for the equality of all humans.

THE SABBATICAL YEAR

23.10 Six years you shall sow your land and gather in its yield;

23.11 but in the seventh you shall let it rest and lie fallow. Let the needy among your people eat of it, and what they leave let the wild beasts eat. You shall do the same with your vineyards and your olive groves.

Every seven years, the Israelites are commanded to stop working the land. This institution, known as the Sabbatical Year, does not exist for the sake of crop rotation or soil replenishment—just as the Kosher laws do not exist to make people healthy. The primary reason—as is true of so many things in the Torah involving the number seven—is, among other things, to remind the Israelites and the world that God created the world. Just as God rested on the Seventh

Day, the Israelites are to rest on the Seventh Day, and in the Seventh Year the land is to rest as well.

Religion, and for that matter, almost anything important from patriotism to weddings, needs rituals.

As explained in Genesis 1:1, the first assertion of the Torah, upon which all else rests, is God created the world. The world, therefore, has design and purpose; it is not the product of random forces.

To this day, there are those in Israel who abide by this law.[6]

23.12 Six days you shall do your work, but on the seventh day you shall cease from labor,

The commandment to keep the Sabbath is reiterated immediately following the law of the Sabbatical Year, making it clear that the Sabbatical Year is to the other six years what the Shabbat Day is to the other six days.

HUMANS ARE TO SANCTIFY THE SABBATH; ANIMALS ARE TO REST ON IT

23.12 (cont.) in order that your ox and your ass may rest, and that your bondman and the stranger may be refreshed.

The Hebrew word *vayinafash* ("refreshed") comes from the word *nefesh*, soul.

The word used for the animals ("your ox and your ass") ceasing from work is the normal word for "rest." But the word used for human beings ("your bondman and the stranger") ceasing from work can be rendered as "en-souled." It is enough for animals to rest their bodies on Shabbat, but not enough for people. The Fourth Commandment is to make Shabbat holy, not just to rest.

This law—the slave ("bondman"), the animals, and the stranger must all rest and have the Sabbath—is unique in ancient history, and perhaps unique in all history.

All the laws from the conclusion of the Ten Commandments until this point have been ethical laws—laws governing the relationship between people. Therefore, this verse treats the Shabbat in that same vein, from an ethical perspective: We, our animals, and servants must rest (and, since the Torah word for "servant" and "slave" is the same, slaves, too, had to be given a day of rest). At other points, the Torah's primary emphasis in discussing the Shabbat is on ritual, holiness, and affirming God as the Creator.

Since the observance of the Sabbath is both an ethical and a ritual/religious obligation, this verse serves as a bridge between the ethical laws preceding it and the ritual laws that now follow.

23.13 Be on guard concerning all that I have told you. Make no mention of the names of other gods; they shall not be heard on your lips.

The prohibition on mentioning the names of other gods is reiterated because some Israelites might be tempted to invoke other gods in observing the festivals outlined in the next verses.

23.14 Three times a year you shall hold a festival for Me:

These three festivals were associated with important moments in the agricultural cycle: the planting, the first harvest, and the second harvest.

23.15 You shall observe the Feast of Unleavened Bread—eating unleavened bread for seven days as I have commanded you—at the set time in the month of Abib, for in it you went forth from Egypt;

The Feast of Unleavened Bread (Matzo) is Passover, the holiday celebrated at the time of planting. In addition to its agricultural significance, Passover is most importantly the celebration of the Exodus. For that reason, it has become the most widely observed Jewish holiday, probably because freedom is a secular value as well as a religious one.

As to how the Hebrew calendar was adjusted to make sure Passover was always observed in the spring, see the commentary on Exodus 13:4.

23.15 (cont.) and none shall appear before Me empty-handed

God commands His people to appear before Him in a sanctuary or other place of worship bearing a ritual offering (see also Deuteronomy 16:17).

23.16 and the Feast of the Harvest, of the first fruits of your work, of what you sow in the field;

This is the holiday of Shavuot, the holiday that takes place at the time of the first harvest. Often referred to as Pentecost, *Shavuot* is the Hebrew word for "weeks." This holiday of "Weeks" was so named because the Torah commands it be celebrated exactly seven weeks after the first day of Passover. In addition to its agricultural significance, Shavuot marks the Jewish people's receiving the Torah.

Of the three festivals specified in these verses, Shavuot is the least widely observed today. One reason is it has the fewest rituals associated with it. Religion, and for that matter, almost anything important from patriotism to marriage, needs rituals. We are physical beings living in a physical universe; physical expression—which is what ritual is—matters. And Passover and Succot (see next verse) are replete with rituals.

The other reason Shavuot might be less widely observed is that moderns relate far more to the idea of freedom (Passover) than to a holiday celebrating the giving of the Torah.

23.16 (cont.) and the Feast of Ingathering at the end of the year, when you gather in the results of your work from the field.

This is Succot, the holiday that takes place at the time of the second harvest. The Torah refers to this holiday as *Hag Ha-asif*, which comes from the Hebrew word for "collect" or "gather in" and refers to the ingathering of the harvested crops. In addition to its agricultural significance, this holiday commemorates the temporary portable huts in which the Israelites lived while wandering in the desert. *Succot* means "booths" or "huts" and the holiday is therefore known in English as Tabernacles (the biblical term for "a fixed or movable habitation usually of light construction").

Deuteronomy 16:15 commands us to "have nothing but joy" on this holiday, which is why later Judaism described Succot as "the time of our happiness." As will be discussed there, happiness is a major *moral and religious* value.

23.17 Three times a year all your males shall appear before the Sovereign, the Lord.

According to a basic principle in traditional Jewish law, women are exempt—because of family responsibilities (the assumption being they are usually the primary caregivers to children)—from all "time-bound" laws, such as this law to appear before God on the festivals. Women as well as men are bound by all negative commands (not to steal, not to slander, not to covet, etc.) and by positive commandments that are not time-bound, such as "Love your neighbor as yourself," and "Honor your father and mother." Having said that, women did indeed often accompany their husbands to the sanctuary, as reflected in the account of Elkanah, Hannah, and Peninah, the story that opens the First Book of Samuel.

23.18 You shall not offer the blood of My sacrifice with anything leavened;

This verse refers to the paschal lamb sacrifice, which was offered each year on the anniversary of the eve of the Exodus. "Paschal" comes from the Hebrew word for the Holiday of Passover, *Pesach*.

23.18 (cont.) and the fat of My festal offering shall not be left lying until morning.

According to Cassuto, the purpose of legislating the sacred meal had to be eaten before morning was to prevent the riotous and unchaste behavior that might occur if a festival was celebrated all night.

23.19 The choice first fruits of your soil you shall bring to the house of the Lord your God.

ESSAY: WHY NOT "BOIL A KID IN ITS MOTHER'S MILK"? THE MEANING OF AN OBSCURE LAW

23.19 (cont.) You shall not boil a kid in its mother's milk.

Centuries ago, Maimonides speculated this prohibition was intended to keep the Israelites away from the idolatrous customs of other peoples. For some time it was believed there was evidence for Maimonides' hypothesis: Ancient Ugaritic texts indicated the Canaanites used to prepare such a dish at festival ceremonies celebrating the fertility of the soil. However, in recent years, a major biblical scholar, Jacob Milgrom, contended the ancient Ugaritic text was mistranslated, and there is, therefore, no evidence of the Ugarits engaging in such a practice.

It would seem Milgrom's knowledge of the Ugaritic text should prevail in this matter. I would, however, add this in defense of Maimonides's explanation: Solely from a common-sense viewpoint, it is difficult to imagine the Torah, or any other body of law, would prohibit a practice no one engaged in. And the Torah states this law three times (here, Exodus 34:26, and Deuteronomy 14:21). If no one engaged in it, all the Israelites might well have shaken their heads wondering what God or Moses was talking about. If some country's parliament prohibited stabbing fish while riding a bicycle, we would assume it was something people in that country did.

However, even if it were proven that other nations did boil goats in their mother's milk, the question would remain: Why would the Torah prohibit the practice, and on three separate occasions, no less?

Clearly, the Torah is sending a message: It is wrong to boil an animal in the substance with which its mother gave it life. Obviously, the prohibition is not for the sake of either animal; neither the mother nor the baby knows whose milk is being used. The purpose of the prohibition must therefore be to affect us—specifically to refine human character. We are never to forget animals are living creatures; and there is something mocking and even cruel about boiling a kid in the milk of its mother.

This is not some modern explanation attempting to make the Torah look modern and moral. The first-century Hellenistic Jewish philosopher, Philo, explained this law in exactly this way. He wrote: "It is grossly improper that the substance which fed the living animal should be used to season or flavor it after its death."[7]

And Milgrom expanded on Philo's observation with an additional moral explanation: "The root rationale behind the kid prohibition is its [the Torah's] opposition to comingling life and death. A substance that sustains the life of a creature (milk) should not be fused or confused with a process associated with its death (cooking)…. Mother's milk, the life sustaining food for her kid, should never become associated with its death."[8]

It is not surprising that the ancient rabbis also did not look upon this law as pertaining only to baby goats. They regarded it as a moral teacher in the same way Philo and Milgrom did—as another attempt of the Torah to teach a major distinction, the distinction between life and death. In part because Egypt's religion was death-oriented (the pyramids are tombs, its holy book was the Book of the Dead, etc.), the Torah is replete with laws banning the comingling of life and death. One such law is this prohibition against boiling a baby goat (death) in its mother's milk (life); another is the prohibition against a priest (who is to be preoccupied with life) from coming into contact with the dead (a law that is probably unique among religions); and another is the prohibition against engaging in sexual intercourse (life) while the woman is menstruating (the blood representing death, or at least the end of a possible new life).

> *God does not fight on behalf of the Israelites per se, but on behalf of those who serve as conduits of His will. God's battle is moral, not ethnic.*

For this reason, though the verse only prohibits the boiling of a kid in its mother's milk, for as long as we know, Jews have not cooked or eaten milk and meat together.[9]

23.20 I am sending an angel before you to guard you on the way and to bring you to the place that I have made ready.

According to Cassuto, God is referring to Himself, since He will guide the people through the desert. Of course, there is always the possibility God really will send an angel.

23.21 Pay heed to him and obey him. Do not defy him, for he will not pardon your offenses, since My name is in him;

It seems to me the least plausible explanation is the "angel" is God. For one thing, God is never elsewhere described as "not pardoning" except in the Third Commandment, which prohibits the worst sin a person can engage in, doing evil in God's name (see commentary to Exodus 20:7). But whether referring to God or not, God is warning the people the stakes are high. He is about to dispossess other nations so the Israelites can enter the land; and the Israelites' right to the land is not at all guaranteed—it is conditional upon their observance of God's laws. In the words of Leviticus: "Do not defile yourselves in any of these ways, for it is by such that the nations I am casting out before you defiled themselves...So let not the land spew you out for defiling it, as it spewed out the nation[s] that came before you" (Leviticus 24:18, 28).

Thus, if the Israelites do not behave appropriately, God will have dispossessed other nations unnecessarily.

On the other hand, if the messenger is Moses, this verse is easier to understand. God is telling the people Moses, who is a human being and is therefore less compassionate than God, will not forgive the people if they disobey God's will.

23.22 but if you obey him and do all that I say, I will be an enemy to your enemies and a foe to your foes.

God's protection, the Israelites are told, is contingent upon their obedience. Unconditional acceptance, support, protection—none of these are Torah concepts. God's response to man, especially to the Israelites, is rooted in their acting decently. God does not fight on behalf of the Israelites per se, but on behalf of those who serve as conduits of His will. God's battle is moral, not ethnic.

NO ONE WAS "ANNIHILATED"

23.23 When My angel goes before you and brings you to the Amorites, the Hittites, the Perizzites, the Canaanites, the Hivites, and the Jebusites, and I annihilate them,

Given the moral problem God "annihilating" these nations appears to raise, four points are worth noting.

First, "annihilate" does not mean kill every Amorite, Hittite, Perizzite, Canaanite, Hivite, and Jebusite. This is made clear seven verses later, in verse 30, where God says, "I will drive them out before you little by little." Furthermore, both the Bible later and modern archaeology affirm many Canaanites were not killed (see, for example, the report, "Fate of Ancient Canaanites Seen in DNA Analysis: They Survived").[10]

> *The follower of the Torah is neither instructed nor allowed to persecute, let alone kill, pagan believers because of their pagan beliefs.*

Second, God is speaking about *a one-time situation* in which He will fight on behalf of the Israelites. There is no notion in the Torah of God promising to always do so. God makes no pledge to always fight against the Jews' enemies.

Third, here it is God doing the fighting—just as in Egypt, where the Torah made clear the angel, not the Israelites, killed the Egyptian firstborn.

Fourth, it has already been established God does not protect the Jews if they cease living by His laws. In ancient religions, the gods' protection was nation-based, not morality-based.

Jews who believe God would automatically fight on their behalf have not come up with helpful ideas. Indeed, they have sometimes been attracted to highly self-destructive ideas. For example, underground Jewish terrorists in Israel in the early 1980s plotted the destruction of the Dome of the Rock mosque in Jerusalem, on the assumption that though it might trigger a worldwide Islamic jihad against Jews and Israel, God would intervene and Israel would win, leading to the building of the Third Temple on the Temple Mount, (on which the mosque stands).

THE TORAH'S ATTITUDE TOWARD IDOLATRY IN THE LAND OF ISRAEL

23.24 you shall not bow down to their gods in worship or follow their practices, but shall tear them down and smash their pillars to bits.

The Torah is philosophically and theologically intolerant of idolatry. Rationally and morally, it could not be otherwise. The moment you assert there is only one God and therefore only one universal moral standard, you are asserting the pagan gods are false. For those who believe tolerance is always a moral virtue, this may be disturbing. But one doesn't have to be an ancient Israelite or a modern monotheist—in fact, one can be an atheist—to assert pagan gods aren't really gods.

Moreover, it is morally inconceivable that tolerance is always a moral virtue. Are we to be tolerant of child sacrifice? The moral answer is self-evident.

A number of other factors should be kept in mind.

First, ethical monotheism's intolerance of false gods does not extend to persecution of followers of other religions. The follower of the Torah is neither instructed nor allowed to persecute, let alone kill, pagan believers because of their pagan beliefs.

Second, even regarding pagan places of worship, this command applies only to the Land of Israel. Jews were never called upon to destroy pagan places of worship outside of Israel. But in this one small land, ethical monotheism, the only solution to evil, is to be established so that "From Zion shall go forth Torah and the word of God from Jerusalem" (Isaiah 2:3). At that time, when ethical monotheism was new and very fragile, the presence of idolatrous places of worship would have made this impossible.

23.25 You shall serve the Lord your God, and He will bless your bread and your water.

DO GOD'S PROMISES OF NO SICKNESS CONFORM TO REALITY?

23.25 (cont.) And I will remove sickness from your midst.

23.26 No woman in your land shall miscarry or be barren. I will let you enjoy the full count of your days.

God promises in return for serving Him, He will eradicate illness, miscarriage, and barrenness. These verses are troublesome to our modern sensibilities, since righteousness has never guaranteed good health.

Obviously, the God who split a sea, delivered water from rocks, and brought ten plagues on Egypt can do anything. And if the Israelites all led the type of life God demanded of them, God might well have abolished illness.

But as this has not happened, it is also possible these promises were made for the theologically primitive Israelites. They needed such promises to take God and ethical monotheism seriously. The Israelites, a group of ex-slaves who had lived among Egyptian idolaters for centuries, needed as clear a motivation as possible to fulfill the commandments. This is not to suggest in any way that God was "bluffing"—God was quite capable of removing sickness from Israelite life if they observed His laws.

It is only to suggest no other promised reward would have been nearly as effective in getting the Israelites, or anyone else 3,000 years ago, to consistently do the right thing.

Today, however, we are expected to understand that the reward for following God's will is not physical health (though there is no doubt an ethical God-centered life does have health benefits), but the act of obeying God. Jews understood this long ago. As the Talmud put it, "The reward for observing a mitzvah [commandment] is not granted in this world."[11] Rather, the Talmud says, "The reward for observing a mitzvah is observing a mitzvah."[12]

No one can rationally believe doing God's will guarantees one will, for example, never develop cancer or die in an earthquake. If that were the case, we would have to draw the irrational and cruel conclusion that anyone who dies prematurely was being punished by God—or the equally irrational conclusion that all those who live long and healthy lives have lived God-centered lives.

In more recent times, Rabbi Emanuel Rackman, the late president of Bar Ilan University, Israel's Orthodox university, maintained there is indeed a

> *God promises in return for serving Him, He will eradicate illness, miscarriage, and barrenness. These verses are troublesome to our modern sensibilities, since righteousness has never guaranteed good health.*

correlation between moral law and natural law: When people act decently, disease is minimized. For example, God wants people to treat the earth well, and when they don't, pollution of the environment leads to poor health conditions. God wants people to engage in monogamous sex, and non-monogamous sexual practices are the ones that cause sexually transmitted diseases such as syphilis, genital herpes, and AIDS. So, too, those nations with the longest life spans are free countries, not tyrannies. Take the dramatic example of North and South Korea—the identical nation and ethnic group divided into two countries, one free and one a tyranny. In 2012, the lifespan of Koreans in the free South was at least twelve years longer than that of North Koreans.

23.27 I will send forth My terror before you, and I will throw into panic all the people among whom you come, and I will make all your enemies turn tail before you

23.28 I will send a plague ahead of you, and it shall drive out before you the Hivites, the Canaanites, and the Hittites.

23.29 I will not drive them out before you in a single year, lest the land become desolate and the wild beasts multiply to your hurt.

23.30 I will drive them out before you little by little,

Even though the word "annihilate" was used in verse 23, it does not mean "wipe out" everyone living in Canaan. This verse makes it clear God does not intend to annihilate all the Canaanites; but they will be gradually removed from the land (owing to their terrible moral conduct). In the eyes of the Israelites, however, it will eventually appear as if those nations were "annihilated."

23.30 (cont.) until you have increased and possess the land.

23.31 I will set your borders from the Sea of Reeds to the Sea of Philistia, and from the wilderness to the Euphrates; for I will deliver the inhabitants of the land into your hands, and you will drive them out before you.

The Torah is outlining here the ideal borders of the Jewish state, borders never fully achieved even during the time of Kings David and Solomon, when the Jewish state was at its largest. And while David and Solomon "asserted political and economic hegemony as far north as the Euphrates (I Kings 5:1), they did not dispossess the local peoples and settle Israelites in their stead" (Sarna). Moreover, it was not up to the Israelites—or Jews thereafter —to set these borders. It is for God to do, in His time: "*I* will set your borders …."

23.32 You shall make no covenant with them and their gods.

23.33 They shall not remain in your land, lest they cause you to sin against Me; for you will serve their gods—and it will prove a snare to you.

As noted above, the goal of the commands to drive out the Canaanites was to develop one small corner of the world in which ethical monotheism could grow. The Bible scholar Yechezkel Kaufmann argued it was only because of these wars against Canaanite nations that Israel "did not assimilate into the indigenous population…. It provided Israel's new religious idea with an environment in which it could grow free of the influence of a popular pagan culture."[13]

As it happens, many Canaanite nations and peoples survived. Judges 1:27-33 lists repeated cases in which the Israelites did not dispossess the Canaanites. And the biblical warning, "it will prove a snare to you," turned out to be correct. Israel's later history is replete with accounts of the Israelites assimilating with pagan tribes and worshipping their idols. To cite one example, Judges 2:11-13 cites instances in which the Israelites forsook the "God of their father Who had brought them out of the land of Egypt" and worshipped Baal and the gods of their neighbors.

CHAPTER 24

24.1 Then He said to Moses, "Come up to the Lord, with Aaron, Nadab and Abihu,

The Hebrew word *aleh* ("come up" or "rise") appears several times in this chapter. The word often implies the act of arising to do something holy. It is used in its noun form, *aliyah*, in the Jewish prayer service to refer to a person "going up" to bless the Torah. The same word, *aliyah*, is also used to describe the act of going to live in Israel—literally, "going up" to Israel.

Nadab and Abihu, mentioned at the end of the verse, are Aaron's two oldest sons (Numbers 3:2). The priesthood has not yet been established, but when it is the Torah ordains it to be transmitted generation to generation from father to son (Exodus 40:12-15). To this day, Jews who know themselves to be priests (*kohanim*) trace their ancestry in a direct line back to Aaron.

THE DEVALUING OF THE OLD MEANS WISDOM ISN'T VALUED

24.1 (cont.) and seventy elders of Israel

Throughout history, not only in ancient Israel, virtually every society greatly valued old people—because old people were associated with wisdom, and wisdom was valued. In the contemporary world, especially in the West, youth is increasingly valued more than age. That is either a reflection of the fact that wisdom is less valued and therefore the old are less valued or the old are less valued and therefore wisdom is less valued. It is hard to know which came first—the devaluing of the old or the devaluing of wisdom. But whichever caused the other, both are tragedies.

In answer to some young people who told the great German-Jewish actor Fritz Kortner he could not understand their problems, Kortner responded, "You were never as old as I am; on the other hand, I was as young as you are now."

The devaluation of old people is a tragedy for their sake, for society's sake, and for the sake of the young who can so benefit from being with and learning from the old. Anyone who has, or who has had, a bond with a grandparent or a mentor knows how true this is. And the devaluation of wisdom is an even greater tragedy. We live in an age that values— or at least claims to value—knowledge. But knowledge without wisdom tells you nothing about how to lead your life. It is like owning a map but having no destination. *If you don't know where you need to go, knowing exactly where you are is useless.*

> *It is hard to know which came first—the devaluing of the old or the devaluing of wisdom. But whichever caused the other, both are tragedies.*

24.1 (cont.) and bow low from afar.

Bowing low involves full prostration, with one's head touching the floor, denoting a sign of total obedience.

24.2 Moses alone shall come near the Lord; but the others shall not come near, nor shall the people come up with him."

The Torah makes a clear distinction between Moses and the others with him; only Moses is allowed to come closer to God. This is consistent with the Torah's posthumous assessment of Moses's unique status: "Never again did there arise in Israel a prophet like Moses—who the Lord singled out, face to face" (Deuteronomy 34:10).

24.3 Moses went and repeated to the people all the commands of the Lord and all the rules;

"The commands" refer to the Ten Commandments (chapter 20, the bulk of the laws written in a similar concise style in 22:17-23:19); and "all the rules" likely refers to those outlined both earlier and in the following chapters.

24.3 (cont.) and all the people answered with one voice, saying, "All the things that the Lord has commanded we will do!"

The Israelites give public assent to all the commandments and laws—a rare moment of agreement and unity in Jewish life.

24.4 Moses then wrote down all the commands of the Lord. Early in the morning, he set up an altar at the foot of the mountain, with twelve pillars for the twelve tribes of Israel.

Moses was just instructed to go up to God, but the Torah now interrupts the story of his ascent for an interlude about a sacrificial offering.

24.5 He designated some young men among the Israelites, and they offered burnt offerings and sacrificed bulls as offerings of well-being to the Lord.

Since these sacrificial offerings take place before a priestly class was designated, no one tribe was directly responsible for preparing them. Moses therefore assigned this task to a group of young men, who were strong enough to lift the heavy bulls.

Most of the sacrifices described in the Torah were public acts of ritual slaughter preceding the eating of the flesh. Only the burnt offering (*olah*) was not eaten; rather it was burned in its entirety.

24.6 Moses took one part of the blood and put it in basins, and the other part of the blood he dashed against the altar.

24.7 Then he took the record of the covenant and read it aloud to the people.

As noted in the commentary to verse 3, what Moses likely read aloud to the people were the laws following the Ten Commandments in chapters 21-23, laws overwhelmingly social and ethical in nature. The only religious laws included in these chapters are the commandments to observe the Sabbath and the festivals, and the prohibition against worshipping false gods.

Essay: Doing and Understanding God's Will

24.7 (cont.) And they said, "All that the Lord has spoken we will faithfully do!"

The English translation here—"All that the Lord has spoken we will faithfully do!"—is not literal. The Hebrew literally says, "All that the Lord has spoken we will do and we will hear (or listen)."

The order of the verbs is significant because they are, obviously, counterintuitive. One has to hear what one is supposed to do before promising to do it. Yet the order here is reversed: "First, we will do and then we will hear."

Because the order of the words seems to make no sense, almost all translations render the verb "hear" to mean "obey." Thus, the oldest and still great English translation, the King James Version, reads: "All that the Lord hath said will we do, and be obedient." Similarly, the highly praised modern translation, the New International Version (NIV), reads: "We will do everything the Lord has said; we will obey."

But logic suggests those translations, while literally accurate, are not what the statement intends to convey. "Obey" is not the correct translation of the word "hear," because the statement would then be essentially redundant: there is no real difference between "we will do" and "we will obey."

For that reason, it would seem in this context (and similar contexts in our own lives) "hear" means "understand." When we tell someone, "I hear you," we are usually not saying our ears are registering their words; we are saying we understand what the person has said. For example, when a parent says to a child, "Did you hear what I said?" they are asking, "Did you understand what I said?"

Therefore, the verse really means, "We will do and we will understand."

This is a major life lesson: Doing leads to understanding. When we act lovingly we understand love. When we see an apple fall from a tree, we understand gravity. We understand marriage only after being married. Only when we experience cold can we understand cold; a year of explaining cold is nothing compared to a few seconds of experiencing it. And this applies to understanding the divine. In the words of the Psalmist, "Taste and see how good the Lord is" (Psalms 34:9).

The Israelites have already affirmed they will do the commandments (verse 3); now they affirm they will then understand.

Understanding after doing is true of all the commandments. But it is especially true of the ritual commandments, those that relate to the relationship between man and God. For example, no amount of explanation of the benefits of observing the Shabbat can compete with living it.

But that is not all the Israelites are saying here. They are committing themselves to understanding the commandments, not just to doing them. This needs to be emphasized because for many religious people, too much of their religious life is habit, not understanding. Therefore, one who commits to doing God's commandments also has to commit to attempting to understand those commandments. Habit and/or "blind faith" is not sufficient when it comes to ritual laws.

> *Knowledge is knowing where you are. Wisdom is knowing where to go. But if you don't know where to go, knowing where you are is useless.*

When it comes to ethical laws, however, observance out of habit or even from "blind faith" is acceptable (though not the ideal: one would hope there is an internal ethical transformation when one commits to leading an ethical life). If you don't steal simply because God said so, the benefits are still enormous both to you and to society. But if you observe religious rituals out of habit with no understanding, they can become meaningless.

In other words, *ethical behavior is an end in itself*; *ritual behavior is a means to an end.* Those ends are holiness, God, and the elevation of the self to a higher plane.

24.8 Moses took the blood and dashed it on the people and said, "This is the blood of the covenant that the Lord now makes with you concerning all these commands."

Blood was used in making a covenant because blood was understood to be the essence of animal and human life.

24.9 Then Moses and Aaron, Nadab and Abihu, and seventy elders of Israel ascended;

The narrative turns to the response to God's commandment at the beginning of the chapter to ascend the mountain.

24.10 and they saw the God of Israel: under His feet there was the likeness of a pavement of sapphire, like the very sky for purity.

> This is to be understood, according to Moses, as a description of a sight so uniquely glorious it seemed they were "seeing" the divine, but not God. Later, in Deuteronomy (4:12), Moses specifically says about this very moment: "Then the Lord spoke to you out of the fire. *You heard the sound of words but saw no form.*" Likewise, God says "No one may see me and live" (Exodus 33:20).
>
> The words, "and they saw the God of Israel" are therefore akin to our saying, "When I see a beautiful sunset or a child born, I see God."

24.11 Yet He did not raise His hand against the leaders of the Israelites; they beheld God, and they ate and drank.

> The Torah mentions the leaders of Israel ate and drank to show they survived the experience of beholding God. The point is they survived precisely because they did not literally see God. Thus, the words translated here as "they beheld God," can be better rendered as "they had a vision of God."

24.12 The Lord said to Moses, "Come up to Me on the mountain and wait there, and I will give you the stone tablets with the teachings and commandments which I have inscribed to instruct them."

24.13 So Moses and his attendant Joshua arose, and Moses ascended the mountain of God.

24.14 To the elders he had said, "Wait here for us until we return to you. You have Aaron and Hur with you; let anyone who has a legal matter approach them."

> Even during an intensely religious period, legal matters and disputes will arise and must be addressed.

24.15 When Moses had ascended the mountain, the cloud covered the mountain.

24.16 The Presence of the Lord abode on Mount Sinai, and the cloud hid it for six days. On the seventh day He called to Moses from the midst of the cloud.

24.17 Now the Presence of the Lord appeared in the sight of the Israelites as a consuming fire on the top of the mountain.

24.18 Moses went inside the cloud and ascended the mountain; and Moses remained on the mountain forty days and forty nights.

> This verse serves as a preamble to the story of the golden calf (chapter 32), which the people will build when they despair at losing their leader for forty days.

CHAPTER

25

25.1 The Lord spoke to Moses, saying:

The remainder of the Book of Exodus is largely about the building of the Tabernacle, the portable sanctuary used by the Israelites in the desert. More chapters are devoted to the Tabernacle and the details of its construction and functioning than to any other subject in the five books of the Torah (Exodus 25-31 and 35-40). Nearly all the material in these chapters is repeated in the final chapters of Exodus. These chapters describe God's instructions to Moses about how to construct the Tabernacle; the later chapters describe the Tabernacle's actual construction.

According to Everett Fox, the great amount of attention devoted to the building of the Tabernacle throughout the second half of Exodus is an indication of the Tabernacle's centrality to Israelite worship. It was the center of grain and animal sacrifice, which was the chief means of religious expression in antiquity.

The Israelites are to engage in making the Tabernacle in the same way God engaged in making the world. In imitation of God, the Israelites are to stop their work on the seventh day. This likely is the reason the laws of the Sabbath are reiterated immediately following the detailed blueprint of the Tabernacle (Exodus 31:12-17).

WHY THE UNPARALLELED AMOUNT OF DETAIL HERE?

One reason for the extraordinarily detailed instructions listed here is the most obvious one: because the Torah records what God says. But, of course, the question remains: Why did God go into such detail?

The most persuasive reason I have heard was offered by Rabbi Saul Berman. By listing every material required and how much was required, there would be no opportunity for those tasked with collecting the gifts to solicit more than was required and pocket the difference. There is a great virtue in openness, particularly in public financial matters. Individuals and especially governments have been notorious for corruption in building projects, by, for example, paying or receiving "kickbacks," bribes officials take from contractors in exchange for hiring them over others who may have submitted lower bids. By listing the precise specifications for the Tabernacle in a document accessible to every person, the officials couldn't later claim more material was required than was recorded.

> *Good actions are good, even if animated by selfishness. And bad actions are bad, even if animated by good intentions.*

One other reason was to communicate the important role aesthetic beauty can play in the worship of God.

ESSAY: IN RELIGIOUS RITUAL—UNLIKE IN ETHICAL BEHAVIOR— INTENTIONS MATTER

25.2 Tell the Israelite people to bring Me gifts; you shall accept gifts for Me from every person whose heart so moves him.

Ordinarily, the Torah gives commandments we must fulfill regardless of whether our heart is in fulfilling them or not. Moral actions must be taken whether or not our heart prompts us to. Accordingly, the Torah commands that every third year we give ten percent of our earnings to the poor (Deuteronomy 26:12) and an additional percentage each year (Leviticus 19:9-10), irrespective of whether our hearts prompt us to do so. But with regard to giving to God, our hearts can determine how much we give.

Charity is given to people. Therefore it is a moral/ethical act. And regarding the ethical, God does not demand the heart. Good actions—actions that help other human beings—are worthwhile in and of themselves because recipients of charity are helped regardless of our intentions.

Or, to put it another way: Good actions are good, even if animated by selfishness. And bad actions are bad, even if animated by good intentions. If a person builds a hospital because he wants to become famous by having the hospital named for him, that hospital saves just as many lives as hospitals built by people animated solely by altruistic motives. Furthermore, people whose lives are saved by a hospital built by a person who wanted to be famous are just as grateful as those whose lives are saved by hospitals built by selfless people. In ethics, what matters most is results, not intentions.

At the same time, good intentions leading to bad results are worthless. Such is the case, for example, when wealthy nations, for altruistic reasons, give large sums of money to poor countries whose corrupt governments are then strengthened. Such "aid" does more harm than good.

This is also true within wealthier nations. Society must, of course, take care of those who are in real need. But a certain percentage of people who are capable of working and providing for themselves will choose not to work, and instead seek to be financially supported by the government. This in turn leads to three awful consequences:

1. It erodes the character of those relying on such aid.

2. It reduces the amount of resources available to care for the truly needy.

3. It literally makes addicts out of many of these people—they become addicted to receiving unearned income. It can be as difficult to wean people off unearned benefits as it is to wean people off drugs.

Each of these destructive consequences is the product of good intentions.

The history of the modern world is filled with people who have done terrible things from sincere and good motives. The large number of individuals in democracies who supported communist tyrannies is one obvious example.

In other words, *regarding morality, intentions matter little; and often, not at all. But when it comes to relating to God (prayer, ritual acts, etc.), intentions matter a great deal.*

The Israelites' gifts will be used to build a place to worship God. This, then, is a ritual act, and when it comes to ritual, our hearts need to be involved if the act is to have significance. Unlike moral actions, which are ends in themselves, *a ritual is not an end in itself* but a means of bringing the individual closer to God and to greater holiness.

Because all the donations given by the Israelites to building the Tabernacle were voluntary, we come across no grumbling, even though until now the Israelites have repeatedly expressed angry complaints against both God and Moses.

That indicates the wisdom of soliciting voluntary contributions in the ritual realm.

God is not restricted to any specific location. This idea about God was another radical innovation of the Torah.

Many hundreds of years later, when the Israelites were firmly ensconced in their homeland, King Solomon set out to build the sequel to the Tabernacle, the *Beit Ha-Mikdash*, the Great Temple, in Jerusalem. Solomon, however, chose not to rely on voluntary contributions and imposed forced labor. Ten thousand men were sent each month to work in timber-rich Lebanon, while seventy thousand porters and eighty thousand stonecutters were assigned to labor in Israel. Some 3,300 officials were appointed to oversee the Temple's erection (I Kings 5:27-30).

ESSAY: BEAUTY CAN BRING PEOPLE CLOSER TO GOD

25.3 And these are the gifts that you shall accept from them: gold, silver, and copper;

The Torah now details the gifts the Israelites may bring (but not until verse 8 do we learn what they are for).

The list that follows includes all the Israelites' most valuable possessions. Although most of these recently-liberated slaves owned only a few precious items, they were willing to part with them. Presumably, they were willing to do so because they wanted to feel connected to God.

Many moderns strongly criticize religions for building ornate temples, churches, and cathedrals. All that wealth would be much better used to help the poor, they argue. The most often cited examples are Catholic cathedrals built in the midst of poverty.

I don't find this a valid criticism. For one thing, the construction and furnishing of those cathedrals employed many thousands of people over the course of decades, and even centuries (it took about 250 years to build the York cathedral in England, for example). But most important, if all the gold in every cathedral in the poorest Catholic countries were melted, and everything of value in those cathedrals were sold off, with the money then dispersed among its neediest citizens, it would have minimal immediate, and no enduring, impact on poverty. A small percentage of the many millions of poor people would benefit, and only for a very limited period. Then they would be left with no more cathedral in their midst—for most of these people, their greatest source of communal pride, and a place that brought them closer to God and uplifted their spirits. These cathedrals have given untold numbers of poor (and wealthy) people peace, meaning, and solace—things for which secular Westerners have little appreciation or empathy.

Like the Israelites in the desert, most of these poor people have preferred to establish an enduring connection to God through their gifts than have a little bit of extra gold for a few days or weeks.

The late British rabbi, Hugo Gryn, recounted a story from when he was a teenage prisoner in the Nazi concentration camp of Auschwitz: "One midwinter evening one of the inmates reminded us that tonight was the first night of Hanukkah, the festival of lights. My father constructed a little Hanukkah menorah out of scrap metal. For a wick he took some threads from his prison uniform. For oil, he used some butter that he somehow procured from a guard. [Although] such observances were strictly *verboten* [forbidden] we were used to taking risks. But I protested at the 'waste' of precious calories. Would it not be better to share butter on a crust of bread than to burn it? 'Hugo,' said my father, 'both you and I know that a person can live a very long time without food. But Hugo, I tell you, a person cannot live a single day without hope.'"

Without God, there is no hope. Only God gives us hope there is something beyond this life—a destination where ultimate justice is achieved, where we reconnect with loved ones, and where life doesn't abruptly end for all eternity. A beautiful religious ritual or a beautiful religious edifice can bring us closer to God and hope.

In my lifetime (unlike in some previous generations), most Jews have, for whatever reason, chosen not to build particularly beautiful synagogues (and, for the most part, Christians are no longer building beautiful churches, much less cathedrals), but Jews who find inspiration and meaning in religious ritual often spend a good deal of money on religious objects such as a Chanukah menorah, a citron for Succot (the holiday of Tabernacles, when Jews say a blessing while holding a palm frond and a citron), a citron box, and a *Havdala* set for the ceremony separating the Sabbath (and other holidays) from the rest of the week.

Beautiful rituals, beautiful places of worship, beautiful art, and music that elevate us and bring us closer to God are worth more than material benefits.

25.3 (cont.) And these are the gifts that you shall accept from them

The Torah now lists seven categories of materials with which to make the tabernacle:

Metals

Dyed yarns

Fabrics

Timber

Oil

Spices

Gems

The number seven recurs throughout the description of the blueprint for the Tabernacle and, as the number seven—repeated over and over in the Torah—always does, recalls God's creation of the world in seven days. Our creative labor in building the Tabernacle is thereby linked to the Creator.

25.3 (cont.) Gold, silver, and copper

In the Tabernacle, these materials are encountered in the opposite order. The entrance area is copper; the next chamber is silver; and the Holy of Holies (the innermost chamber where God's spirit dwells) is gold. "The closer the object is to the Holy of Holies, the more valuable the metal of which it is made" (Sarna).

Iron is not mentioned because it was used as a weapon of war and therefore had no place in God's sanctuary. The Talmud explains: "For iron [used in making weapons] was created to shorten man's days, while the altar was created to lengthen man's days, and it does not seem right that that which shortens life should be wielded against that which prolongs it."[1]

25.4 blue, purple, and crimson yarns, fine linen, goats' hair;

Each of these colors has symbolic significance. Blue represents the heavens and the creation of the world; purple represents royalty (the high cost of purple dye due to its rare source generally meant only the wealthiest individuals, usually royalty, owned purple garments); and crimson represents sin, as reflected in Isaiah's statement: "Be your sins like crimson, they can turn snow-white" (i.e., if you repent; Isaiah 1.18).

These colors represent the major themes Israelites were supposed to think about during worship: God's creation, God's kingship, and God's acceptance of atonement for sin.

25.5 tanned ram skins, dolphin skins, and acacia wood;

25.6 oil for lighting, spices for the anointing oil and for the aromatic incense;

25.7 lapis lazuli and other stones for setting, for the ephod and for the breastpiece.

The ephod was a vest worn by the high priest when he presided at the altar (see Exodus 28:4-12 and 39:2-7). Two onyx stones, upon which were engraved the names of the twelve tribes of Israel, were placed on the shoulder of the ephod.

WHERE IS GOD?

25.8 And let them make Me a sanctuary that I may dwell among them.

We would expect this verse to read, "And let them make Me a sanctuary that I may dwell *in it*." Instead, this verse states God will dwell "among them." God wants the Israelites to know that while He is invisible, He is not remote; He dwells in their midst, wherever they are. The portability of the Tabernacle is a reminder God is not restricted to any specific location—another revolutionary innovation of the Torah.

Everett Fox comments that the Tabernacle is God's resoundingly positive answer to the question asked by the Israelites shortly after leaving Egypt: "Is the Lord present among us or not?" (Exodus 17:7)

The nineteenth-century rabbi Menachem Mendel of Kotzk challenged his followers one day with a question: "Where does God exist?"

Puzzled by what sounded almost heretical, they answered: "God exists everywhere."

"No," the rabbi responded: "God exists wherever man lets Him in."

God's statement that He will dwell among the people emphasizes the Tabernacle is not for Him, but for them. God can be found everywhere, but there are certain settings in which it is easier for us to encounter Him. The Tabernacle is intended to serve as one such setting. Today, we each must seek out a place or places in which we are able to feel close to God, whether it is a synagogue sanctuary, a cathedral, or an open field (though this risks people confusing God with nature—God can be experienced through nature, but God is not in nature, He is above it; it is His handiwork). But the rabbi's response was the best of all—God is wherever we let Him in, meaning God is most present whenever we are good and just to other human beings. Nothing inspires people to believe in God as much as God-centered people doing good, just as nothing alienates people from belief in God as much as people doing evil in God's name.

ESSAY: WITHOUT STANDARDS, EVERYTHING GOOD WILL FAIL

25.9 Exactly as I show you—the pattern of the Tabernacle and the pattern of all its furnishings—so shall you make it.

This is one of those verses in the Torah that does not seem particularly significant, but is actually one of the most significant.

To understand why, let's pose a question: Why doesn't God stop speaking after verse 8? Why doesn't He simply give an instruction, "Let them make Me a sanctuary that I may dwell among them," and stop there? Wouldn't there be great Israelite artists, designers, and architects who could have designed and built something beautiful?

Perhaps they could have. But there would have been two possible problems.

First, leaving it completely up to the subjective tastes of some Israelites might well have led to the building of a Tabernacle that would be uninspiring—or, worse, looked just like a pagan house of worship. Or, it could have led to building something simply ugly—as much guideline-free, and God-free, architecture and art produced in the twentieth and twenty-first centuries do (see the discussion concerning art in the commandment against worshipping false gods—Exodus 20:3).

Second, as noted above, the Israelite elite could have kept some of the precious jewels they requisitioned for the Tabernacle for themselves.

The highest achievement of art is to elevate man. But that, of course, presumes there is something higher than man to elevate him to. And if that is true of art, it is particularly true regarding the place where people go to experience God. Therefore, God gives the instructions. The design of the Tabernacle is not left to men, no matter how artistically talented they may be.

Of course, God can't give every artist in every generation instructions on how to build places of worship, let alone how to make art or compose music. But there is nevertheless an important lesson here about art and religion: *Both need standards* or they become useless and even destructive (for more on this topic, see the commentary to Exodus 20:2, the prohibition on worshipping false gods).

Regarding religion, the Torah provides guidelines on how to lead a religious life. While there is room for spontaneity in religion—prayer being an obvious example—such spontaneity must be within the context of the Torah's ethical monotheism. In our time, many people believe they need no guidance on how to express religiosity or, as many put it, "spirituality." They attempt to be religious without adhering to any religious standards or even just to biblical ethical monotheism. While it is certainly possible to be a Torah-based ethical monotheist without identifying with any religion, there is, nevertheless, much truth to what the twentieth-century American philosopher, George Santayana, said: "To attempt to be religious without practicing a specific religion is like trying to speak without speaking a specific language."

Without the Torah, we would not know how to become God-centered. Without the Torah, we would not even know what "God" means. In the Canaanite societies surrounding the Israelites, people thought gods wanted children sacrificed to them and the Egyptians thought their gods wanted elaborate tombs constructed by slave labor.

The great lesson of this verse is individuals and societies need ethical, moral, artistic, and religious standards that transcend them or there will be no more ethics, morality, art, or good religion.

A rabbi challenged his followers one day: "Where does God exist?" Puzzled by what almost seemed to be a heretical question, they answered: "God exists everywhere." "No," the rabbi responded: "God exists wherever man lets Him in."

25.10 They shall make an ark of acacia wood, two and a half cubits long, a cubit and a half wide, and a cubit and a half high.

The Torah here lists the items to be built and placed in the Tabernacle. These items are listed in order from the most holy to the least holy, starting with the Ark. The Ark is the holiest object because it contains the Ten Commandments, which is the centerpiece of the Tabernacle (to this day, the holiest object in every synagogue is the ark [the *aron kodesh*] which contains Torah scrolls. And in many synagogues, the Ten Commandments are listed on the front of the ark).

A cubit is a standard biblical measurement. In ancient times, it was generally thought to be the distance between the tip of the middle finger and the elbow of a person of average height. The Hebrew word for cubit, *amah*, also means "forearm." It is assumed to be about 18 to 21 inches (45 to 53 centimeters).

25.11 Overlay it with pure gold—overlay it inside and out—and make upon it a gold molding round about.

Gold is the most valuable and expensive metal, and thus it is used for the most important structure in the Tabernacle.

25.12 Cast four gold rings for it, to be attached to its four feet, two rings on one of its side walls and two on the other.

> The structure of the Tabernacle is characterized by order and symmetry—reflecting order in the universe, which in turn reflects on God, the Creator of order.

25.13 Make poles of acacia wood and overlay them with gold;

25.14 then insert the poles into the rings on the side walls of the ark, for carrying the ark.

25.15 The poles shall remain in the rings of the ark: they shall not be removed from it.

> The Ark required poles so, like everything else in the Sanctuary, it could be portable. Unlike the Holy Temple, which was built hundreds of years later in Jerusalem and which was a large stationary structure, the Tabernacle was constructed in the desert, and had to be made in a way that allowed for the Israelites to take it with them throughout their forty-year journey.

THE TEN COMMANDMENTS: THE MOST IMPORTANT WORDS IN THE TORAH

25.16 And deposit in the Ark [the tablets of] the Pact which I will give you.

> Only the Ten Commandments are placed in the Ark; no other words from the Torah. This is another indication from within the Torah itself—the first, of course, being the Ten Commandments were revealed by God Himself, and revealed to the entire assembly at Sinai—that the Ten Commandments are a uniquely important part of the Torah. Within the Jewish tradition, there has long been a belief that, because the Torah is divine, all its words are of equal importance. But one should not infer that, if all the words are divine, they are,

therefore, of equal importance. They *are* all important; but they not *equally* important. (See the commentary to Exodus 32:16.)

The special status of the Ten Commandments was demonstrated again hundreds of years later when Solomon built the Holy Temple in Jerusalem: "There was nothing inside the Ark but the two tablets of stone which Moses placed there...when the Lord made [a covenant] with the Israelites after their departure from the land of Egypt" (I Kings 8:9).

There is a powerful message in the placing of the Ten Commandments—the core document of ethical monotheism—in the ark, which is in the holiest part of the Tabernacle. It is a physical representation of a major Torah teaching: *the holy protects the ethical.*

Ever since the French Enlightenment, Western man has believed ethics can survive without the holy, meaning without God. But "the death of God" along with the death of the holy inevitably leads to a moral collapse. It is an open question whether Western societies will survive "the death of God" (as famously declared in 1882 by Friedrich Nietzsche); and if those societies die, there is no reason to believe they will be replaced by something morally superior—and a great deal of reason to believe they will not.

25.17 You shall make a cover of pure gold, two and a half cubits long and a cubit and a half wide.

The Hebrew word for cover, *kaporet*, comes from the same root as the Hebrew word for atonement, *kippur*. Perhaps atonement is a way of covering our iniquities by burying them under the weight of good deeds. The association between the cover and the act of atonement serves as a reminder that just as the cover was one of the centerpieces of the Tabernacle, atonement was one of its central purposes.

A rabbinic text posits the cover is made of gold as a form of atonement for the sin of the golden calf (see Exodus, chapter 32), thereby reminding us gold can be used for idolatry or for holiness: It is our choice.

Atonement is fundamental to the Torah, but much of the modern world has either forgotten its importance or deliberately rejected it. The message of the sanctuary was we are all guilty to varying degrees, and have all committed offenses for which we must atone, but the message today—in part due to the widespread substitution of the therapeutic for the moral—is we should not burden ourselves with feelings of guilt. In addition, personal guilt is often rejected in favor of societal guilt—the argument being that people who commit violent crimes, for example, do so because of social inequality, racism, poverty, or other forces outside the criminal. But a society that raises people to think they are not responsible for the evil they do will, quite simply, raise many people who do evil acts.

> *Without the Torah we would not know how to become God-centered. Without the Torah we wouldn't even know what "God" means.*

THE CHERUBIM

25.18 Make two cherubim of gold—make them of hammered work—at the two ends of the cover.
The Torah does not say anything about the appearance of the cherubim, presumably because the Israelites would have been familiar with this image. In the Book of Ezekiel (10:9-14), the cherubim are described as winged creatures with four faces: that of a man, a lion, an ox, and an eagle.

Cherubim are first mentioned in Genesis 3:24, where they guard the entrance to the Garden of Eden. The cherubim thus allude to the place where man dwelled free of sin. As such, they are a link to the *kaporet*, the cover symbolizing atonement.

Today the idea of golden cherubim seems primitive and idolatrous, but the Israelites regarded the cherubim as powerful physical reminders of God's presence. The cherubim of the temple functioned much as rituals do today, providing physical reminders of God's presence.

Rabbi Menachem Liebtag explained the images on the cherubim represented the most valuable beings of each class of life. The ox is the most valuable working creature; the eagle is the greatest flying creature; the lion is the greatest of the predators; and man is the highest being of all.

25.19 Make one cherub at one end and the other cherub at the other end; of one piece with the cover shall you make the cherubim at its two ends.

25.20 The cherubim shall have their wings spread out above,

Cassuto explains the outstretched wings of the cherubim were thought to form the base of God's symbolic heavenly throne: "an empty throne on which God, invisible to the human eye, would sit. It is just the empty seat that clearly indicates that God has no likeness whatsoever."

25.20 (cont.) shielding the cover with their wings.

Everything in the Tabernacle functions to shield and protect the holier structure beneath it. The wings of the cherubim shield the cover; the cover shields the Ark; the Ark shields the tablets; and the tablets, i.e., the Ten Commandments, shield and safeguard civilization.

25.20 (cont.) They shall confront each other, the faces of the cherubim being turned toward the cover.

The cherubim face toward the cover beneath them so as not to gaze upon God, Who is enthroned upon their wings. This gesture recalls the way in which Moses shielded his face when he encountered God at the burning bush (see Exodus 3:6).

25.21 Place the cover on top of the Ark, after depositing inside the Ark of the Pact that I will give you.

25.22 There I will meet with you, and I will impart to you—from above the cover, from between the two cherubim that are on top of the Ark of the Pact—all that I will command you concerning the Israelite people.

Above the cover of the Ark and between the two cherubim is the place in the Tabernacle from which God will issue His royal decrees. God does not only speak from the majestic thundering heavens above Mount Sinai (Exodus 20:15-16); He can also be heard from an area no larger than a small desk or table. And still later, in the Book of I Kings (19:11-12) God is heard in the form of a still, small voice.

25.23 You shall make a table of acacia wood, two cubits long, one cubit wide, and a cubit and a half high.

Some Bible scholars suggest the table and its implements are holdovers from pagan models of worship, in which the gods were seen as needing nourishment. Pagan worshippers prepared food for the gods and left it on the table. However, there is no parallel. In the Israelite sanctuary, the parts of the sacrifices designated "for God" were burned in the sanctuary courtyard. The table played no role.

The holy protects the ethical. When standards of holiness die, morality begins to die shortly thereafter.

25.24 Overlay it with pure gold, and make a gold molding around it.

25.25 Make a rim of a hand's breadth around it, and make a gold molding for its rim round about.

25.26 Make four gold rings for it, and attach the rings to the four corners at its four legs.

25.27 The rings shall be next to the rim, as holders for poles to carry the table.

25.28 Make the poles of acacia wood, and overlay them with gold; by these the table shall be carried.

25.29 Make its bowls, ladles, jars and jugs with which to offer libations; make them of pure gold.

It has also been argued that vessels for libations (a drink poured out as an offering to a god) might well have been a holdover from the pagan model, in which worshippers poured an offering of water and wine onto the ground to quench the thirst of the gods. In contrast, the Torah maintains God has no physical form (Deuteronomy 4:12) and therefore requires no physical sustenance. In the Israelite sanctuary, these vessels were all empty.

> *The Torah, over and over, emphasizes the central and fundamental importance of Genesis 1:1—"In the beginning God created the heavens and the earth."*

25.30 And on the table you shall set the bread of display, to be before Me always.

Although the bread was theoretically intended for God, it was eaten by the priests. It is known as the "bread of display" because it was left on the table for a full week. The priests then had the privilege of eating from God's table. This ritual represents an inversion of the standard pagan practice whereby human worshippers would leave bread for the gods: In the Torah, it is men who eat the bread, symbolizing God is the provider of all food and nourishment.

The bread of display also served as a reminder of the incorporeality of God, since it made it clear God does not need nourishment from human beings. The bread, after all, just sits there. (For more on God's incorporeality and its significance, see commentary to Deuteronomy 4:15).

25.31 You shall make a lampstand of pure gold; the lampstand shall be made of hammered work; its base and its shaft, its cups, calyxes, and petals shall be of one piece.

What is being described here is the menorah, or candelabra, which was the first symbol of the Jewish people. Today it is used as the coat of arms of the State of Israel.

Unlike the table, which was made of acacia wood and overlaid with gold, the menorah is hammered from a single block, or ingot, of pure gold.

25.32 Six branches shall issue from its sides; three branches from one side of the lampstand and three branches from the other side of the lampstand.

25.33 On one branch there shall be three cups shaped like almond-blossoms, each with calyx and petals, and on the next branch there shall be three cups shaped like almond-blossoms, each with calyx and petals; so for all six branches issuing from the lampstand.

Sarna notes the almond tree is the earliest spring plant to flower in the Land of Israel, and its blossom is used here as a symbol of renewed and sustained life.

The combination of blossoms, petals, and calyx renders the menorah like a tree, and in the Bible a tree symbolizes life (see, for example, Proverbs 3:18; in the Jewish liturgy, the Torah, basing itself on this verse and on Proverbs 4:2, is described as a Tree of Life [*etz chaim*]).

25.34 And on the lampstand itself there shall be four cups shaped like almond-blossoms, each with calyx and petals:

25.35 a calyx, of one piece with it, under a pair of branches; and a calyx, of one piece with it, under the second pair of branches, and a calyx, of one piece with it, under the last pair of branches; so for all six branches issuing from the lampstand.

25.36 Their calyxes and their stems shall be of one piece with it, the whole of it a single hammered piece of pure gold.

25.37 Make its seven lamps—the lamps shall be so mounted as to give the light on its front side—

Unlike the Chanukah menorah, which contains nine lamps (eight representing the eight days of the holiday, and one that holds the candle used to light the others), the menorah in the Tabernacle has seven. The central lamp represents the Sabbath, and the other six represent the days of the week. Once again, we encounter the number seven in the Torah. The Torah, over and over, emphasizes the central and fundamental importance of Genesis 1:1— "In the beginning God created the heavens and the earth."

25.38 and its tongs and fire pans of pure gold.

25.39 It shall be made, with all these furnishings, out of a talent of pure gold.

25.40 Note well, and follow the patterns for them that are being shown you on the mountain.

God acknowledges the description provided thus far is insufficient to build the menorah; after all, He has not even specified any measurements. He therefore promises to show Moses an image of this object.

CHAPTER

26

THE TORAH TURNS FROM A DISCUSSION OF THE OBJECTS AND VESSELS INSIDE the Tabernacle to a description of the tapestries surrounding and covering it. Verse 1 describes the innermost covering, linen. Verse 7 describes the next layer, made of goat's hair; and verse 14 describes both the third layer—ram's skin—and the outmost layer, "a covering of dolphin skins."

ONCE AGAIN, THE IMPORTANCE OF AESTHETIC BEAUTY IN THE WORSHIP OF GOD

26.1 As for the Tabernacle, make it of ten strips of cloth; make these of fine twisted linen, of blue, purple, and crimson yarns,

The elaborate details in this chapter once again attest to the importance the Torah attached to the place of great art in religious life. With the destruction of the Temple, however, art became much less significant in Jewish life, which came to emphasize the intellect and morality. The aesthetic has often been viewed as irrelevant to Jewish religiosity (except for some stunning synagogues, almost all of them built before the beginning of the twentieth century), and as "not Jewish" given its importance in the non-Jewish—specifically the Christian, Muslim, and secular—world.

That this estrangement from art need not be inherent to traditional Judaism is demonstrated by a story Jonathan Sacks uncovered in the writings of Rabbi Abraham Isaac Kook, the chief rabbi of pre-state Israel. Rabbi Kook spent several years in London during World War I, and wrote the following:

When I lived in London I would visit the National Gallery, and the paintings I loved most were those of Rembrandt. In my opinion, Rembrandt was a saint. When I first saw Rembrandt's paintings, they reminded me of the rabbinic statement about the creation of light. When God created light, it was so strong and luminous that it was possible to see from one end of the world to the other. And God feared that the wicked would make use of it. What did he do? He secreted it for the righteous in the world to come. But from time to time there are great men whom God blessed with a vision of that hidden light. I believe that Rembrandt was one of them....[1]

26.1 (cont.) with a design of cherubim worked into them.

26.2 The length of each cloth shall be twenty-eight cubits, and the width of each cloth shall be four cubits, all the cloths to have the same measurements.

26.3 Five of the cloths shall be joined to one another, and the other five cloths shall be joined to one another.

26.4 Make loops of blue wool on the edge of the outermost cloth of the one set; and do likewise on the edge of the outermost cloth of the other set:

26.5 make fifty loops on the one cloth, and fifty loops on the edge of the end cloth of the other set, the loops to be opposite one another.

ONE GOD, ONE SANCTUARY

26.6 And make fifty gold clasps, and couple the cloths to one another with the clasps, so that the Tabernacle becomes one whole.

The words translated as "so that the Tabernacle becomes one whole" literally mean, "And the Tabernacle will be one." Richard Elliott Friedman comments that this rendering fits better in connecting "the centrality of the Tabernacle to Israel's monotheism"; along with the one God, there is only one Tabernacle, one altar, and only one place of worship (see Leviticus 17:1-8, which directs all sacrifices to be offered at the Tabernacle altar and not elsewhere).

> *More than one place to worship God might suggest that there is more than one God.*

At this sensitive moment in history, when the idea of monotheism was beginning to plant roots in a polytheistic world, it was imperative "there not be more than one place to worship God, because that might suggest there is more than one God." A new religion with a single deity required a single sanctuary. Friedman argues Bible critics who claim Israel's religion became a pure monotheism only many hundreds of years later, perhaps only during the Second Temple period, "have not appreciated the significance of the commandment of centralization of worship at a single location."

26.7 You shall then make cloths of goats' hair for a tent over the Tabernacle; make the cloths eleven in number.

The second layer of coverings is referred to as a tent.

The cloths of goats' hair served as protection against rain, wind, dust, and heat.

26.8 The length of each cloth shall be thirty cubits, and the width of each cloth shall be four cubits, the eleven cloths to have the same measurements.

26.9 Join five of the cloths by themselves, and the other six cloths by themselves; and fold over the sixth cloth at the front of the tent.

26.10 Make fifty loops on the edge of the outermost cloth of the one set, and fifty loops on the edge of the cloth of the other set.

26.11 Make fifty copper clasps, and fit the clasps into the loops, and couple the tent together so that it becomes one whole.

26.12 As for the overlapping excess of the cloths of the tent, the extra half-cloth shall overlap the back of the tabernacle,

26.13 while the extra cubit at either end of each length of tent cloth shall hang down to the bottom of the two sides of the Tabernacle and cover it.

26.14 And make for the tent a covering of tanned ram skins, and a covering of dolphin skins above.

> The creature translated as "dolphin" might refer to a creature known as the dugong, a sea mammal related to the manatee, found in the Red Sea.

26.15 You shall make the planks for the Tabernacle of acacia wood, upright.

> The Torah does not explain why acacia trees were used for the building of the Ark. But one likely reason is acacia trees are not fruit-bearing, and God, it would seem, did not want fruit trees cut down even for the building of the Ark. Later Torah law formally forbade the cutting down of fruit trees (Deuteronomy 20:19-20). For the implications of this regulation regarding acacia trees in our daily lives, see commentary on Exodus 36:20.

26.16 The length of each plank shall be ten cubits and the width of each plank a cubit and a half.

26.17 Each plank shall have two tenons, parallel to each other; do the same with all the planks of the Tabernacle.

26.18 Of the planks of the Tabernacle, make twenty planks on the south side:

26.19 making forty silver sockets under the twenty planks, two sockets under the one plank for its two tenons and two sockets under each following plank for its two tenons;

26.20 and for the other side wall of the Tabernacle, on the north side, twenty planks,

26.21 with their forty silver sockets, two sockets under the one plank and two sockets under each following plank.

26.22 And for the rear of the Tabernacle, to the west, make six planks;

26.23 and make two planks for the corners of the Tabernacle at the rear.

God, it would seem, did not want fruit trees cut down even for the building of the Ark.

26.24 They shall match at the bottom, and terminate alike at the top inside one ring; thus shall it be with both of them: they shall form the two corners.

26.25 Thus there shall be eight planks with their sockets of silver: sixteen sockets, two sockets under the first plank, and two sockets under each of the other planks.

26.26 You shall make bars of acacia wood: five for the planks of the one side wall of the Tabernacle,

26.27 five bars for the planks of the other side wall of the Tabernacle, and five bars for the planks of the wall of the Tabernacle at the rear to the west.

26.28 The center bar halfway up the planks shall run from end to end.

26.29 Overlay the planks with gold, and make their rings of gold, as holders for the bars; and overlay the bars with gold.

26.30 Then set up the Tabernacle according to the manner of it that you were shown on the mountain.

> According to Cassuto, "what was left unexplained in words was clarified by the vision he [Moses] saw [on the mountain]."

26.31 You shall make a curtain of blue, purple, and crimson yarns, and fine twisted linen; it shall have a design of cherubim worked into it.

> This curtain, described in verses 31–35, separates the inner sanctum known as the Holy of Holies (where God's spirit dwelled) from the holy place outside it.

26.32 Hang it upon four posts of acacia wood overlaid with gold and having hooks of gold, [set] in four sockets of silver.

26.33 Hang the curtain under the clasps, and carry the Ark of the Pact there, behind the curtain, so that the curtain shall serve you as a partition between the Holy and the Holy of Holies.

26.34 Place the cover upon the Ark of the Pact in the Holy of Holies.

26.35 Place the table outside the curtain, and the lampstand by the south wall of the Tabernacle opposite the table, which is to be placed by the north wall.

26.36 You shall make a screen for the entrance of the Tent, of blue, purple, and crimson yarns, and fine twisted linen, done in embroidery.

> This screen separates the tent from the courtyard.

26.37 Make five posts of acacia wood for the screen and overlay them with gold—their hooks being of gold—and cast for them five sockets of copper.

CHAPTER
27

27.1 You shall make the altar of acacia wood, five cubits long and five cubits wide—the altar is to be square—and three cubits high.

> The text moves to the description of the Tabernacle's courtyard, where sacrifices were offered.

ESSAY: WAS ANIMAL SACRIFICE IN THE TORAH IMMORAL?

The sacrificial system strikes many moderns, perhaps most of us, as primitive and even cruel. But there are several reasons to reevaluate this initial reaction.

First, anyone who eats meat—in other words, the great majority of humanity—has no legitimate reason to oppose animal sacrifice on moral grounds. Since the large majority of the biblical sacrifices were eaten by human beings, they were, essentially, public religious slaughtering.

People today eat beef and chicken without thinking twice about the life of the animal taken. In the world of the Torah, however, the killing and eating of animals was taken extremely seriously and imbued with sanctity. Moreover, the animals sacrificed were not subjected to the cruelties of modern slaughterhouses or factory farming, the fate of the large majority of animals eaten in our time.

In light of that, only a vegetarian could morally object to the sacrificial system—and any such objection would have to be made against every secular or religious society that allowed meat eating.

Second, animal sacrifice was, of course, an immeasurable moral advance over human sacrifice, *which was universal* in the ancient world—another example of the how the Torah changed the world.

According to Maimonides, the animal sacrifices prescribed in the Torah were a concession on God's part, since animal (and, alas, human) sacrifice was universal. Of course, the Torah repeatedly prohibits human sacrifice, which God declares a moral abomination (see Leviticus 20:2-3), but does allow animal sacrifice. One might add, considering the number of immoral (as opposed to morally justified) wars nations, religions, and tyrannical regimes have waged, child sacrifice never really died. Only the age of the sacrificed children may have changed. And what else would one call sending young men and women on suicide terror missions?

> *Anyone who eats meat—in other words, the great majority of humanity—has no legitimate reason to oppose animal sacrifice on moral grounds.*

Third, unlike meat-eating generally, sacrifices were performed for noble goals: to atone for sins and to come closer to a moral God. The Hebrew word for sacrifice, *korban*, comes from the Hebrew word for "close" (*karov*). The sacrificial system is predicated on the notion we must give up—sacrifice—something precious as a way of getting closer to God. The giving up of an animal, and not just any animal, but a very fine one—the best of one's herd, or the best specimen one could buy, which had a significant practical and financial value— constituted such a sacrifice.

The fundamental idea behind the sacrificial system—giving to God something precious to us—thus remains relevant. The reason is *nothing worthwhile comes without sacrifice.* Parents sacrifice a great deal on behalf of their children; spouses sacrifice on behalf of their marriage; friends make sacrifices to maintain their friendships; and we sacrifice to be better at our professions. If we didn't make sacrifices, we would lose our children, our spouses, our friends, and our jobs. But when it comes to God and religion, most people don't think in terms of sacrifice. They think closeness to God and a religious life should come automatically, no sacrifice needed. The sacrificial system taught ancient Israelites the truth that sacrifice was necessary for a meaningful religious life.

Of course, religious sacrifice today does not involve giving up livestock. It involves giving up money and time. In terms of money, this is generally understood to mean financial contributions to religious institutions and other charities. In terms of time, it means engaging in Bible study, other religious study, prayer, ritual observance, celebration of holy days, working to build a religious community, and doing volunteer work.

It is not trite to point out that one of the great lessons of the sacrificial system is the importance of sacrifice to a good life and to a religious life.

27.2 Make its horns on the four corners, the horns to be of one piece with it; and overlay it with copper.

27.3 Make the pails for removing its ashes, as well as its scrapers, basins, flesh hooks, and fire pans—make all its utensils of copper.

27.4 Make for it a grating of meshwork in copper; and on the mesh make four copper rings at its four corners.

27.5 Set the mesh below, under the ledge of the altar, so that it extends to the middle of the altar.

27.6 And make poles for the altar, poles of acacia wood, and overlay them with copper.

> Richard Elliott Friedman notes: "The quantity of detail in these chapters is an indication that these are authentic descriptions of the Tabernacle and its accoutrements. What motive would there be to make all this up? The dominant view in critical biblical scholarship for over a hundred years has been the Tabernacle is fiction. The character of the text, however, argues against that view as much as the content does."

27.7 The poles shall be inserted into the rings, so that the poles remain on the two sides of the altar when it is carried.

27.8 Make it hollow, of boards. As you were shown on the mountain, so shall they be made.

27.9 You shall make the enclosure of the Tabernacle: On the south side, a hundred cubits of hangings of fine twisted linen for the length of the enclosure on that side—

27.10 with its twenty posts and their twenty sockets of copper, the hooks and bands of the posts to be of silver.

27.11 Again a hundred cubits of hangings for its length along the north side— with its twenty posts and their twenty sockets of copper, the hooks and bands of the posts to be of silver.

27.12 For the width of the enclosure, on the west side, fifty cubits of hangings, with their ten posts and their ten sockets.

27.13 For the width of the enclosure on the front, or east side, fifty cubits:

27.14 fifteen cubits of hangings on the one flank, with their three posts and their three sockets;

27.15 fifteen cubits of hangings on the other flank, with their three posts and their three sockets;

27.16 and for the gate of the enclosure, a screen of twenty cubits, of blue, purple, and crimson yarns, and fine twisted linen, done in embroidery, with their four posts and their four sockets.

27.17 All the posts round the enclosure shall be banded with silver and their hooks shall be of silver; their sockets shall be of copper.

27.18 The length of the enclosure shall be a hundred cubits, and the width fifty throughout; and the height five cubits—[with hangings] of fine twisted linen. The sockets shall be of copper:

27.19 all the utensils of the Tabernacle, for all its service, as well as all its pegs and all the pegs of the court, shall be of copper.

27.20 You shall further instruct the Israelites to bring you clear oil of beaten olives for lighting, for kindling lamps regularly.

27.21 Aaron and his sons shall set them up in the Tent of Meeting, outside the curtain which is over [the Ark of] the Pact, [to burn] from evening to morning before the Lord. It shall be a due from the Israelites for all time, throughout the ages.

The twelfth-century commentator Rashbam noted this is the only commandment pertaining to the Tabernacle that applies for all time: "At the beginning of the passage about the Tabernacle, it says, 'Tell the Israelite people to bring Me gifts' [Exodus 25:2]. This was to provide whatever was needed for the one-time construction of the Tabernacle. But here, since the Israelites are being commanded for all time to bring oil for lighting year after year, the language is changed to 'You shall further command' the Israelites. Every time the word 'command' is used it applies to [the current generation and to] future generations."

Further substantiating Rashbam's point are the words, "throughout the ages."

> *"The quantity of detail in these chapters is an indication that these are authentic descriptions of the Tabernacle and its accoutrements."*
> —Richard Elliott Friedman

To this day, synagogues throughout the world have a constantly-burning light known as an "eternal lamp" or "eternal light" (*Ner Tamid*) that takes the place of the regularly-kindled lamps in the Tabernacle.

"This is the only commanded practice associated with the ancient Tabernacle that is still with us."[1]

CHAPTER 28

28.1 You shall bring forward your brother Aaron, with his sons, from among the Israelites, to serve Me as priests: Aaron, Nadab and Abihu, Eleazar and Ithamar, the sons of Aaron.

ESSAY: THE BENEFITS OF A HEREDITARY PRIESTHOOD

The priesthood is a hereditary institution. Only the descendants of Aaron, all of whom come from the tribe of Levi, are designated as priests, and this remains true to this day. However, this is not how the modern world views the making of leaders. We believe in choosing leaders, hopefully based on their abilities and values, and not in individuals attaining positions of authority solely through birth.

Despite all the problems with democracy, we would not have leaders chosen any other way. As Sir Winston Churchill pithily noted (quoting an unknown source), "Democracy is the worst form of government—except for all [the] other[s]."

Nevertheless, there are benefits to having a hereditary priesthood.

First, unlike societal leaders who are given political and military power, priests are to have no power. Their role is to serve to help the community come closer to God.

Second, by making the priesthood a hereditary institution, the chances for corruption entering the religious leadership of the nation are reduced. Simply put, no one can buy or force his way into the priesthood.

A third benefit is priests do not have to worry about popularity. They never have to run for election or re-election.

With regard to hereditary institutions being non-democratic, while democracy is indispensable to civil society, it is irrelevant to (and potentially even destructive of) religion. When religion becomes democratic, it ceases to be religion. Members of a religion can vote for one's clergy (obvious examples include cardinals of the Roman Catholic Church choosing their pope, and synagogue boards voting on who to employ as rabbi), but they cannot vote on what their religion demands. Members of religion do not get to vote, for example, on whether or not to remove one of the Ten Commandments. Had the Israelites been able to vote on the Ten Commandments, they may well have voted against some of them. (A well-known Jewish joke relates that when Moses descended with the second set of the Ten Commandments, he announced: "Israelites, I have good news and bad news. The good news is I got Him down to ten. The bad news is adultery stays.")

> By making the priesthood a hereditary institution, no one could buy or force his way into the priesthood.

A remarkable Talmudic passage makes this point rather emphatically: The Israelites, the Talmud records, only accepted the Ten Commandments when God held Mount Sinai over their heads and threatened to drop it on them if they didn't accept them.[1]

Most of the British people, the founders of modern democracy, have been comfortable with a hereditary monarchy for over a thousand years. It may ultimately be rejected as more and more British reject the concept of a hereditary monarchy—even one that doesn't really rule them. But that would be a pity, since little would be gained, and a nation-uniting institution would be lost.

James Burton Coffman, author of a thirty-seven-volume verse-by-verse commentary on the Bible, noted the priesthood "introduced a dramatic change into the religious [life] of Israel." Until now, Coffman explained, only individuals played the role of priest—Moses as high priest, sprinkling the blood upon the people to signal the formal ratifying of the covenant (Exodus 24:8); and before Moses, Abraham had in effect acted as a priest (see Genesis 15:7-19). But from this point on, the responsibilities of carrying out the sacrifices shifted to Aaron, his sons, and their descendants.

THE ROLE OF THE PRIEST

The modern Bible scholar Jacob Milgrom makes the important point that the welfare of Israel depended on both Moses and Aaron. Moses served as the prophet, the sublime ethical voice conveying God's word to the people, while Aaron served as the priest, the ritual leader responsible for helping people connect individually to God. Both are necessary for a meaningful religious life.

The priest had four major duties:

1. The priest dedicated himself to living a holy life and helping other Jews come closer to God through Jewish ritual, which at that time consisted primarily of sacrifice. As noted, other rituals performed by priests included blessing the people with "the priestly benediction" (Numbers 6:22-26); redeeming the firstborn son (Numbers 18:15-16); and blowing trumpets to convene the people, both on joyous festivals and at times of war (Numbers 10:1-10; that the trumpets were sounded by priests is made clear in Numbers 31:6).

2. The priest treated physical ailments such as disease and plague, which were thought to be not only physiological phenomena but also sometimes embodiments of spiritual imperfection (see Leviticus, chapters 13-15; also Numbers 12, which depicts Miriam as afflicted with a serious skin disease for speaking ill of her brother Moses).

3. The priest judged disputes (Deuteronomy 21:5) and instructed the people and the king in the laws of the Torah (Deuteronomy 17:18, 31:9-13).

4. The High Priest, by wearing an object known as the "Urim and Thummim" on his breastplate, provided the medium through which God would communicate positive or negative responses to major national questions (see verse 30 in this chapter, and also Numbers 27:21). Jacob Milgrom notes the Torah does not make clear how the *Urim* and *Thummim* worked.

The insignia of Yale University is the breastplate the high priest wore—complete with the words *Urim* and *Thummim* in Hebrew. Yale, like nearly all the old prestigious American universities, was founded by Christians rooted in the Torah and the rest of the Hebrew Bible, initially for training clergy.

Since the priests were regarded as mediators between man and God (as well as between man and man in the case of disputes), there was always the chance they might become intoxicated by their power and abuse their authority. Indeed, this happened. First Samuel describes how the sons of the priest Eli, himself a righteous man, misappropriated meat from the sacrifices being offered at the Shiloh Temple and slept with women who worked there (see I Samuel 2:12-4:22). To prevent these and other abuses, and ensure the priests' behavior was in the service of God, the Torah provides extensive, detailed laws governing the conduct of the priests. These laws include the following:

> *Yale University's insignia to this day is the breastplate the high priest wore—complete with the words Urim and Thummim in Hebrew. Like nearly all the old prestigious American universities, Yale was founded by Christians rooted in the Torah and the Hebrew Bible.*

a) Priests were not allowed to have any contact with a dead body. In this important regard, they were fundamentally different from Egyptian priests, who were responsible for ministering to the dead. Egyptian religion and culture were focused on death. The Torah, on the other hand, wants its adherents to be preoccupied with sanctifying this life. Thus, an absolute barrier was erected between the Israelite priesthood and death.

b) Priests had to wash their hands and feet prior to entering the temple or approaching the altar. They also had to be dressed in a manner that radiated sanctity.

c) A priest could not marry a woman who had been a prostitute or who was divorced (Leviticus 21:7). Regarding the first instance, priests were expected to serve as models of holiness, and, fairly or unfairly, if it became known the priest's wife was a former prostitute, it could hinder his efforts to be regarded as a holy man.

As regards the ban on a priest marrying a divorced woman, this had nothing to do with her worth as a human being. The issue was, again, the priest's stature being compromised if there were another man—one, moreover, undoubtedly known to the community—who had sexual relations with the priest's wife.

Analogously, throughout most of modern history it was expected the king of England would marry a woman who was a virgin. As recently as 1938, King Edward III had to abdicate the throne of England in order to marry the twice-divorced Wallis Simpson. One suspects what disturbed the English was there would have been two men, both living, who could claim they slept with the woman who was now queen.

Of course, all other Israelite men could marry a divorced woman. The Torah attached no stigma to a divorced woman, or, for that matter, to divorce.

The biblical restrictions regarding priests are still observed by Orthodox and some non-Orthodox Jews.

In addition to the prohibition on marrying a divorced woman, a Jew who knows himself to be a priest (*kohain*) is not allowed to attend a funeral or go to a burial except in the case of an immediate relative.

When the Second Jewish Temple was destroyed (in the year 70), the priests, for obvious reasons, lost their formal religious role, and the Jewish priesthood became largely symbolic. However, within the Hasidic movement (which arose in the eighteenth century), the *rebbe* (the leader of a Hasidic sect) became a sort of modern incarnation of the High Priest—a person who could mediate, or at least uniquely facilitate, people's connection to God.

Nevertheless, priests still play several distinctive roles within Judaism:

- When the Torah is read aloud in synagogue, the first person called to bless the Torah is always a *kohain*.
- At daily services in Israel and holiday services outside of Israel, all the priests present in the congregation wrap themselves in their prayer shawls and bless the congregation, reciting the words with which God tells

Moses to instruct Aaron and his descendants to bless the Israelites (Numbers 6:22-27; the words are known in Jewish life as the *Birkat Kohanim*, the priestly benediction).

- A firstborn son (one who is both male and the first child born to his mother) is supposed to be dedicated to God (Exodus 13:1-2), and to perform religious services for the priests. On the thirty-first day after the child's birth, however, the father can pay a priest five silver shekels (see Numbers 18:16; today five dollars in silver coins is generally used) to have the child released from this obligation. The ceremony of redeeming the firstborn is still practiced among observant Jews.

Later in the Torah, God tells the Israelites they are to be "a kingdom of priests and a holy nation" (Exodus 19:6). In the same manner Aaron and his sons were supposed to lead an especially holy life and help bring Jews closer to God, the Jewish people, in turn, are supposed to lead a holy life and help bring humanity to God.

THE PRIESTHOOD AS A MALE INSTITUTION

The priesthood is an exclusively male institution. The primary reason is the Torah was adamant about de-sexualizing religion; having priests and priestesses would have made that impossible. That is why, for example, the Torah commands priests to dress in modest clothing (see verses 40-43): priests were meant to be seen solely as vehicles to holiness.

The surrounding polytheistic religions all had male and female priests and ritual sexual activity was a major feature of their religions. Few would argue women had a more elevated status in pagan society than in Israel. The Torah's de-sexualization of God, religion, and the family played a fundamental and world-changing role from which both women and men immeasurably benefited.

In addition, the Torah's depiction of women was often remarkably egalitarian. The first woman, Eve, is described as "a helper equal to" Adam (see commentary to Genesis 2:18). The matriarchs play a decisive role in determining the destiny of the Jewish people—it is Rebecca, for example, and not Isaac, who guarantees Jacob becomes the third patriarch (Genesis, chapter 27). Women are the heroes in resisting Pharaoh's attempt to kill all male Israelite babies. It is a woman who saves Moses. Mother and father are always depicted as equals. Women, along with men, serve as prophets who convey God's word. And so on.

ESSAY: THE IMPORTANCE OF CLOTHING

28.2 Make sacral clothing for your brother Aaron, for dignity and adornment.

We would expect God's first instruction regarding the priests to deal with their role and duties. Instead, God begins with a description of the priests' clothing, a subject occupying this entire chapter. The large majority of the chapter deals with the clothing of the high priest and the final verses with the clothing of the other priests.

As noted above, the first—and certainly the most important—task of the Torah regarding the priesthood was to desexualize it. That began with allowing only male priests and then with specifying exactly what they would wear. It was not left up to the priests to decide what they would wear. In other words, the priests had a dress code. That is why the verse says one of the reasons for the following instructions regarding priestly clothing is "dignity." The other was "adornment," yet again placing an emphasis on aesthetic beauty in religious life.

Clearly, the Torah wants us to understand clothing is of immense significance. This is as true today as it was 3,000 years ago. First, clothing is a distinctive sign of being human; it sets people apart from animals. Animals walk around unclothed, people should not. Genesis teaches the first thing God made for Adam and Eve were garments: "And the Lord God made garments of skin for Adam and his wife, and clothed them" (3:21). Benno Jacob makes the point that whereas God required people to invent or discover fire, agriculture, and all other aspects of culture and civilization, God Himself gave them clothing. In so doing, He consecrated human beings for a holier purpose than the unclothed animals, just as Moses consecrated the priests for a holier purpose than the rest of the Israelites.

The single greatest argument against public nudity may not even be about sex *per se*, but about holiness: Clothing distinguishes human beings from animals.

Second, clothing inspires respect. When worshippers entered the Tabernacle and saw the priest dressed in strikingly beautiful garments, they were undoubtedly impressed, in a manner befitting the solemnity of the priesthood and the service.

The effect and importance of clothing have not changed. Clothes affect how people are viewed by others. People dressed conservatively—meaning, essentially, with "dignity"—are consistently judged as more reliable. That is why people going for a job interview are almost always advised to dress conservatively. Whether conservative or not, they are told they should "dress to impress." The fact is we are assessed by how we dress. How could it not be? Other than our faces, almost all one sees of us is what we wear, and how we choose to dress makes a statement about our attitude toward whatever it is we are doing.

The first—and certainly the most important—task of the Torah with regard to the priesthood was to de-sexualize it. That began with only allowing male priests, and then with specifying exactly what they would wear.

Third, clothes are a sign of the respect or lack of respect we have for the activities in which we are engaged and for the people around us. It would be a sign of great disrespect to attend a wedding wearing a t-shirt and shorts.

Fourth, clothing is a sign of self-respect. Studies consistently show that when a school requires its students to wear school uniforms, or even just has a dress code, grades rise and violence declines.

The fact that a chapter of the Bible is devoted to priestly garments is testimony to the immense significance the Torah attaches to dress.

28.3 Next you shall instruct all who are skillful, whom I have endowed with the gift of skill, to make Aaron's vestments, for consecrating him to serve Me as priest.

The words "for consecrating him to serve Me" literally mean, "in order to make him holy" —words reinforcing the Torah's belief that the clothing we wear affects our spiritual state.

28.4 These are the vestments they are to make: a breastpiece, an ephod, a robe, a fringed tunic, a headdress, and a sash. They shall make those sacral vestments for your brother Aaron and his sons, for priestly service to Me;

Nelson's Illustrated Bible Dictionary offers a comprehensive and accessible definition of what is perhaps the most important of these garments, the ephod (pronounced "ay-FODE"):

> A vest worn by the High Priest when he presided at the altar. Worn over a blue robe (see verses 31-35), the ephod was made of fine linen interwoven with some threads of pure gold and other threads that were blue, purple and crimson in color. The ephod consisted of two pieces joined at the shoulder and bound together at the bottom by a woven band of the same material as the ephod.... Upon the shoulders of the ephod, in settings of gold, were two onyx stones. Upon these stones were engraved the names of the twelve tribes of Israel. The front of the vest, or the breastplate, was fastened to the shoulder straps by two golden chains (verse 14) and by a blue cord (verse 28).

Centuries later, in post-Torah times, the ephod was worn by many, perhaps all, priests, not just the High Priest (see I Samuel 22:18), and in one famous instance, King David, though not a priest, wore the ephod when he brought the Ark with the Ten Commandments to Jerusalem (II Samuel 6:14-15). Other than on that unique occasion, the wearing of the ephod was restricted to priests.

28.5 they, therefore, shall receive the gold, the blue, purple, and crimson yarns, and the fine linen.

28.6 They shall make the ephod of gold, of blue, purple, and crimson yarns, and of fine twisted linen, worked into designs.

28.7 It shall have two shoulder-pieces attached; they shall be attached at its two ends.

28.8 And the decorated band that is upon it shall be made like it, of one piece with it: of gold, of blue, purple, and crimson yarns, and of fine twisted linen.

28.9 Then take two lazuli stones

These are semi-precious stones with a deep blue color.

28.9 (cont.) and engrave on them the names of the sons of Israel:

The priests represent all twelve tribes, not just their own tribe of Levi.

28.10 six of their names on the one stone, and the names of the remaining six on the other stone, in the order of their birth.

28.11 On the two stones you shall make seal engravings—the work of a lapidary—of the names of the sons of Israel. Having bordered them with frames of gold,

28.12 attach the two stones to the shoulder-pieces of the ephod, as stones for remembrance of the Israelite people, whose names Aaron shall carry upon his two shoulder-pieces for remembrance before the Lord.

28.13 Then make frames of gold

28.14 and two chains of pure gold; braid these like corded work, and fasten the corded chains to the frames.

28.15 You shall make a breastpiece of decision, worked into a design; make it in the style of the ephod: make it of gold, of blue, purple, and crimson yarns, and of fine twisted linen.

The "breastplate of decision" refers to the *Urim* and *Thummim*—see verse 30 below for explanation.

28.16 It shall be square and doubled, a span in length and a span in width.

28.17 Set in it mounted stones, in four rows of stones. The first row shall be a row of carnelian, chrysolite, and emerald;

28.18 the second row: a turquoise, a sapphire, and an amethyst;

The use of the Urim and Thummim is another example of the Torah using an evolutionary, rather than revolutionary, approach to abolish what God opposed.

28.19 the third row: a jacinth, an agate, and a crystal;

28.20 and the fourth row: a beryl, a lapis lazuli, and a jasper. They shall be framed with gold in their mountings.

28.21 The stones shall correspond [in number] to the names of the sons of Israel: twelve, corresponding to their names. They shall be engraved like seals, each with its name, for the twelve tribes.

28.22 On the breastpiece make braided chains of corded work in pure gold.

28.23 Make two rings of gold on the breastpiece, and fasten the two rings at the two ends of the breastpiece,

28.24 attaching the two golden cords to the two rings at the ends of the breastpiece.

28.25 Then fasten the two ends of the cords to the two frames, which you shall attach to the shoulder-pieces of the ephod, at the front.

28.26 Make two rings of gold and attach them to the two ends of the breastpiece, at its inner edge, which faces the ephod.

28.27 And make two other rings of gold and fasten them on the front of the ephod, low on the two shoulder-pieces, close to its seam above the decorated band.

28.28 The breastpiece shall be held in place by a cord of blue from its rings to the rings of the ephod, so that the breastpiece rests on the decorated band and does not come loose from the ephod.

28.29 Aaron shall carry the names of the sons of Israel on the breastpiece of decision over his heart, when he enters the sanctuary, for remembrance before the Lord at all times.

28.30 Inside the breastpiece of decision you shall place the Urim and Thummim, so that they are over Aaron's heart when he comes before the Lord. Thus Aaron shall carry the instrument of decision for the Israelites over his heart before the Lord at all times.

The *Urim* and *Thummim* were worn by the High Priest and functioned as a kind of oracle, providing yes-or-no answers to important national questions.

According to the Italian Jewish scholar Umberto Cassuto, the *Urim* and *Thummim* were the Torah's response to the magic and divination practices common in all parts of the ancient world. Ancient Near Eastern cultures sought to know the divine will by examining the movements of birds, inspecting the livers of animals, and engaging in other forms of magic. The Torah sought to abolish all such practices, but it would have been impossible to do so at a time when they were universally practiced. The *Urim* and *Thummim* may thus be considered a temporary indulgence to satisfy the people's innate yearning to receive messages from God. Moreover, such inquiries could only be addressed to the High Priest, and only, as Cassuto notes, by "the leader of the people, and only in respect of public needs." So even the *Urim* and *Thummim* were thereby limited in their ability to discover God's will—only the leader could do so, and only on behalf of the whole nation. That ended all individual divination.

And all use of the *Urim* and *Thummim* was discontinued after the time of King David, when prophecy replaced oracle as the chief means of knowing God's will.

This is, as I understand it, another example of the Torah using an evolutionary, rather than a revolutionary, approach to abolish what God opposed. The former approach works because the best (in this case, the immediate elimination of anything smacking of oracles) is almost always the enemy of the better.

28.31 You shall make the robe of the ephod of pure blue.

28.32 The opening for the head shall be in the middle of it; the opening shall have a binding of woven work round about—it shall be like the opening of a coat of mail—so that it does not tear.

28.33 On its hem make pomegranates of blue, purple, and crimson yarns, all around the hem, with bells of gold between them all around:

28.34 a golden bell and a pomegranate, a golden bell and a pomegranate, all around the hem of the robe.

28.35 Aaron shall wear it while officiating, so that the sound of it is heard when he comes into the sanctuary before the Lord and when he goes out—that he may not die.

This warning is repeated at the end of the chapter as well (see verse 43). God is reminding the priests their entire purpose is to fulfill His will. If they deviate from His instructions in any way, when they come into His presence in the Holy of Holies, He will not let them live. Later, in Leviticus 10:1-3, Aaron's two oldest sons, Nadab and Abihu, offer at their own initiative an "alien fire," which God had not commanded, and God sends forth a fire which consumes them.

The priests were entrusted with keeping ethical monotheism alive in its earliest days. If they did what they wanted in the sanctuary, as opposed to what God expressly directed, it would have likely meant the end of Israel's ethical monotheist experiment. This is especially true at the outset of something as new and utterly different as Israel's religion. But it can happen at any time in a religion's life. When the religious leaders do what they wish—even with the best intentions—the religion slowly but surely erodes. This does not mean no changes are possible; it simply means when God's direct instructions are involved, they must be observed. Otherwise the leaders end up replacing God.

God will put to death priests who defy His rules, but only when they do so in the sanctuary. And, it is critical to note, it is God Who will put the sinning priest to death, not man.

28.36 You shall make a frontlet of pure gold and engrave on it the seal inscription: "Holy to the Lord."

28.37 Suspend it on a cord of blue, so that it may remain on the headdress; it shall remain on the front of the headdress.

28.38 It shall be on Aaron's forehead, that Aaron may take away any sin arising from the holy things that the Israelites consecrate, from any of their sacred donations; it shall be on his forehead at all times, to win acceptance for them before the Lord.

28.39 You shall make the fringed tunic of fine linen. You shall make the headdress of fine linen. You shall make the sash of embroidered work.

28.40 And for Aaron's sons also you shall make tunics, and make sashes for them, and make turbans for them, for dignity and adornment.

28.41 Put these on your brother Aaron and on his sons as well; anoint them, and ordain them and consecrate them to serve Me as priests.

28.42 You shall also make for them linen breeches to cover their nakedness; they shall extend from the hips to the thighs.

28.43 They shall be worn by Aaron and his sons when they enter the Tent of Meeting or when they approach the altar to officiate in the sanctuary, so that they do not incur punishment and die. It shall be a law for all time for him and for his offspring to come.

CHAPTER
❧29❧

29.1 This is what you shall do to them in consecrating them to serve Me as priests.

This chapter describes the induction ceremony of the priests. Moses, in what can be viewed as his final act as priest (for an earlier example of Moses acting as a priest see Exodus 24:8), is commanded to preside over the induction ceremony.

Everett Fox describes the process: "First, sacrificial animals and bread are brought and prepared; then the priests are systematically clothed in their sacred vestments. After the first animal is slaughtered, its blood is dashed against the altar and the innards are burned as an offering; then the sacred ram is slain."

Having come out of pagan societies and surrounded by paganism, there was always the danger the priests might deviate from God's specifications and, in so doing, lapse into paganism. The Torah therefore outlines each step of the ceremony in detail to ensure it is performed in the service of God alone.

29.1 (cont.) Take a young bull of the herd and two rams

Bulls and rams were worshipped as gods in ancient Egypt. The induction ceremony of the priests therefore involved sacrificing Egyptian gods to God—another attempt to turn the people away from polytheism and pagan worship.

29.1 (cont.) without blemish;

Without this stipulation, many—perhaps most (depending on one's view of human nature)—people would have brought their least healthy, most blemished, animals for sacrifice, which wouldn't extract much in the way of a cost and would thereby cheapen the concept of sacrifice.

29.2 also unleavened bread, unleavened cakes with oil mixed in, and unleavened wafers spread with oil—make these of choice wheat flour.

The priests ate unleavened bread as part of their induction ceremony. According to historical and archeological evidence, the leavening process—in other words, the making of bread—was invented in Egypt. Like the sacrificing of the bulls and rams, the eating of unleavened bread symbolized a rejection of Egypt and its values. It was also an affirmation of Israelite identity, since it was the food associated with the exodus from Egypt.

29.3 Place these in one basket and present them in the basket, along with the bull and the two rams.

29.4 Lead Aaron and his sons up to the entrance of the Tent of Meeting, and wash them with water.

29.5 Then take the vestments, and clothe Aaron with the tunic, the robe of the ephod, the ephod, and the breastpiece, and gird him with the decorated band of the ephod.

29.6 Put the headdress on his head, and place the holy diadem upon the headdress.

29.7 Take the anointing oil and pour it on his head and anoint him.

Anointing with oil symbolized the consecration of priests to the service of God. The oil was sprinkled except in the instance of the High Priest, where the oil was poured on his head (see Leviticus 8:12). The formula for the oil and various regulations surrounding the anointing are found in Exodus 30:22-33; in later Israelite history, kings, like priests, were anointed with oil (see, for example, I Samuel 16:1).

The word "Messiah"—a transcription from the Hebrew *Moshiach*—literally means anointed.

29.8 Then bring his sons forward; clothe them with tunics

29.9 and wind turbans upon them. And gird both Aaron and his sons with sashes. And so they shall have priesthood as their right for all time. You shall then ordain Aaron and his sons.

29.10 Lead the bull up to the front of the Tent of Meeting, and let Aaron and his sons lay their hands upon the head of the bull.

29.11 Slaughter the bull before the Lord, at the entrance of the Tent of Meeting,

29.12 and take some of the bull's blood and put it on the horns of the altar with your finger; then pour out the rest of the blood at the base of the altar.

> As Jacob Milgrom explains, Jews are forbidden to eat the blood of animals because blood represents life. So, while the animal's dead body may be eaten, the animal's life-blood must, as it were, be "returned" to God—either by sprinkling it on the altar or by pouring it on the ground (see Deuteronomy 12:16 and 15:23).

29.13 Take all the fat that covers the entrails, the protuberance on the liver, and the two kidneys with the fat on them, and turn them into smoke upon the altar.

> The burning of the entrails symbolized another rejection of pagan values—in this instance ancient Near Eastern divination practices. In those cultures, priests killed animals and examined the liver to divine signs from the gods.
>
> *The induction ceremony of Israelite priests involved sacrificing Egyptian gods.*
>
> Nahum Sarna: "Numerous clay models of the liver have been uncovered in Mesopotamia, some divided into fifty sections and inscribed with omens and magical formulas for the use of diviners."
>
> A reference to the king of Babylon inspecting the liver of a sacrificed animal appears in Ezekiel 21:26.

The Torah insists on burning the entrails to ensure these magical practices would have no place in the Tabernacle. In reading these accounts of the Tabernacle, perhaps the most important point to keep in mind is the Torah's obsession with ridding the Israelites of idolatrous beliefs. Maimonides identified fifty-one of the Torah's 613 commandments as directed against idolatry.

This is just one more example of how meaningful the details of the sacrificial system were to the Jews of ancient times and how infused they were with civilization-changing values.

29.14 The rest of the flesh of the bull, its hide, and its dung shall be put to the fire outside the camp; it is a sin offering.

29.15 Next take the one ram, and let Aaron and his sons lay their hands upon the ram's head.

29.16 Slaughter the ram, and take its blood and dash it against all sides of the altar.

By turning the ram into smoke, the priest powerfully demonstrated the gods of Egypt can disappear in a puff of smoke, whereas the God of Israel has no physical form that can be obliterated.

29.17 Cut up the ram into sections, wash its entrails and legs, and put them with its quarters and its head.

The details of the sacrificial system seem gory and unintelligible to us. But animal sacrifices were as widely accepted as a way of relating to God among ancient Jews (and to just about every other ancient culture of which we are aware) as prayer services are to people today.

Nevertheless, as noted earlier, Maimonides was almost surely right in his belief that animal sacrifices were instituted to wean people from the universal practice of human sacrifice. This substitution of animals for humans was made clear when, after God stopped Abraham from sacrificing his son Isaac, Abraham immediately sacrificed a ram (Genesis 22:11-13).

29.18 Turn all of the ram into smoke upon the altar. It is a burnt offering to the Lord, a pleasing odor, an offering by fire to the Lord.

By turning the ram into smoke, the priest powerfully demonstrated the gods of Egypt can disappear in a puff of smoke, whereas the God of Israel has no physical form that can be obliterated.

Like the ten plagues, which were directed at Egyptian gods, many of the sacrifices do the same thing—undermine belief in Egyptian gods (rams and bulls) and religious superstitions (reading animal entrails).

29.19 Then take the other ram, and let Aaron and his sons lay their hands upon the ram's head.

29.20 Slaughter the ram, and take some of its blood and put it on the ridge of Aaron's right ear and on the ridges of his sons' right ears, and on the thumbs of their right hands, and on the big toes of their right feet; and dash the rest of the blood against every side of the altar round about.

Sarna notes this practice may have had a purifying role, since the Torah prescribes a similar procedure for people recovering from an impure state (see Leviticus 14:14).

The marking of the ear, hand, and foot of the priest with blood is likely meant to convey the notion the priest is to serve God and the people with all his body. This is another Torah practice exemplifying that ritual is used to embody (literally) the religious and the holy. Many people today believe they can keep religious values alive without accompanying rituals, but the Torah is emphatic about ritual being necessary to keep religion alive. To use an American example, consider what would happen to the holiday of Thanksgiving if there were no Thanksgiving dinner.

29.21 Take some of the blood that is on the altar and some of the anointing oil and sprinkle upon Aaron and his vestments, and also upon his sons and his sons' vestments. Thus shall he and his vestments be holy, as well as his sons and his sons' vestments.

29.22 You shall take from the ram the fat parts—the broad tail, the fat that covers the entrails, the protuberance on the liver, the two kidneys with the fat on them—and the right thigh; for this is a ram of ordination.

29.23 Add one flat loaf of bread, one cake of oil bread, and one wafer, from the basket of unleavened bread that is before the Lord.

29.24 Place all these on the palms of Aaron and his sons, and offer them as an elevation offering before the Lord.

29.25 Take them from their hands and turn them into smoke upon the altar with the burnt offering, as a pleasing odor before the Lord; it is an offering by fire to the Lord.

29.26 Then take the breast of Aaron's ram of ordination and offer it as an elevation offering before the Lord; it shall be your portion.

29.27 You shall consecrate the breast that was offered as an elevation offering and the thigh that was offered as a gift offering from the ram of ordination—from that which was Aaron's and from that which was his sons'—

29.28 and those parts shall be a due for all time from the Israelites to Aaron and his descendants. For they are a gift; and so shall they be a gift from the Israelites, their gift to the Lord out of their sacrifices of well-being.

29.29 The sacral vestments of Aaron shall pass on to his sons after him, for them to be anointed and ordained in.

29.30 He among his sons who becomes priest in his stead, who enters the Tent of Meeting to officiate within the sanctuary, shall wear them seven days.

29.31 You shall take the ram of ordination and boil its flesh in the sacred precinct;

29.32 and Aaron and his sons shall eat the flesh of the ram, and the bread that is in the basket, at the entrance of the Tent of Meeting.

This verse describes the sacrificial meal eaten by the priests.

29.33 These things shall be eaten only by those for whom expiation was made with them when they were ordained and consecrated; they may not be eaten by a layman, for they are holy.

29.34 And if any of the flesh of ordination, or any of the bread, is left until morning, you shall put what is left to the fire; it shall not be eaten, for it is holy.

29.35 Thus you shall do to Aaron and his sons, just as I have commanded you. You shall ordain them through seven days,

> Once again there is the number seven, the most important and recurrent number in the Torah because it hearkens back to the creation of the world in seven days. Acknowledging God as the Creator is to acknowledge, among many other things, that life is ultimately meaningful; it is not a haphazard series of coincidences, which is all life is if there is no Creator.
>
> In this verse, "seven" suggests the initiation of the priests involves the creation of something new, namely the ritual service of God in the Tabernacle.

29.36 and each day you shall prepare a bull as a sin offering for expiation; you shall purge the altar by performing purification upon it, and you shall anoint it to consecrate it.

29.37 Seven days you shall perform purification for the altar to consecrate it, and the altar shall become most holy; whatever touches the altar shall become consecrated.

29.38 Now this is what you shall offer upon the altar: two yearling lambs each day, regularly.

> These daily sacrifices continued to be offered until the Temple was destroyed in the first century in the year 70. Orthodox Jews continue to pray for the rebuilding of the Temple and the restoration of sacrifice. Outside Orthodoxy, however, it is generally assumed sacrifices are no longer necessary because they were a temporary means of weaning the Israelites away from pagan forms of worship, most particularly child sacrifice (see discussion on verse 17).
>
> In the absence of the Great Temple (*Beit Ha-Mikdash*) in Jerusalem, Orthodox Jews do not bring sacrifices to God, but the Orthodox Siddur (prayer book)

repeatedly expresses the hope that one day the Temple will be rebuilt and sacrifices offered there: "And there we shall bring before you our obligatory sacrifices" (Shabbat service). As for other denominations within Judaism, the prayer book of the Conservative movement retains the prayers concerning the sacrifices, but reframes them in the past tense: "and there our ancestors sacrificed to you." And the Reform movement's Siddur drops mention of the sacrifices altogether.

The God of the Torah is not a remote god.

29.39 You shall offer the one lamb in the morning, and you shall offer the other lamb at twilight.

29.40 There shall be a tenth of a measure of choice flour with a quarter of a hin of beaten oil mixed in, and a libation of a quarter hin of wine for one lamb;

29.41 and you shall offer the other lamb at twilight, repeating with it the meal offering of the morning with its libation—an offering by fire for a pleasing odor to the Lord,

29.42 a regular burnt offering throughout the generations, at the entrance of the Tent of Meeting before the Lord. For there I will meet with you, and there I will speak with you,

29.43 and there I will meet with the Israelites, and it shall be sanctified by My Presence.

29.44 I will sanctify the Tent of Meeting and the altar, and I will consecrate Aaron and his sons to serve Me as priests.

29.45 I will abide among the Israelites, and I will be their God.

This verse is a variation on the theme of the verse that began the description of the building of the Tabernacle: "Let them make Me a sanctuary that I may dwell among them" (25:8).

29.46 And they shall know that I the Lord am their God, who brought them out from the land of Egypt that I might abide among them, I the Lord their God.

God will abide among the people; He is not remote. God wants to be close to people.

The affirmation that God took the Israelites out of Egypt reveals several characteristics of God:

1. God did not just create the world; He also continues to take an active role in human history. That is just one of the great differences between the Unmoved Mover god of Aristotle and the God of Israel.

2. God cares about human suffering.

3. God wants people to be free.

4. God has a special role for the Jewish people, which is why He took them out of Egypt.

CHAPTER

30

30.1 You shall make an altar for burning incense; make it of acacia wood.

30.2 It shall be a cubit long and a cubit wide—it shall be square—and two cubits high, its horns of one piece with it.

30.3 Overlay it with pure gold: its top, its sides round about, and its horns; and make a gold molding for it round about.

30.4 And make two gold rings for it under its molding; make them on its two side walls, on opposite sides. They shall serve as holders for poles with which to carry it.

30.5 Make the poles of acacia wood, and overlay them with gold.

30.6 Place it in front of the curtain that is over the Ark of the Pact—in front of the cover that is over the Pact—where I will meet with you.

30.7 On it Aaron shall burn aromatic incense: he shall burn it every morning when he tends the lamps,

> The ritual service of God in the Tabernacle involved all five senses. The priests smelled the incense; they tasted the sacrificial offerings; they felt the sacrificial blood on their hands; they saw the light of the menorah; and they heard the bells on their clothing.

According to Maimonides, the purpose of the incense was to block out the unpleasant odors that came from the sacrifices.

Nahum Sarna explains the incense represented God's invisible, active presence, much like the cloud accompanying the Israelites during the Exodus and during their time in the desert. It was in a cloud of incense God appeared before the High Priest on the holiest day of the year, the Day of Atonement.

30.8 and Aaron shall burn it at twilight when he lights the lamps—a regular incense offering before the Lord throughout the ages.

30.9 You shall not offer alien incense on it, or a burnt offering or a meal offering; neither shall you pour a libation on it.

30.10 Once a year Aaron shall perform purification upon its horns with blood of the sin offering of purification; purification shall be performed upon it once a year throughout the ages. It is most holy to the Lord.

30.11 The Lord spoke to Moses, saying:

While many people assert God and religion have been responsible for more evil than anything else, in the modern world it is the powerful state—almost always a secular one— that has been the greatest source of evil.

30.12 When you take a census of the Israelite people according to their enrollment, each shall pay the Lord a ransom for himself on being enrolled, that no plague may come upon them through their being enrolled.

Taking a census provided the opportunity to have each Israelite pay an "atonement" tax for the upkeep of the Tabernacle. (See verse 15)

30.13 This is what everyone who is entered in the records shall pay: a half-shekel by the sanctuary weight—twenty *gerahs* to the shekel—a half-shekel as an offering to the Lord.

In the time of the Torah, a shekel was a specific weight of gold or silver. The half-shekel was likely silver and was a small amount (perhaps a half-ounce), thereby enabling all Israelites to participate in the census. The shekel has been resurrected as the currency of the modern State of Israel.

A *gerah* was a weight equivalent to one-twentieth of a shekel.

30.14 Everyone who is entered in the records, from the age of twenty years up, shall give the Lord's offering:

Twenty was the minimum age for military service.

30.15 the rich shall not pay more and the poor shall not pay less than half a shekel when giving the Lord's offering as expiation for your persons.

The small contribution enabled every Israelite to participate. In that way, the Tabernacle would belong equally to each Israelite, regardless of wealth or social status: the rich could not make large contributions and be regarded as having played more of a role in the maintenance of the Tabernacle.

30.16 You shall take the expiation money from the Israelites and assign it to the service of the Tent of Meeting; it shall serve the Israelites as a reminder before the Lord, as expiation for your persons.

30.17 The Lord spoke to Moses, saying:

30.18 Make a laver of copper and a stand of copper for it, for washing; and place it between the Tent of Meeting and the altar. Put water in it,

30.19 and let Aaron and his sons wash their hands and feet [in water drawn] from it.

30.20 When they enter the Tent of Meeting they shall wash with water, that they may not die; or when they approach the altar to serve, to turn into smoke an offering by fire to the Lord,

This warning is repeated throughout this chapter. In each case, God reminds Moses that priests fulfill their holy role only insofar as they follow His instructions exactly. If they deviate from God's directives in any way, they will be struck down as if they have lapsed into pagan worship. Any deviation can end up leading to pagan worship (see commentary on Leviticus 10:1-2, in which two of Aaron's sons, Nadab and Abihu, are executed by God for offering "alien fire").

The small contribution enabled every Israelite to participate. In that way, the Tabernacle would belong equally to each Israelite, regardless of wealth or social status.

30.21 they shall wash their hands and feet, that they may not die. It shall be a law for all time for them—for him and his offspring—throughout the ages.

30.22 The Lord spoke to Moses, saying:

30.23 Next take choice spices: five hundred weight of solidified myrrh, half as much—two hundred and fifty—of fragrant cinnamon, two hundred and fifty of aromatic cane,

30.24 five hundred—by the sanctuary weight—of cassia, and a hin of olive oil.

30.25 Make of this a sacred anointing oil, a compound of ingredients expertly blended, to serve as sacred anointing oil.

Sarna explains that in the time of the Torah, oils and perfumes were very costly due to the enormous amounts of raw materials required for their manufacture—some of which had to be transported from as far away as Arabia and even India—and the considerable level of skill and experience involved.

30.26 With it anoint the Tent of Meeting, the Ark of the Pact,

30.27 the table and all its utensils, the lampstand and all its fittings, the altar of incense,

30.28 the altar of burnt offering and all its utensils, and the laver and its stand.

30.29 Thus you shall consecrate them so that they may be most holy; whatever touches them shall be consecrated.

30.30 You shall also anoint Aaron and his sons, consecrating them to serve Me as priests.

30.31 And speak to the Israelite people, as follows: This shall be an anointing oil sacred to Me throughout the ages.

30.32 It must not be rubbed on any person's body, and you must not make anything like it in the same proportions; it is sacred, to be held sacred by you.

30.33 Whoever compounds its like, or puts any of it on a layman, shall be cut off from his kin.

30.34 And the Lord said to Moses: Take the herbs stacte, onycha, and galbanum—these herbs together with pure frankincense; let there be an equal part of each.

30.35 Make them into incense, a compound expertly blended, refined, pure, sacred.

30.36 Beat some of it into powder, and put some before the Pact in the Tent of Meeting, where I will meet with you; it shall be most holy to you.

30.37 But when you make this incense, you must not make any in the same proportions for yourselves; it shall be held by you sacred to the Lord. Whoever makes any like it, to smell of it, shall be cut off from his kin.

> This incense is designated solely for ritual worship, and must therefore not be used for any other purposes. The misappropriation of a ritual item for any other purpose is regarded as a serious sin (much as Christians would react if someone took a cross and used it as a backscratcher) and while the punishment, "shall be cut off from his kin," is not precisely defined, it clearly refers to being cast out of the community in some way.

31.1 The Lord spoke to Moses:

31.2 See, I have singled out by name Bezalel son of Uri son of Hur, of the tribe of Judah.

Only after God fully laid out the design of the Tabernacle did He designate the artisan who would execute the plan. This was a very special circumstance in which the normal process for building was reversed. Normally, first we hire architects and artists, then we see their designs. In the building of the Tabernacle, first we are told what the design and artwork is to be, and then the artisan is hired. The artist is secondary to the artwork. According to the Torah, the artist, at least in this case, is not the source of the creative vision, but a vehicle for implementing the vision of the Creator.

31.2 (cont.) Bezalel son of Uri son of Hur,

In Hebrew, the name Bezalel means "in the shadow of God." The Torah would seem to be teaching that ideally, artists should see themselves as working in the shadow of God. (That is exactly how the greatest composer, Johann Sebastian Bach, viewed his work—see the commentary on art in Exodus 20:3). Otherwise, given the power of art and aesthetic beauty, they may start to see themselves— and others might see them—as higher than, and superior to, other human beings.

31.3 I have endowed him with a divine spirit of skill, ability, and knowledge in every kind of craft;

Bezalel is an artist because God has endowed him with particular gifts. Only when people understand their singular abilities are gifts can they remain humble and put their gifts to noble use. But when people come to regard their gifts as something they have made, they often lose all humility. In the case of the artist, if he believes he is great, rather than merely the recipient of great gifts, he will use his gifts to elevate himself, not society.

There is a parallel to this in the field of medicine. A famous Talmudic statement about doctors says: "The best physicians go to hell."[1] While this was obviously hyperbole, the Talmud was warning that the best physicians might well come to believe they alone, i.e., without God's help, are the healers of the sick—and might to see themselves as gods.

31.4 to make designs for work in gold, silver, and copper,

31.5 to cut stones for setting and to carve wood—to work in every kind of craft.

31.6 Moreover, I have assigned to him Oholiab son of Ahisamach, of the tribe of Dan; and I have also granted skill to all who are skillful, that they may make everything that I have commanded you:

31.7 the Tent of Meeting, the Ark for the Pact and the cover upon it, and all the furnishings of the Tent;

31.8 the table and its utensils, the pure lampstand and all its fittings, and the altar of incense;

31.9 the altar of burnt offering and all its utensils, and the laver and its stand;

31.10 the service vestments, the sacral vestments of Aaron the priest and the vestments of his sons, for their service as priests;

31.11 as well as the anointing oil and the aromatic incense for the sanctuary. Just as I have commanded you, they shall do.

31.12 And the Lord said to Moses:

31.13 Speak to the Israelite people and say: Nevertheless, you must keep My sabbaths, for this is a sign between Me and you throughout the ages, that you may know that I the Lord have consecrated you.

This Hebrew word, *ach*, translated here as "nevertheless," may be considered a combination of the words "and" and "but."

God is telling Moses that despite the extraordinary importance of building the Tabernacle, the Israelites must still keep the Sabbath; they are not to violate the Sabbath for the sake of completing the Tabernacle. The Torah considers the sanctification of time (the Sabbath) more important than the sanctification of place (the Tabernacle). In addition, the Sabbath, being time-bound rather than place-bound, can be observed anywhere, while the priestly service can only be performed in the Tabernacle. By privileging the Sabbath over the Tabernacle, the Torah thus laid the foundations for a faith not dependent on a place, one that is timeless and universal.

Benno Jacob offers two additional reasons that keeping the Sabbath was more important than building the Tabernacle. First, the Sabbath represents a higher degree of holiness: It was created by God Himself at the beginning of time, whereas the Tabernacle was made by human hands (albeit at God's direction) at a particular historical moment. The Sabbath is the first thing God ever designates as holy (Genesis 2:3). Second, the entire edifice of Judaism collapses without the Sabbath, because the observance of this day is an affirmation of Judaism's fundamental message that God created the world. The Tabernacle, in contrast, can be (and has been) replaced by other forms of worship.

Historically, the Sabbath has functioned as the practice that perhaps most distinguished Jews from non-Jews. Both Christianity and Islam have a weekly

In Hebrew, the name Bezalel means "in the shadow of God." The Torah would seem to be teaching that ideally, artists should see themselves as working in the shadow of God.

day of rest with religious study and prayer, but neither has observed the Sabbath as the commemoration of creation as the Jews have. Christianity celebrates Sunday as the Lord's Day, the day of the Resurrection; and it has often served as a weekly holy day on which normal work is not performed and religious services are attended. But Christian scholars have often noted it is the only one of the Ten Commandments not specifically repeated as a commandment in the New Testament.

> *The Torah considers the sanctification of time (the Sabbath) more important than the sanctification of place (the Tabernacle).*

Nor does Islam's weekly holy day, Friday, commemorate creation. It is the day of the week when Muslims are expected to pray with other Muslims at a mosque, and hear a religious scholar preach from the Quran.[2]

One non-Jewish religion, Seventh Day Adventism, a Protestant denomination, does observe a Sabbath from Friday sunset to Saturday sunset, just as the Jews do. But, as the religion's name makes clear, it is Advent-centered (in reference to the Second Coming), not creation-centered.

CAPITAL PUNISHMENT FOR VIOLATION OF THE SABBATH

31.14 You shall keep the sabbath, for it is holy for you. He who profanes it shall be put to death: The Torah does not prescribe capital punishment for the violation of any ritual commandment except for the Sabbath (though Torah law—and later on Talmudic law—regarding capital crimes generally essentially assured Shabbat violators were not executed).[3]

Why the exception for violating the Shabbat? Why is it a uniquely grave religious offense?

First, the Shabbat is the only ritual observance in the Ten Commandments. That alone assures it a uniquely important status among Torah rituals.

Second, what is described here is not a mere violation of the Sabbath, but one rising to the level of "profaning" this holy day. What might that be? The Sabbath is the primary means of expressing the most fundamental of all Torah teachings, namely that God created the world. Therefore, the Israelite who violated the Sabbath *in public* undermined the most fundamental teaching of the Torah. An Israelite who openly and flagrantly desecrated the Shabbat was intentionally leading others to deny God created the world at the very time Moses was attempting to inculcate the basis of ethical monotheism in the Israelite people. It was the element of publicity added to the Sabbath violation that took it to the level of "profane." If a Jew violated the Sabbath in private, he would not be punished, as he could not be considered to have undermined this fundamental teaching.

Commenting on this verse, Ovadia ben Jacob Sforno (1475–1550), an Italian rabbi and biblical commentator, wrote: "The reason for such a penalty is that anyone violating the concept of the Sabbath prohibitions thereby denies that *I, God*, created the universe out of no preexisting tangible substance."

For the record, except for the man who was executed for publicly gathering wood on the Sabbath (Numbers 15:32-36), there is no record of Jews putting a Jew to death for violating the Sabbath. And they are hardly about to begin today. If Jews put Sabbath violators to death, it would amount to a form of auto-genocide. Moreover, no Jewish high court has existed in the last 2,000 years with any authority to execute anyone for anything.

As elsewhere in the Torah, we have the death penalty decreed by the Torah primarily to emphasize how severe the offense is. The one Israelite (the woodgatherer in Numbers) who was executed for violating the Sabbath committed a deliberate act of public defiance of the very legitimacy of the Ten Commandments and the ethical monotheist experiment.

31.14 (cont.) whoever does work on it, that person shall be cut off from among his kin.

To be "cut off from his kin" likely does not mean to be executed. If it did, this part of the verse would merely be a repetition of the first part. As noted earlier, since being "gathered to one's kin" is one of the Torah's ways of expressing death, being cut off from one's kin means not being with them in the afterlife. Again, Sforno: "[Cut off] from those members of his people who are destined to live on in the world to come after their bodies are left behind on earth by their souls." So, the Torah is stating that even if one wasn't executed for violating the Sabbath (because the violation was done privately), the violation will still carry a serious consequence: the offender will be "cut off" from the afterlife.

THE WORD "WORK" IN THE TORAH

The Hebrew word used in this verse is not *avodah*, which is the standard Hebrew word for "work," but *melacha*, which is not precisely translatable. It can mean "profession" (as in, one's line of work), but it usually signifies a category of activities Jewish law prohibits on the Sabbath.

The Talmud enumerated thirty-nine types of *melacha* forbidden on the Sabbath, based on the thirty-nine types of *melacha* involved in the construction of the Tabernacle.

The Chabad website has this to say about the thirty-nine prohibited forms of *melacha*: "The principle behind [the forbidden activities] is that they represent constructive, creative effort, demonstrating man's mastery over nature. Refraining from *melacha* on Shabbat signals our recognition that, despite our human creative abilities, God is the ultimate Creator and Master."

31.15 Six days may work be done, but on the seventh day there shall be a sabbath of complete rest, holy to the Lord; whoever does work on the sabbath day shall be put to death.

Accompanying the commandment not to work on the Sabbath is a directive to work on the other six days of the week. Even retired people or those who are independently wealthy should engage in some sort of productive labor during the week.

Not resting on the Sabbath generally means working seven days a week—precisely what slaves do. Therefore, by not resting on the Sabbath, an Israelite was not only negating that God created the world, but also negating that he was a free man (and, by implication, also negating that God took him out of slavery). While they were slaves in Egypt, the Israelites could not rest once a week. By desisting from work on the Sabbath, they affirm they are free people, solely thanks to God having liberated them.

31.16 The Israelite people shall keep the sabbath, observing the sabbath throughout the ages as a covenant for all time:

> The Hebrew word *la'asot* (translated here as "observing") literally means "to make." It is the same word used throughout the description of the building of the Tabernacle. The Israelites are commanded to "make" the Sabbath just as they were commanded to make the Tabernacle. Both the Sabbath and the Tabernacle affirm God, and both are man-made. God created the "original" Sabbath, but it is now up to people to make it each week.

> By keeping the Sabbath, the Jewish people affirm they have a covenantal relationship with God. Prior to the giving of the Ten Commandments and its command of the Sabbath, circumcision served as the sign of the covenant. However, circumcision is not unique to Jews; it has been practiced all over the world. And though circumcision remains a cornerstone of Judaism, it is the Sabbath that serves as the chief sign of the unique relationship between God and Israel. Furthermore, while circumcision applies only to males, the Sabbath applies to both men and women. And, of course, in terms of influencing people's behavior, circumcision is a one-time act, while the Sabbath is observed weekly. The late Pinchas Peli, a prominent Israeli theologian and dear friend, once noted a seventy-year-old Jew has spent ten years observing the Sabbath.

31.17 it shall be a sign for all time between Me and the people of Israel. For in six days the Lord made heaven and earth, and on the seventh day He ceased from work and was refreshed.

> Once again, the Torah appends the great reason for keeping the Shabbat: affirming God's creation of the world. That is why Jews recite the verses from Genesis describing the Seventh Day as part of the Friday evening prayer over the wine (Kiddush); and those present stand—a reflection of the ancient practice of standing while giving testimony in court.

31.18 When He finished speaking with him on Mount Sinai, He gave Moses the two tablets of the Pact, stone tablets inscribed with the finger of God.

> The Torah includes only one verse about the way in which God communicates these ideas to the people. Most of this part of the Torah is instead concerned

with the content of the ideas themselves. We are not told exactly how God's revelation of the Law to Moses at Sinai occurred. I am convinced one reason is the Torah does not deem the details of how it was transmitted important; what is important is *that* it occurred, not *how* it occurred.

That is true about everything related to God. We do not know how God operates, only that He exists. And we do not know anything about the afterlife, only that it exists.

CHAPTER
32

32.1 When the people saw that Moses was so long in coming down from the mountain, the people gathered against Aaron

At this point in the Torah's narrative, Moses is still on the mountain receiving the Ten Commandments. The Israelites can be likened to children whose parent goes out of sight for too long and become anxious about whether he/she is ever coming back.

32.1 (cont.) and said to him, "Come, make us a god who shall go before us,

The Hebrew word translated here as "come" (*kum*) literally means, "Get up." It is a command, implying both impatience and disrespect.

Cassuto notes the absurdity of the Israelites' request: They believe human beings can make a god, yet they do not realize that whatever human beings make has less power than they have.

The people's demand does not make sense for another reason as well, since they seem to be confusing the idea of a leader with the idea of a god. Either they should be saying, "Moses is gone, so make us a leader," or "God is gone, so make us a god." Their desire to replace Moses with a god might signify that, having come from a culture that deified Pharaoh, and after seeing all the miracles God performed through Moses, they have come to regard Moses as divine. The deification—real or potential—of Moses will play a decisive role in God's subsequent decision not to allow Moses into Israel (see commentary to Numbers 20:12).

32.1 (cont.) for that man Moses, who brought us from the land of Egypt—we do not know what has happened to him."

> The Israelites have spent much of the Book of Exodus complaining to Moses about his leadership. Yet, shortly after he disappears, they become angry he is no longer leading them.

32.2 Aaron said to them, "Take off the gold rings that are on the ears of your wives, your sons, and your daughters, and bring them to me."

> Aaron is in a terrible quandary. On the one hand, he fears what has become a mob—and who knows what this mob will do to him? On the other hand, he does not want to betray God and his brother Moses. So he tries several times to stall and undermine the people's plans without directly opposing them. Here, for example, he insists the people surrender their precious jewelry, in the hope that having to part with their most valuable material possessions will dissuade them from idolatry.

Their desire to replace Moses with a god likely signifies the Israelites have come to regard Moses as divine.

> As for how this band of recently freed slaves acquired all this jewelry, undoubtedly it was the gold and silver they were given by the people of Egypt. The Egyptians were generous with their jewelry of precious metals in their desire to quickly be rid of the Israelites, whose presence brought such disaster upon them (Exodus 12:35-36).

32.3 And all the people took off the gold rings that were in their ears and brought them to Aaron.

> It is not just some or even most Israelites who are willing to part with their jewelry, but "all the people." They are clearly lost without Moses, desperate to regain a sense of security.
>
> People will happily trade valuables for security. And security is not only physical; there is also security in having some transcendent meaning. People will not only trade in their valuables for meaning, many will give their lives for it. After food and water, the greatest human desire is for meaning (this truth is explained in Viktor Frankl's classic work, *Man's Search for Meaning*).

On a more prosaic level, the Israelites may have also simply concluded their precious jewelry would be worth nothing if they never made it to Canaan.

Cassuto explains Aaron's actions in this way: The peoples of the ancient Near East often portrayed their deities standing or sitting on wild beasts or cattle, and Aaron may therefore have been trying to satisfy the people's need for a physical symbol of God's presence by fashioning a vacant seat for God. Perhaps Aaron reasoned (hoped?) the molten calf would not be worshipped as a god, but only serve as a throne on which God would sit. A golden calf wouldn't be all that different from the cherubim in the Tabernacle (see Exodus 25:18-22), whose body was supposed to serve as a throne for God.

However, Cassuto provides an insightful explanation of the difference. Though the Second Commandment forbids constructing any likeness of "what is in the heavens above, or on the earth below, or in the waters under the earth" (Exodus 20:4), the cherubim do not represent anything that exists in those realms. What is expressly prohibited is to ascribe divinity to an image of something in the world—in this case, for instance, a calf.

There may be a simpler explanation. Since God instructed the making of the cherubim, they could not possibly be a false god. But the people, acting on their own, made the calf; it is therefore a false god.

ESSAY: REASON AND BELIEF

32.4 This he took from them and cast in a mold, and made it into a molten calf. And they exclaimed, "This is your god, O Israel, who brought you out of the land of Egypt!"

It is difficult for us today to believe the people really believed a calf made from molten metals brought them out of Egypt.

First, they already ascribed this to Moses: "that man Moses, who brought us from the land of Egypt..." (verse 1).

Second, they witnessed Aaron fabricate the calf with their own eyes from jewelry they gave him; surely, they had to realize it was not in existence prior to and during their exodus from Egypt.

And third, as Nachmanides writes: "No one in the world could be so stupid as to think that the gold in their ears brought them out of Egypt."

But coming from a pagan culture, one that revered the calf (the sacred bull known as Apis or Hapis was an Egyptian god), they apparently did believe it. The ability of people to suspend reason in order to believe what they want to believe is limitless.

To understand what is wrong here, one must distinguish between the non-rational and the anti-rational (or the "irrational"). There is most certainly a place for the non-rational in life. Much of what is beautiful—love and art, for example—transcends reason. And a great deal of good is achieved by not following the dictates of pure reason. It is not fully rational, for example, to risk one's life to save another person. But there is no place for the *anti*-rational—and ascribing divinity to a molten calf is anti-rational.

Of course, some atheists argue belief in a God Who created the world, acted in history, and revealed His moral will through the Ten Commandments is also contrary to reason. But they equate lack of scientific proof with irrationality. While not scientifically provable, there is nothing anti-rational about believing in a Creator. On the contrary, what is anti-rational is the belief the universe came about by itself, intelligence was not created by intelligence, and life sprang from non-life, even though we have not the slightest evidence it did. Furthermore, there is no comparison between the belief in the Creator God and the God of Exodus and people believing a gold statue just produced from their own jewelry was responsible for freeing them from slavery and leading them out of Egypt.

> *There is most certainly a place for the non-rational in life. Much of what is beautiful—like love and art—transcends reason. But there is no place for the anti-rational.*

The latter belief is contrary to reason—a fact that neither troubled the Israelites then nor vast numbers of people today. And one can find belief in the anti-rational in the secular world as well as in the religious world. Think of all the people, especially secular intellectuals, who believed in communism, the ideology that enslaved and murdered more people than any other in history.

And think of all the people in Germany and elsewhere who believed in racism, an idea as contrary to reason as belief in a golden calf.

The idea the Israelites, who announced their faith in God and in His servant Moses (Exodus 14:31), suddenly believed a molten calf was the god who took them out of Egypt struck the ancient rabbis as so implausible they held that it emanated from the "mixed multitude" of other oppressed, non-Israelite peoples in Egypt who joined the Exodus (the *erev rav*; see Exodus 12:38). This explanation was not some chauvinistic attempt to avoid blaming the Israelites; the Torah constantly blames the Israelites for their bad conduct. It was based on the language of the verse. The speakers did not say "our god"; they said, "your god," implying they were addressing the Israelites as outsiders.

Bible commentator Professor Jeffrey Tigay notes the "declaration that the calf is the god who brought them out of Egypt contrasted ironically with God's [earlier] declaration that it is through the Tabernacle that He will abide among the Israelites and that *they will know that He is their God who brought them out of Egypt*" (Exodus 29:42-46; emphasis added).

Finally, the verse does not actually say, "This is your god, O Israel." It says, "These are your gods, O Israel." Why the plural, given that only one "god" has been built?

In Cassuto's view, the Israelites regarded "the calf [as] a partner, as it were, of the Lord. Hence the plural." He is probably right. Though strict monotheism characterized biblical thought from the very beginning, it took a long time to become fully and universally rooted among the Israelites. What existed among many ancient Israelites was henotheism—a belief in the one God of Israel, but not *only* in the God of Israel. In other words, the plural sentence implies the Israelites were worshipping the golden calf *and* God.

32.5 When Aaron saw this, he built an altar before it; and Aaron announced: "Tomorrow shall be a festival of the Lord!"

When Aaron's first delaying tactic—asking for all the Israelites' valuables—doesn't work, he employs another tactic to prevent the idol worship: he tries to postpone the Israelites' worship of the calf until the next day. Perhaps the Israelites will change their minds by the morning, or perhaps Moses will return by then.

He also tries to steer the ceremony to God-worship. Aaron invokes God's proper name, "Jehovah" (which is what the term "Lord" always signifies). Perhaps he can convince the people to worship God in the presence of the calf instead of worshipping the calf as a god.

32.6 Early next day, the people offered up burnt offerings and brought sacrifices of well-being; they sat down to eat and drink.

The people agree to wait until the next day, as Aaron proposed, but they are so eager to begin worshipping the calf they wake up early to do so. (The insertion of the word "early" is one of those many subtle insights of the Torah many readers, understandably, overlook.)

The range of activities to follow suggests the people did whatever they wanted in their worship of the calf. When people create their own gods, they also create their own rules—of worship, and of other behaviors. Perhaps the reader can now better appreciate the reason for all the detail in the priestly code, the sacrificial system, and the building of the Tabernacle. God did not want to risk having people make up their own rituals. Among other things, He knew inappropriate sexual activity would ensue—as it does.

32.6 (cont.) and then rose to dance.

The Hebrew word *l'tzachek* (translated here as "to dance") is a combination of the Hebrew words "to play" and "to laugh" and is a euphemism almost definitely connoting sexual behavior (the same word is used in Genesis 26:8 in what is definitely a sexual context). The rendering of the 1917 Jewish Publication Society translation, "and rose up to make merry," suggests an orgy.

32.7 The Lord spoke to Moses, "Hurry down, for your people,

God almost always refers to the Israelites as "My people." But at this moment, He refers to them as "your [Moses's] people." The covenant is clear: the Israelites are God's people only if He is their God.

32.7 (cont.) whom you brought out of the land of Egypt, have acted basely.

When referring to the Exodus, God nearly always identifies Himself as the one Who "took the Israelites out of Egypt" (as in the opening verse of the Ten Commandments, Exodus 20:2). Here, however, God ascribes the Exodus to Moses; He communicates a disappointment so profound He no longer wishes to take credit for it.

God did not take the Israelites out of Egypt so they could be free to do whatever they wanted, but rather to worship the one God and to establish ethical monotheism in the world. That is why Moses did not simply say to Pharaoh, "Let My people go," but, "Let My people go that they may worship Me" (Exodus 9:1).

The words translated as "have acted basely," are literally "have destroyed [everything, or themselves]." As Sarna explains, the people are now destroying the Torah's fundamental idea that God is not in nature. Instead of worshipping God, Who is above and outside the natural world, they are worshipping a calf, which is, of course, part of the natural world: "By putting God back into nature, the people have violated and nullified the fundamental distinctive idea of the religion of Israel."

MIRACLES, FAITH, AND GRATITUDE

32.8 They have been quick to turn aside from the way that I enjoined upon them. They have made themselves a molten calf and bowed low to it and sacrificed to it, saying: 'This is your god, O Israel, who brought you out of the land of Egypt!'"

Less than two months have passed and already the Israelites have turned away from God. The very people who witnessed all the miracles of the Exodus—in Egypt and after leaving Egypt—are now building the Golden Calf. There is a particularly important lesson regarding human nature here.

Most people believe if God performed a miracle—just *one* miracle—for them, they would surely and permanently believe in God. But, as explained in the commentary to Exodus 16:2, human nature doesn't work that way. The power of witnessing a miracle wears off quickly, and most individuals soon need (or merely want) another miracle. Over time, most people's attitude toward those who have done something good for them is: "What have you done for me lately?"

Therefore the Torah repeatedly emphasizes the need for Jews to remember the Exodus. Without constantly reminding themselves—through study, prayer, and ritual (most obviously the Passover Seder)—most Jews would have long ago largely forgotten the Exodus.

In many ways, gratitude is the most important of all the good character traits. It is the most indispensable trait to both happiness and goodness. One can neither be a happy person nor a good person without gratitude. The less gratitude one has, the more one sees oneself as a victim; and nothing is more likely to produce a bad person or a bad group than defining oneself or one's group as a victim. Victims, having been hurt, too often believe they have a license to hurt others. As for happiness, if you think of all the people you know, you will not be able to name one who is ungrateful and happy. The two are mutually exclusive.

But gratitude is difficult to sustain. Just about everyone is grateful when someone does something particularly kind for him or her. But the more time passes, the less gratitude most people have. *Most people remember the bad done to them far longer than the good done to them.* It took the Israelites all of two months to forget the greatest set of miracles ever performed for a people.

If you think of all the people you know, you will not be able to name one who is ungrateful and happy. The two are mutually exclusive.

The story of the Golden Calf is another example of the Hebrew Bible depicting its people, the Hebrew people, in an honest—and therefore often negative and unflattering—way. That is one of the most compelling reasons I believe in the historicity of the Torah and that it is not a man-made document. In the history of religion, there is no parallel.

Having said that, it is important to stress that no other group would likely have reacted differently. Ingratitude is a universal trait. And animal worship was a universal practice.

ESSAY: FAITH AND WORKS: HOW WE KNOW WHETHER PEOPLE REALLY BELIEVE IN GOD

The Israelites built an idol and worshipped it as a god. Yet, God says to Moses the Israelites "turn[ed] aside *from the way* that I enjoined upon them"; God does not say, "the Israelites turned aside from *Me*."

One of the most crucial lessons in the whole Bible is contained in this statement: There is no distinction between God and God's way. If you think you believe in God but you reject "God's way," you do not believe in God. You believe in your way, which essentially means you believe you are your own god.

What is "God's way?" It has already been made clear—first and foremost, it is the Ten Commandments.

This also answers the question posed by anti-religious individuals: "What god are you talking about?"

Here is the answer:

God is the God of the Ten Commandments and of creation, and the God introduced to the world by the Bible. Any other "god" using the word "God" is a misuse of the term. If people want to introduce another god into the world, it is their right to do so. But they should not use a word that has meant something quite specific for thousands of years. It would be as if three new countries arose, all calling themselves "France." They may be countries, but none of them is France.

There is an additional lesson here. What matters most to God is that we "not turn aside from the way I enjoined." In other words, as important as faith is, what God demands is right behavior. (Moreover, keeping God's laws is likely to bring people back to faith in God. As the Talmud later put it: "Better that they abandon Me [God] and keep My laws—because through My laws they will come back to Me.")[1]

What is faith in God if it does not mean living according to His way? It is meaningless.

People who murder innocents in the name of "God" do not believe in God. Most obviously, they certainly do not believe in the God of the Ten Commandments—and *that* God is the God of the Torah.

This is one reason, as important as faith in God is, the Torah constantly stresses moral behavior, as do God's prophets later in the Bible. As the Prophet Isaiah put it: "'What need have I of all your sacrifices?' says the Lord" (Isaiah 1:11).

This theme is also repeated in the New Testament in James (2:14-17 NKJV), for example:

> What does it profit, my brethren, if someone says he has faith but does not have works? Can faith save him? If a brother or sister is naked and destitute of daily food, and one of you says to them, "Depart in peace, be warmed and filled," but you do not give them the things which are needed for the body, what does it profit? Thus also *faith by itself, if it does not have works, is dead*" (emphasis added).

32.9 The Lord further said to Moses, "I see that this is a stiffnecked people.

THE COMPLETE ABSENCE OF ETHNIC CHAUVINISM IN THE TORAH

32.10 Now, let Me be, that My anger may blaze forth against them and that I may destroy them, and make of you a great nation."

God formed the Israelites as a nation and made them His Chosen People to lead the world to ethical monotheism and away from polytheistic superstition and its accompanying evils. If they reject that purpose, they no longer have any purpose. And God might as well destroy them. To understand this morally troubling idea, we need to consider the following:

First, God wants a good world. The purpose of human life is not merely to live—that is the purpose of an animal's life—but to live a moral life. The same moral calculation took place when God decided to destroy the world in the time of Noah. God made man to live a good life; if mankind chooses evil, God will start all over, which He did with Noah. God tells Moses He is contemplating something very similar now—starting all over with Moses.

Second, if nothing else, God's threat to destroy the Israelites should make it more than clear—once again—the Torah is not ethnically chauvinistic. God's first concern is goodness.

Third, it is likely God did not seriously intend to destroy the Israelites. If He had, it is unlikely He would have telegraphed His intention to Moses, essentially inviting him to intervene. Yet, that is exactly what God did: "*Let me be,* that my anger may blaze forth," He said to Moses.

As Sarna put it, God's telling Moses what He intends to do is an invitation for a counter-argument. If Moses offers a counter-argument, God will positively respond to his pleas on behalf of the people. It may even be a test of Moses: How will Moses react to God's offer to become the father of his own "great nation"?

If it was a test, Moses immediately passed it.

32.11 But Moses implored the Lord his God, saying,

This verse actually means, "Moses endeavored to calm and soften God's angry countenance" (Cassuto). In effect, Moses reaches out to comfort God because he understands God's pain.

Can God experience pain? No human being can know the answer to such an anthropomorphic question. However, the possibility God experiences pain should not be discounted. After all, since man feels emotional pain, and God made man in His image, it is reasonable to believe God has the same capacity for emotional

> *If you think you believe in God but you reject "God's way," you do not believe in God. You believe in your way, which essentially means you believe you are your own god.*

feeling He instilled in humans. The Bible speaks frequently of God's emotions. Genesis 6:6, for example, speaks of God's response to the evil human beings were committing: "And the Lord regretted that He had made man on earth, and His heart was saddened."

It is, therefore, possible God does experience pain and other "feelings." Nevertheless, we cannot know. A medieval Hebrew saying wisely put it, "If I knew Him, I would be Him" (*lu yidativ hayitiv*).

Regarding the expression, "the Lord his God," God is, of course, everybody's God, not just Moses's. The term may be used here to highlight the uniquely intimate relationship between God and Moses.

MOSES'S THREE ARGUMENTS TO PERSUADE GOD NOT TO DESTROY THE ISRAELITES

Moses offers three arguments to dissuade God from destroying the people.

The First Argument

32.11 (cont.) "Let not your anger, O Lord, blaze forth against Your people, whom You delivered from the land of Egypt with great power and with a mighty hand.

First, he reminds God the Israelites are His people (not Moses's, as God just said)—and they are the people He delivered from Egypt.

The Second Argument

32.12 Let not the Egyptians say, 'It was with evil intent He delivered them, only to kill them off in the mountains and annihilate them from the face of the earth.' Turn from your blazing anger, and renounce the plan to punish your people.

Moses's second argument is that God's reputation is at stake. If God destroys the Israelites, the miracles of the Exodus will be ascribed to a malevolent deity who took His people out of Egypt solely to annihilate them.

And while Moses doesn't say so, it would also confirm to the Egyptians they had every right to treat the Israelites as they did, as they hardly treated them worse than their own God.

Moses's argument draws upon two fundamental concepts in the Jewish tradition: "the desecration of God's name" (*chillul Hashem*) and "the sanctification of

God's name" (*kiddush Hashem*). An example of *chillul Hashem* would be a religious person who robs a bank; his behavior would reflect not only on himself, but on his religion and most of all on the God in whom he professes to believe. Conversely, *kiddush Hashem* takes place when a religious person does particularly kind things; his actions bring honor to his religion and to the God he professes to believe in. Here Moses contends even God can sanctify or desecrate His name— and His killing off the Israelites would surely desecrate it.

The Third Argument

32.13 Remember your servants, Abraham, Isaac, and Israel, how You swore to them by Your Self and said to them: I will make your offspring as numerous as the stars of heaven, and I will give to your offspring this whole land of which I spoke, to possess forever."

Moses's third argument is to remind God of His promise to the patriarchs that their descendants will be as numerous as the stars. Moses insists God be bound by His own promises—just as Abraham insisted, on the eve of the destruction of Sodom, that God be bound by His own rules: "Shall not the Judge of all the earth deal justly?" (Genesis 18:25).

Once again, the Torah makes it clear the believer is allowed to argue with God. There is not a hint in the Torah that God finds arguing with Him objectionable or sinful. On the contrary, it makes God all the more real and all the more believable—and the Torah all the more rational and therefore believable.

32.14 And the Lord renounced the punishment He had planned to bring upon His people.

The Hebrew word *va-yinachem*, translated here as "renounced," may also be translated as "regretted." One can therefore translate this verse to mean, "God regretted that He wished to destroy His people." In any event, Moses's arguments had their intended effect.

Note, too, God reverts to referring to the Israelites as "His people," not as Moses's people.

32.15 Thereupon Moses turned and went down from the mountain bearing the two tablets of the Pact,

Once God decided not to go through with His punishment, Moses realized he did not have anything more to say. A successful businessman said one secret to his success in negotiating was that as soon as he achieved the result he sought, he ended the meeting. As this negotiation with God reveals, Moses knew what to say, when to say it, and when to say no more.

32.15 (cont.) tablets inscribed on both their surfaces: they were inscribed on the one side and on the other.

The most logical interpretation of this description is the tablets were double-sided, with half of the commandments written on one side and half on the other.

32.16 The tablets were God's work, and the writing was God's writing, incised upon the tablets.

The words *ma'aseh Elohim*—"the makings of God"—are a direct echo of the people's demand to Aaron in verse 1, "make us a God" (*aseh lanu Elohim*).

The double emphasis in this verse—"The tablets were God's work, and the writing was God's writing"—is a statement made about nothing else in the Torah. *Once again, the Torah emphasizes the unique importance of the Ten Commandments.*

For reasons I do not fully understand, many traditional Jews have objected to this conclusion, maintaining it is wrong to categorize any of the Torah's words as more significant than any others.

The prominent Jewish philosopher, Ernst Simon, did not agree with that view. He argued that while all of the Torah is divine and binding, certain chapters and verses are more religiously significant than others.

Responding to Simon's argument, another Jewish writer, defending the view that all the Torah's words are equally significant and holy, wrote the words of the *Sh'ma*—the Jewish credo, "Hear O Israel, the Lord is our God, the Lord is one" (Deuteronomy 6:4)—have no greater sanctity than the words, "And Timnah was a concubine" (Genesis 36:12).

To which Simon responded (I paraphrase):

On some theoretical level, perhaps you are right. But throughout history thousands upon thousands of Jews went to their deaths with the words "Hear, O Israel, the Lord is our God, the Lord is one" on their lips. I have yet to hear of any Jews going to their death with the words, "And Timnah was a concubine," on their lips.

32.17 When Joshua heard the sound of the people in its boisterousness,

Joshua was neither at the top of Mount Sinai with Moses nor involved in the Golden Calf proceedings.

32.17 (cont.) he said to Moses, "There is a cry of war in the camp."

The people were engaged in a ritualistic orgy, the sounds of which struck Joshua as those of a war camp.

32.18 But he answered, "It is not the sound of the tune of triumph, or the sound of the tune of defeat; it is the sound of song that I hear!"

32.19 As soon as Moses came near the camp and saw the calf and the dancing, he became enraged;

The same Hebrew words, "he became enraged" (*va-yichar af*), were used to describe God's reaction to the Golden Calf in verse 10. Moses reacted exactly as God did.

Moses had already heard from God about the people's idolatry, but only when he saw it with his own eyes did he become enraged; until then his primary concern was protecting the Israelites from God's rage. Now that he knew they were in no danger of being destroyed, he allowed his anger to emerge. This is reminiscent of a parent who is worried sick when a child has broken curfew by many hours. Only once the child has finally come home safe can the parent let his or her fury emerge.

The verse demonstrates the truism that seeing is more emotionally powerful than hearing. Indeed, seeing is so compelling it can block rational or intellectual perception. For this reason, the Torah trusts the ear more than the eye. It therefore strongly cautions us against being led astray by our eyes. For example, the literal translation of Numbers 15:39 is, "Do not prostitute yourselves by following your heart *and your eyes*"; and the Ten Commandments forbid making graven images. This may also be why the Torah's credo reads, "*Hear*," not "*See*," "O Israel...."

> *God's threat to destroy the Israelites should make it more than clear—once again—the Torah is not in the least ethnically or religiously chauvinistic.*

32.19 (cont.) And he hurled the tablets from his hands and shattered them at the foot of the mountain.

It is hard to know whether God was pleased or displeased at Moses's shattering of the tablets. In Exodus 34:1, God adds the words "which you shattered" when describing the first set of the Ten Commandments. Those words were not necessary, thereby implying some annoyance on God's part.

On the other hand, God never actually rebuked Moses for breaking the tablets. Moreover, the Bible commentator Benno Jacob suggests God might not have forgiven the Israelites' sin had Moses not gotten as angry as he did. It was, in Jacob's view, Moses's three rational arguments combined with his raw emotional reaction that softened God's judgment of the people. Righteous anger is legitimate anger.

Moses may have broken the tablets not just out of anger, but also in a deliberate attempt to make a statement to the people about the gravity of their sin.

And perhaps Moses wanted to make the statement that, after having broken at least one, and possibly two, of the Ten Commandments—the prohibitions against idolatry and adultery (verse 6 strongly implies sexual misconduct; see also the commentary to verse 21)—the Israelites no longer deserved the Ten Commandments.

32.20 He took the calf that they had made and burned it;

Moses does not say anything to the people by way of rebuke: what is there to say? They surely knew they were guilty. And in this case certainly, his actions spoke louder than any words.

32.20 (cont.) he ground it to powder and strewed it upon the water and so made the Israelites drink it.

Moses forced the people to drink of the waters containing the ashes of the calf to rub their faces in their sin. Gunther Plaut declares this "an immediate psychological punishment."

32.21 Moses said to Aaron, "What did this people do to you that you have brought such great sin upon them?"

Moses did not address the Israelites directly; he simply made them drink the water. His first words were directed at Aaron. Although God never told Moses Aaron was responsible for the building of the calf, Moses faults his brother because he was the one left in charge of the people. In accusing Aaron, Moses is teaching his older brother an important lesson: A leader is deemed responsible for what happens under his leadership. If a leader does not want his followers to do something, he must do whatever he can to stop them.

The expression "great sin" is a legal term found in ancient Near Eastern marriage documents: "It always refers to adultery, suggesting here that the worship of the Golden Calf is an act of gross infidelity."[2] Joseph uses a similar term when Potiphar's wife tries to seduce him (Genesis 39:9).

32.22 Aaron said, "Let not my lord be enraged.

Although Aaron is Moses's older brother, he refers to Moses as "my lord" because he realizes Moses is the people's, and therefore Aaron's, leader. He is also probably terrified of Moses's anger. He just saw his brother destroy something made by God; he can only wonder what Moses might now do to him.

Aaron is in many ways a tragic figure, even before losing his two sons (Leviticus 10:1-2). He is saddled with the burdens of leadership, but does not get any of the benefits Moses received. He must lead a difficult, quarrelsome people in Moses's absence, but he has only a few personal encounters with God (and one of them is particularly unpleasant: see Numbers 12:2). And perhaps most difficult of all, Moses is Aaron's younger brother (and calling one's younger brother "my lord" cannot be an easy thing to do).

32.22 (cont.) You know that this people is bent on evil."

Aaron knows Moses has also been frustrated by the Israelites, so he first tries to elicit Moses's sympathy by blaming the people. This is not likely to work, however. For one thing, Moses repeatedly stood up to the Israelites and expected Aaron to do so as well. For another, if Moses was able to stand up to God in the people's defense, he will certainly be able to stand up to his brother.

32.23 They said to me, 'Make us a god to lead us; for that man Moses, who brought us from the land of Egypt—we do not know what has happened to him.'

Cassuto explains that Aaron is very worried Moses will think he participated in idolatry—about as serious a sin as he could commit. So he stresses to Moses the calf was intended not as a substitute for God, but as a substitute for Moses.

In quoting the Israelites, Aaron may also be leveling a subtle criticism at Moses for failing to come down the mountain sooner, thereby causing the people to panic in his absence.

32.24 So I said to them, 'Whoever has gold, take it off!'

This is the only time Aaron mentions any of the tactics he used to delay or discourage the people.

32.24 (cont.) They gave it to me and I hurled it into the fire and out came this calf!"

Aaron speaks like a young child trying to evade responsibility. There is probably no child yet born who, after spilling, let us say, grape juice on an expensive tablecloth, said to his parent, "I spilled it." Rather, every child says, "It spilled."

Instead of admitting he was the one who fashioned the calf out of the people's jewelry, he instead suggests the calf simply "came out."

After offering this irrational final plea, and again receiving no response, Aaron realizes he has nothing more to say.

32.25 Moses saw that the people were out of control—

Between idolatry and ritual sex, the people are indeed out of control.

32.25 (cont.) since Aaron had let them get out of control

We get Moses's reaction immediately: The reason the people were out of control was "Aaron had let them get out of control."

Aaron is guilty.

Benno Jacob calls attention to the self-critical nature of this verse and of the Hebrew Bible in general. The Jews never tried to expunge negative descriptions of themselves from the Torah. And, one might add, if the Jews did not always believe the Torah was a divine document, they almost surely would have attempted to alter the text to whitewash their past.

Seeing is more emotionally powerful than hearing.

32.25 (cont.) —so that they were a menace to any who might oppose them.

Anyone who does not control himself is a menace to others. Self-control is the mother of virtues. In our time, generations of young people have been raised by parents who have stressed self-esteem far more than self-control. And the results have not been good. Self-esteem derived from having self-control is a good thing; self-esteem without self-control is dangerous.

32.26 Moses stood up in the gate of the camp and said, "Whoever is for the Lord, come here!" And all the Levites rallied to him.

It seems unlikely no one from any other tribe rallied to Moses. Perhaps this verse should be interpreted to mean the Levites were the only ones to come forward as a group.

32.27 He said to them, "Thus says the Lord, the God of Israel: Each of you put sword on thigh, go back and forth from gate to gate throughout the camp, and slay brother, neighbor, and kin."

Instead of following His original plan to destroy the entire people, God instructed the Levites to kill off those who were, presumably, the leading offenders. God singles out "brother, neighbor, and kin" so the Levites do not engage in nepotism. They are supposed to kill even those wrongdoers who are closest to them. This might be one reason why God wants all the executioners to be from this one tribe, since few of those who will be executed will be their relatives.

Self-control is the mother of virtues. In our time, generations of young people have been raised by parents who have stressed self-esteem far more than self-control. And the results have not been good.

This is most certainly a difficult order for us to read today. But one should recall this was a one-time order in a time of emergency, with the future of ethical monotheism on the line, and only those directly involved in creating the Golden Calf were to be killed.

32.28 The Levites did as Moses had bidden; and some three thousand of the people fell that day.

32.29 And Moses said, "Dedicate yourselves to the Lord this day—for each of you has been against son and brother—that He may bestow a blessing upon you today."

Moses assures the Levites he understands how difficult it was for them to kill family, fellow Levites, and Israelites. The Levites are soon honored with the role of serving the priests in the Tabernacle. It would appear from Moses's description no one killed—or would have been allowed to kill—a parent.

32.30 The next day Moses said to the people, "You have been guilty of a great sin.

Moses has finally calmed down enough to address the people directly about the nature of their sin.

Rarely does a leader condemn his people as a whole. Yet Moses realizes there is such a thing as collective guilt—a subject discussed previously (see the

Exodus 7:4 essay, "Is There Such a Thing as Collective Guilt?"). Abraham Joshua Heschel put it this way: "Some are guilty, but all are responsible."

32.30 (cont.) Yet I will now go up to the Lord; perhaps I may win forgiveness for your sin."

Moses does not say perhaps God will forgive the people; he says perhaps he will be able to win them forgiveness. This statement demonstrates Moses is well aware that even his power is limited when it comes to negotiating with God. While God dropped His threat to destroy the people, He had not yet forgiven them.

32.31 Moses went back to the Lord and said, "Alas, this people is guilty of a great sin in making for themselves a god of gold.

32.32 Now, if You will forgive their sin [well and good]; but if not, erase me from the record You have written!"

Despite his revulsion at the people's behavior, Moses puts himself on the line for their sake. If God will not forgive the Israelites, Moses no longer wants to be a part of God's plan.

32.33 But the Lord said to Moses, "He who has sinned against Me, him only will I erase from My record.

Despite Moses's tremendous boldness, God never tells him to remember his place. God promises not to erase the record of the entire Israelite nation; He will only wipe out those who have sinned.

The notion of being wiped out from God's book cannot simply refer to death, since, after all, we all die. This, then, is probably another Torah indication that there is an afterlife. What else can "erased from My record" mean?

32.34 Go now, lead the people where I told you. See, My angel shall go before you. But when I make an accounting, I will bring them to account for their sins."

Every generation tends to remake God in its own image. In modern times, with its psychological and therapeutic mindset, many people tend to think of God as a loving therapist Who is always there to listen, to understand, and most importantly, not to judge us. This verse reminds us that above all, the God of the Torah is a moral judge. He demands certain behavior, and holds people accountable when they fail to live accordingly.

32.35 Then the Lord sent a plague upon the people, for what they did with the calf that Aaron made. This chapter closes by holding both Aaron and the people responsible for the Golden Calf. Why, then, wasn't Aaron killed as well? The only reason would seem to be Aaron was in no way a leader in making the calf. He was the leader who failed to prevent the making of the Calf.

CHAPTER

33

33.1 Then the Lord said to Moses, "Set out from here, you and the people that you have brought up from the land of Egypt,

> God is still angry. Once again, not wanting to take credit for liberating the Israelites, He refers to them as Moses's people— "the people that *you* have brought"—not His people. God's choice of words is reminiscent of an angry parent saying to his or her spouse, "Do you know what your son/daughter did?"

33.1 (cont.) to the land of which I swore to Abraham, Isaac, and Jacob, saying, 'To your offspring will I give it' —

> Though still angry at the Israelites, God does not renege on the promise He made to their forefathers. Even if we are justifiably angry, we still have to do the right thing—such as, in this case, keeping our word.

33.2 I will send an angel before you, and I will drive out the Canaanites, the Amorites, the Hittites, the Perizzites, the Hivites, and the Jebusites—

> Although the Hebrew word *malach* has come to mean "angel," in the Torah it means a messenger sent by God to accomplish His will. Sometimes these messengers are humans who are not even aware they are playing this role.
>
> The idea of God driving these nations from the land to make way for His Chosen People certainly appears morally troubling. However, elsewhere in the Torah, God makes it clear the nations dwelling in Canaan will only be

removed once their behavior becomes so evil they deserve to be expelled (see, for example, Genesis 15:16 and Deuteronomy 9:4-5). Furthermore, later in the Torah, God warns the Israelites that if they do not behave decently, they, too, will be forced out of the land (see, for example, Leviticus 18:28). There, is, however, one difference: The land remains a permanent inheritance of the Jewish people, even when they are expelled from the land.

> *The Torah does not refer to Israel as a "holy land" because the land is not inherently holy. It is the responsibility of the Jews to make the land holy through their behavior.*

33.3 a land flowing with milk and honey.

Significantly, the Torah does not refer to Israel as a "holy land" because the land is not inherently holy. Rather, it is the responsibility of the Jews to make the land holy through their behavior.

33.3 (cont.) But I will not go in your midst, since you are a stiffnecked people, lest I destroy you on the way."

The Torah view is the purpose of the Chosen People is to bring the world to God and His moral law. When Jews abandon God, they have abandoned their reason for existence. In the words of one of Judaism's earliest philosophic works, the ninth-century *Book of Beliefs and Opinions* (*Emunot ve-Deot*), Saadia Gaon wrote: "Our nation is only a nation by virtue of its Torah."

The Jews are not a people defined by a distinct ethnicity (there are Jews of every ethnicity). They are a people defined by a distinct idea and set of principles.

33.4 When the people heard this harsh word, they went into mourning, and none put on his finery.

The people are deeply distressed to learn of God's reaction to them—He no longer wishes to dwell among them.

This phrase is out of chronological order. It should come after the next verse, verse 5, in which God tells Moses the people should remove their ornaments.

33.5 The Lord said to Moses, "Say to the Israelite people, 'You are a stiffnecked people. If I were to go in your midst for one moment, I would destroy you. Now, then, leave off your finery, and I will consider what to do to you.'"

33.6 So the Israelites remained stripped of the finery from Mount Horeb on.

Umberto Cassuto points out this Hebrew word, *vayitnatzlu*, is closely similar to the one used to describe the Israelites stripping the Egyptians of their jewelry before leaving Egypt, *vayinatzlu* (in 12:36; see also 3:22). This literary parallel suggests the finery the Israelites are now removing from their bodies is the loot they took from the Egyptians during the Exodus.

Mount Horeb is another name for Mount Sinai.

> *God's essence is goodness. Many people say "God is love." However, while goodness and love are often related, they can be very different from one another.*

33.7 Now Moses would take the Tent and pitch it outside the camp, at some distance from the camp. It was called the Tent of Meeting, and whoever sought the Lord would go out to the Tent of Meeting that was outside the camp.

Verses 7-11 describe the nature of Moses's relationship with God. Although they interrupt the narrative, they serve as a parenthetical introduction to Moses's attempt to get to know God better in verses 12-23.

33.8 Whenever Moses went out to the Tent, all the people would rise and stand, each at the entrance of his tent, and gaze after Moses until he had entered the Tent.

33.9 And when Moses entered the Tent, the pillar of cloud would descend and stand at the entrance of the Tent, while He spoke with Moses.

33.10 When all the people saw the pillar of cloud poised at the entrance of the Tent, all the people would rise and bow low, each at the entrance of his tent.

33.11 The Lord would speak to Moses face to face, as one man speaks to another.

As the Torah says God has no face and no physical form (Deuteronomy 4:12), this verse is not to be taken literally—anymore than we would take the expression "to lose face" literally. The expression is meant to convey that the communication between Moses and God was as direct as that of one person to another—not, for example, via a dream (see Genesis 20:3-7) or a vision (Isaiah 1:1 is commonly translated as "the prophecies of Isaiah," but literally means, "the visions of Isaiah"). The unparalleled intimate nature of God's relationship to Moses is described at the Torah's end: "Never again did there arise in Israel a prophet like Moses—whom the Lord singled out face to face" (Deuteronomy 34:10).

33.11 (cont.) And he would then return to the camp; but his attendant, Joshua son of Nun, a youth, would not stir out of the Tent.

33.12 Moses said to the Lord, "See, You say to me, 'Lead this people forward,' but You have not made known to me whom You will send with me.

Moses does not know the identity of the "angel" to whom God refers in verse 2.

33.12 (cont.) Further, You have said, 'I have singled you out by name, and you have, indeed, gained My favor.'

33.13 Now, if I have truly gained Your favor, pray let me know Your ways, that I may know You and continue in Your favor.

Although Moses is closer to God than any other human being (Deuteronomy 34:10), he still has questions about Him. If this is true regarding human beings—as close as we may be to other people, we never feel we understand them completely—it is infinitely more so with regard to understanding God.

33.13 (cont.) Consider, too, that this nation is Your people."

Moses is responding to God's statement the Israelites are "the people that you [Moses] have brought up from the land of Egypt" (verse 1). He is reminding God it was God Who took them out of Egypt, and they are His people.

33.14 And He said, "I will go in the lead and will lighten your burden."

33.15 And he said to Him, "Unless You go in the lead, do not make us leave this place.

Moses and God are engaged in a give-and-take. In this verse, Moses asks God to resume His place in front of the people, to lead them through the wilderness, before the Israelites continue their journey.

What Has Distinguished—and Sustained—the Jews?

33.16 For how shall it be known that Your people have gained Your favor unless You go with us, so that we may be distinguished, Your people and I, from every people on the face of the earth?"

Moses's statement embodies a profound truth about the Jews: The Israelites then, and the Jewish people later, have indeed been "distinguished...from every people on the face on the earth" because they have affirmed God and "His way." When Jews have abandoned God and the Torah, little or nothing has remained distinctive about them, and they simply assimilated into their host societies.

Ultimately, there can be no lasting, exclusively secular Jewish culture. Nothing secular ever united the Jews for an extended period. In the early twentieth century, an effort was made to unite Jews around the Yiddish language, but the Yiddish language and culture were shared only by Central and Eastern European Jews. Yiddish was unknown to the Jews of the Arab and Spanish world, just as the Ladino language spoken by Spanish Jews and many Jews in the orbit of Islam was unknown to Central and Eastern European Jews.

Zionism (the Jewish national movement to re-establish the Jewish state in its ancient homeland) came close to uniting nearly all Jews. Secular Jews founded and led Zionism, and almost all religious Jews came to strongly identify with Israel. But over time, many secular Jews have lost interest in Zionism (and a small number of ultra-Orthodox Jews never accepted it).

Only their religious essence has, as the verse says, "distinguished" Jews and thereby sustained them.

CAN HUMANS CHANGE GOD'S MIND?

33.17 And the Lord said to Moses, "I will also do this thing that you have asked; for you have truly gained My favor and I have singled you out by name."

Moses has succeeded in changing God's mind: God has agreed to resume leading the people again. The notion that a human being can change God's mind may at first seem logically impossible (and generally it is true God does not change His mind: Numbers 23:19). After all, isn't God infallible?

God is indeed infallible. But the human ability to change God's mind or behavior does not mean God makes mistakes; it means God is affected by human beings.

The notion that God is open to human influence is, of course, what animates prayer in all religions that believe in the God of the Torah. The God of the Torah is not Aristotle's "unmoved mover." He is a "movable mover."

In other words, God takes human beings very seriously.

33.18 He said, "O, let me behold Your Presence!"

Even with all the intimate interaction he's had with God since the burning bush, Moses yearns to better know God.

ESSAY: IS GOD GOOD OR IS GOD LOVE?

33.19 And He answered, "I will make all My goodness pass before you,

When Moses asks God to allow him to behold God's presence—to reveal His essence—what is it God reveals?

His goodness.

God's essence is goodness.

Many people say, "God is love." However, while goodness and love are often related, they can be very different from one another.

Many people who have been filled with love—for country, for humanity, for the planet, for their religion, for their god—have not been good people. This is also true regarding love for people. It is possible to feel love for another person and treat him or her badly. Many men and women who feel love for their spouses abuse them physically or verbally. Many abusive parents love their children (or at least think they do).

> *Good people, by definition, do good—whether or not they happen to have loving feelings.*

As beautiful as love can be, it is, in fact, amoral. Love is moral depending on what or whom one loves, and how one expresses it. Vast numbers of people have loved bad individuals—think of the millions who have loved Hitler, Stalin, and other murderous tyrants. On a micro level, think of the women who fall in love with terrible men.

On the other hand, while many people who feel loving do bad things, good people, *by definition*, do good—whether or not they happen to have loving feelings.

That God chooses to define Himself as good constitutes one of the most important statements in the entire Bible. God does not say, "I will make my love pass before you." In fact, the expression, "God is love," is not to be found in the Hebrew Bible.

While love can (and should) mean loving action, it is usually understood to mean a feeling. Goodness, on the other hand, always implies action. And the Torah is first and foremost concerned with how humans act, not how we feel. Whether or not we love others, what matters most is whether we do good for them. (Regarding the best-known verse in the Torah, "Love your neighbor as yourself," see the commentary to Leviticus 19:18.)

This verse is of extreme significance for another reason.

The most important leap of faith we humans must make vis-à-vis God is not believing that He exists. That a Creator exists is more a logical deduction than a leap of faith. The evidence for a Creator is logical; the atheist position that everything exists by sheer accident—everything came from nothing, life somehow sprang from non-life—is less logical.

But the belief that God is good *is* a statement of faith. Given all the unjust suffering in the world, logic alone does not necessarily lead one to conclude the Creator is good. The title character in Archibald MacLeish's play *J.B.* summed up the problem of believing in God's goodness in these words: "If God is God, He is not good; if God is good, He is not God."

So, given the understandable human questioning of God's goodness, God asserts here, first and foremost, He is good.

Now, putting faith aside, are there *reasons* to believe God is good? I think there are.

First, the only alternative is to believe God is indifferent to suffering or evil. But the amount of good on earth, the fact humanity only thrives when good thrives, the fact the great majority of people are happiest when they are good, all argue for a good God.

And second, the supreme revelation—the Ten Commandments—God introduced to the world in the Torah is very strong evidence God is good. Only a good God would give humanity laws of goodness.

Finally, a good God means a judging God, a God who ultimately dispenses justice—meaning reward for the good and punishment for the evil.

33.19 (cont.) and I will proclaim before you the name Lord, and the grace that I grant and the compassion that I show.

DOES GOD HAVE A FACE?

33.20 "But," He said, "you cannot see My face, for man may not see Me and live."

What does God mean by the words, "My face"? The phrase in this context is ambiguous. Either God really has a face, but people would die if they saw it, or else God does not have a face—at least, as we know a face—and only after death can people have any knowledge (if there is any such knowledge to be had) of God's "appearance."

The latter explanation seems more plausible since it is consistent with the notion of an invisible and incorporeal God. Richard Elliott Friedman notes Moses told the Israelites "you saw no shape when the Lord your God spoke to you out of the fire," (Deuteronomy 4:15) yet just one chapter he later declares, "Face to face the Lord spoke to you out of the mountain from the fire" (Deuteronomy 5:4).

"This is further confirmation," Friedman notes, "that 'face-to-face' is not a literal expression. Like many Hebrew expressions involving the word 'face,' it is an idiom. It is used metaphorically to mean direct, personal communication, not mediated by any third party."[1]

33.21 And the Lord said, "See, there is a place near Me. Station yourself on the rock

33.22 and, as My Presence passes by, I will put you in a cleft of the rock and shield you with My hand until I have passed by.

33.23 Then I will take My hand away and you will see My back; but My face must not be seen."
God tells Moses he can only see God's back but not His face. Clearly, whatever it was Moses experienced is, like Moses's other interactions with God, something that cannot be described in terms understandable to us. On a more metaphorical level, perhaps God's statement may be interpreted to mean man can see what God has wrought in the past. Generally speaking, man can perceive God's involvement only after such involvement, but not during it.

CHAPTER
~34~

34.1 The Lord said to Moses: "Carve two tablets of stone like the first, and I will inscribe upon the tablets

> God carved the first set of tablets. But Moses has to carve the second set. He broke them; he must replace them.

34.1 (cont.) the words that were on the first tablets, which you shattered.

> God could have simply said, "the first tablets." That He added the words "which you shattered" suggests God is at least somewhat displeased with Moses for losing his temper and breaking the first set.
>
> The other famous loss of temper by Moses (Numbers 20) resulted in his being forbidden to enter the Promised Land. To be fair, on both occasions, it was the result of completely understandable exasperation with his people.

34.2 Be ready by morning, and in the morning come up to Mount Sinai and present yourself there to Me, on the top of the mountain.

34.3 No one else shall come up with you, and no one else shall be seen anywhere on the mountain; neither shall the flocks and the herds graze at the foot of this mountain."

34.4 So Moses carved two tablets of stone, like the first, and early in the morning he went up on Mount Sinai, as the Lord had commanded him, taking the two stone tablets with him.

34.5 The Lord came down in a cloud; He stood with him there,

God provides Moses with an answer to his request in the previous chapter: "Pray let me know Your ways" (Exodus 33:13).

34.5 (cont.) and proclaimed the name Lord.

ESSAY: THE ATTRIBUTES OF GOD

34.6 The Lord passed before him and proclaimed: "The Lord! the Lord! a God compassionate and gracious, slow to anger, abounding in kindness and faithfulness,

34.7 extending kindness to the thousandth generation, forgiving iniquity, transgression, and sin;

> Friedman notes, "this is possibly the most repeated and quoted formula" in the Hebrew Bible: Numbers 14:18-19; Jonah 4:2; Joel 2:13; Micah 7:18; Psalms 86:15, 103:8, 145:8; 2 Chronicles 30:9; and Nehemiah 9:17, 31.

34.7 (cont.) yet He does not remit all punishment, yet He does not clear the guilty but visits the iniquity of parents upon children and children's children, upon the third and fourth generations."

> Verses 6 and 7 consist of a list of the attributes God ascribes to Himself. Although Judaism traditionally divides this list into thirteen attributes, there are nine distinct characteristics enumerated here.
>
> 1. Compassionate
>
> The Hebrew word for compassionate, *rachum*, comes from *rechem*, the Hebrew word for "womb." The use of this term suggests God's feelings toward humanity resemble those of a mother toward the children who come out of her womb.
>
> 2. Gracious
>
> 3. Slow to anger
>
> God gets angry at people, but it takes a great deal to make Him angry (otherwise, given the state of human behavior, He would presumably be in a permanent state of anger). And because God is slow to anger, people have time to repent before He exacts any harsh punishments.
>
> 4. Abounding in kindness

The Hebrew word *chesed*, translated here as "kindness," refers to a form of extraordinary kindness above and beyond the call of duty (hence, it is often translated as loving-kindness). A prime example of *chesed* offered by the Jewish tradition is the act of preparing dead bodies for burial—because the dead cannot express gratitude, let alone return the favor.

> *A prime example of chesed (kindness) offered by the Jewish tradition is preparing dead bodies for burial—because the dead cannot express gratitude, let alone return the favor.*

5. Abounding in faithfulness

The word translated as "faithfulness" literally means truth. God is true to His word, promises, vows, and standards. One of God's attributes is truth because goodness cannot exist without truth. Indeed, most great evils are based on lies. (See the essay, "The Ninth Commandment: Lies Cause the Greatest Evils," in the commentary to Exodus 20:13.)

6. Extending kindness to the thousandth generation

7. Forgiving sin

8. Not clearing the guilty

Friedman comments that though the central focus of most of these attributes is kindness and graciousness, this attribute, "not clearing the guilty...conveys that this does not mean that one can just get away with anything; there is still justice."

That God does not "clear" the guilty means there is ultimate justice—another strong hint there is an afterlife where the guilty are punished (and the good rewarded) because that is surely not the rule in this life.

9. Remembering the sins of parents unto the third and fourth generation

As noted in the comments to Exodus 20:5, the Hebrew word *po-ked*, often translated as "visits," actually means "remembers," or "takes account of." The second part of the verse therefore literally reads, "God remembers the iniquity of parents upon children and children's children, upon the third and fourth generations."

This verse does not mean God punishes children for their parents' sins. The Torah itself commands that "Parents shall not be put to death for children, nor children for parents. A person shall be put to death only for his own sins" (Deuteronomy 24:16).

> *The children of people who do evil often suffer more shame than the parents of people who do evil.*

The intent is to communicate that, though God takes into account the good done by people for a thousand generations, He remembers the bad done by people for only three to four generations. It may simply be a poetic statement of God's favoring the good.

Nevertheless, life—not necessarily God—does often punish children for parents' sins. The children of people who do evil often suffer even more shame than the parents of people who do evil.

This verse describes another way in which the world works. When parents do bad things, their children, knowing no other model, often follow in their footsteps. Children born to abusive parents, for example, often go on to abuse children (their own and/or others'). Children who have a parent in prison or addicted to alcohol or drugs, or who have been abandoned by a parent, often suffer lifelong psychic and emotional damage. This verse may therefore be understood as a warning to parents to avoid evil for the sake of their children, if for no other reason.

34.8 Moses hastened to bow low to the ground in homage,

34.9 and said, "If I have gained Your favor, O Lord, pray, let the Lord go in our midst,

Moses is reacting to God's declaration He is too angry with the people to walk among them, and will therefore send a messenger in His stead (see 32:34). Moses now beseeches God to revoke this pronouncement.

Moses says, "in our midst," not "in their midst," because he considers himself a part of the people. Whatever the Israelites' misbehavior, Moses remains dedicated to them and continues to include himself among them.

34.9 (cont.) even though this is a stiffnecked people. Pardon our iniquity and our sin, and take us for Your own!"

Moses echoes God's assessment of the people as "stiff-necked" (see 32:9). However, he disagrees with how to respond to this failing. God wants to withdraw from them, but Moses asks God to forgive them and to walk among them.

Moses's plea lends itself to two possible interpretations.

He may be saying that given the Israelites' stubborn nature, God should consider forgiving their sins and walk among them. In life, we all occasionally do this: understand that someone we love has a certain undesirable characteristic, yet we forgive him or her the behaviors that arise from that characteristic.

Alternatively, Moses may be saying that since the Israelites are so stubborn, they need God to walk in their midst to guide them and help them learn to behave in a way worthy of forgiveness.

34.10 He said: I hereby make a covenant.

In a covenant, each side has responsibilities to the other. In this verse and the next, God tells Moses what He will do to fulfill His half of the covenant. In all the subsequent verses in this chapter, God tells Moses what the people will have to do in exchange.

34.10 (cont.) Before all your people I will work such wonders as have not been wrought on all the earth or in any nation;

God once again refers to the Israelites as "your people" rather than "My people," thereby making it clear He is still angry with them. Although God is slow to anger (see verse 6), it might be said when He does not see true repentance, His anger is slow to abate.

34.10 (cont.) and all the people who are with you shall see how awesome are the Lord's deeds which I will perform for you.

The Hebrew word used here, *imach* ("for you"), is in the singular, which suggests God will perform wonders for Moses's sake rather than for the sake of the nation. Though still angry at the people, God is willing to establish a covenant with them because of the merit of their leader, who has interceded on their behalf.

34.11 Mark well what I command you this day. I will drive out before you the Amorites, the Canaanites, the Hittites, the Perizzites, the Hivites, and the Jebusites.

34.12 Beware of making a covenant with the inhabitants of the land against which you are advancing, lest they be a snare in your midst.

The pagan values and beliefs of the Canaanite nations would simply be too tempting to a people new to ethical monotheism (clearly demonstrated by their behavior just two chapters earlier with the Golden Calf). Hence, God does not want the Israelites making any treaties with them. However, it is important to note the ban on making covenants refers to specific nations; there is no ban in perpetuity on making covenants with non-Israelite nations.

Only in the Holy Land Must Pagan Places of Worship Be Destroyed

34.13 No, you must tear down their altars, smash their pillars, and cut down their sacred posts;

God commands the Israelites to destroy the Canaanites' places of worship, not to kill the Canaanites. The only divinely sanctioned violence here is against inanimate objects. (With regard to Deuteronomy 20:17, where Moses—not God—instructs the Israelites to kill the Canaanites, see the commentary there.)

As noted previously, neither the Israelites then nor the Jewish people later are ever commanded to destroy pagan places of worship outside Israel. But it would have been impossible to establish ethical monotheism in the Holy Land if pagan places of worship—with their human sacrifices and cult orgies—were allowed to remain.

34.14 for you must not worship any other god, because the Lord, whose name is Impassioned, is an impassioned God.

> If the Israelites worship other gods, they are nullifying the purpose of the Exodus and of their existence as a nation.

PROSTITUTES ARE NOT THE WORST FORM OF PROSTITUTION

34.15 You must not make a covenant with the inhabitants of the land, for they will lust after their gods and sacrifice to their gods and invite you, and you will eat of their sacrifices.

> Regarding covenants with the Canaanite nations, see comments to 34:12.
>
> The word translated as "they will lust" literally means "and they will prostitute themselves." Among the abhorrent practices to ensue if the Israelites followed the Canaanite gods was the Israelite God and religion would become sexualized. Pagan worship often involved cult prostitution and sexual displays on the altar. The Torah, in contrast, insists God is not a sexual being and sex has no place in religious worship.
>
> Metaphorically speaking, people "prostitute themselves" whenever they compromise their higher values, whether for money, success, fame, or anything else people crave. A prostitute sells her body for money. A crook sells his character for money. A crooked politician sells his influence for money. People sell their souls—prostitute themselves—for a whole host of desired things. And one might say such individuals are considerably worse than a prostitute. She sells her body, they sell their souls; and crooks and others who prostitute their values do greater harm to society than prostitutes.
>
> Note:
>
> a) the positive way in which the Hebrew Bible depicts the prostitute Rahab (Joshua 2). (The Talmud went so far as to claim Rahab became a Jew, married

The later depiction by various religious groups of prostitution as among the greatest of sins and of prostitutes as among the lowest of people is more a cultural construct than a Bible-based value.

Joshua, Moses's successor, and that generations later the Prophet Jeremiah descended from her)[1];

b) the sympathetic depiction of Tamar who, though not a prostitute, on one occasion acted as a prostitute for a noble end (Genesis 38);

c) the Torah never depicts a prostitute as evil (although, of course, child prostitution [Leviticus 19:29] and cult prostitution are declared evil).

The Torah does deplore prostitution: The verse just cited (Leviticus 19:29) reads in full: "Do not profane your daughter, to cause her to be a whore; lest the land fall to whoredom, and the land become full of wickedness." Nevertheless, the post-biblical assessment by various religious groups and cultures of prostitution as among the greatest of sins, and of prostitutes as among the lowest of people, is more a cultural construct than a Bible-based value.

THE PROBLEM WITH MARRYING CANAANITE WOMEN

34.16 And when you take wives from among their daughters for your sons, their daughters will lust after their gods and will cause your sons to lust after their gods.

The Israelites are warned if their sons marry Canaanite women, their sons will end up following the Canaanite religion. To say women have an immense impact on their husbands is an understatement. And God knew the Israelites were not yet strong in their monotheistic faith (see comment on following verse). Israelite men could easily be led astray by Canaanite wives.

This diversion of Israelite men away from ethical monotheism need not even involve marriage. Just consorting sexually with Canaanite women could easily have led Israelite men to abandon, even if only temporarily, worship of God (see Numbers 25:1-3)—which tells us as much about the power of the male sexual drive as it does about the tenuous hold of the Israelite religion over the Jews at that time.

34.17 You shall not make molten gods for yourselves.

This is, of course, an allusion to the Golden Calf.

WHY WE NEED RELIGIOUS RITUALS

34.18 You shall observe the Feast of Unleavened Bread—eating unleavened bread for seven days, as I have commanded you—

> The rest of this chapter deals with the rituals the Israelites must observe once they enter the Promised Land. These rituals are intended as a way for the Israelites to keep faith in God alive once the land has been conquered and God is no longer intervening with miracles on their behalf. This is one of the major reasons for rituals—to keep faith alive once regular and apparent divine intervention ends.
>
> The following list of ritual commandments comes right after the prohibition against making molten gods. This suggests another important reason for religious rituals. One way people guard against the temptation to create idols and other false gods is by observing regular rituals that keep them focused on the One True God. One of the appeals of idols is they exist physically, whereas God does not. The practice of physical rituals helps keep people attuned to the reality of God's presence; otherwise, God can become too abstract and difficult to connect to. Humans, being physical beings, need some physical connection to God.
>
> This helps explain why Christianity has many fewer ritual laws than Judaism. For Christians, God has taken on a physical form that provides them with a physical connection to God. But for Jews, since God is always non-physical, the way to have a physical connection to God is through ritual.
>
> The Feast of Unleavened Bread, Passover, is mentioned first because, having just experienced the Exodus from Egypt, it is the ritual observance most immediately relevant to the Israelites. Also, eating unleavened bread is a symbolic rejection of Egypt and its values. Given that the Egyptians invented the process of leavening, bread was a symbol of Egypt (just as eating pasta would be banned if one wanted a society to reject Italy).

The seven days of Passover are an echo of the seven days of creation (as is always the case with the number seven in the Torah). The Exodus signifies a new creation—God's Chosen People and ethical monotheism.

For reasons having to do with calculating the new moon—and thereby the date of the holidays—in ancient Israel, and transmitting that information to other Jewish communities, Jews outside of Israel long ago developed the tradition of observing Passover for eight days (and adding a day onto other biblical holidays as well).[2] This led many Jews to overlook the direct connection between Passover and Creation.

34.18 (cont.) at the set time of the month of Abib, for in the month of Abib you went forth from Egypt.
The Hebrew word *Abib* means spring, which is when the holiday of Passover falls each year. The Israelites are commanded to observe this holiday during the spring in order to re-experience the Exodus from Egypt.

34.19 Every first issue of the womb is Mine, from all your livestock that drop a male as firstling, whether cattle or sheep.

34.20 But the firstling of an ass you shall redeem with a sheep; if you do not redeem it, you must break its neck.
See the explanation for this law in Exodus 13:13.

34.20 (cont.) And you must redeem every first-born among your sons. None shall appear before me empty-handed.

Jews today still perform the ritual of the redemption of the firstborn son, which is known as *pidyon ha-ben* (see the commentary to Numbers 18:15-16).

THE SABBATH DEMANDS SACRIFICES

34.21 Six days you shall work, but on the seventh day you shall cease from labor; you shall cease from labor even at plowing time and harvest time.

Living according to God's will generally, and the Ten Commandments specifically, demands making sacrifices. Everything good—every achievement—demands sacrifices. In the case of the Shabbat, that sacrifice is abstaining from work one day each week when doing so may diminish one's income or even employability (for example, in the Jews' early years in America, there were factory owners who would tell Jewish employees on Friday, "If you don't come in on Saturday, don't come in on Monday").

However, as those who observe the Sabbath are well aware, the rewards usually far exceed the sacrifices. No practice in the Torah brings as much joy and elevates a life as does observance of the Shabbat. Leaving the world and its material concerns one day every week is literally and figuratively life-saving. Having prolonged meals with family and/or friends every week is uniquely bonding. And the Shabbat creates a communal life. No wonder it is the one ritual commanded in the Ten Commandments.

34.22 You shall observe the Feast of Weeks, of the first fruits of the wheat harvest;

The Feast of Weeks—in Hebrew, *Shavuot* ("Weeks")—is so named because it is observed exactly seven weeks after Passover. It is also known as Pentecost.

34.22 (cont.) and the Feast of Ingathering at the turn of the year.

The "Feast of Ingathering" is Sukkot, also known as Tabernacles. Since the Israelites will soon be living in an agricultural society, the festivals are connected to the agricultural cycle. But for millennia, Jewish tradition has identified the "Feast of Weeks" with the giving of the Law at Sinai, and the "Feast of Ingathering" with Sukkot, during which Jews are commanded to eat and dwell in temporary booths ("tabernacles") to commemorate the booths in which Jews dwelt during their forty years in the desert.

34.23 Three times a year all your males shall appear before the Sovereign Lord, the God of Israel.

Except for those few men who lived within easy walking distance of the Temple, all the men had to leave their homes three times a year to gather with other men to worship God. Compared to what often draws men together—drinking, gambling, and carousing—this was a rather wholesome activity. There was, however, no prohibition on women—and children, for that matter—joining their husbands on the holiday, and many did. But the commandment was only directed to men.

For Jews, since God is always non-physical, the way to have a physical connection to God is through ritual.

34.24 I will drive out nations from your path and enlarge your territory; no one will covet your land when you go up to appear before the Lord your God three times a year.

Lest the men worry about leaving their homes vulnerable to theft and seizure in their absence, God promises to protect their land while they are away. Otherwise, men would fear leaving their families, livestock, and land.

34.25 You shall not offer the blood of My sacrifice with anything leavened; and the sacrifice of the Feast of Passover shall not be left lying until morning.

34.26 The choice first fruits of your soil you shall bring to the house of the Lord your God. You shall not boil a kid in its mother's milk.

According to the Torah, one is not permitted to boil a kid in the same substance (milk) with which the animal's mother gave it life. This law exists not for the sake of the animal, which is already dead, but to elevate the Israelites. There is something perverse—even mocking and cruel—in cooking a baby animal in its mother's milk. This injunction was considered so important that the Torah states it three times (in this verse, Exodus 23:19; and Deuteronomy 14:21—see the commentary to Exodus 23:19).

The Torah is rooted in distinctions: God-man; male-female; human-animal; and life-death. This law likely concerns the last. God does not want us to symbolically combine death (the dead animal) with life (milk—especially that of its mother, which sustained it). Judaism expanded this law into a general ban on consuming milk and meat at the same time.

34.27 And the Lord said to Moses: Write down these commandments, for in accordance with these commandments I make a covenant with you and with Israel.

34.28 And he was there with the Lord forty days and forty nights; he ate no bread and drank no water; and he wrote down on the tablets the terms of the covenant, the Ten Commandments.

As with the first set of tablets, Moses spent forty days on Mount Sinai. This time, however, the people knew better than to try to replace him or God with an idol.

Under ordinary circumstances, of course, a human being cannot go for forty days without eating, let alone without drinking. The number forty, which recurs throughout the Torah, is a term most likely reflecting something highly significant—usually divinely significant—is taking place: the flood lasts for forty days, the Israelites are in the desert for forty years, and Moses is on Sinai for forty days. All of them are divine miracles and world-altering.

34.29 So Moses came down from Mount Sinai. And as Moses came down from the mountain bearing the two tablets of the Pact, Moses was not aware that the skin of his face was radiant,

Umberto Cassuto points out the many repetitions in the concluding verses of this chapter: the radiant face of Moses is referred to three times; the veil Moses places on his face, three times; and seven references to speaking (in verses 29 to 35).

That the Torah mentions a name three or seven times in a given section cannot be coincidental. Seven, as we have repeatedly seen, almost always hearkens back to creation. But whatever the significance of the number, each serves as a type of embedded code denoting the section is a unified story with a single author.

The Hebrew word for ray (or "radiant"), *karan*, is spelled with the same Hebrew letters as the word for horn, *keren*. As a result, this verse has been misinterpreted to mean Moses came down from Mount Sinai with horns on his face, resulting, for instance, in the famous Michelangelo statue of Moses with horns.

Sarna notes the use of the word *karan* (radiant), so similar to the word *keren* (horn) "is probably a pointed allusion to the golden calf...[and] subtly emphasizes that the true mediator between God and Israel was not the fabricated, lifeless image of the horned animal, as the people thought (Exodus 32:1-4), but the living Moses."

34.29 (cont.) since he had spoken with Him.

34.30 Aaron and all the Israelites saw that the skin of Moses' face was radiant; and they shrank from coming near him.

34.31 But Moses called to them, and Aaron and all the chieftains in the assembly returned to him, and Moses spoke to them.

The Torah does not specify what Moses said to Aaron and the leaders, but it is reasonable to assume he tried to calm and reassure them.

34.32 Afterward all the Israelites came near, and he instructed them concerning all that the Lord had imparted to him on Mount Sinai.

34.33 And when Moses had finished speaking with them, he put a veil over his face.

34.34 Whenever Moses went in before the Lord to speak with Him, he would leave the veil off until he came out; and when he came out and told the Israelites what he had been commanded,

34.35 the Israelites would see how radiant the skin of Moses' face was. Moses would then put the veil back over his face until he went in to speak with Him.

Presumably, Moses does not want the rays of light radiating from his face to intimidate the people.

CHAPTER
～❩35❨～

35.1 Moses then convoked the whole Israelite community and said to them: These are the things that the Lord has commanded you to do:

35.2 On six days work may be done, but on the seventh day you shall have a sabbath of complete rest, holy to the Lord;

> The remainder of Exodus is concerned with the building of the Tabernacle. First, however, the laws of the Sabbath are reiterated to provide the Israelites with an important stipulation: Even though the building of the sanctuary is the holiest work they will engage in, they are not allowed to do it on the Sabbath. In the Torah and later Judaism, time is holier than place, and thus the observance of the holiest day of the week takes precedence over the building of the holiest place. (Mishnah *Shabbat* 7:2 lists thirty-nine types of labor done at the Tabernacle, all of which are forbidden on the Sabbath.)
>
> Abraham Joshua Heschel notes that in the Hebrew Bible, "not even the Promised Land is called holy. While the holiness of the land and the holiness of the festivals depends on the actions of the Jewish people, the holiness of the Shabbat preceded Israel's existence (Genesis 2:3). Even if people fail to observe the Shabbat, it remains holy."[1]

35.2 (cont.) whoever does any work on it shall be put to death.

> The Torah prescribes such a severe punishment for violating the Sabbath to emphasize the severity of the infraction. The Sabbath affirms God created the world—the foundational belief of ethical monotheism, of the new Israelite

nation, and the new and better world that should emanate from them. Without the Sabbath, there will ultimately be no Jewish religion, and no Jewish people.

Hence, the aphorism of the Jewish philosopher Ahad Ha'am, "More than Israel has kept the Sabbath, the Sabbath has kept the Jews." Such an observation has not been made about any other ritual law in the Torah, including kashrut and Yom Kippur.

In the Torah, time is holier than place. Therefore, the observance of the holiest day of the week takes precedence over the building of the holiest place.

In the Ten Commandments, Commandment Two and Commandments Four through Nine carry the death penalty. No Jewish ritual other than the Sabbath is in the Ten Commandments in part because there is no other Jewish ritual for which violators are given the death penalty (though, it is important to add, we have only one instance of this ever being carried out—see the next paragraph). Such is the unique importance of the Shabbat.

Nevertheless, as noted elsewhere, in every case but murder, the overwhelming preponderance of evidence suggests the death penalty was on the books to teach the severity of the offense rather than as an actual punishment to be enacted. With but one exception, we know of no case of an Israelite executed for working on the Sabbath. That exception takes place later (Numbers 15: 32-36), when an Israelite gathers wood in public on the Sabbath. What is noteworthy about that case is that despite this verse—"whoever does any work on it shall be put to death" —the Israelites did not know what to do with the Sabbath violator in Numbers. God had to tell Moses to put the man to death. At the very least, that bears testimony to how rare it was, even 3,000 years ago, to put a person to death for violating the Sabbath.

ESSAY: WHY NO FIRE ON THE SABBATH?

35.3 You shall kindle no fire throughout your settlements on the sabbath day.

There is very little specific legislation in the Torah concerning the Sabbath. The most significant prohibitions, alongside this one, are the ban against plowing and harvesting (Exodus 34:21) and an unclearly-defined prohibition against leaving one's "place" on the Sabbath (which later Jewish law understood as a prohibition against going outside one's city limits [Exodus 16:29]). Today, when a small percentage of the population engages in agricultural work, the prohibition against kindling a fire remains the most relevant Sabbath prohibition in the Torah.

The question, then, is, why? Why is making a fire singled out as forbidden? The key to understanding why is this: whereas the actions the Torah prohibits on Shabbat are also prohibited on the festivals (Passover, Shavuot, and Sukkot), the one exception is making a fire. The Torah prohibits making a fire only on Shabbat.

(The Jerusalem Talmud, citing this verse, states: "'On the Sabbath day you may not light, but you may light on a festival."[2] Observant Jews, however, do not light a fire on a festival, though they permit transferring flame from a pre-existing fire, something forbidden on the Sabbath.)

And why does the Torah ban making a fire on Shabbat but on no other holy days (except Yom Kippur, which is considered "the Sabbath of Sabbaths," and has all the laws pertaining to the Sabbath)?

The answer must lie in the meaning of the Sabbath: to affirm that God is the Creator (by not working or creating on the day God ceased working and creating).

Aside from making new life (conceiving a child, which I will address), making a fire is the ultimate symbolic act of human creation. (Animals, too, make new life, but they do not make fire.)

As only God creates *ex nihilo* (out of nothing), the kindling of fire is the closest humans come to creating. By kindling fire, humans are engaging in an act uniquely close to creating, whereas the purpose of the Sabbath is to refrain from such acts in order to affirm the one Creator is God.

Not only does fire seem to come from nothing; it also has the unique power to transform everything it touches. Everett Fox alludes to this: "Since the Shabbat was apparently to be static in nature, or at least transformative of time alone, fire (which by its nature causes chemical changes) could not be employed." The Sabbath is a time to enjoy the world as it is. The uniquely transformative entity—fire—thus becomes the archetypal Sabbath prohibition.

So, then, why doesn't the Torah prohibit making a child, the only other act that creates something from nothing? For four possible reasons:

First, as noted, animals also make new life. Therefore, making a new life is not uniquely human.

Second, unlike fire, a new human life does not physically transform everything it touches.

Third, as noted, Jewish law understands the Sabbath prohibition on work as applying to the thirty-nine types of work carried out in the building of the Tabernacle. Sexual relations were, of course, not one of those thirty-nine types of work.

Fourth, and most important, the Torah affirms life. Therefore, just as every Torah prohibition may—indeed, must—be violated to save a human life, the prohibition on creating on Shabbat is suspended in order to make a new human life.

The Torah adds the qualification, "Throughout your settlements," because the kindling of fire was allowed in the Tabernacle, and later in the Temple, for the special Sabbath sacrifices. (See Talmud *Shabbat* 20a: the Tabernacle and Temple were not regarded as "settlements.")

One might further ask: If fire is an act of creation, why did the Torah allow it in the Temple?

Because the purpose of the sacrificial fires in the Temple was to affirm the Creator, whereas all other fires—fires "throughout your settlements" —had other purposes.

35.4 Moses said further to the whole community of Israelites: This is what the Lord has commanded:
The Torah now returns to the subject of the Tabernacle.

The instructions for building the Tabernacle were provided in chapters 25–31, where this structure was identified as the means through which God would "dwell amidst the people." The narrative was then interrupted because the people built the Golden Calf, and God threatened He would no longer dwell in their midst. Since Moses has successfully petitioned God to forgive the people and dwell among them, the building of the Tabernacle can resume.

From this point until the end of the Book of Exodus, the actual building of the Tabernacle, as opposed to instructions for how it is to be built, is recorded.

Regarding this repetition, some Bible scholars explain the Torah was written in accordance with different literary conventions than we are accustomed to today. For instance, Umberto Cassuto argues ancient Near Eastern religious texts often dealt with the founding and building of a shrine and most of these narratives would contain two parallel passages: The first passage would describe the plan of the shrine in minute detail and the second would give an account of the construction using identical or similar phrasing. In this regard, this repetition is typical of literary texts of its time.

> *Why is kindling a fire prohibited on the Sabbath? By kindling a fire, humans are acting as if they create, whereas the purpose of the Sabbath is to affirm that the one Creator is God.*

Benno Jacob points out that whereas chapters 25–31 represent a continuous, uninterrupted address given by God to Moses, chapters 35–40 are filled with dramatic action. Therefore, the narratives supplement rather than solely replicate one another (though there is, as repeatedly noted in chapters 36–40, much replication).

35.5 Take from among you gifts to the Lord; everyone whose heart so moves him shall bring them—gifts for the Lord: gold, silver, and copper;

The laws of donating to the Tabernacle are very different from the laws concerning donating to the poor. Given that God has no need of gifts, He wants gifts offered to Him to be voluntary. In contrast, the poor do need donations, and therefore such help must be commanded (Deuteronomy 26:12) and not be dependent on voluntary contributions.

Since the people were instructed to bring only as much as they felt moved to contribute, the following account of what they brought seems to reflect a deep desire to connect with God. The list of items in this chapter is therefore not merely a repetition of the list provided earlier by God (see 25.1-7), but also a testament to the depth of that desire.

35.6 blue, purple, and crimson yarns, fine linen, and goats' hair;

35.7 tanned ram skins, dolphin skins, and acacia wood;

35.8 oil for lighting, spices for the anointing oil and for the aromatic incense;

35.9 lapis lazuli and other stones for setting, for the ephod and the breastpiece.

35.10 And let all among you who are skilled come and make all that the Lord has commanded:

35.11 the Tabernacle, its tent and its covering, its clasps and its planks, its bars, its posts, and its sockets;

35.12 the ark and its poles, the cover, and the curtain for the screen;

35.13 the table, and its poles and all its utensils; and the bread of display;

35.14 the lampstand for lighting, its furnishings and its lamps, and the oil for lighting;

35.15 the altar of incense and its poles; the anointing oil and the aromatic incense; and the entrance screen for the entrance of the Tabernacle;

35.16 the altar of burnt offering, its copper grating, its poles, and all its furnishings; the laver and its stand;

35.17 the hangings of the enclosure, its posts and its sockets, and the screen for the gate of the court;

35.18 the pegs for the Tabernacle, the pegs for the enclosure, and their cords;

Given that God has no need of gifts, He wants gifts offered to Him to be voluntary. In contrast, the poor do need donations, and therefore such help must be commanded.

35.19 the service vestments for officiating in the sanctuary, the sacral vestments of Aaron the priest and the vestments of his sons for priestly service.

35.20 So the whole community of the Israelites left Moses' presence.

35.21 And everyone who excelled in ability and everyone whose spirit moved him came, bringing to the Lord his offering for the work of the Tent of Meeting and for all its service and for the sacral vestments.

35.22 Men and women, all whose hearts moved them, all who would make an elevation offering of gold to the Lord, came bringing brooches, earrings, rings, and pendants—gold objects of all kinds.

The Torah repeatedly states both men and women were involved in the building of the Tabernacle. In addition to bringing jewelry, yarn, and other gifts, women also took responsibility for spinning the goats' hair used to make one of the protective coverings for the Tabernacle.

35.23 And everyone who had in his possession blue, purple, and crimson yarns, fine linen, goats' hair, tanned ram skins, and dolphin skins, brought them;

35.24 everyone who would make gifts of silver or copper brought them as gifts for the Lord; and everyone who had in his possession acacia wood for any work of the service brought that.

35.25 And all the skilled women spun with their own hands, and brought what they had spun, in blue, purple, and crimson yarns, and in fine linen.

35.26 And all the women who excelled in that skill spun the goats' hair.

35.27 And the chieftains brought lapis lazuli and other stones for setting, for the ephod and for the breastpiece;

35.28 and spices and oil for lighting, for the anointing oil, and for the aromatic incense.

35.29 Thus the Israelites, all the men and women whose hearts moved them to bring anything for the work that the Lord, through Moses, had commanded to be done, brought it as a freewill offering to the Lord.

35.30 And Moses said to the Israelites: See, the Lord has singled out by name Bezalel, son of Uri son of Hur, of the tribe of Judah.

35.31 He has endowed him with a divine spirit of skill, ability, and knowledge in every kind of craft

35.32 and has inspired him to make designs for work in gold, silver, and copper,

35.33 to cut stones for setting and to carve wood—to work in every kind of designer's craft—

35.34 and to give directions. He and Oholiab son of Ahisamach of the tribe of Dan

35.35 have been endowed with the skill to do any work—of the carver, the designer, the embroiderer in blue, purple, crimson yarns, and in fine linen, and of the weaver—as workers in all crafts and as makers of designs.

CHAPTER

~❧ 36 ❧~

Chapters 36–40 largely recapitulate chapters 25–28 and 30. Those earlier chapters record God's instructions to Moses on how to build the Tabernacle (the Mishkan), while these chapters record its actual building. Because much of this material is repetitious, the commentary here is briefer, and restricted to new material. In each instance, I briefly note where the earlier, original, recording of this material can be found.

36.1 Let, then, Bezalel and Oholiab and all the skilled persons whom the Lord has endowed with skill and ability to perform expertly all the tasks connected with the service of the sanctuary carry out all that the Lord has commanded.

This verse could easily have read, "Let, then, all the skilled persons perform expertly." Why are the words "whom the Lord has endowed with skills and ability" added?

The likely reason is the Torah wishes to emphasize that people who have special skills and abilities do not have themselves to thank or praise for those abilities. They have them because God gave them these abilities. Even those who do not believe God is the source of their abilities should not attribute their innate talents to anything they have done. If they don't want to credit God, they should at least credit their good luck. Otherwise they become like the man of whom it is said, "He is a self-made man, and he worships his creator."

There is nothing intrinsically wrong with recognizing a special ability one has. In fact, it is an exercise in false modesty not to. A great singer who denies that he or she has a great voice is engaging in false modesty, not humility. The humble person recognizes his or her specialness and thanks God (or simple good fortune) for it. And if that person is religious, he or she asks how God would want that talent to be used.

People with exceptional talents or abilities are therefore not to be praised for those abilities or talents, but for what they do with them.

36.2 Moses then called Bezalel and Oholiab, and every skilled person whom the Lord had endowed with skill, everyone who excelled in ability, to undertake the task and carry it out.

36.3 They took over from Moses all the gifts that the Israelites had brought, to carry out the tasks connected with the service of the sanctuary.

"The donations of the people are represented as lying in a heap before Moses, and the [artisans] took what they required" (Hertz).

36.3 (cont.) But when these continued to bring freewill offerings to him morning after morning,

There is nothing intrinsically wrong with recognizing a special ability one has. In fact, it is an exercise in false modesty not to.

36.4 all the artisans who were engaged in the tasks of the sanctuary came, each from the task upon which he was engaged,

36.5 and said to Moses, "The people are bringing more than is needed for the tasks entailed in the work that the Lord has commanded to be done."

36.6 Moses thereupon had this proclamation made throughout the camp: "Let no man or woman make further effort toward gifts for the sanctuary!"

This may be the only time in recorded history a leader told his people, "The government has enough money; don't give us any more."

36.6 (cont.) So the people stopped bringing:

36.7 their efforts had been more than enough for all the tasks to be done.

Since the Torah routinely depicts the Israelites in a negative light, when it shows them in a positive light—as it does here for their generosity—it has credibility.

Like most of us, the Israelites had their good traits and their bad traits. This is worth remembering when we assess individuals or groups. At the same time, it is also important not to fall into the trap of excusing truly evil people or groups by saying "everyone has their faults," or "we're all a mixed bag," or "I try to find the good in everyone." There are individuals and groups whose evil so outweighs whatever good they have done it is wrong to lump them with the rest of humanity, which is largely made up of people and groups who do both good and bad—but not true evil. And there are people whose good so outweighs whatever sins they have committed they, too, should not be lumped in with the rest of humanity.

6.8 Then all the skilled among those engaged in the work made the Tabernacle of ten strips of cloth, which they made of fine twisted linen, blue, purple, and crimson yarns; into these they worked a design of cherubim.

These verses concerning the curtains of the Tabernacle (verses 8-19) correspond to Exodus 26:1-11, 14 (thus, for example, 36:9 is a precise restatement of 26:2).

36.9 The length of each cloth was twenty-eight cubits, and the width of each cloth was four cubits, all cloths having the same measurements.

36.10 They joined five of the cloths to one another, and they joined the other five cloths to one another.

36.11 They made loops of blue wool on the edge of the outermost cloth of the one set, and did the same on the edge of the outermost cloth of the other set:

36.12 they made fifty loops on the one cloth, and they made fifty loops on the edge of the end cloth of the other set, the loops being opposite one another.

36.13 And they made fifty gold clasps and coupled the units to one another with the clasps, so that the Tabernacle became one whole.

36.14 They made cloths of goats' hair for a tent over the Tabernacle; they made the cloths eleven in number.

36.15 The length of each cloth was thirty cubits, and the width of each cloth was four cubits, the eleven cloths having the same measurements.

36.16 They joined five of the cloths by themselves, and the other six cloths by themselves.

36.17 They made fifty loops on the edge of the outermost cloth of the one set, and they made fifty loops on the edge of the end cloth of the other set.

36.18 They made fifty copper clasps to couple the Tent together so that it might become one whole.

36.19 And they made a covering of tanned ram skins for the tent, and a covering of dolphin skins above.

36.20 They made the planks for the Tabernacle of acacia wood, upright.

The description of the wooden planks in the Tabernacle which runs from 36:20-34 corresponds to the earlier description in Exodus 26:15-29.

The Midrash has an interesting environmentalist take on the injunction to build the Tabernacle with wood from the acacia, a non-fruit bearing tree:

"God set an example for all time, that when a man is about to build his house from a fruit-bearing tree, he should be reminded: If, when the supreme King of kings commanded the Temple to be erected, His instructions were to use only such trees as are not fruit-bearing—even though all things belong to Him, how much more should this be in our case" (see commentary on Deuteronomy 20:19, the prohibition against destroying fruit-bearing trees).[1]

36.21 The length of each plank was ten cubits, the width of each plank a cubit and a half.

36.22 Each plank had two tenons, parallel to each other; they did the same with all the planks of the Tabernacle.

36.23 Of the planks of the Tabernacle, they made twenty planks for the south side,

36.24 making forty silver sockets under the twenty planks, two sockets under one plank for its two tenons and two sockets under each following plank for its two tenons;

36.25 and for the other side wall of the Tabernacle, the north side, twenty planks,

36.26 with their forty silver sockets, two sockets under one plank and two sockets under each following plank.

This may be the only time in recorded history a leader told his people, "The government has enough money; don't give us any more."

36.27 And for the rear of the Tabernacle, to the west, they made six planks;

36.28 and they made two planks for the corners of the Tabernacle at the rear.

36.29 They matched at the bottom, but terminated as one at the top into one ring; they did so with both of them at the two corners.

36.30 Thus there were eight planks with their sockets of silver: sixteen sockets, two under each plank.

36.31 They made bars of acacia wood, five for the planks of the one side wall of the Tabernacle,

36.32 five bars for the planks of the other side wall of the Tabernacle, and five bars for the planks of the wall of the Tabernacle at the rear, to the west;

36.33 they made the center bar to run, halfway up the planks, from end to end.

36.34 They overlaid the planks with gold, and made their rings of gold, as holders for the bars; and they overlaid the bars with gold.

36.35 They made the curtain of blue, purple, and crimson yarns, and fine twisted linen, working into it a design of cherubim.

> The description of the curtain to section off the Holy of Holies (the area that will enshrine the Ark) and the screen for the door of the tent in verses 35-38 corresponds to Exodus 26:31-37.

36.36 They made for it four posts of acacia wood and overlaid them with gold, with their hooks of gold; and they cast for them four silver sockets.

36.37 They made the screen for the entrance of the Tent, of blue, purple, and crimson yarns, and fine twisted linen, done in embroidery;

36.38 and five posts for it with their hooks. They overlaid their tops and their bands with gold; but the five sockets were of copper.

CHAPTER
～ 37 ～

37.1 Bezalel made the ark of acacia wood, two and a half cubits long, a cubit and a half wide, and a cubit and a half high.

> As noted in the introduction to chapter 36, much of the material covered in the last chapters of Exodus repeat details about the building of the Tabernacle recorded earlier. This applies to chapter 37 in its entirety (parts of which are found in chapters 25 and 30).
>
> The opening verses, 1-9, which detail the building of the Ark, parallel chapter 25:10-15, and chapters 18-20. Any commentary on this material is found there.

37.2 He overlaid it with pure gold, inside and out; and he made a gold molding for it round about.

37.3 He cast four gold rings for it, for its four feet: two rings on one of its side walls and two rings on the other.

37.4 He made poles of acacia wood, overlaid them with gold,

37.5 and inserted the poles into the rings on the side walls of the ark for carrying the ark.

37.6 He made a cover of pure gold, two and a half cubits long and a cubit and a half wide.

37.7 He made two cherubim of gold; he made them of hammered work, at the two ends of the cover:

37.8 one cherub at one end and the other cherub at the other end; he made the cherubim of one piece with the cover, at its two ends.

37.9 The cherubim had their wings spread out above, shielding the cover with their wings. They faced each other; the faces of the cherubim were turned toward the cover.

37.10 He made the table of acacia wood, two cubits long, one cubit wide, and a cubit and a half high;

> The construction of the table in the Tabernacle, (verses 10-16), corresponds to Exodus 25:23-29.

37.11 he overlaid it with pure gold and made a gold molding around it.

37.12 He made a rim of a hand's breadth around it and made a gold molding for its rim round about.

37.13 He cast four gold rings for it and attached the rings to the four corners at its four legs.

37.14 The rings were next to the rim, as holders for the poles to carry the table.

37.15 He made the poles of acacia wood for carrying the table, and overlaid them with gold.

37.16 The utensils that were to be upon the table—its bowls, ladles, jugs, and jars with which to offer libations—he made of pure gold.

37:17 He made the lampstand of pure gold. He made the lampstand—its base and its shaft—of hammered work; its cups, calyxes, and petals, were of one piece with it.

> Verses 17-24 describe the making of the lampstand (in Hebrew, the Menorah), whose construction was commanded in Exodus 25:31-40.

37.18 Six branches issued from its sides: three branches from one side of the lampstand, and three branches from the other side of the lampstand.

37.19 There were three cups shaped like almond-blossoms, each with calyx and petals, on one branch; and there were three cups shaped like almond-blossoms, each with calyx and petals, on the next branch; so for all six branches issuing from the lampstand.

37.20 On the lampstand itself there were four cups shaped like almond-blossoms, each with calyx and petals:

37.21 a calyx, of one piece with it, under a pair of branches; and a calyx, of one piece with it, under the second pair of branches; and a calyx, of one piece with it, under the last pair of branches; so for all six branches issuing from it.

37.22 Their calyxes and their stems were of one piece with it, the whole of it a single hammered piece of pure gold.

37.23 He made its seven lamps, its tongs, and its fire pans of pure gold.

37.24 He made it and all its furnishings out of a talent of pure gold.

37.25 He made the incense altar of acacia wood, a cubit long and a cubit wide—square—and two cubits high; its horns were of one piece with it.
> Verses 25-27, describing the altar of incense, correspond to Exodus chapter 30:1-9.

37.26 He overlaid it with pure gold: its top, its sides round about, and its horns; and he made a gold molding for it round about.

37.27 He made two gold rings for it under its molding, on its two walls—on opposite sides—as holders for the poles with which to carry it.

37.28 He made the poles of acacia wood, and overlaid them with gold.

37.29 He prepared the sacred anointing oil and the pure aromatic incense, expertly blended.

The final verse of this chapter is a one-verse summary of Exodus 30:22-33 and 34-37.

38.1 He made the altar for burnt offering of acacia wood, five cubits long and five cubits wide—square—and three cubits high.

> Verses 1-7, dealing with the altar for burnt offerings, correspond to Exodus 27:1-8 and 30:18-21.

38.2 He made horns for it on its four corners, the horns being of one piece with it; and he overlaid it with copper.

38.3 He made all the utensils of the altar—the pails, the scrapers, the basins, the flesh hooks, and the fire pans; he made all these utensils of copper.

38.4 He made for the altar a grating of meshwork in copper, extending below, under its ledge, to its middle.

38.5 He cast four rings, at the four corners of the copper grating, as holders for the poles.

38.6 He made the poles of acacia wood and overlaid them with copper;

38.7 and he inserted the poles into the rings on the side walls of the altar, to carry it by them. He made it hollow, of boards.

38.8 He made the laver of copper and its stand of copper, from the mirrors of the women who performed tasks at the entrance of the Tent of Meeting.

This is a reference to the tent (mentioned in Exodus 33) Moses pitched outside the camp, and where he would go to commune "face-to-face" with God (Exodus 33:7-11). Later, after the Tabernacle was completed, the Tent of Meeting became the inner area—where the Ark resided, and which became the Holy of Holies.

There is no other reference in the Torah to the women who worked at the entrance to the tent (nor is it clear what they did). But reference to women doing this type of work hundreds of years later is found in I Samuel 2:22 (in a passage about two corrupt priests who took advantage of these women).

38.9 He made the enclosure: On the south side, a hundred cubits of hangings of fine twisted linen for the enclosure—

Verses 9-20 describe the building of the outer courtyard of the Tabernacle, and correspond to Exodus 27:9-19.

When complimenting or criticizing, the more specific we are, the more meaningful the compliment or criticism; and the more likely the individual who is complimented or criticized will hear you.

38.10 with their twenty posts and their twenty sockets of copper, the hooks and bands of the posts being silver.

38.11 On the north side, a hundred cubits—with their twenty posts and their twenty sockets of copper, the hooks and bands of the posts being silver.

38.12 On the west side, fifty cubits of hangings—with their ten posts and their ten sockets, the hooks and bands of the posts being silver.

38.13 And on the front side, to the east, fifty cubits:

38.14 fifteen cubits of hangings on the one flank, with their three posts and their three sockets,

38.15 and fifteen cubits of hangings on the other flank—on each side of the gate of the enclosure—with their three posts and their three sockets.

38.16 All the hangings around the enclosure were of fine twisted linen.

38.17 The sockets for the posts were of copper, the hooks and bands of the posts were of silver, the overlay of their tops was of silver; all the posts of the enclosure were banded with silver.—

38.18 The screen of the gate of the enclosure, done in embroidery, was of blue, purple, and crimson yarns, and fine twisted linen. It was twenty cubits long. Its height—or width—was five cubits, like that of the hangings of the enclosure.

38.19 The posts were four; their four sockets were of copper, their hooks of silver; and the overlay of their tops was of silver, as were also their bands.—

38.20 All the pegs of the Tabernacle and of the enclosure round about were of copper.

38.21 These are the records of the Tabernacle, the Tabernacle of the Pact, which were drawn up at Moses' bidding—the work of the Levites under the direction of Ithamar son of Aaron the priest.

38.22 Now Bezalel, son of Uri son of Hur, of the tribe of Judah, had made all that the Lord had commanded Moses;

38.23 at his side was Oholiab son of Ahisamach, of the tribe of Dan, carver and designer, and embroiderer in blue, purple, and crimson yarns and in fine linen.

> The Torah regularly credits those who do good. For example, in Exodus, we learn the names of the two midwives—Shifra and Puah—who courageously resisted Pharaoh's order to kill the newborn male Israelites. Here the Torah credits by name, several times, Bezalel and Oholiab. And we are told specifically what Oholiab did: He was a "carver and designer, and embroiderer in blue, purple, and crimson yarns and in fine linen."
>
> There is a lesson to be drawn: When giving a compliment or when criticizing, the more specific we are, the more meaningful the compliment or critique will be, and the more likely the person receiving the compliment or criticism will take it to heart.

38.24 All the gold that was used for the work, in all the work of the sanctuary—the elevation offering of gold—came to 29 talents and 730 shekels by the sanctuary weight.

> Verses 24-29 detail the exact quantities of precious metals used in constructing the Tabernacle. I have previously cited Rabbi Saul Berman's fine conjecture that by detailing these quantities the Torah intended to foreclose the possibility of corrupt priests insisting on the need for more gold and silver than necessary, which they could then "pocket."

38.25 The silver of those of the community who were recorded came to 100 talents and 1,775 shekels by the sanctuary weight:

38.26 a half-shekel a head, half a shekel by the sanctuary weight, for each one who was entered in the records, from the age of twenty years up, 603,550 men.

> Once again, the Torah repeats the details concerning the half-shekel and the number of men of fighting age (see, as well, Numbers 1:46). What is remarkable here is the specific number of men given—not rounded off to the nearest hundred thousand, but precise to the nearest ten. It doesn't appear to be a made-up number, but actual documentation.

38.27 The 100 talents of silver were for casting the sockets of the sanctuary and the sockets for the curtain, 100 sockets to the 100 talents, a talent a socket.

38.28 and of the 1,775 shekels he made hooks for the posts, overlay for their tops, and bands around them.

38.29 The copper from the elevation offering came to 70 talents and 2,400 shekels.

38.30 Of it he made the sockets for the entrance of the Tent of Meeting; the copper altar and its copper grating and all the utensils of the altar;

38.31 the sockets of the enclosure round about and the sockets of the gate of the enclosure; and all the pegs of the Tabernacle and all the pegs of the enclosure round about.

39.1 Of the blue, purple, and crimson yarns they also made the service vestments for officiating in the sanctuary; they made Aaron's sacral vestments—as the Lord had commanded Moses.

Nearly all of this chapter, verses 1-31, is devoted to the priests' garments. Once again, this is material covered earlier in Exodus.

39.2 The ephod was made of gold, blue, purple, and crimson yarns, and fine twisted linen.

The description of the priests' ephod (breastplate) in verses 2-7 corresponds to the previous description in Exodus 28:6-12, the difference being that in the earlier chapter it was described in the future tense: "And they shall make the *ephod*…" while here it is described after the fact, "And he made the ephod…."

39.3 They hammered out sheets of gold and cut threads to be worked into designs among the blue, the purple, and the crimson yarns, and the fine linen.

The earlier passage (Exodus 28:6-12) does not mention the hammering out of sheets of gold; the verse here describes how the gold was worked into the garments.

39.4 They made for it attaching shoulder-pieces; they were attached at its two ends.

39.5 The decorated band that was upon it was made like it, of one piece with it; of gold, blue, purple, and crimson yarns, and fine twisted linen—as the Lord had commanded Moses.

39.6 They bordered the lazuli stones with frames of gold, engraved with seal engravings of the names of the sons of Israel.

39.7 They were set on the shoulder-pieces of the ephod, as stones of remembrance for the Israelites—as the Lord had commanded Moses.

39.8 The breastpiece was made in the style of the ephod: of gold, blue, purple, and crimson yarns, and fine twisted linen.

> The making of the breastplate described here in verses 8 to 21 corresponds to the equally detailed earlier description ordaining how the breastplate is to be made (Exodus 28:15-28).

39.9 It was square; they made the breastpiece doubled—a span in length and a span in width, doubled.

39.10 They set in it four rows of stones. The first row was a row of carnelian, chrysolite, and emerald;

39.11 the second row: a turquoise, a sapphire, and an amethyst;

39.12 the third row: a jacinth, an agate, and a crystal;

39.13 and the fourth row: a beryl, a lapis lazuli, and a jasper. They were encircled in their mountings with frames of gold.

39.14 The stones corresponded [in number] to the names of the sons of Israel: twelve, corresponding to their names; engraved like seals, each with its name, for the twelve tribes.

39.15 On the breastpiece they made braided chains of corded work in pure gold.

39.16 They made two frames of gold and two rings of gold, and fastened the two rings at the two ends of the breastpiece,

39.17 attaching the two golden cords to the two rings at the ends of the breastpiece.

39.18 They then fastened the two ends of the cords to the two frames, attaching them to the shoulder-pieces of the ephod, at the front.

39.19 They made two rings of gold and attached them to the two ends of the breastpiece, at its inner edge, which faced the ephod.

39.20 They made two other rings of gold and fastened them on the front of the ephod, low on the two shoulder-pieces, close to its seam above the decorated band.

39.21 The breastpiece was held in place by a cord of blue from its rings to the rings of the ephod, so that the breastpiece rested on the decorated band and did not come loose from the ephod—as the Lord had commanded Moses.

39.22 The robe for the ephod was made of woven work, of pure blue.

> Verses 22-26, describing the robe made for the ephod, correspond to Exodus 28:31-34.

39.23 The opening of the robe, in the middle of it, was like the opening of a coat of mail, with a binding around the opening, so that it would not tear.

39.24 On the hem of the robe they made pomegranates of blue, purple, and crimson yarns, twisted.

39.25 They also made bells of pure gold, and attached the bells between the pomegranates, all around the hem of the robe, between the pomegranates:

39.26 a bell and a pomegranate, a bell and a pomegranate, all around the hem of the robe for officiating in—as the Lord had commanded Moses.

39.27 They made the tunics of fine linen, of woven work, for Aaron and his sons;

> The tunics and headdress described in verses 27-29 were earlier described in Exodus 28:39-42.

39.28 and the headdress of fine linen, and the decorated turbans of fine linen, and the linen breeches of fine twisted linen;

39.29 and sashes of fine twisted linen, blue, purple, and crimson yarns, done in embroidery—as the Lord had commanded Moses.

39.30 they made the frontlet for the holy diadem of pure gold, and incised upon it the seal inscription: "Holy to the Lord."

> A diadem, mentioned earlier in Exodus 29:6, is a jeweled crown or headband.

39.31 They attached to it a cord of blue to fix it upon the headdress above—as the Lord had commanded Moses.

39.32 Thus was completed all the work of the Tabernacle of the Tent of Meeting. The Israelites did so, just as the Lord had commanded Moses, so they did.

> The rest of the chapter is a summary of what the children of Israel accomplished in constructing all the many parts of the Tabernacle, while the following chapter (the last in Exodus) describes the setting up of the Tabernacle.

39.33 Then they brought the Tabernacle to Moses, with the Tent and all its furnishings: its clasps, its planks, its bars, its posts, and its sockets;

39.34 the covering of tanned ram skins, the covering of dolphin skins, and the curtain for the screen;

39.35 the Ark of the Pact and its poles, and the cover;

39.36 the table and all its utensils, and the bread of display;

39.37 the pure lampstand, its lamps—lamps in due order—and all its fittings, and the oil for lighting;

39.38 the altar of gold, the oil for anointing, the aromatic incense, and the screen for the entrance of the Tent;

39.39 the copper altar with its copper grating, its poles and all its utensils, and the laver and its stand;

39.40 the hangings of the enclosure, its posts and its sockets, the screen for the gate of the enclosure, its cords and its pegs—all the furnishings for the service of the Tabernacle, the Tent of Meeting;

39.41 the service vestments for officiating in the sanctuary, the sacral vestments of Aaron the priest, and the vestments of his sons for priestly service.

39.42 Just as the Lord had commanded Moses, so the Israelites had done all the work.

39.43 And when Moses saw that they had performed all the tasks—as the Lord had commanded, so they had done—Moses blessed them.

Perhaps because of previous disappointments with the Israelites, Moses withheld his blessing until the work was completed. There is an old Jewish proverb, "A mitzvah (a commandment/good deed) is attributed to the one who completes it."[1] Many people start projects and never complete them. But, to their credit, the Israelites did complete the construction of the Tabernacle and Moses, who was not hesitant to criticize the Israelites, now finally has reason to bless them.

CHAPTER
~40~

40.1 And the Lord spoke to Moses, saying:

40.2 On the first day of the first month you shall set up the Tabernacle of the Tent of Meeting.
Verse 17 will specify the exact day the Tabernacle was set up. It is the first day of the Hebrew month of Nisan—the month in which the Israelites exited Egypt and the month in which Jews have ever since celebrated Passover—at the beginning of the second year following the Exodus.

40.3 Place there the Ark of the Pact, and screen off the ark with the curtain.

40.4 Bring in the table and lay out its due setting; bring in the lampstand and light its lamps;

40.5 and place the gold altar of incense before the Ark of the Pact. Then put up the screen for the entrance of the Tabernacle.

40.6 You shall place the altar of burnt offering before the entrance of the Tabernacle of the Tent of Meeting.

40.7 Place the laver between the Tent of Meeting and the altar, and put water in it.

40.8 Set up the enclosure round about, and put in place the screen for the gate of the enclosure.

40.9 You shall take the anointing oil and anoint the Tabernacle and all that is in it to consecrate it and all its furnishings, so that it shall be holy.

40.10 Then anoint the altar of burnt offering and all its utensils to consecrate the altar, so that the altar shall be most holy.

40.11 And anoint the laver and its stand to consecrate it.

40.12 You shall bring Aaron and his sons forward to the entrance of the Tent of Meeting and wash them with the water.

40.13 Put the sacral vestments on Aaron, and anoint him and consecrate him, that he may serve Me as priest.

40.14 Then bring his sons forward, put tunics on them,

40.15 and anoint them as you have anointed their father, that they may serve Me as priests.

The anointing of Aaron's sons as priests might well have been a bittersweet moment for Moses, whose sons, it would appear, were not actively involved in carrying on his mission. (See commentary to Exodus 6:23, "Prominent Parents and Their Children.")

40.15 (cont.) This their anointing shall serve them for everlasting priesthood throughout the ages.

The high status assigned to the priests in the Torah and in later Jewish life motivated Jews who were priests (*kohanim*) to make sure their children were aware of their identity. Even though women did not have priestly duties, the daughter of a priest (*bat kohain*) also had a high status and, in case of divorce, was to be awarded a much greater amount of money than a woman of non-priestly lineage. Unlike Jewish identity, which traditional Jewish law holds to be transmitted through the mother (the child of a Jewish mother is a Jew), tribal identity, as in the case of the *kohanim* (priests), who are all of the tribe of Levi, is transmitted through the father.

Research conducted by Dr. Michael Hammer of the University of Arizona, a scholar in molecular genetics and chromosome research, confirmed the presence of special genetic markers in Jews who identify as *kohanim* which point to a common descent from a priestly lineage. Hammer's conclusion was, "Our estimates…lend support to the hypothesis that the extended CHM (Cohen Modal Haplotype) represents a unique founding lineage of the ancient Hebrews that has been paternally inherited along with the Jewish priesthood."[1]

All of which suggests, to a statistically improbable extent, the descendants of Aaron have maintained their priestly lineage. For example, there is a strong likelihood Jews named Cohen (if their name did not come about through a name change) are direct descendants of Aaron, Judaism's original priest.

> *Research conducted by Dr. Michael Hammer of the University of Arizona, a scholar in molecular genetics and chromosome research, confirmed the presence of special markers in Jews who identify as kohanim (priests) which point to a common descent from a priestly lineage.*

40.16 This Moses did; just as the Lord had commanded him, so he did.

40.17 In the first month of the second year, on the first of the month, the Tabernacle was set up.

40.18 Moses set up the Tabernacle, placing its sockets, setting up its planks, inserting its bars, and erecting its posts.

40.19 He spread the tent over the Tabernacle, placing the covering of the tent on top of it—just as the Lord had commanded Moses.

40.20 He took the Pact and placed it in the ark;

The Pact refers to the Ten Commandments.

40.20 (cont.) he fixed the poles to the ark, placed the cover on top of the ark,

40.21 and brought the ark inside the Tabernacle. Then he put up the curtain for screening, and screened off the Ark of the Pact—just as the Lord had commanded Moses.

40.22 He placed the table in the Tent of Meeting, outside the curtain, on the north side of the Tabernacle.

40.23 Upon it he laid out the setting of bread before the Lord—as the Lord had commanded Moses.

40.24 He placed the lampstand in the Tent of Meeting opposite the table, on the south side of the Tabernacle.

40.25 And he lit the lamps before the Lord—as the Lord had commanded Moses.

Exodus begins with a tale of darkness, misery, and oppression, and closes with the brilliant illumination of God's glory.

40.26 He placed the altar of gold in the Tent of Meeting, before the curtain.

40.27 On it he burned aromatic incense—as the Lord had commanded Moses.

40.28 Then he put up the screen for the entrance of the Tabernacle.

40.29 At the entrance of the Tabernacle of the Tent of Meeting he placed the altar of burnt offering. On it he offered up the burnt offering and the meal offering—as the Lord had commanded Moses.

40.30 He placed the laver between the Tent of Meeting and the altar, and put water in it for washing.

40.31 From it Moses and Aaron and his sons would wash their hands and feet;

40.32 they washed when they entered the Tent of Meeting and when they approached the altar—as the Lord had commanded Moses.

40.33 And he set up the enclosure around the Tabernacle and the altar, and put up the screen for the gate of the enclosure. When Moses had finished the work,

40.34 the cloud covered the Tent of Meeting, and the Presence of the Lord filled the Tabernacle.

> The cloud is God's glory, which now dwells among the people.
>
> "The function of the Tabernacle was to create a portable Sinai, a means by which a continued avenue of communication with God could be maintained. As the people move away from the moment of revelation, they need a visible, tangible symbol of God's ever-abiding presence in their midst" (Sarna).

40.35 Moses could not enter the Tent of Meeting, because the cloud had settled upon it and the Presence of the Lord filled the Tabernacle.

> Everett Fox points out that Exodus ends not with a tribute to the beauty of the Tabernacle or to the skill of its builders, but with a description of how "its purpose was fulfilled." The Tabernacle was built so God could dwell among the Israelites; now that it has been completed, the Torah affirms God is indeed in their midst.

40.36 When the cloud lifted from the Tabernacle, the Israelites would set out, on their various journeys;

> Whereas the story of Exodus began with a people in servitude to an earthly king, it ends with a people in servitude to a Divine King (Everett Fox).

40.37 but if the cloud did not lift, they would not set out until such time as it did lift.

40.38 For over the Tabernacle a cloud of the Lord rested by day, and fire would appear in it by night, in the view of all the house of Israel throughout their journeys.

> Nahum Sarna, Benno Jacob, and Everett Fox all point out Exodus begins with a tale of darkness, misery, and oppression, and closes with the brilliant illumination of God's glory. The book thus functions as an organic, literary unit tracing the development of the Israelites from a nation Pharaoh enslaved and tried to annihilate to a nation sheltered by God's presence.

NOTES

Chapter 1

1. Bruce Feiler, *America's Prophet: How the Story of Moses Shaped America* (New York: William Morrow, 2009).

2. "This lack of knowledge in American history is not limited to college students. Studies over the years show Americans of all ages fail to answer the most simple of questions .... The 2014 National Assessment of Educational Progress (NAEP) report found that only 18 percent of 8th graders were proficient or above in U.S. History." Saba Naseem, May 28, 2015, https://www.smithsonianmag.com/history/how-much-us-history-do-americans-actually-know-less-you-think-180955431/.

Chapter 2

1. Talmud *Sanhedrin* 19b, based on verse 10.

2. Talmud *Ethics of the Fathers* 2:5.

Chapter 3

1. Winston Churchill, "Moses," in *Thoughts and Adventures: Churchill Reflects on Spies, Cartoons, Flying, and the Future,* (Greenville, DE: ISI Books, 2009).

2. Exodus Rabbah 2:5.

3. Elizabeth Browning, from "Aurora Leigh."

4. Joseph P. Carter, "The Universe Doesn't Care About Your 'Purpose," *New York Times,* July 31, 2017, https://www.nytimes.com/2017/07/31/opinion/the-universe-doesnt-care-about-your-purpose.html.

5. Charles Guignon and David R. Hiley eds., *Richard Rorty* (*Contemporary Philosophy in Focus*) (Cambridge: Cambridge University Press, 2003), 131.

6. See, for example, "Official 'Well-Being' Statistics Show Religious People Are Happier Than Atheists," HuffPost UK, February 2, 2016, http://www.huffingtonpost.co.uk/2016/02/02/office-for-national-statistics-well-being-data_n_9138076.html.

7. *Relationships in America Survey, 2014,* The Austin Institute for the Study of Family and Culture, http://relationshipsinamerica.com.

8. "Universe shouldn't exist, CERN physicists conclude," *Cosmos Magazine*, October 23, 2017.
9. John Adams to James Warren, April 22, 1776.
10. Talmud Ethics of the Fathers 3:15.

Chapter 5

1. Based on a Midrash in *Exodus Rabbah* 5:17

Chapter 6

1. The famous Hebrew phrase is *shtika k'hoda'ah* – "silence is agreement." Talmud *Yevamot* 87b.
2. This is one of a number of examples of pre-Torah Jews not observing some of the laws that are later forbidden by the Torah. It is true that since the time of the Talmud many traditional Jews have argued that pre-Torah Jews such as Abraham and the patriarchs kept all the ritual laws found in the Torah. But if the pre-Torah patriarchs did observe ritual laws given to the Jews after they lived, the Torah never mentions this. Rather, the Torah describes a number of instances in which the patriarchs and other righteous Jews of the pre-Sinai period violated subsequent Torah laws. To cite just a few examples: Jacob marries two sisters, a violation of Leviticus 18:18 (a man is permitted to marry two sisters only after one of them has died—which was not the case with Jacob, who was deceived into marrying Leah, and a week later married her sister Rachel); Amram, Moses's father, marries his aunt Yocheved, a violation of Leviticus 18:12; Abraham is depicted as serving milk and meat at the same meal (Genesis 18:8), a violation of the rabbinic understanding of Exodus 23:19, which Jewish law understands as forbidding eating meat and dairy at the same meal; and Judah marries a Canaanite woman (Genesis 38:2) though this was prohibited both by Abraham (Genesis 24:3) and by later Torah law (Deuteronomy 7:3).
3. Moses's sons are mentioned two other times in the Hebrew Bible: in 1 Chronicles 23:15-17 and 26:24-25. But nothing is related about their lives.
4. "Nelson Mandela: The Long Walk is Over," *The Economist*, December 5, 2013, https://www.economist.com/blogs/baobab/2013/12/nelson-mandela.

Chapter 7

1. Slavery caused the American Civil War. See the video, "Was the Civil War about Slavery?" by Colonel Ty Seidule, Professor of History at the United States Military Academy at West Point, at www.prageru.com.
2. Thomas Jefferson, Merrill D. Peterson, ed., *Thomas Jefferson: Writings* (Library of America, 1984), 289.
3. Abraham Lincoln, Second Inaugural Address, March 4, 1865.
4. Abraham Lincoln to Thurlow Weed (March 15, 1865); Abraham Lincoln, Don E. Fehrenbacher, ed., *Abraham Lincoln: Speeches and Writings*, 1859-1865 (New York: Library of America, 1989), 689.

5. Abraham Lincoln, " 'Reply to the Loyal Colored People of Baltimore upon Presentation of a Bible,' September 7, 1864," in Roy P. Basler, ed., *Collected Works of Abraham Lincoln*, Volume VII (New Brunswick: Rutgers University Press, 1953).

6. For the names of specific Egyptian gods, see, for example, http://www.biblecharts.org/oldtestament/thetenplagues.pdf and http://www.khouse.org/articles/2000/263/.

7. Alfred Lord Tennyson, *In Memoriam A.H.H.*, 1850.

Chapter 8

1. Song by Shirley Cohen Steinberg.

2.   Ernest van den Haag, *The Jewish Mystique* (New York: Stein & Day, 1977).

3. Talmud Mishnah *Sanhedrin* 4:5.

4. Joanna Bourke, "Staring at the Void: Joanna Bourke reviews *The Human Predicament* by David Benatar, Oxford 2017," *Wall Street Journal*, August 30, 2017, https://www.wsj.com/articles/staring-at-the-void-1504132971.

5. Clarence Darrow, "Remarks from a Debate on Capital Punishment with Judge Alfred J. Talley," New York City October 27, 1924, http://etc.usf.edu/lit2go/185/civil-rights-and-conflict-in-the-united-states-selected-speeches/5059/remarks-from-a-debate-on-capital-punishment-with-judge-alfred-j-talley-new-york-city-october-27-1924/.

6. Henry Bamford Parkes, *The Divine Order: Western Culture in the Middle Ages and the Renaissance* (New York: Knopf, 1969).

Chapter 10

1. Talmud *Bava Mezia*, 71a.

Chapter 12

1. See "Sacrificing a Lamb in Egypt" by Jan Assmann and Zev Farber in the www.thetorah.com. Assmann was Professor of Egyptology at the University of Heidelberg (1976–2003), and Farber is a rabbi with a doctorate in biblical studies.

2. Talmud Mishnah *Megillah* 1:5

3. Boyd Seevers, "How Big Was Israel's Army? Dealing with Large Numbers in the Bible," adapted from *Old Testament Warfare* (Kregel, 2012), https://unwsp.edu/documents/13231/88501/BATS_BoydSeevers-HowBigWasIsraelsArmy.pdf/166f720f-0730-472f-b04a-b451e7583436.

Chapter 14

1. This slave mentality was powerfully described by the former American slave, Booker T. Washington, at the end of the American Civil War when all the slaves were freed. He told of how their joy at being free almost immediately turned into fear at being free: "The great responsibility of being free, of having charge of themselves, of having to think and plan for themselves and their children, seemed to take possession of them. It was very much like suddenly turning a youth of ten or twelve years out

into the world to provide for himself.... These were the questions of a home, a living, the rearing of children, education, citizenship, and the establishment and support of churches. Was it any wonder that within a few hours the wild rejoicing ceased and a feeling of deep gloom seemed to pervade the slave quarters? To some it seemed that, now that they were in actual possession of it, freedom was a more serious thing than they had expected to find it." Booker T. Washington, *Up From Slavery* (New York: Dover Publications, Inc., 1995), 10-11.

Chapter 15

1. Talmud Sanhedrin 39b.
2. Talmud *Kiddushin* 19b.
3. Talmud *Ethics of the Fathers* 4:2.

Chapter 17

1. Talmud Mishnah, *Rosh Hashana* 3:8.

Chapter 18

1. Talmud *Pesachim* 6b.

Chapter 19

1. Alexis de Tocqueville, *The Old Regime and the Revolution* (New York: Harper and Brothers, 1856). My translation from the French: "Qui cherche dans la liberté autre chose qu'elle-même est fait pour servir."
2. Walter Kaufmann, *The Faith of a Heretic,*(New York: Doubleday Anchor, 1963).
3. Talmud *Shabbat* 88a.
4. Cited in Herman Rauschning's preface to Armin Robinson, ed., *The Ten Commandments* (New York: Simon and Schuster, 1944). Rauschning was present when Hitler said this.

Chapter 20

1. The most comprehensive listing of the human toll of communism, which killed about one hundred million people in the twentieth century, is found in *The Black Book of Communism*, written by French scholars and published in the United States by Harvard University Press in 1999.
2. Peter Merkl, *Political Violence under the Swastika* (Princeton: Princeton University Press, 1975).
3. Erwin Lutzer, *Hitler's Cross: The Revealing Story of How the Cross of Christ Was Used As a Symbol of the Nazi Agenda* (Chicago: Moody Publishing 1995). Lutzer is the senior pastor of the Moody Church in Chicago.
4. Hans T. David & Arthur Mendel, eds., *The Bach Reader* (New York: Norton, 1972), 33.
5. James Webster and Georg Feder eds., *The New Grove Haydn* (New York: Norton, 1982).
6. *The Humanist*, November–December 1974.

7. Father George Florovsky, "The Epistle of St. James and Luther's Evaluation," (available on the web, http://www.oodegr.com/english/protestantism/louther_grafi1.htm). Father Florovsky was Emeritus professor of Eastern Church History at Harvard University.

8. *Midrash Sifre*, Deuteronomy 54.

9. Talmud, *Sanhedrin* 56a.

10. See Douglas Murray, *The Strange Death of Europe* (New York: Bloomsbury Continuum, 2017). Though Murray is an atheist, he describes the likely fatal consequences of godlessness to Europe.

11. Gunther Plaut ed., *The Torah: A Modern Commentary* (Boston: CCAR Press, 1981).

12. Maimonides, "Laws of Kings," chapter 11.

13. Talmud *Berachot* 31b and elsewhere.

14. Talmud *Yevamot* 5b-6a.

15. Maimonides "Laws Concerning Rebels" 6:11.

16. Charles Pigden, ed., *Russell on Ethics* (New York: Routledge, 1999), 165. Pigden's book is an anthology of Russell's writings on ethical issues.

17. Timothy Snyder, *Black Earth: The Holocaust as History and Warning* (New York: Crown/Archetype, 2016), Kindle Edition (Locations 168-170).

18. See, for example, W. Bradford Wilcox of the University of Virginia, "Don't be a bachelor: Why married men work harder, smarter and make more money," *Washington Post*, April 2, 2015; and the video at www.prageru.com/courses/life-studies/be-man-get-married.

19. Talmud *Sanhedrin* 86a.

20. Talmud *Ethics of the Fathers* 6:6. The Mishna consists of the earliest major rabbibic writings (third century CE).

21. Saint Augustine, "On Lying," R. J. Deferrari, ed., in *Treatises on Various Subjects*, 67.

22. Immanuel Kant, "On a Supposed Right to Lie from Altruistic Motives," https://pdfs.semanticscholar.org/9575/d0993ae726215f16244ac69f333d807492e9.pdf.

23. Maimonides, *Guide for the Perplexed*, Part III, Chapter 45.

Chapter 21

1. Forough Jahanbaksh, *Islam, Democracy and Religious Modernism in Iran, 1953-2000* (Leiden: Brill, 2001), cited in BBC "Slavery in Islam," http://www.bbc.co.uk/religion/religions/islam/history/slavery_1.shtml.

2. Abbot Emerson Smith, *Colonists in Bondage: White Servitude and Convict Labor in America, 1607-1776* (Chapel Hill: Chapel Hill, 1947), 336. Cited in David W, Galenson, "The Rise and Fall of Indentured Servitude in the Americas: An Economic Analysis," in *The Journal of Economic History* (Cambridge: Cambridge University Press, March 1984).

3. According to Jewish law, a person would not, however, be sold into slavery if he made restitution but lacked the money to pay the 100 percent fine that Exodus 22:6 imposed on thieves. Talmud *Kiddushin* 18a.

4. *Mishneh Torah*, "Laws of Slavery," 4:2

5. See Talmud *Kiddushin* 19a.

6. See Maimonides, "Laws of Murder and the Preservation of Life," 1:4.

7. Talmud *Sanhedrin* 84b.

8. Talmud *Mo'ed Kattan* 17a.

9. Joachim Jeremias, *Jerusalem in the Time of Jesus* (London: SCM Press, 1969).

10. Talmud *Ketubot* 33a.

11. Harold Fisch ed., *The Holy Scriptures*, English text (Jerusalem: Koren Publishers, 1997).

12. For a thorough review of the terms used in these verses, see Gregory Koukl, "What Exodus 21:22 Says about Abortion," https://www.str.org/articles/what-exodus-21-22-says-about-abortion#.WhED7kqnH-g.

13. *Hilkhot Melakhim* 9:4; 10:11.

14. Union for Reform Judaism, "What is the Reform perspective on abortion?" https://web.archive.org/web/20080323092722/http://urj.org/ask/abortion/.

15. See Talmud, *Bava Kamma* 84a.

16. Gandhi, Mohatma, *Non-Violence in Peace and War* (Ahmedabad: Navajivan Publishing House, 1948).

Chapter 22

1. Sanhedrin 72a. In Hebrew the well-known phrase is *im ba l'horgecha, hashkeym l'hargo*.

2. Talmud Sanhedrin 72a.

3. Talmud Mishnah Bava Mezia 4:10.

4. Cited in W. Bradford Wilcox, "Don't be a bachelor: Why married men work harder, smarter and make more money," *Washington Post*, April 2, 2015.

5. Steven Nock, *Marriage in Men's Lives*, (Oxford University Press, 1998).

6. Robyn L. Fielder et al., "Sexual Hookups and Adverse Health Outcomes: A Longitudinal Study of First-Year College Women," *The Journal of Sex Research* vol. 51 (2014), https://www.ncbi.nlm.nih.gov/pmc/articles/PMC3946692/

7. Ugo, Uche, "A Link Between Sexual Promiscuity and Depression in Teens," *Psychology Today*, January 14, 2013.

8. Nancy Jo Sales, "Tinder and the Dawn of the Dating Apocalypse: As romance gets swiped from the screen, some twenty-somethings aren't liking what they see," *Vanity Fair*, September 2015.

9. Richard Elliott Friedman, Shawna Dolansky, *The Bible Now* (Oxford University Press, 2011).

10. I promise, I did not make this up.

11. Irving Kristol, *On Jews and Judaism*, (Mosaic Books, 2014).

12. Jonathan Glover, *Humanity: A Moral History of the Twentieth Century* (New Haven: Yale University Press, 2000).

Chapter 23

1. Robert Egner and Lester Denonn edsl, *The Basic Writings of Bertrand Russell 1903-1959* (Routledge, 2001), 38–39.

2. Simcha Raz, *A Tzaddik in Our Time: The Life of Rabbi Aryeh Levin*, Revised edition (Philipp Feldheim, 2008).
3. Midrash *Tanhuma B*, Mishpatim #1.
4. See, for example, "Misplaced charity: Aid is best spent in poor, well-governed countries. That isn't where it goes," *The Economist*, June 11, 2016.
5. Talmud Mishnah *Ethics of the Fathers* 2:4.
6. See, for example, Jeremy Sharon,"Diaspora Sabbatical year to commence with start of New Year with involvement of thousands of farmers," *Jerusalem Post*, September 22, 2014, http://www.jpost.com/Diaspora/Sabbatical-year-to-commence-with-start-of-New-Year-with-involvement-of-thousands-of-farmers-376064.
7. Philo, *De Virtute,* 13.
8. Jacob Milgrom, "You Shall Not Boil a Kid in its Mother's Milk," in the *Bible Review* (Fall 1985).
9. See Talmud *Chullin* 115b.
10. Nicholas St. Fleur, "Fate of Ancient Canaanites Seen in DNA Analysis: They Survived," *New York Times*, July 27, 2017, https://www.nytimes.com/2017/07/27/science/ancient-canaanites-bible-lebanon.html.
11. Talmud *Kiddushin* 39b.
12. Talmud Mishnah *Ethics of the Fathers* 4:2.
13. Yechezkel Kaufmann, *The Religion of Israel* (Chicago: University of Chicago Press, 1960).

Chapter 25

1. Talmud Mishnah *Middot* 3:4.

Chapter 26

1. *Jewish Chronicle*, September 9, 1935.

Chapter 27

1. *Etz Hayim* Torah Commentary.

Chapter 28

1. Talmud *Shabbat* 88a.

Chapter 31

1. Talmud *Kiddushin* 82a.
2. Quran 62:9—"O you who believe! When the call to prayer is proclaimed on Friday hasten earnestly to the remembrance of God, and leave aside business. That is best for you if you but knew."
3. The Talmud did so by demanding that two witnesses had to first warn the would-be Sabbath desecrator that he was about to commit a capital crime, and the accused had to acknowledge that he

heard and understood the warning; and then he had to perform the act. It has struck me that anyone who would act in such a manner would have likely been spared execution on the grounds of insanity. Moreover, the Sabbath violator had to do so publicly. There were no "religious police" going into people's homes to check on their observance.

Chapter 32

1. Jerusalem Talmud *Haggigah* 1:7.
2. *Etz Hayim* Commentary

Chapter 33

1. Richard Elliott Friedman, *Commentary on the Torah* (New York: HarperOne, 2003), Deuteronomy 5:4.

Chapter 34

1. Talmud *Megillah* 14b.
2. For an explanation of this added day to Torah holidays, see https://www.myjewishlearning.com/article/extra-festival-days-in-the-diaspora/.

Chapter 35

1. Abraham Joshua Heschel, *The Sabbath* (New York: Farrar, Straus, and Giroux, 1951).
2. Jerusalem Talmud *Beitzah* 5:2.

Chapter 36

1. Exodus Rabbah 35:2.

Chapter 39

1. Based on the Midrash, *Genesis Rabbah* 85:4.

Chapter 40

1. Michael Hammer, "Extended Y chromosome haplotypes resolve multiple and unique lineages of the Jewish priesthood," *Human Genetics* 126 no. 5 (November 2009), https://www.ncbi.nlm.nih.gov/pmc/articles/PMC2771134/.